Coaching Basketball Successfully

THIRD EDITION

Morgan Wootten
Joe Wootten

Human Kinetics

Library of Congress Cataloging-in-Publication Data

Wootten, Morgan.
  Coaching basketball successfully / Morgan Wootten, Joe Wootten. -- 3rd ed.
    p. cm.
  Includes index.
  1. Basketball--Coaching. I. Wootten, Joe, 1972- II. Title.
  GV885.3.W67 2012
  796.323--dc23

                                        2012020094

ISBN-10: 0-7360-8372-3 (print)
ISBN-13: 978-0-7360-8372-0 (print)

Developmental Editor: Laura E. Podeschi; **Assistant Editor:** Tyler Wolpert; **Copyeditor:** Patrick Connolly; **Indexer:** Alisha Jeddeloh; **Permissions Manager:** Martha Gullo; **Graphic Designer:** Nancy Rasmus; **Graphic Artist:** Julie L. Denzer; **Cover Designer:** Keith Blomberg; **Photograph (cover):** Courtesy of Bishop O'Connell High School/Tommy Orndorff; **Photographs (interior):** © Human Kinetics, unless otherwise noted; **Photo Asset Manager:** Laura Fitch; **Visual Production Assistant:** Joyce Brumfield; **Photo Production Manager:** Jason Allen; **Art Manager:** Kelly Hendren; **Associate Art Manager:** Alan L. Wilborn; **Illustrations:** © Human Kinetics; **Printer:** Sheridan Books

On the cover: 2012 NBA first-round draft pick Kendall Marshall is shown here at an earlier stage in his career, playing at Bishop O'Connell High School under coach Joe Wootten.

We thank Bishop O'Connell High School in Arlington, Virginia, for assistance in providing the location for the photo shoot for this book.

Human Kinetics books are available at special discounts for bulk purchase. Special editions or book excerpts can also be created to specification. For details, contact the Special Sales Manager at Human Kinetics.

Printed in the United States of America   10 9 8 7 6 5 4 3 2 1

The paper in this book is certified under a sustainable forestry program.

Human Kinetics
Website: www.HumanKinetics.com

United States: Human Kinetics
P.O. Box 5076
Champaign, IL 61825-5076
800-747-4457
e-mail: humank@hkusa.com

Canada: Human Kinetics
475 Devonshire Road Unit 100
Windsor, ON N8Y 2L5
800-465-7301 (in Canada only)
e-mail: info@hkcanada.com

Europe: Human Kinetics
107 Bradford Road
Stanningley
Leeds LS28 6AT, United Kingdom
+44 (0) 113 255 5665
e-mail: hk@hkeurope.com

Australia: Human Kinetics
57A Price Avenue
Lower Mitcham, South Australia 5062
08 8372 0999
e-mail: info@hkaustralia.com

New Zealand: Human Kinetics
P.O. Box 80
Torrens Park, South Australia 5062
0800 222 062
e-mail: info@hknewzealand.com

E4850

This book is dedicated to my number one team of all time—my wife, Kathy; our children, Cathy, Carol, Tricia, Brendan, and Joe; our sons-in-law, Steve and Mike; our daughters-in-law, Elizabeth and Terri Lynn; and our grandchildren, who are adding quality depth to our team.

—Morgan Wootten

This book is dedicated to my incredible wife, Terri Lynn, whose support, love, and friendship mean everything, and to our wonderful children, Alexa, Reese, and Jackson, who make family time the most memorable time.

—Joe Wootten

CONTENTS

FOREWORD

Two primary things drew me to coaching the game of basketball. One was a desire to teach and to play a role in the development of young people the way so many teachers and coaches had done for me in my life. Joy and satisfaction come with that, and, over the years, I have received more in the way of motivation and inspiration from my players than they could have ever received from me.

But another very basic reason I pursued a life as a basketball coach is that I love the game. To me, it is beautiful. Each year, I am excited to take the new group of individuals I have on my team and coaching staff and work with them to become the best team we can be when we face competition on the basketball court.

I have long admired Morgan Wootten as a pioneer in coaching, a family man, and a loyal friend. The time we have spent together over the years has made me a better man and a better teacher. His longevity in coaching speaks to the enduring nature of his values and the universality of his coaching principles. He is an absolute legend of the game.

One shining example of Coach Wootten's legacy is *Coaching Basketball Successfully*. This third edition of his classic book is a terrific aid to anyone interested in becoming a basketball coach or improving as one. Morgan, with valuable assists throughout the book from his son Joe, scores key points on every subject. From teaching players the fundamentals and the Xs and Os to handling game situations and many essential off-court coaching duties, this is a complete manual for running a championship high school program. But what stands out most to me throughout the book is the concern for developing the players as athletes, as teammates, as students, and as people.

That focus—helping each player to be his or her personal best and getting those athletes to commit fully to the team—is the essence of coaching. And it's what I love most about being a basketball coach.

Mike Krzyzewski
Head Men's Basketball Coach
Duke University

ACKNOWLEDGMENTS

I could not begin this book without acknowledging the deep debt I owe so many people for so many reasons:

All the fine young men I have had the privilege of teaching and coaching.

Rochelle McCoy, who gave me and six other people the gift of life by being an organ and tissue donor, and her husband, Ray, and children, Randall and Ray Jr., for honoring and supporting her choice.

The teams at Johns Hopkins and the University of Maryland Medical Center, especially Drs. Thulavath and Gelb.

The great coaches who have coached both with me and against me.

That special group of coaches who gave so much of their time and wisdom to teach me the game of life as well as basketball: John Wooden, Red Auerbach, Joe Gallagher, Jim Kehoe, Vic Bubas, Dean Smith, Ken Loeffler, Bud Millikan, John Ryall, and so many others.

My mother, for passing on to me her intense drive and love of competition; and my father, for teaching me to tell the truth and to be myself—always.

My sisters, Clare and Helen Lee, and my brother, Angus, who all helped me in so many ways.

My late Uncle Jack and my Uncle Robert, who were like second fathers to me.

Physicians and friends Dr. Hanley, Dr. Berard, and the late Drs. Gaffney, Sullivan, Scalessa, and Lavine.

The parents of all the young men I have had the privilege of teaching and coaching.

All of the great men and women who were my teachers from the first grade on.

The three men who coached me in high school and college: Reno Continetti, Tony Crème, and Frank Rubini.

The Holy Cross nuns who gave me my start as a coach.

The Christian brothers, who gave me my start as a teacher and enabled me to advance my career as a coach.

The Trinitarians and all of the DeMatha family. The Trinitarians saw something in a young man who dreamed of being a coach, and they hired me and stood beside me my entire career. There were so many great brothers and priests over the years from this terrific order, but I especially must recognize my great friends, Father Damian and Father James, our rector.

DeMatha continues to flourish under the leadership of the incomparable principal Dr. Dan McMahon.

And the many people, too numerous to mention, who touched my life and inspired me to touch the lives of others.

And God, for allowing me to be a teacher and a coach.

Morgan Wootten

Basketball allows us to meet so many great people and build so many great relationships. I would like to thank a few people who have had a profound impact on me:

My mother, whose passion, compassion, selflessness, and kindness not only inspired me but made our family go. For this I am eternally grateful.

My father, whom I have coached with, played for, been a business partner with, and who above all has been a role model for me and taught me how to compete in all that I do.

My brother, Brendan, and my sisters, Cathy, Carol, and Tricia, who made growing up a lot of fun.

All the young men I have had the privilege to coach and work with as both a head coach and as an assistant coach.

Joe Cantafio Sr., who gave me an incredible opportunity as a Division I assistant at a young age. I learned so much from him.

The late Jack Bruen and Mike Brey, who always had time to share a word or two with a young coach.

Mike Gielen Sr., who coached me in grade school, worked me out as a player for over 10 years, and is still a good friend.

Al Burch, the principal who hired me as a 26-year-old and gave me an opportunity to be a head coach.

Katy Prebble, O'Connell's president, for her outstanding vision and leadership.

Joe Vorbach, O'Connell's principal, for his leadership and for being a good teammate on Sunday night hoops.

Terry and Kay Bogle, my in-laws, who have been at 98 percent of the games I have coached and have been supportive every step of the way. They are family.

All of the great faculty and staff whom I am privileged to work with at O'Connell every day.

All of the great coaches whom I have had the opportunity to work with at O'Connell and as an assistant at DeMatha.

All of the great coaches whom I have worked with at our camp over the years. The friendships have been great!

Joe Wootten

INTRODUCTION

Nearly 20 years ago, when I wrote the first edition of this book, I explained the primary purpose for doing so:

> What convinced me to go ahead with the book was my desire to pay at least some portion of the debt that I owe to the game of basketball, which has been such a big and rewarding part of my life . . . I figured if I could play a part in other coaches' lives the way that so many coaches have played a part in mine, it would be worth it.

Since then, more than 120,000 copies of the book have been read by coaches all over the world, and I've heard from many of them. The comments, questions, compliments, and suggestions I continue to receive confirm the merit of the first edition. And that input has also helped me determine that this new edition of the book needed to be even better and more useful than the first two editions.

Coaching is an investment. But rather than showing a financial gain, a coach's balance sheet is full of intangibles with dividends that cannot be measured. What about wins, you say? Though my DeMatha teams won 1,274 games, I can assure you that the value of those victories comes nowhere near the satisfaction of witnessing the development and achievements of the hundreds of young men I was privileged to coach over the course of my 46-year career.

The great Notre Dame football coach Knute Rockne was once asked this about a just-completed season: "How do you think the season went?" To me, his answer embodies the true spirit of coaching. Rockne told the questioner to check back with him in 10 or 15 years. Then, he said, he would know what kinds of young men he had produced and what kinds of citizens they had become. Only at that point and judging by that standard, said Rockne, would he be able to evaluate his season.

Records and honors also pale in comparison to the great relationships built during a coaching career. Within a staff, among competing peers, and at all levels of basketball, coaches can and should have a mutual respect—an appreciation of the time, talents, and teaching they've put forth in their role.

Two greatly admired friends have passed away since I wrote the second edition of *Coaching Basketball Successfully*. Red Auerbach and John Wooden had a lifelong influence on my coaching career. They are the legendary coaches considered to be the best-ever pro and college coaches, respectively.

Red Auerbach orchestrated the most dominant dynasty in NBA history, but what I'll remember more is his engaging personality and his astute assessment of basketball talent. Tuesday lunches with Red and the gang at China Doll restaurant were some of the best moments of my life. I never stopped learning from Red. Among the many great lessons I learned from him, I always kept in mind his most important rule: When it comes to discipline, *there are no rules.* Rather than using a fixed set of rules for discipline, Red always made sure to address each issue in such a way as to enforce discipline, improve the individual, and strengthen the team.

And, of course, John Wooden set the standard for how to comport oneself as a teacher and a coach. The principles by which he lived and that he taught to his players, along with the pearls of wisdom he shared on topics ranging from proper work habits to precise execution of an offensive play, generated even greater regard for Coach than his unmatched number of NCAA championships. It is why I was so humbled when, in the foreword to this book's previous edition, Coach had these kind words for me:

> It has long been my expressed opinion that Morgan Wootten was one of the finest coaches in the sport of basketball. And he might have been the best.

I always said that when I spent time with Coach, I came away feeling as though I had been to the mountaintop and received the Word. It is hard to pick just one example of the many words of wisdom he shared with me, but one of the greats was this: "I have noticed that really good teams do only a few things, but they do those few things really well."

Though I no longer coach, I will always remain close to the game. Not only is it the most exciting sport around, but I have so many former players and assistants to root for. Plus, my son Joe has become a very successful coach in his own right at Bishop O'Connell High School in Arlington, Virginia.

Joe played on some outstanding DeMatha teams in high school and early on showed interest and aptitude in coaching. After college he returned as an assistant for me and soon demonstrated a knack for coaching that he would later apply to turn O'Connell into a top program.

It was in 2006, after Joe had been with O'Connell for seven seasons, that he performed a deed that far surpassed any number of wins or championships on a coaching resume. On October 11 of that year, Joe donated a kidney to me that I wouldn't have survived long without. His sacrifice on my behalf will always be one of the true highlights of my life.

This third edition is extra special because Joe agreed to coauthor the book with me. His insights on the challenges of coaching today, innovative approaches to managing a program, new Xs and Os, and interesting stories add a current perspective you're sure to appreciate. Joe is also O'Connell's athletic director, so he places great emphasis on the development of the student-athlete.

The challenges in making a positive impact in classrooms and on basketball courts today are many. Societal and institutional changes have placed even greater responsibilities on coaches. Yet, in every generation, educators and coaches have faced some type of adversity. The teaching and coaching job I accepted at the age of 24 wasn't exactly easy. I would have one coach, Buck Offutt, help me work with every sport on all levels (freshman, junior varsity, and varsity) at a 10-year-old school named DeMatha that was so noncompetitive it had to drop out of the Catholic League. Formerly a school for seminarians, DeMatha was at a transitional point as it was becoming established as a school for all young men. Today DeMatha is a world-renowned powerhouse in sports. More important, it is a two-time Blue Ribbon school of excellence, a top-ranked school for music, and a legendary educational institution. It is hard to remember those humble beginnings. It does prove to me what I have long believed is true: Facilities do not make a school or an athletic program. It is the *people* who are key.

At DeMatha I was fortunate to be surrounded by great individuals: Reverend Lou Amica and the Trinitarians, great coaches, and top educators. I really believed it was possible, with the support of the administration, faculty, and community, to build a program that would not only produce winners on the court but also build young men into solid, Christian citizens. And so we did.

Coaching Basketball Successfully contains all the principles and practices essential to achieving and sustaining a top-notch program. It covers both off-court and on-court measures to ensure a winning approach—one that develops people, not just players.

After all, the real game we are preparing our athletes for is the game of life. And it's the one game they can't afford to lose.

KEY TO DIAGRAMS

All diagrams

———→ = Path of player

- - - → = Path of ball

∿∿∿→ = Dribble

———┤ = Screen

Offensive diagrams

① = Point guard

② = Shooting guard

③ = Small forward

④ = Power forward

⑤ = Center

① = Offensive player with ball

X = Defensive player

Defensive diagrams

X₁ = Player assigned to 1

X₂ = Player assigned to 2

X₄ = Player assigned to 3

X₃ = Player assigned to 4

X₅ = Player assigned to 5

◯ = Offensive player

◯ = Offensive player with ball

Drill diagrams

C = Coach

C = Coach with ball

M = Manager

M = Manager with ball

General situations:

◯ = Offensive player

X = Defensive player

Specific situations:

Numbers used when perimeter vs. post distinction is made

Example:

② = Perimeter offensive player, perhaps the shooting guard

X₄ = Post defensive player, perhaps the power forward

PART I

COACHING FOUNDATION

CHAPTER 1

Developing a Basketball Coaching Philosophy

As father and son, we share many similar views about coaching, especially on a core set of issues. There is no more rewarding, satisfying, or fulfilling job than working with young people on the basketball court. Whether at DeMatha High School in Hyattsville, Maryland; Bishop O'Connell High School in Arlington, Virginia; or the school where you coach, the development of the student-athletes on that team must be the coaching staff's primary objective.

Forming a coaching philosophy is the first, and perhaps most important, step toward becoming a successful basketball coach. Without a philosophy, you will lack the road map and direction necessary to achieve your goals. This is true in any endeavor that you undertake in life.

Philosophical Foundation

People who become coaches typically develop a love of the game and develop ideas about the role of a coach at an early age when they are athletes. Other facets of the philosophy emerge through the years and are incorporated through personal experiences and educational pursuits.

Though a coach isn't required to have played competitive basketball, most coaches do have personal experience as a player. Your philosophy starts forming the first time you pick up and dribble a basketball. It expands as you participate in games and observe them in person and on television. And it will continue to grow as you learn more about the game and how to work with players.

The sum of your experiences as a player, the information you've gained through observing games, the lessons you've learned through reading, and the ideas you've picked up by listening and asking questions at clinics, in combination with your personality, constitute your unique coaching philosophy. But

THOUGHT FOR THE DAY

If you don't stand for something, you will fall for anything.* –Malcolm X

*The thought for the day is a great way to teach your players about the value of teamwork, dedication, preparation, hard work, and proper values. For a more detailed explanation of how I use the thought for the day, see chapter 6.

Morgan Wootten's Big 5 in Coaching

Over nearly 50 years, I concluded that these five principles supersede all others when it comes to fulfilling one's coaching duties:

1. Our goal must be to provide a wholesome environment in which young men or women can develop themselves spiritually, socially, and academically.

2. As coaches, we should be the kind of coach we would want our sons or daughters to play for.

3. We must never lose sight of the fact that basketball is a game and it should be fun. We should never put winning ahead of the individual.

4. Because basketball is a great teaching situation, we must use this opportunity to educate the young men or women on our teams. We must prepare them for the many decisions they will be making that will have long-range effects on the quality of their lives.

5. As coaches, the underlying question that we all must strive to be able to answer affirmatively is this: Did we make our players' sport experience as rewarding as possible?

Joe Wootten's Big 6 in Coaching

These are the core elements of my approach to coaching. Notice the overlap in principles with my father:

1. Use basketball to teach players the intrinsic value of hard work, as well as what this type of effort makes possible. Teach players to always outwork the opposition.

2. Teach players to embrace adversity. When challenges are met head-on, this fosters growth. Teach players to come back stronger than ever after being knocked down.

3. Demonstrate and emphasize to players that if you give more than you get, you will get more than you give. Gain great satisfaction from helping others reach their goals.

4. Teach players to focus on the task at hand. Notice and take care of the little things.

5. Nurture the following values in your players: belief, trust, honesty, and collective responsibility. Developing these values will help players in the game of basketball, and more important, it will help them in the game of life.

6. Are you the kind of coach you would want your son or daughter to play for?

don't be misled; simply playing, observing, reading, and listening more does not guarantee you'll have a better coaching philosophy. The quality—not just the quantity—of your experiences and how you implement your philosophy are equally important in determining your success.

At the heart of every sound philosophy is a set of important and unchanging beliefs called the philosophical foundation. We, for example, share the core views that a coach should emphasize the fundamentals, that practice is where most teaching and learning occur and where habits are formed, that proper physical conditioning is essential, and that players and the coaching staff must treat one another with a high level of respect.

This is where you establish a value system as a coach. What do you emphasize—winning a basketball game or winning in life? What priorities do you have regarding the development of your athletes as people, not just as basketball players?

Be Yourself

In determining where your philosophical foundation rests, keep in mind that you must be yourself. You can't be John Wooden, Red Auerbach, Mike Krzyzewski, or Dean Smith—you have to be you. It's all right to adopt certain ideas from other coaches, but if you try to be somebody you're not, you'll be inconsistent in your thoughts and actions, your players and assistants will question your honesty, and you will not be as successful as you could be. If you try to be someone else, the best you can do is only second best.

One of my favorite sayings is "I am me, and I want to be the best me that I can be." If all of us try to be the best we can be, we will be successful.

My favorite definition of success comes from John Wooden, the coaching legend from UCLA. He said, "Success is a peace of mind which comes as a direct result of knowing that you did the best you could to be the best you are capable of becoming."

My coaching philosophy benefited from the positive influence of a number of other coaches. My philosophical development got off to a great start with the help of my high school coach, Tony Creme. He was an excellent coach who stressed fundamentals and communicated well with his players, almost like a father figure. Later, in my first coaching job at St. Joseph's Orphanage, I was fortunate to meet Ken Loeffler, the brilliant former head coach at LaSalle University. He was 25 or 30 years ahead of his time in many areas, including the development of the 1-4 offense, which we started using at DeMatha in 1956.

Another man who influenced me greatly was Red Auerbach, the legendary coach and general manager of the great Boston Celtic teams. He taught me the importance of having the feel of the game—of observing closely and knowing what was happening out on the court rather than just being a spectator from the bench. He was also influential in the development of my conviction that each player has a certain role on a team, and that the ideal team consists of players who understand and fulfill their roles.

John Wooden was a dear friend for many years. He unselfishly shared many, many hours with me, all the while helping me determine where I was, where I was going, and how I should get there. I've often said that when Dr. James Naismith invented the game of basketball and perhaps dreamt of the perfect coach, the dream became a reality when John Wooden came along.

Coaching as a Career

I was working at my father's day camp after my freshman year at Maryland, and quite honestly, I had never contemplated getting into coaching as a career. I heard that the JV coach at my father's school was taking a head coaching job and that my father was going to move the freshman team's head coach up to coach the JV team. So I went to my dad and asked him who his freshman assistant coach was going to be. He said he had not decided, and I told him that I would like to do it. And that is how I started coaching. I then coached the JV summer league team and absolutely loved the connection with the players. From that point on, I knew I wanted to coach, but I also realized that I had to develop my coaching philosophy.

The many hours that North Carolina coach Dean Smith spent with me were some of the most valuable for expanding my knowledge of the game of basketball. Trapping defenses, four-corner offenses, foul line huddles, and changing defenses are just a few elements of the game that he helped me with by sharing his ideas. In addition to considering Dean a great friend, I also consider him one of the greatest coaching innovators the game has ever known.

Many other people helped me at different points in my career, and not all of them were basketball people. Jim Kehoe, the long-time athletic director at the University of Maryland, taught me the importance of discipline, of getting things done ahead of time, and of doing things well and doing them wholeheartedly. It was Coach Kehoe who told me, "If you don't have time to do it right the first time, you better make sure you have double the time to do it the second time."

Duke coach Mike Krzyzewski, "Coach K," has also been a great help to me. Mike is a good example of a coach who has adopted much of what he learned from others, then adapted those teachings to fit his own special style. Bob Knight, former Indiana and Texas Tech coach whom Krzyzewski played for and coached under while at West Point, has

"Is Morgan Wootten Your Father?"

I believe in my father's motto of "Be yourself." If coaches are not themselves, their players can spot it right away. Many people were surprised that I would want to get into coaching after having a hall of fame coach as a father. I was constantly asked, "Is Morgan Wootten your father?" Many thought I would feel pressure trying to follow in his footsteps or feel the burden of his success. I actually view it as good fortune that my entire life has been spent around a hall of fame coach. This allowed me to spend a lifetime developing my philosophy without even knowing it.

Any young coach can benefit from spending time around successful coaches and successful people in other walks of life. Ask questions. So many people think that they have to have all the answers. One thing I learned from my father was that coaches need to ask as many questions and observe as much as they can. By doing this, you will find out what to do, and more important, what not to do.

To truly be myself, I had to develop my own coaching philosophy and not try to be my father. When my father was coaching, he often sat during the games. Over 46 years of coaching, he mellowed and became a calm man who rarely displayed fire or emotion on the sidelines. I am very enthusiastic and intense when I coach, often standing during a good portion of the game. But in 13 years of coaching, I have felt myself become more mellow and calmer on the sidelines. Perhaps by the end of my own coaching career, I will find myself as calm as my father was during the games.

© Edward Potskowski

Morgan instructs his players as Joe, his assistant coach at the time, looks on.

been instrumental in Mike's career; Mike's great Duke teams have reflected many of the principles he learned from Knight. But Mike also added his own beliefs and experiences to come up with an approach to the game that is uniquely his. For example, Coach Knight will not run set plays designed to get the ball to his outstanding players, because he believes that everything comes from within the structured offense itself. Coach K, however, believes that a coach should have a special play to get the ball into the hands of a great player.

I met many of these men who influenced me so greatly at various clinics and basketball functions. Because of my respect for them and my desire to be the best coach I could possibly be, I frequently took the initiative to approach these men and pick their brains in an effort to increase my expertise. Not once was I disappointed by their knowledge or their kindness.

As a coach, you should find great value in the advice from people you respect, but you must construct your own distinct approach to life and to basketball. You will be better off developing your own philosophy as a coach and as a person, rather than simply trying to emulate someone else.

Parts of your philosophy will continue to evolve through the years. These will be primarily tactical elements that change with your personnel and with the game itself. The institution of the three-point shot is one example. Another is the shot clock, which is already being used in many situations, and I expect it to soon be used in all high school leagues. As it has done in the NBA and NCAA, the shot clock will speed up the high school game, making it more entertaining for fans and resulting in better basketball players. On the other hand, it will clearly affect a coach's ability to use delay tactics in the closing minutes of a half or game (or if his team is less talented than the opponent).

Developing My Philosophy

My philosophy was developed, much like my father's, from being around great people and learning from them. A coach's philosophy is constantly in a state of growth. This growth results from being in a basketball environment, whether working at camps, attending clinics, chatting with friends in coaching, or getting together with other coaches to share ideas.

John Wooden showed my father and me how to attend to every detail. I was 8 years old, and my family had referred to me as Joey for my entire life. We were at the McDonald's All-American game, and Coach Wooden walked up to my father and said the simplest sentence. "Morgan, I noticed that Joey is now introducing himself as Joe." We both found it amazing that a legend such as John Wooden would pick up on that small detail from a little boy, but that was the genius of John Wooden. No detail was too small; no job was too small. This was a man who swept the floor before practice every single day! Some coaches think there is a magic pill or secret to success. The secret is that there is no secret. Attending to details is a huge difference maker that is achievable by anyone who is willing to do it.

But the people who are influences on a coaching philosophy do not need to be big-name coaches; in fact, they might not be coaches at all. A coach's philosophy can be influenced by anyone who makes a lasting contribution to the coach's perspective. I recall my high school history teacher, Rich Macheski, who taught with more enthusiasm and passion than I ever saw from a teacher. His example encouraged me to be passionate when I coach.

Continue to Learn

To ensure that the philosophy you develop is a positive one, you should examine the approaches taken by successful coaches. Talk with them, read their books, and attend their clinics. Books and clinics are especially important to your growth and development as a coach.

Reading books allows you to find out what other coaches think, what they've done through the years, and what has worked for them. All types of publications are helpful, but a book—because of its depth—provides real insight into a coach's philosophical approach.

Attending clinics is an absolute necessity. Not only do you hear what respected coaches think, but you also have a chance in private sessions to talk with them, ask questions, and receive feedback about your own ideas. These gab sessions will contribute significantly to your philosophical development and growth as a coach.

The wealth of knowledge available is immense. Therefore, you need to seek as much advice and knowledge from other coaches as you possibly can. But being willing to learn is not enough—you must be *eager* to learn.

When I speak at clinics, coaches frequently come up to me and tell me what they are doing. I appreciate them sharing their approaches, but many of these coaches don't ask me anything. When they merely tell me what they do, I may learn from them, but they won't learn from me without seeking my feedback. Remember, learning stops when you think you have all the answers.

And don't limit your learning to clinics, books, and discussions with other head coaches. Chances are you may have great resources right in your own building in the form of one or all of your assistant coaches. I have had the privilege of working with and learning from some great assistants. In fact, over a dozen former DeMatha coaches or players are now college coaches (I believe this is an all-time record). What an opportunity I would have missed had I not been alert enough to learn from these talented people.

Touch People's Lives

As coaches, we are extremely fortunate to have the opportunity and ability to work with and positively influence young people. That's why coaches should follow this general rule: Be the kind of coach that you would want your own sons and daughters to play for. That is a good basis from which to evaluate and correct yourself. All of us should be determined to be that kind of coach.

Never lose sight of the tremendous impact you are having on young people's lives. We are with young people at their emotional heights and their emotional depths, the times when they are most impressionable. Teachers of other subjects would love to have the classroom situation that we do, because we have a class that young people are pleading to get into and be a part of. It is our moral responsibility to use this unique opportunity in a positive manner to help prepare our young people for life.

We live in an instant gratification society where even McDonald's is not fast enough anymore, but coaching is a profession that will reap rewards well down the road. Coaches often cannot tell how well their teams have done until they see how their players are doing 15 to 20 years later and see if they have become productive citizens. As a coach, you have the perfect classroom for teaching the players values that they can take with them for the game of life. You must always keep in mind that in the end your players will have an impression of you as a coach based on how you treated them, how you conducted yourself, and what you taught them—for example, if you taught them to prepare, to be punctual, to give a great effort, to win and lose with class, and so on.

As a coach, you must always be aware of the influence you have on your players. Because of their keen interest and emotional involvement in sports, your athletes will be hanging on every word you say. Many times, you may think you're not reaching them, but what you say to them in practice can determine how good their dinner will taste and how well they will sleep that night. An incidental

My first job as a basketball coach was at St. Joseph's Orphanage in Washington, DC. At that time, Rocky Marciano had just won the heavyweight boxing championship, and we were fortunate to have him visit the orphanage not too long after he had won the title. Marciano gave a nice talk and then took questions from the youngsters. Some of the questions were quite astute, such as whether he would recommend boxing as a career, or how his mother felt when he decided to become a boxer. Of course, there were also the typically humorous questions, and one of those almost got me killed. I cringed when one of the fourth graders at the orphanage asked, "Rocky, do you think you could beat Morgan?"

Fortunately for me, Rocky Marciano was a kind man. He looked at the youngster and said, "Well, I think it would probably be the toughest fight I've ever had, and I don't know which way it would go. If I won, it would probably be because I'm a little bigger than he is." Since then, I've always told people I'm the only person Rocky Marciano didn't say he could definitely beat. But what made me cringe even more than the boy's question was his response to Marciano's answer. He said, "I think Morgan would kill you."

At that point, I realized just how much of an impact I was having on these youngsters and the tremendous responsibility that goes along with that. We, as coaches, will touch our athletes' lives by what we say, what we do, and even what we think because the athletes can read us. We must never forget the impact we're having, even when it is not readily visible.

cutting remark, which you forgot about as soon as you said it, can stay with that young person and be a source of pain for a longer time than you may ever know.

At St. Joseph's, one of my best athletes was leaving the eighth grade and was destined to be sent to a trade school. But I thought he had too much talent for that, so I brought him home to stay with the Wootten family. The young man went on to St. John's College High School in Washington, DC, where he had an outstanding career both academically and athletically. He continued on to college, and today is a successful sales executive. I was truly honored when, years after he had played for me, he asked me to be the best man at his wedding and then to be godfather to his first son.

In fact, I have been asked to be in the weddings of more than a dozen of my former athletes and have been godfather to many of their children.

Priorities and Objectives

With a solid philosophy in place, you can then establish objectives for your players, your team, and yourself. Most important of these are the objectives for your athletes. Always keep in mind that the game is for the players, and that they are the most important part of any program. The coach provides the leadership, but the athletes must be the main focus.

Player Objectives

A fundamental job of a coach is to help the athletes get their priorities in order. We encourage players to devote themselves to four things:

1. God
2. Family
3. School
4. Basketball

Everything else must come after these. Young people who have their priorities in order will have the best chance of getting the most out of their lives, both on and off the court.

These priorities are one element of our coaching philosophy that has endured and will remain unchanged over the years. These four cornerstones came as a result of stepping back and taking a look at the characteristics desired in a player.

The primary emphasis on a strong spiritual commitment results from experience; those with such a conviction are better able to meet life's challenges than those without one. Second, we have found that young people who are loyal and devoted to their families are more capable of becoming loyal and devoted members of a team. Third, academics are the purpose of school; a student who is willing to work hard toward that purpose is more likely to work hard toward becoming a better basketball player and helping the team. And fourth, basketball is the sport that the athlete is playing, so obviously a strong commitment to that is necessary as well.

Players who demonstrate these priorities are far superior to those with equal talent who do not have such objectives. We've all seen teams with the proper priorities beat much more talented teams whose players are only interested in individual statistics and scoring their 25 points. That kind of player is not a winner in any sense of the word.

Instead, we'll take someone like Bill Bradley, former New York Knick and U.S. senator for New Jersey. Bradley was capable of scoring 50 points a game, a feat he performed on several occasions. But he did not care if he scored only 2 points, as long as his team won. Give a good coach a dozen such players, and that team will be successful, regardless of the level of talent.

Kids today want the same things as kids did when I started coaching over 50 years ago. They seek guidance, discipline, and people who are interested in them. We, as coaches, must be both teachers and guides, because kids sometimes have no one else to help them establish priorities. To reach these young people, I demonstrate to them what the proper priorities should be and give them examples of the kind of positive results such objectives can produce. I then try to make sure that they taste success when they attempt to put things in the proper order. Because once they've seen it work, they're convinced.

THOUGHT FOR THE DAY

God gave us people to love and things to use. When we reverse this, tragedy strikes.
—Morgan Wootten

One of the most flattering moments in my life came in 1990 when Adrian Dantley, a former player of mine who went on to Notre Dame and a very successful career in the NBA, spoke at my summer basketball camp. One of the campers asked him, "Who is the best coach you ever played for?" and I kind of gulped. But Adrian pointed at me and said, "That man sitting right over there." I was touched when I thought of all the great college, Olympic, and pro coaches for whom Adrian had played. However, the camper tried

Former DeMatha star Adrian Dantley defends Larry Bird in the 1988 NBA playoffs.

to burst my bubble by telling Dantley, "You're just saying that because he's sitting there."

"No," Dantley replied. "I'm saying that because he taught me two things. He taught me the importance of priorities, and he taught me the fundamentals of the game of basketball."

I use success stories like these to help convince young people that their priorities must be in order. Once they see how these personal objectives have helped other players, they quickly understand the importance of proper priorities in their own lives.

THOUGHT FOR THE DAY

Be concerned with process and the results will take care of themselves.
–Morgan Wootten

Team Objectives

After your athletes establish their priorities and have a good idea where they're heading, then you must establish objectives for the team. Our team objectives are very simple, and they never change:

1. Play hard.
2. Play smart.
3. Play together.
4. Have fun.

How a team approaches the game makes all the difference in the world. A team can take the floor with one of three perspectives:

Team A goes out on the court thinking that it must win at all costs, which places an unbelievable pressure on the athletes. This team will rarely play anywhere near its potential.

Team B comes into games with a fear of losing. Therefore, the players play the game trying not to lose rather than trying to play their best. Again, this is an unhealthy attitude that will prevent the players on the team from playing up to their potential.

Team C enters a game with the attitude that we stress: Play hard, smart, and together, and have fun. This is the best approach because it promotes maximum effort from all members of the team while allowing them to enjoy the thrill of competition. In this situation, the players don't feel the pressure of winning at all costs, nor do they fear losing. Rather, they simply try to give their best effort and to have fun, and, as a result, they play up to their potential.

Play hard. When you tell players to "play hard," you want them to give everything they have every second out on the basketball floor. If they give anything less than 100 percent, then they are not getting the most out of their abilities. They cannot reach their potential without putting maximum effort into everything they do.

Play smart. To encourage smart play, we try to get each player to work within the offense that we spend so much time on in practice and to play within his own physical limitations. To accomplish this, players must fully understand their roles on the team, and that starts with the coach. You must identify each player's strengths; this will help you define the players' roles. Then you need to communicate these to each player. If the player is one of your top scorers, make sure he knows he is your "go to" guy. If the player is your best defender, assign him the role of defensive stopper. By focusing on their strengths, players will make the biggest contribution to the team.

If both coach and players have a good understanding of the different roles and who will fill them, you're well on your way to having your team play smart. As a general rule, you do not want inventors out there (inventors are players who try to make a spectacular play rather than the simple, effective one). Tell the players to just make the basic plays and let the overall flow of the play take care of itself.

How much structure you want your players to play within, and how much freedom you give them, will depend both on your nature and on the personnel you have. Generally, teams with less talent and experience do better with more structure and control. Ultimately, when all five players are performing their roles within the team offense and defense and are playing within their own physical limitations, then you have a team that is playing smart.

Play together. Simply put, your team will play together if your players are as thrilled with a teammate's accomplishments as they are with their own. No one should care who gets the credit. If the team does well, everyone does well. Every player must be as excited when another player scores a basket as when he makes one himself—including players who don't play as much. As Ben Franklin told his colleagues in the Continental Congress, "We must all hang together, or we will surely hang separately." That's chemistry, which we'll talk more about in chapter 3. Instill it in your players, and you will find them playing together.

Have fun. When emphasizing that the players should have fun, we merely want to remind them that basketball is a game and that their primary reason for participating in the sport is simply for the pleasure they experience while playing it. But players won't get any enjoyment if they play the game afraid that they might lose or believe that they must win at all costs. Players should play with this mind-set: Basketball is simply a game, it's supposed to be fun, and we can have fun while we are busy playing hard and playing smart.

Practice as You Play

The best way to get your athletes to enter games with the proper perspective is to help them approach each practice with a positive mind-set. Stress that the players should play hard, play smart, and have fun while practicing. Conduct your practices in an upbeat manner. Your practices should move quickly and emphasize the repetition and proper execution of fundamentals.

One of the commandments of coaching is "As you practice, so shall you play." Because

Morgan begins his winning tradition at DeMatha in 1961.

Courtesy of DeMatha Catholic High School

our players follow this advice (we believe they practice as hard as anybody in the country), our teams are as well prepared as they can be when it's time to play a game. The players, consequently, enter the game with a feeling of confidence that inspires them to really get after the task at hand. They take the floor knowing that they will not beat themselves.

More teams lose because they have beaten themselves through poor preparation than for any other reason. Conversely, players who take the floor confident that they can win the game because of their preparedness—if they play hard, play smart, play together, and have fun—almost always come out on top in the end.

As you develop a winning tradition, your players will learn that maximum effort, intelligent play, and enjoyment of the game are the keys to the success of the program. After all, success is the greatest motivator; players who see what previous teams have done to be successful respond to the challenge because they want to be successful too.

Put Forth a Winning Effort

One of the all-time great sportswriters, Grantland Rice, once wrote, "It's not whether you win or lose, but how you played the game." And there is a lot of truth in that. Therefore, I never talk to my players about a game in terms of winning it. For example, I'll never say in a pregame talk, "Let's go out and win this game."

Adrian Dantley recalls a pregame talk I gave before we played St. John's one year for the league championship. According to Dantley, the only comment I made was "Everyone knows what DeMatha does in big games. Let's go." I did not tell the team to go out, win the game, and win the championship. Still, Dantley says that remark really fired him up.

And what do we want our teams to do in big games? More than anything, we want them to give a winning effort.

We keep score during games so that the team with the most points at the end is recognized for its achievement. And, without question, I want each game to go in the books as a "W" as much as anybody. But winning has

a prominent place in my coaching philosophy only if it is accompanied by a winning effort. A winning effort is more important than the actual outcome. When we can look back at a game and know we did the best we possibly could, then we know we made a winning effort. That is all any coach can ask of his players, his assistants, and himself.

A trap that every coach must avoid falling into is evaluating the success of the program in terms of wins and losses. This could result in the old cycle: If you win, everything is wonderful; if you lose, everything is terrible. But, again, if you and the players evaluate performance strictly on winning and losing, the team will not reach its potential. You will never acknowledge the mistakes made in the games you win, so you won't work to correct them. Conversely, the only thing you'll think about after losses is how poorly the team played. Then the players' confidence is bound to suffer. As a result, the task of improving seems overwhelming because the players see and hear no glimmer of hope for a turnaround.

What you should keep in mind and stress is that sometimes you can learn more from a loss than a win. The players may be more motivated to improve, and they may be more receptive to the constructive criticism that will help them do so. So maintain an even keel. Work on the mistakes you make even in a win, but also praise the successes even in the games you lose.

THOUGHT FOR THE DAY

A man may fail many times, but he isn't a failure until he begins to blame somebody else. –John Burroughs

Coaching Objectives

Once we've established objectives with our athletes as individuals and with the team as a whole, we must then look at ourselves. What is it that you want to accomplish through coaching?

As a coach, your biggest personal goal should be to do the best you can to have your team as well prepared as possible. You owe this to your school, your assistants, your players, and their parents.

From a professional point of view, coaches, like their players, should work hard to become the best that they can possibly be. Coaches need to continue to add to their knowledge of the game through reading as many books as they can get their hands on, attending as many clinics as possible, exchanging information freely with fellow coaches, and asking intelligent questions of the right people.

Basketball is full of nice people, and coaches at every level are ready and willing to share information. Whether you're doing the talking or the listening, you will become a better coach by discussing this great game with wise and experienced counterparts.

The Big Upset

When we were preparing to play Power Memorial High School from New York City (undefeated with their star Lew Alcindor), I went to an old friend, Ken Loeffler, for advice. Ken, who had been former president Gerald Ford's roommate at Yale Law School, was then coaching at LaSalle University. I told him we were playing against Alcindor, who was 7 feet 2 inches tall, and discussed what a tough task it was going to be. Loeffler said in response, "No problem. Just put a 7-footer in front of him and a 7-footer in back of him."

But, I told him, we didn't have a couple of 7-footers hanging around the DeMatha gym.

"Still no problem," he said. "Do it with a couple of 6-10 guys."

"But I don't have a couple of 6-10 players either," I responded. This went on until I finally admitted the best I could come up with was a 6-6 player. It was then that Ken asked the question I had already been contemplating, namely, "Why are you playing the game?"

That little bit of kidding aside, he then sat down and helped me devise the strategy that resulted in one of the biggest upsets in basketball history. Power Memorial's 71-game winning streak was to be snapped, and DeMatha High School was on its way to national acclaim.

Six Challenges of Coaching

When you become a basketball coach, you accept certain things that go along with the job. We have identified six primary challenges that a coach should be prepared to address:

1. *Your success is dependent on the abilities of other people.* Admiral Hyman Rickover, the father of the nuclear navy, believed that endeavors succeed or fail because of the people involved. Only by attracting the best people, he believed, would you accomplish great things. This is also true of coaching. You've got to surround yourself with good people. To a great extent, your success is dependent on the abilities of other people and how you can mold them, direct them, guide them, work with them, and lead them.

2. *Coaches are evaluated by everyone.* In almost any other profession, few or no people see the results of the work. But if a player misses a layup, everybody sees it, and the coach gets blamed (often correctly, but sometimes not) if the team doesn't play well. The coach is always in the spotlight.

3. *Everyone believes they have knowledge about coaching sports.* Outside influences have made our job more difficult. For example, some parents think that their child is the next Michael Jordan and that the only way he can achieve is if they control every step. Parents, fans, faculty members—pretty much everyone who attends games or has a connection to the program—will offer opinions and advice. It's easy coaching from the bleachers. People forget that we all learn from the ups and downs that life throws at us. Stick to your philosophy, priorities, and tactics.

4. *The highs are incredibly high, and the lows are amazingly low.* Athletes' self-images are tied to their athletic performances. And coaches are there when young men and women are most

pliable. In fact, players need coaches most at down times. A former player once came back to visit me and said, "Morgan, I'll never forget one time after we lost a heartbreaker and were really down, you walked into the locker room and said, 'Fellas, get your heads up, because we played a great game. If you think you feel bad now, how would you feel if you lost your soul?'" Players need you most when they're really low.

5. *The coach has a personal relationship with every player and has a dramatic impact on every player's life.* At DeMatha, every senior fills out an exit form before graduation. The form includes space for the student to write about any teacher at the school who had an impact on the student, and those comments are then forwarded to the teachers. If you're coaching at a school, you should recommend this exercise to your principal. After looking at those comments, you remember why you're coaching. Coaches have dramatic impacts on players' lives. Be the kind of coach you always wanted to play for, and treat your players the way you always wanted to be treated.

6. *Success is based on the unusual paradox of getting an individual to work to develop skills and then getting him to sacrifice that for the well-being of the team.* That just about sums up coaching right there, and what a wonderful and rewarding challenge it is.

These six factors need to be taken into account as you examine your strengths and your professional objectives. Some coaches find them to be a burden, but we believe they are the reasons why coaching is so special.

Summary

If you do the following, you'll form an effective coaching philosophy and help your players and teams reach their full potential:

- Be eager to learn, and work hard to be as up-to-date as possible by reading, attending clinics, and talking with fellow coaches.
- Be yourself, and strive to be the best you that you can be.
- Never lose sight of the impact that you are having on young people's lives.
- Teach your players the importance of having proper priorities that allow for maximum personal, academic, and athletic development.
- Emphasize team objectives of playing hard, playing smart, playing together, having fun, and giving a winning effort in games and practices.
- As a coach, make it your goal to have your team as well prepared as possible.
- Evaluate wins and losses objectively, focusing more on effort and execution than on the outcome of the game.

CHAPTER 2 | Communicating Your Approach

Your style of communication should be based on who you are and what your philosophy is. That's what you will be most comfortable with, so that's what will make your communication most effective.

No one way of communicating is successful for everyone in all situations. That means you should communicate in a manner consistent with your personality and the circumstances. If you are a vocal, fired-up kind of person, then be that kind of coach. Never abuse the players, but feel free to be animated if that's what you're all about. If you're a relaxed, father figure kind of person, then be that kind of coach. Perhaps you are somewhere in between.

Although styles of communication will and should vary from coach to coach, the one common ingredient should always be enthusiasm. Nothing worthwhile has ever been accomplished without enthusiasm. You can be animated or laid back and still be enthusiastic; so be enthusiastic in your teaching, preparation, and individual and team work with your players.

Communicating With Players

In communicating with the players on the court, a good rule is to precede any constructive criticism with praise. This *sandwich technique* starts with a base consisting of a compliment regarding a specific aspect of the player's performance. Then comes a constructive comment concerning an area in which improvement is needed. This is followed by more praise.

An example of this is "Hey, Bill, great rebound! But you failed to look up and missed the opportunity to throw a wide-open pass to your teammate, who could have triggered the break. On the other hand, you did a great job of protecting the ball, and that at least assured us of keeping possession."

The two things people like to hear the most are the sound of their own name and a compliment—preferably together. So when talking to your players, if you call their name and pay them a compliment, you know you're going to have their full attention. And that is communication at its best.

Honesty and humility are also important. Coaches shouldn't think that they can reach every player or that they have all the answers. A coach is not expected to know every single thing about basketball, and you should never be afraid to admit to a player that you aren't sure of an answer to the player's question. If a player asks a question that you don't know how to answer, do not be afraid to say, "That is a great question; let me give that some thought." This will give you a chance to call a friend in coaching and get some advice. If, for example, a player asks you to identify the best way to guard another player in a particular situation, you might say, "I'm not sure. Let's look at a couple of ways and see which one seems to work the best for you."

Don't assume that you must have an instant answer to every question. No one ever does, yet many coaches think they have to. When coaches start inventing answers, they lose a certain degree of integrity with the players, thereby reducing the effectiveness of their communication.

Treat every player exactly the way you want to be treated. Try never to make players feel embarrassed or that they are being treated improperly. And if they do think that you've been unfair, make sure they know that you have an open-door policy that encourages them to come and talk to you about it.

Try to remind players every week that they may come and talk with you about any problems they might have. And explain to them that if you seem a little harsh at times, it is simply because of your enthusiasm to see them become better players and people.

THOUGHT FOR THE DAY

Enthusiasm creates heroism.
–Morgan Wootten

Never Humiliate

My style of communicating to players on the court is not one of hollering or screaming. I may get a little loud sometimes, but I tell my players at the first meeting that when I get loud, it's because I'm enthusiastic.

Humiliating players by screaming at them has no place in coaching, not only because it is wrong, but also because it will not achieve the desired results. You need to treat your

Courtesy of DeMatha Catholic High School

Morgan communicates with his team in the locker room during a game in 1974.

players as the young men and women they are, and you need to treat them with the dignity they deserve. Also, though you may never intentionally humiliate your players, you must be careful that you aren't doing it unwittingly.

One day after practice, Chris Gildea, a player on the team, asked to see me. On the verge of tears, Chris told me, "Coach, you're really embarrassing me in practice. You're constantly harassing me to rebound stronger and to get more rebounds. I know you're doing this to help make me a better player, but it's having the opposite effect and driving me into a shell. I think the quiet type of encouragement will work better with me."

I thanked Chris for letting me know how he felt, and I made a conscious effort to provide more of that "quiet type of encouragement." Chris eventually became the team's leading rebounder and went on to a fine career at the University of New Hampshire. I learned a lesson from Chris and became more convinced than ever that the open-door policy is the best one for players and coaches.

The Chris Gildea example also illustrates the importance of flexibility. Be willing to learn from the talks you have with players and to make the necessary changes.

Instruct, Don't Dictate

Coaches must be teachers, so your style of communication on the court should be the same style of communication you would use in a classroom. When you work with your team, think of yourself as a teacher working with students. Give some direction, but promote an atmosphere of interaction and self-discovery.

When Wilt Chamberlain was traded to the Los Angeles Lakers, a reporter asked him if he thought Coach Bill van Breda Kolff could handle him. Chamberlain's answer was "No one handles Wilt Chamberlain. They work with him." When communicating with players, you must remember these words. You're not handling your players. You're working with them, helping them to become the best they can be.

Coaching as a Parent

I had the opportunity to coach both of my sons, and I believed that I did not have to be any different with them because I tried to coach all players as if they were my children. I did, however, make it a point not to talk basketball outside of the team setting unless the topic was first brought up by either boy. I would then discuss what was on their mind if they had a question. I have what I refer to as my "all-parent team." The all-parent team consists of those parents who tried to relive their athletic life through their child. When my children were playing the game, I made sure that I allowed them to enjoy basketball and allowed it to be their experience, not mine.

Be Forthright

As a coach, you always want to act and interact in ways that are true to who you are. When you do this, a natural line will be drawn between yourself and players without a word being said. This will lead to a healthy coach–player relationship. Coaches run into problems when they try to be "cool" with their players. Players will quickly notice if you are pretending to enjoy certain music or speaking in the latest lingo just to make them think you are more like them. They will respect you more if you have different interests because you are being yourself.

As coaches, we need to understand that we are with the players when they are at their emotional highs and emotional lows. We need to use this opportunity to be honest with them and tell them what they need to hear. Those who truly care about young people will not tell them only the positive but will also point out areas where improvement is needed. A coach sometimes needs to tell players that they have to work on a certain area of their game (their left hand, their jump shot, their defense) or that they need to work on their grades.

In today's culture, the perception of the coach can be a negative one. Many in the basketball world have the attitude that coaches hold players back or do not know what they are doing. In reality, the only people who do not know what they are doing are the ones feeding young players the quick fix or the easy way out. This may be easier at the time, but ultimately, it will not lead to the player's long-term success.

Encourage Player Interaction

Red Auerbach would always ask his team this question when they came to the sideline: "What do you guys see out there?" Similarly, after every workout and every game, we get together as a team and allow the players to talk first. We start this gathering by asking, "What did you guys think?" This allows someone to step up and say something positive about a teammate. One player may say, "I thought that Dave was really good on the boards today." Dave would then in turn compliment another player, who would then compliment someone else

We have found that this approach does a few things. First, as coaches, we always want our players to talk more, yet we are usually the ones doing all the talking. This approach prompts players to work on their communication skills with each other. Second, it allows the players to hear positive things from their teammates. This helps build chemistry and develop a positive feeling among the team. Third, it allows leaders to develop, which is crucial to a team's success. Every successful team has great player leadership. Fourth, it helps prevent players from getting tired of hearing the coaches' voices. When that happens, they'll tune the coaches out. Finally, players will gain confidence that they can speak their mind with no backlash. One player might say, "Hey John, you are really doing well on offense, but you have to guard someone for us to be a good team."

A coach does not have to control everything that goes on in the gym or within the team. It's great when, during a practice, a player turns to a teammate and says, "Forget the coach, just go out and play the way you know how." Players must be able to talk to each other and motivate each other to excel. Some coaches might not like this, but a coach often needs to sacrifice control and allow the players to work things out among themselves. When engaged properly, those informal interactions between players—which sometimes occur in the heat of the battle—are elements of the "glue" that holds a cohesive team together. That's one reason why well-coached, veteran squads are so tough to beat.

John Wooden said that when he first started coaching, he had a lot of rules, had very few suggestions, and commented on everything. After years of experience, he revised that statement to say that he had very few rules, had a lot of suggestions, and commented on a few things. Take it from Coach Wooden—you must know when to intervene and when to leave players alone to work things out.

THOUGHT FOR THE DAY

The art of being wise is the ability to know what to overlook. –William James

Be Available

The greatest gift that one person can give to another is time. Players respect a coach for giving them his time. We always enjoy driving players home (in a school vehicle, per school rules) or sitting down with them over a meal. This allows the coach and players to have a longer conversation and get to know one another better.

As a coach, you should also try to be in the gym and weight room when your players are working on skills and conditioning. The players will be aware of your presence and will appreciate the hours you devote to them. This investment also reflects an all hands on deck mentality that reinforces to the team that the coaching staff and players are in this together. The time you spend together interacting in a respectful manner and working toward the same goals will only enhance the trust between the players and staff.

Part of my job at O'Connell is to go to the local parochial schools and tell the students about O'Connell. We were out on a visit on the other side of the city, and I wouldn't get back to school until an hour after school ended. We had called a study hall for the team that day; my assistant coach ran the study hall in my absence. When I returned, he informed me that the team had complained about the study hall, that many players spent the time listening to their iPods, and that some had not done any work.

We were scheduled to lift weights the next morning, but before we began the lift, I had the team go into the gym and do some extra running to make up for their behavior the day before. Before the players ran, I told them that if any of their parents wanted to send me a note stating they did not want them in a study hall, I would happily excuse them from attending it. But if we were going to have a study hall, then we were there to study and get our work done. I could have ignored this small detail, but instead, I showed the kids that we cared about how they were doing in school.

Use Technology Effectively

Players now have cell phones that go with them everywhere and Facebook and Twitter accounts where they do most of their communication. Coaches need to embrace this new technology while never forgetting that a one-on-one talk will always be the best way to communicate with anyone.

Coaches can now talk to their players through the use of text messages. This form of communication allows a coach to stay in constant contact with players. The coach can provide an encouraging word after a tough practice or game, check on a player's injury, or remind players to get their homework done or to study for a big test. Players prefer text messages, and they typically respond quickly to any message sent. Texting allows players to stay in touch using a form of communication they are comfortable with. However, remem-

ber that an individual talk is still the best way to communicate.

We talk to our players about how the decisions they make can have long-term effects on their life, and technology is no different. We tell them that colleges and potential employers are now going on Facebook, Twitter, and MySpace to find out more about a person. Opinions can be formed about a person based on a picture that shows a negative act or something that is written on the person's page. As coaches, we are role models and need to reinforce to our players the need to use technology in an appropriate, honorable, and safe manner.

Streamline Game Communication

Communication on the court during an actual game is also very important but can sometimes be difficult. A head coach must be able to send messages to, and receive messages from, the players on the floor and the players observing from the bench. The coach must use both verbal and nonverbal means.

Most coaching staffs develop code words or short terms for plays. This helps expedite communication when a time-out in the action is not possible or advised. Use of these words and phrases should become so practiced over time that players respond instantly to their use.

When you're coaching a game, the groundwork of trust you've built through practice will cause players to respond to your communication. Your players have to be prepared to accept what you say without question, particularly in the crucial moments of big games. The groundwork for this effective communication is laid through the trust they develop toward you and through preparation in practices. Even though a player might think his coach is a few cards short of a full deck, the player should react to the communication instead of questioning it. In a tight game when time is a crucial factor, communication from the coach and reaction from the players can be the difference between winning and losing.

We try to practice the situations that the players will be in. For example, on the day before a game that will take place in front of a large crowd, we practice with crowd noise blaring from our speakers. This enables us to practice our relay system. For example, we will have an inbounder practice getting the call from the point guard (except in cases when the point guard is our inbounder) and then passing that call along so the other players know what we are running. This is an effective tool that works better than having the point guard try to yell over the din of the crowd. It also teaches the players to use their communication skills.

Right on Cue

Our O'Connell team was playing in the Beach Ball Classic Tournament, one of the finest high school tournaments in the country. In our game against Dunwoody, the score was tied, and we had the ball to inbound under our own basket with 1.6 seconds left. Kendall Marshall, who went on to star at the University of North Carolina and now plays in the NBA after being drafted in the first round by the Phoenix Suns, was the inbounder. We have a rule that players do not move to run the play until the ball is hit by the inbounder. As he slapped the ball, Kendall noticed that the defender, Chris Singleton (now a fellow NBA player) was face guarding our 6-6 wing, Dave Eismeier, who was lined up on the ball-side block. Recognizing that Chris did not have the ball in his vision, Kendall lobbed the ball over Chris's head, and Dave, ready for the pass, laid the ball in at the buzzer for the win. Chris never reacted. This was our team following a rule we had put in. This simple nonverbal cue won us the game.

Off-Season Communication

Perhaps the most important off-court communication between coaches and players is during the off-season. After the last game, we can't just tell our players, "So long, see you next year." It doesn't work that way.

Frequent off-season communication with players is important from an academic point of view, but it's also important in building rapport with your players. Coaches should ask their players how their lives are going, maybe talk about college choices with juniors, and certainly work hard with seniors as they prepare for college. Constant communication between the players and the coach during the off-season helps to build a strong bond, which in turn builds strong teams.

Whether you offer a friendly smile when passing one of your players in the hall, say a simple "hello" to acknowledge a player's presence, or show interest when an athlete comes to you with a problem, you can—through effective communication—help build enduring relationships that will last long after players have finished playing for you.

In fact, one way to determine whether you've been a successful communicator and coach is by the achievements of your former players and by whether they seek to remain in touch with you. The legendary coach Joe Lapchick once said that the greatest thrill in coaching comes when a player returns some years later and, with a big smile, says, "Hi, Coach!" Nothing else needs to be said.

You need to keep open your lines of communication with players, parents, and assistant coaches. Remind them that your office door is always open, and encourage them to come see you about any issue or problem.

In the long run, player–coach communication off the court is more important than on the court. Many players will remember the coach's pep talk that helped them get better grades long after they've forgotten the instructions on how to handle a zone press.

Communication Failures

One of the greatest obstacles to effective communication is assuming that a player, or even your entire team, already knows certain things. At the first practice of every football season, Notre Dame coach Knute Rockne would hold up a ball in front of his team and say, "Gentlemen, this is a football." That may sound overly simplistic, but you can't argue with success. Knute Rockne knew the value of not taking anything for granted.

No matter how hard we try to be great communicators, there will be times when we fail. But we should always strive to stay in touch with our players, coaches, and everyone connected with the success of our basketball teams.

You're always going to have some communication problems, but the key is to head off as many of them as possible. Learn to anticipate problems, and address them quickly and directly when they occur. Most of them will then remain manageable.

A Capital Miscommunication

At the end of the 1990 basketball season, our championship team was invited to the White House to help President Bush kick off May as Physical Fitness Month. Basketball was to be one of 10 sports represented on the South Lawn of the White House when President Bush made the rounds to view each sport. What a great honor for DeMatha High School to be the only high school team included in this gala affair!

However, try as I did to change it, the organizers told me that I could only bring 10 players from our 13-man team. Three of our players were seniors; one had already been to the White House two years earlier to meet President Reagan when he greeted our city championship team of 1988, and all three had secured college scholarships as a reward for their athletic and academic efforts in high school. So I thought the fairest approach would be to take the 10 underclassmen, and I assumed that the 3 seniors would understand that they were victims of the numbers game.

The mistake I made was that I failed to talk to each senior individually, and I found out later that there were some hurt feelings. I then met with the seniors and explained to them how hard we had tried to get permission to bring all 13 players, but that we just could not. The seniors understood, and the problem was resolved, but better communication on my part could have avoided the problem in advance.

Communication Among Coaches

As coaches, we must realize that it takes the entire team to get things accomplished. Not just one or two players or only the head coach, but the entire player roster and everyone on the coaching staff must contribute to the effort.

Morgan's basketball team, including Joe (number 20), in 1990.

Courtesy of DeMatha Catholic High School

Interaction between all coaches—from the varsity head coach down to the assistant freshman team coach—should be frequent, free flowing, and respectful. Coaches should also maintain professional confidentiality and never undermine their colleagues.

As the head coach, you must communicate effectively and often with assistant coaches so that they are prepared and comfortable with their roles. Part of the practice plan (which is discussed in chapter 6) should include a prepractice meeting among the coaching staff. At that meeting, seek the assistant coaches' input and make them aware of what you want them to do, such as when they should step in and correct mistakes. Good advance communication with your coaches will prevent misunderstandings and will improve the efficiency of your staff.

A coach who is followed by "yes-men" will never grow beyond a certain point. Encourage assistants to interject their ideas and to offer any constructive suggestions they might have. Even if you don't use a particular idea from your assistants, you need to let them know that you appreciate that they've taken the time and made the effort to come up with the idea.

One year at DeMatha, I suspected one of my assistants of being disloyal to the program. I never thought he was doing so deliberately, but I felt certain that he was giving others the wrong impression. So I arranged a meeting, the two of us sat down, and we worked everything out. Today we are the greatest of friends. From that incident, though, I started a tradition of passing out a poem titled "Loyalty" by Elbert Hubbard at the first staff meeting every year:

> If you work for a man, in heavens name work for him: speak well of him and stand by the institution he represents. Remember, an ounce of loyalty is worth a pound of cleverness. If you must growl, condemn, and eternally find fault, resign your position and when you are on the outside, damn to your heart's content . . . but as long as you are part of the

institution, do not condemn it. If you do, the first high wind that comes along will blow you away, and you probably will never know why.

Promote an environment in which your coaches feel free to give their comments. They'll like their jobs more, and your program will benefit from their input.

In addition, you should coach your coaches. As the head coach, it is your job to lead the entire program. Give your assistants opportunities to grow by giving them the lead in areas such as scouting, weight room, community outreach, travel, schedule, and so on. This will allow them to grow and have ownership of what takes place in the program.

Be clear with your coaches regarding the duties that they are responsible for. For example, give them specific tasks to handle during the games so that the staff is being effective overall (an example is provided in figure 2.1).

These duties allow the coaches to focus on specific areas and give the head coach specific feedback. Otherwise, some coaches might turn spectator and just start watching the game. The head coach can get the overall feel of the game while the assistants look at

Getting Involved

Jason Donnelly, now an assistant at Villanova, came to work with us at O'Connell directly from college graduation. He was the head freshman team coach, but he wanted to get involved with the varsity, so he came to me and asked how he could get more involved. I told him to take ownership of the scouting department for me. He took it and ran with it. He was able to give me a complete scouting report on each and every team that we were about to play. This information was invaluable to the team my first year at O'Connell. Sometimes we need to give our assistants the opportunity to make things happen. Subsequently, Jason moved on to Villanova from O'Connell and was part of the coaching staff for the Wildcats' 2009 Final Four team.

Game Responsibilities

1. Book: Spencer Westemeier (student manager)
2. Stats: Mike Adkins (student manager)
3. Comments: Eric Edwards
4. Time chart: Mike Cresson (freshman coach)
5. Shot chart: Joey Cantafio (JV coach)
6. Matchups (book): Bryant Majors
7. Overall defense: Bryant Majors
8. Overall offense: Matt Mihalich
9. Post play: Dave Neal
10. Guard play: Matt Mihalich
11. Referee at time-out: Dave Neal
12. Camera: Donald Darang (student manager)
13. Water: Jackie Myers (student manager)
14. Warm-ups: Dave Neal
15. Edit film during game: Joe Blaser

FIGURE 2.1 Game responsibilities.

their specific assignments. This allows each assistant coach to not only give immediate feedback to the head coach, but also take responsibility for and feel like a part of the team.

Communicating With Officials

Basketball is the most difficult game in the world to officiate. And, having officiated for 10 years, I can make that claim based on direct experience. Officiating is a thankless job, yet this great game would not be what it is without the dedicated officials who work night after night and do their job so well.

The coaching staff must maintain effective communication with officials. And it is not

that difficult to do, because the same communication philosophy that applies to players and coaches also works for officials: Treat them with the proper respect, and they will treat you the same way.

Coaches who bait, scream, and holler are not enhancing their relations with officials (or their team's chances). In addition, they are setting a bad example for their players, who will often follow their cue. On the other hand, the coach who treats officials with respect will almost always maintain a good relationship with them.

One of the best opportunities to get a point across to the officials is in the pregame chat. This is a chance for a head coach and members of the staff to generate good will between themselves and the officials—and perhaps get a message to them. For example, you can talk about a play in a previous game and say something like, "Can you imagine the official in this situation awarding two free throws for that kind of foul?" Most of the time, the officials will respond, "He must not have known the rules."

Pregame talks are also an opportunity to subtly remind officials about certain elements of the game that you think could become important in that particular contest. If you have a pressing team, one aspect of officiating that will figure prominently into your games is the inbounds rule. The rule states that a player must pass the ball inbounds within five seconds or the team loses possession. The official who hands the player the ball is required to give a visible hand count of each of the five seconds. So, in the pregame chat, you should ensure that the officials intend to give the hand count and that they will call a violation when the ball is not inbounded within five seconds.

Also, let referees know when they are doing a good job. As a coach, you shouldn't limit your communication with officials to times when you're trying to make a point. We try to compliment them every time we believe they deserve it, even after games we lose. They are human beings, so they like a compliment as much as the next guy. Plus, keep in mind that

When communicating with officials, one of my rules at O'Connell is to ask them questions rather than tell them that they've made a mistake or that they're wrong. You can get your point across much better by creating a dialogue with the officials than by attacking them.

officials talk to each other. If they consider you a fair coach and a gentleman—someone who treats them fairly even when you don't agree with them—they will be more positive working your games.

THOUGHT FOR THE DAY

What is right is more important than who is right. –John Wooden

Above all, treat officials with the respect they deserve. This approach is both morally right and strategically more effective. Basketball can sometimes bring out the best and the worst in all of us; we need to strive to bring out the best, especially in our behavior toward officials. When we do this, it's better not only for those who officiate, but also for our players, ourselves, and our sport.

Communicating With Parents

Coaches must make themselves available to the parents of their young athletes. Set aside time to talk with the parents individually or collectively. Remember, parents are rightfully involved in the progress of their children, and it is your duty to speak with them and patiently answer all of their questions.

As coaches, we sometimes expect parents to be a problem. And the problems that do arise often stem from parents' unrealistic views of their children's athletic abilities. However, if you tactfully and positively communicate a more realistic assessment of their child's talent, you can usually keep the problems under control, if not entirely eliminate them. That's important, because parents can be tremendous assets to your program.

I have had good luck with parents, with only a few exceptions. One of those exceptions first became evident at a tournament in a neighboring state during two games I had to miss (something that happened only five times in my career). My assistant, Jack Bruen, who went on to become the head coach at Colgate, took the team to the tournament and brought them home with two victories. As I was congratulating him, he said, "Morgan, everything went great except time-outs. Only four players would sit on the bench and listen to me. One of the fathers would actually come over and grab his son and talk to him during the time-outs." I found it difficult to believe that a parent would do that, and I realized that I was in for a yearlong problem if I didn't correct the situation.

During the first time-out of our next game, all five of the players sat down on the bench to face me as they are supposed to do. However, this one young man's father, sitting in the first row behind the bench, jumped up and started hollering instructions to his son. I stood up, looked the father dead in the eye, and said, "If you're going to coach your son, you're going to have to find a team for him to play on. Because you're not going to coach him here." I then went back to the huddle and started talking to the players. I never had a problem with that parent again.

I want to emphasize that my desire in this situation was not to embarrass the young man, but to solve a problem that I thought could only become more harmful to the player and the team if allowed to continue. If you don't address such problems immediately, all they do is get worse.

We must remember that each young person we are coaching is the most precious thing in the world to his or her parents. Consequently, it is very difficult for parents to be completely objective. For this reason, I often start conferences with parents by saying, "Look, I know this is an emotional subject. I promise you that I will treat you with respect, and I expect you to treat me with the same respect. Let's work hard together to do what is best for your child."

One useful strategy is to get all of the parents and players to sign a letter of understanding before the season starts (an example is provided in figure 2.2). This letter helps the parents understand how they can support their child but also how they need to allow the child and his coach to develop a relationship. As coaches, we want our players' parents to work with and support their child and team—but not try to micromanage every decision. We want them to understand that there will be ups and downs in every season and that they need to allow their child to go through those highs and lows. This ability to face adversity will help the child come out a stronger person.

When a player has a problem, we also want that player to deal directly with the coach. The player–coach relationship will be strengthened by communication and trust will develop. Today, many parents want to jump in and solve every issue that comes up for their son or daughter; in the end, these parents are not helping their children develop the skills that they will need in life.

Generally, coaches should view parents the same way they view the players—as part of the team. And good communication will help make the parents positive contributors. So try to make the parents feel as if they are a part of the program early in the year.

Once the team is selected, we invite the players' parents to attend a team mass at the school after a regular practice session. When mass is over, we have a social hour in which we all get to know each other a little bit better, followed by a dinner. At the end of the dinner,

Letter of Understanding

This will serve as a letter of understanding between ____________________ and the coaching staff at O'Connell.

To allow for ____________________ and the O'Connell team to have the most productive year possible, the following parameters are agreed to by the O'Connell coaching staff and ____________________ and his parents:

That all questions about playing time, role on the team, and the way the coach wants ____________________ to play will be handled directly between ____________________ and Coach Wootten first. The family may meet with the coach after ____________________ has done so.

That the family agrees to give positive support to the team and ____________________ regardless of how the team and ____________________ are playing.

That ____________________ will attend all team functions.

That the family agrees to say absolutely nothing negative in the stands about any player or coach, to have no communication with ____________________ during the course of the game, and to not say anything negative about the program.

FIGURE 2.2 Letter of understanding.

From M. Wootten and J. Wootten, 2013, *Coaching basketball successfully, third edition* (Champaign, IL: Human Kinetics).

I generally give a short speech. I talk about the rules the players have voted on, encourage parents to be active participants with the team, and emphasize that we all must work together to make it a successful year. At that point, we distribute the Commandments of Players' Parents. I also reinforce the point that my door is always open to parents and players any time they wish to come and talk to me.

Commandments of Players' Parents

Following are 10 commandments I ask of players' parents:

1. Make sure that your child knows that win or lose, scared or heroic, you love him, appreciate his efforts, and are not disappointed in him.

2. Try your best to be as objective as possible about your child's athletic capability, competitive attitude, sporting behavior, and *actual* skill level.

3. Be supportive, but don't coach your child on the way to the court, on the way back, or at home.

4. Teach your child to enjoy the thrill of competition. Don't say "Winning doesn't count," because it *does*.

5. Try not to relive your athletic life through your child in a way that creates pressure. Don't pressure him because of *your* pride.

6. Get to know the coach so that you can be sure that his philosophy, attitudes, ethics, and knowledge are such that you are happy to expose your child to him.

7. Don't compete with the coach. You'll end up either undermining your child's respect for the coach, putting your child in the uncomfortable position of having to take sides, or alienating your child and making the coach a hero who can do no wrong while your authority is shot down.

8. Don't compare the skill, courage, or attitudes of your child with those of other members of the team. And if you must do so, do it outside of your child's hearing and in confidence with someone you can trust.

9. Keep in mind that children tend to exaggerate, both when praised and when criticized. Temper your reactions when they bring home tales of woe or heroics.

10. Make a point of understanding courage and the fact that it is relative. Some of us climb mountains but fear a fight; some of us fight but turn to jelly if a bee buzzes nearby. A child must know the meaning behind Mark Twain's well-known saying, "Courage is not absence of fear, but rather doing something in spite of fear."

And recently, I've added an 11th commandment:

11. Don't force the coaches to think about you while they are trying to coach your child.

We've found this preseason gathering to be a great way to start the year on a positive note. It allows the parents to meet each other as well as the coaches who will be working with their children. And it helps begin building team unity among the coaches, players, and parents, which is essential to any successful basketball program.

At Bishop O'Connell, we also take time at the beginning of the year to stress to parents that before they make an appointment to see a coach, they first allow their child to speak with him, since the most important relationship is between coach and player. We also ask parents that they express their concerns about the coach directly to him and never to the player (just as the coach would never express any concerns about a parent to a player). Finally, we institute a rule that parents and the coach should take 24 hours to cool off after a game before meeting.

One of the cornerstones of the Bishop O'Connell program is belief. To build a winning team, not only must players and coaches have belief, but parents should as well. This belief should exist in good times and in bad, extending not only to their own child but also to the coach and program in general.

Audrey Clark Shows Her Son Belief

During Jason Clark's freshman year, we had been practicing about three weeks when I received a call from his mom, Audrey. She told me that Jason had come home saying that practices were too hard and that he was unsure whether he was good enough to play. Audrey told me that her response to him was, "Listen to your coach and tough it out."

Jason went on to an illustrious career at O'Connell, being named the Washington, DC, player of the year as a senior. He then proved himself at Georgetown, where he played for John Thompson III. As a senior there, he won the Big East sportsmanship award and was first team All-Big East.

I believe a big reason for Jason's success was his mother and grandmother, the late Janetta Clark, who taught him to listen to his coaches and work through the tough times. Audrey and Janetta never missed a game, yet believed in our coaching staff and never questioned us in front of him. They believed not only in Jason but also in us during both ups and downs. Their parenting helped Jason become such the classy, likeable man he is today.

Communicating With School Faculty

Stay in constant contact with your school faculty, including the classroom teachers of your players. Every teacher in your school can help your program in some way, even if it's just by coming to the games and showing support. You'll be amazed at how many people are eager to help your program if you only ask.

For years, all of our games at DeMatha were filmed by Rocco Manella, the head of our computer programming department. As a technician and as a friend, his interest was invaluable to me and to our program. Other teachers have kept statistics for us, and the art department makes posters for our games. Though not always possible, it is ideal if some or all of your assistants are members of the faculty. This helps increase the interaction between the basketball staff and teachers throughout the year. Your assistants can also easily check on the players to see how they're doing, both in season and out.

The faculty supports us because they know I do not put basketball ahead of academics. They know that I pass along this philosophy to my players: The classroom is more important than the court. They see our players taking the same course load as every other DeMatha student. And they know that I do not expect them to give our athletes any special treatment; they appreciate that I will allow players to miss practice for tutoring or to take an exam. Our coaching staff demonstrates its willingness to work with the faculty and reinforces the priority of academics over athletics.

We closely monitor our athletes' course work. Every two weeks, my players take a form to all of their classes. The teachers are asked to provide the student's current grade and any other relevant comments. This way, there are no surprises when report cards are distributed at the end of the term.

Any time a bad grade shows up on a two-week report, I have a personal chat with the teacher to find out what I can do to help the situation. And because the lines of communication between the faculty and me are open, the reverse is often true. I have teachers come to me and ask me to talk with a player who may be having trouble in a certain subject.

I also monitor the kinds of courses the players register for every year to ensure that they are taking the core courses required by DeMatha High School. Fortunately, these school-mandated courses are in accordance with NCAA bylaws regarding eligibility for college athletic scholarships.

Academic File

At O'Connell, we keep an academic file on each player. This file contains an updated transcript and biweekly progress reports. In addition, we make sure that players are aware of any rule changes that the NCAA Clearinghouse might have made in the past year. We review these files and rule changes with the players' parents at a year-end meeting to ensure that the players are making progress toward graduation and are meeting NCAA standards. This is another important means of communication with your players, and it shows that you care about them as complete people.

Also to help players meet the NCAA standards, I have all players take the college entrance exams in the spring of their junior year. At DeMatha, we were once fortunate enough to have Dr. Charles "Buck" Offutt, who was an expert on the Scholastic Aptitude Test (SAT); before his passing, he regularly conducted an SAT preparation course for basketball players and anyone else who wanted to attend.

We have had tremendous success in preparing athletes to play in college through our close monitoring of their academic standing and our strong recommendations that our players take the SAT prep course. It is a coach's moral obligation to prepare players for life after school. If you do not, then you are using your players.

That's why you need to make the faculty part of your basketball team. Let them know they are important and that you appreciate their contribution. I love it when a teacher comes up to me and says, "Hey, I saw we won a big one last night." Everyone likes to be part of a good team—one whose players are good people, have their priorities in order, and represent the school in the right way.

Communicating With the Student Body

From what I have said, you can see that I encourage players to take active roles as members of the student body. I encourage them to go to the school's other athletic events, support the school's teams, and interact with the other students. One year I called off practice so the whole team could watch our soccer team play in a championship game.

James Brown, a longtime national sportscaster now with CBS, made our basketball team as a sophomore. He did not play much that year, but at almost every home game, the crowd would chant, "We want James! We want

Mark Goldman/Icon SMI

James Brown interviews his former coach in 2003.

James!" The reason everybody loved James was that he always had a big smile and "hello" for everyone he met in the hallway, from the littlest freshman to the biggest senior.

While you are encouraging your players to get involved in the activities of the rest of the student body, also make an effort to keep the student body informed and enthused about the basketball team. The student body is so important in supporting the team from the stands and will be more eager to get involved if you make coming to the games fun. At one of our first home games each year, we give a DeMatha basketball T-shirt to all students who show up and support us. We also have different students dress up as the school mascot. This has become such a popular part of games that seniors vie for the privilege of being Buck, the stag. At our last home game of the season, we honor all of the seniors who will graduate that year. At O'Connell, we might give away free T-shirts or a slice of pizza to the first 100 students to enter a game. We've even given away shirts with individual letters on them to spell out our team name: *KNIGHTS*. This ensures that each student involved will be at the game; otherwise, the team name would be misspelled! All of these ideas lead to the students being more involved with the team.

When you urge students to attend games, also urge them to show their support in the proper way. Ask them to cheer for your team, not boo or harass the opponent. Then, when they really turn out and support the team positively, show your appreciation. For example, during morning announcements at DeMatha, we sometimes have our players come on the loudspeaker and thank the students for their support at the previous game. At O'Connell, the players sometimes pass out free pizza at school the next day, or the players may walk through the cafeteria, thanking the students for coming out and supporting the team.

Finally, and perhaps most important, let all of the students know that those who participate in the basketball program will receive no academic favors. The student body will be more supportive when they find that the basketball players do not get special treatment. Consequently, there is little or no jealousy or animosity from other students toward the student-athletes.

Communicating With Community Members

At DeMatha, we are proud that so many community-minded people in Hyattsville, Maryland, have chosen to be a big part of our teams over the years and have contributed to our success. If you're willing to spend time cultivating these relationships, you can drum up great community support.

For example, the local automobile dealer, Sport Chevrolet, has supported the school financially through advertising and donating cars for raffles. A nearby restaurant, Ledo's, has been another big booster. The owner's son graduated from DeMatha, and our basketball coaches gather there after every home game. The local Subway and McDonald's support us, as do many other business people, service organizations, and clubs in the area.

Community Service

At O'Connell, we have done several community service projects, such as having our program buy a Christmas gift for each student at a nearby school in a low-income area. We then go to the school, give out the gifts, and talk to the students about the importance of education.

We have also adopted a unit in the Army overseas and sent them such items as magazines, board games, and playing cards.

Another way that you can communicate with community members is to develop ties with the local youth community. For each home game, we select an elementary or middle school in the area and invite the students from that school to come to the game as our guests. This allows the youth to see the team in action and helps build strong community support. We also hold a community tournament at a facility called Hoop Magic, where we have over 60 teams compete at various age levels and divisions. Our players work the book and the clock. Through their involvement with the tournament, our players are able to support the local youth teams.

During the summer of 1977, I had an opportunity to take the team to compete in Brazil. With little prompting on my part, the community helped us raise the necessary funds to give our young athletes an experience of a lifetime. That team went on to become one of the five national champions we had at DeMatha.

Communicating With the Media

Whether it's on a regular basis or only a couple of times a season, you will at some point have to communicate with the local media. It can mean a great deal to your program if you make yourself available for interviews and take the time to courteously answer all of the media's questions.

Demonstrate to the reporters your understanding that they have a job to do, and that you view their job as important. Keep your answers to questions positive, and remember to promote the team and your players, not yourself. Because many media organizations have limited staffs to cover the high schools, you may want to reach out to them if you have a story that they might be interested in.

Try not to give preference to one reporter or to one media outlet over another. Several media sources cover our games, from small local papers to the *Washington Post*. Make yourself equally accessible to reporters from every news organization that shows an interest in the basketball program. Accessibility to the media can help your program attract more coverage. And equal treatment of all reporters can help ensure that your program receives fair coverage from the press.

Our players are available to the media. We do not believe in shielding or hiding the players; in fact, we encourage reporters to talk with them. This is part of their education (even at the high school level). Learning how to speak with members of the press is another aspect of their development. Though most of our players won't be doing media interviews the rest of their lives, the ability to think on their feet in a situation like that will serve them well, whatever vocation they choose in life.

We even like to provide media training for our players. A former team manager at DeMatha, Andre Jones, became a producer with a local television station. Each year Andre comes to the school with a camera and conducts interviews with the players to help them get used to being in that situation. If any of our players need a little extra work at it, we bring Andre back for another practice interview or two. The only rule for speaking to the media is that players must keep their comments as positive as possible. It serves no purpose to voice negative comments about others through the media.

Summary

The keys to communicating effectively as a basketball coach are as follows:

- Communicate your approach in a style that is comfortable to you and fits your personality and philosophy.
- Learn to anticipate problems, and correct them quickly through good communication.
- When offering constructive criticism, use the *sandwich technique* (compliment–critique–compliment).
- Be enthusiastic but not overbearing in your communication. Never intentionally embarrass a player.
- Be honest when communicating, even if it means admitting you don't know something.
- Always keep your door open to your players, their parents, your assistants, faculty members, your student body, and individuals from the community. Treat each group as an important part of your program.
- Treat officials with the respect they deserve. Use the pregame chat to your benefit.
- Be accessible and accommodating to members of the media. Promote the team, not yourself or only one or two players.

CHAPTER 3

Motivating Players

When your team does not play well, it may have nothing to do with the offense or defense you're using; rather, it may be because your players lack the necessary desire, enthusiasm, and eagerness to achieve. Your ability to increase their level of motivation will go a long way toward determining how successful your team will be.

Before we begin, let me first issue a word of caution against using a packaged approach. Do not try to treat all of your players the same, because they are not the same. Just as they stretch differently to warm up for practice, they will be motivated differently. Some are self-starters; others need a push. But the one area in which every coach should remain consistent is in applying rewards and punishments fairly.

Let's first consider when and what you should reward and punish, both on and off the court. I try to reward whenever possible; players love to hear compliments, so rewards really grab their attention. And I try never to punish, but instead to use discipline to teach. In the rare instances when I do punish, it is for improper conduct or a violation of a team rule.

As for what to reward, an obvious choice is good performance. But perhaps more important, always try to reward players who are working hard and putting forth a good effort, both on and off the court.

Once you know when and what to reinforce, you need to know how to go about it. The rest of this chapter describes the approaches that have worked best for me.

Verbal Reinforcement

The most effective means of reward on the court is a simple one: verbal reinforcement. You can praise this player for the outstanding pass or that player for the great defensive play. But if you praise only for the show of athletic skill, how are you going to reward the less athletically inclined players who give great effort? Chances are, you wouldn't, which is an obvious mistake. So keep in mind the different abilities of players and praise them for demonstrating hustle, too.

A player feels especially rewarded when his coach praises him in front of the rest of the team. Therefore, when a player makes an outstanding effort, I stop practice and single out the individual. Over time, the message that effort draws my praise spreads throughout the team; the players become motivated to earn that praise, and a greater team effort is the result.

On the opposite end of the spectrum from positive verbal reinforcement is punishment. I don't even like the word *punishment.* Yet some coaches punish more than they praise.

I strongly suggest that you never discipline to punish; rather, discipline to teach. This will allow you to complement your use of rewards with a disciplinary system that leaves no doubt regarding what is unacceptable in terms of effort, conduct, and court decorum. And it won't cause your players to be so frightened of the consequences after a miscue that they become hesitant or refuse to even try.

I've often said that it is not so much what you coach but what you emphasize that really counts. Your coaching philosophy will tell you what you want to emphasize, but remember that your players will react to what you are emphasizing. In their eagerness to please, they will try to do what they know is important to you.

For example, if you believe defense is important, your players will pick up on that by what you say and by what you reward. Every year I tell my players, "I don't know who will start this year, but I do know that the best defensive player will. And I'm not sure that the second-best defensive player won't also start. If it's a close call between two players as to who will start, the better defensive player will get the nod." This straightforward talk sends a clear message to my players about the importance I assign to defense. It doesn't just motivate my top two defensive players to excel, it motivates all the players to become better defensively, which means we will play better team defense. I also tell my players that the best rebounder will be in the starting lineup. And, as a result, everyone attacks the boards in our practices.

All players want to play, and they want to play as many minutes as possible. I frequently use this desire as leverage when I talk to the team about what I want them to do. I may then say, "If you noticed the other night, Joe played

three and one-half quarters. He's consistently been our defensive stopper. He's dived for every loose ball. He's our blue-collar worker. And we know that every good team has some blue-collar guys."

Right away, the players know what's important to me. If you take the same approach, pretty soon you will see more and more of your players playing better defense and diving for loose balls (or performing whatever skill you've emphasized). It becomes contagious.

The opposite is also true. Your players will know what not to do and what is unimportant to you by what you de-emphasize. If you don't glorify the three-point shooter, or if you don't play a member of the squad who never passes the ball, the team will realize that the long shot is of little importance, whereas passing is very important to you.

Joe cheers on his players during a game.

Once you've defined each player's role, you have to praise those who perform their jobs well. After each game, I make it a point to single out who led the team in rebounding, who dived for the most loose balls, who took the most charges, who did the best defensive job, and so forth. This helps the players who aren't getting the headlines to feel good about their contribution to the team, and it helps those who are getting the headlines appreciate their teammates. That puts you one step closer to creating the chemistry that every coach strives for, when the success of the team is more important to your players than their own individual achievements.

I remember hearing about an exchange between former Minnesota Vikings coach Bud Grant and his star quarterback, Fran Tarkenton. Bud was showing film of a reverse that went for a touchdown, and Tarkenton threw the key block that sprung the play. Bud praised every player involved with the success of that play, except he didn't point out Tarkenton's block. After the meeting, Tarkenton went up to Grant and said, "Coach, how come you didn't mention my block?"

Grant replied, "Fran, I know you're always going to do that." To which Tarkenton said, "Not if you're not going to mention it."

Remember this: Players pick up on everything you say and do. I have seen teams that come out and shoot around for warm-ups with no organization or structure whatsoever. Somewhere along the line, the coaches of those teams have communicated to the players (perhaps unintentionally) that warm-up is not very important.

I let my players know that the pregame warm-up is significant, and that they must go about it properly. On the other hand, hardly any of our players ever warm up before the second half. That's because I tell them that they can warm up if they wish, but it's not essential; I let each player determine what he feels most comfortable with. So most of my players sit on the bench and get mentally prepared for the second half. And if anyone gets the impression that halftime warm-ups are not that important to Morgan Wootten, they would be absolutely correct.

Coaches as Models

No written word,

No oral plea,

Can tell our players

What they should be;

Nor all the books

On the shelves,

It's what their coaches

Are themselves.

You're writing the gospel,

A chapter each day,

By the deeds that you do

And the words that you say.

Men read what you write,

Whether faithless or true;

Say, what is the gospel

According to you?

Play on a short verse by Rudyard Kipling.

Postpractice Meetings

I tell my players that I am responsible for their physical conditioning and behavior on the court. However, I also tell them that for the remaining 22 or so hours in the day, it is their job to keep themselves in shape and to conduct themselves appropriately.

One way I've found to have a positive impact on players' off-court behavior is through brief team meetings at the end of almost every practice. I use these meetings to talk about how the just-concluded practice went. I also use the time to cover any other points that I think are important, such as the rules that the team has voted on.

These postpractice discussions serve three purposes. First, they remind the players of their own team rules. Second, they allow me to emphasize to the players what I believe is acceptable or unacceptable behavior. Third, they help to establish a certain amount of control through peer pressure.

Note Cards and Notebooks

As coaches, we are always borrowing good ideas from other coaches. I borrowed the following idea from my coaching colleague, Tommy Orndorff, who is one of the top coaches in girls' softball in the nation. He has won state titles 19 of the last 26 seasons!

At O'Connell, we have long used note cards to give the players weekly goals. Some of these goals are assigned by the coaches, while others are assigned by the players themselves. We talk about these weekly goals after practice with both the individuals and the team. Letting the players know what their fellow teammates are trying to improve on builds great chemistry.

Recently, we have added Tommy's idea of using notebooks to this practice. The notebooks are a place for the players to write down anything related to that day's practice—for example, the diagram of a play or their thoughts on various topics, such as *What is success? What is mental toughness?* or *What does consistency mean?*—and a place to put their weekly note cards.

The coaches read the players' notebooks and can use them to discuss things with the players either privately or collectively after practice. Tommy told me that this also allows him to teach life skills.

Never be afraid to borrow from other coaches!

My teams traditionally spend much of their social time together. Consequently, the players tend to monitor each other in these off-court situations. I don't mean to suggest that they spy on each other, but rather that they keep each other focused on their goals and reinforce the proper behavior to achieve those goals.

I encourage players to come talk to me if they see improper behavior from anyone on the team. However, I do not ask them to tell me the name of the player violating the rules or the specifics of the incident. I am careful not to create the unhealthy situation in which teammates are squealing on teammates. The players feel comfortable coming to talk to me because they know that the conversation will be kept in confidence and that they will not be getting a specific teammate in trouble.

If a player feels the need to talk to me about such a situation, he will usually say something like, "Coach, can you make a general statement to the team regarding smoking?" That's all I need to know—no names, dates, or phone numbers. I'm not conducting a police investigation.

I will then use one of the meetings after practice to send a message to the team. "It has come to my attention," I will say, "that a few of you are not abiding by the curfew that the team set." Or, "We know we have a no smoking rule on this team, and apparently some of you have forgotten that." They usually get the message.

One-on-One Talks

One of my favorite means of reaching young people is through motivational, thought-provoking poems. Some of my greatest players, such as Adrian Dantley and Danny Ferry, have told me how much some of these poems have helped them.

But perhaps the best way to motivate a young person to reach his potential is through one-on-one talks. Occasionally take a player aside, pat him on the back, and let him know he is special to you and the team. Praise his effort, and encourage him to give an even better effort. You'll be amazed at how much a seemingly small talk can do. It can work wonders.

An MVC: Most Valuable Conversation

During Adrian Dantley's senior year at DeMatha, we went to Cumberland, Maryland, for the Alhambra tournament, the most prestigious Catholic high school tournament in the country. By the time we reached the finals to play St. Leo's, an undefeated team from Chicago, it had become fairly evident that our senior guard, Billy Langloh (who later went on to start for four years at Virginia), would probably be voted the outstanding player in the tournament. Dantley had won the MVP trophy the year before, but this particular year he had been slowed by a knee injury and forced to wear a knee wrap for the first time in his life. Understandably, he was discouraged.

On the afternoon of the championship game, I took Adrian aside in the hotel lobby and spoke to him for about five minutes. I told him that I thought Langloh would be the MVP, but I also reminded him that this was his own last high school game. "Why don't you go out like the All-American you are?" I asked him.

That night, Dantley showed up for the game without the knee wraps. He scored 38 points and grabbed 22 rebounds in 16 minutes, and we beat undefeated St. Leo's by a record margin for that tournament. It was the only loss of the year for St. Leo's, who went on to win the Illinois state championship.

The previous example is living proof of what a one-on-one talk can accomplish. Of course, I had a big advantage with Adrian Dantley, the kind of player who had that competitive fire burning in him all the time. But even the best of us need a boost at times.

I believe that coach–player talks prompt more positive responses because players like being dealt with individually. It demonstrates to them that they are important to you as individuals, and they appreciate your willingness to help them solve their particular problems.

A lot of coaches are skeptical about how much a simple talk can mean to a player and a team. Instead they focus their energies on

Kirk Sides/Icon SMI

Danny Ferry, a former DeMatha player under Morgan, plays for the Spurs in 2001.

looking for that secret offense or that magic defense that will win games. But I believe that individual communication is far more important, and I encourage you to give it a try. You'll find these one-on-one interactions more helpful to the team, both on and off the court.

Nonverbal Reinforcement

In addition to verbal forms of motivation, I use a system of behavioral rewards called "permissions." The system is based on the amount of effort and the quality of performance demonstrated during practice. Outstanding efforts and accomplishments earn players permissions, which allow them to get

Honesty

Earlier in the book, we talked about philosophy and the four cornerstones of belief, trust, honesty, and collective responsibility. At O'Connell, we use these terms to talk about the type of players, coaches, and team we want to be.

An incident that occurred involving Bryant Majors, my current assistant coach and a former player, is a good example of the cornerstone of honesty. At the end of the summer going into his junior year at O'Connell, I asked to meet with Bryant and his mother. In this meeting, I told Bryant that I did not think he was working hard enough on his individual skills. I told him that he had three months until the season started and that he needed to make a significant change or he was unlikely to play.

We won the regular season and tournament title that year in our league, and Bryant was our first sub at guard. The honest and direct conversation that we had allowed him to listen and make the change that was needed. If I had not been honest or if I had sugarcoated things, he might not have heard the message the same way. Also, my honesty created more trust in the relationship.

out of a certain amount of running at the end of practice. Failure to put forth total effort or to remain alert throughout the practice, however, may result in extra running.

At the end of practice, we add up the permissions to determine how many double separators each player must run. (A separator involves running the length of the floor in short sprints from foul line to baseline, half-court to baseline, the other foul line to baseline, and finally baseline to baseline. A double separator involves completing this sequence twice. We call them separators because they separate who is in shape and who is not.)

Another way permissions are granted is through our three foul-shooting sets during the practice:

1. Players shoot 10 free throws at the start of practice.
2. Halfway through, players shoot 5 two-shot fouls.
3. And at the end of practice, players shoot 5 one-and-ones.

If a player makes 9 or 10 free throws in any of the sets, he will pick up a permission. If he makes fewer than 7, he will pick up a double separator.

We assign permissions and separators to other elements of our practices as well, such as the half-court offense (which will be discussed in chapters 10 and 11). We make a game out of it; the winning side picks up a permission, while the losing side gets a double separator.

You can assign permissions or separators to any activity during practice. This will encourage your players to concentrate and practice as hard as possible, which is essential to player development. Coaches who have watched our workouts are amazed at the effort put forth by the players. I think this reward system is one of the major reasons why the players work so hard.

THOUGHT FOR THE DAY

There is no elevator to success—you have to take the stairs.

I also encourage hustle by allowing players to reduce their running at the end of practice in ways independent of permissions and separators. Most of our conditioning work is done during the practice itself, so the amount players run at the end of practice varies with how much conditioning I think the players actually got during practice. If, for example, we're running 20 sprints in two minutes after a particularly tough practice, I may decide that the leader after 10 will get to drop out, then the leader after 12, and so on.

At the end of practice, some players have more permissions than separators and do not have to do the extra running at all. Those who have the extra running try to borrow permissions from the players who have a surplus by offering to stand in line for the teammate's lunch, carry his books, or shovel snow off his car. But any player who does finish in a deficit will have to run at least one double separator.

It always works out that we issue more permissions than separators, however, so most players who end up running only run one double separator, which they must complete in one minute. But I do not view this extra running at the end of practice as a punishment; rather, I tell the players that it is an opportunity for them to get in a little better condition.

The system of permissions is actually designed for training the mental, more than the physical, condition of players. Players' awareness of permissions and separators increases their concentration and effort during practice. They perform with maximum intensity because they know it can result in permissions and therefore fewer separators. Additionally, the bartering between players who have extra permissions and those who need them increases the camaraderie among the players and invariably leads to some of the more amusing moments of practice.

Problem Behaviors

The permission system works well on the court in practice. But how do you administer rewards and punishment relative to compliance with or violation of team rules?

Because I believe that the team is not my team, but rather the players' team, I let the players make the rules. However, I do encourage the team to set as few rules as possible. And I've learned not to fall into the trap of designating exactly what punishments will be applied if the rules are broken. If you announce what the punishment is before an infraction occurs, you'll paint yourself into a corner. Any situation that arises should be dealt with in the context of its own circumstances.

You can ruin or at least damage future athletic and academic careers when you paint yourself into a corner by announcing penalties in advance. Penalties can only be fairly arrived at after all the facts have been weighed.

Flexibility Is a Must

When I was a young coach, I asked the players to set the night curfew for a road trip. When the curfew was established, I foolishly announced that anyone missing the curfew would be off the team.

Wouldn't you know it, my six-foot-eight star center, Sid Catlett, and a young sophomore named Billy Hite missed the curfew by 15 minutes. At the team breakfast the next morning, I announced that both of them were off the team because I had said that would be the penalty.

But after talking to the two players individually, I found out that they had had a legitimate reason for being late. Now my problem was to solve the bad situation that I had created by announcing a penalty without extenuating circumstances in advance.

The next school day, I called a meeting of the team and had both Sid Catlett and Billy Hite attend. I told the rest of the players that if Catlett was kicked off the team, all the college coaches who were recruiting him would think he was a bad person, and we all knew that wasn't true. I could not, I said, put myself in the position of playing God and possibly ruining a young man's future. I told them that Sid would be reinstated, and that, because Sid was being reinstated, Billy Hite had to be brought back as well.

Sid went on to a great career at Notre Dame. Billy had a great football career at the University of North Carolina and is now the associate head football coach at Virginia Tech.

For less serious infractions that come up along the way, you have to use your good judgment. If a player is slightly late for practice, I merely say, "You've missed some of your conditioning. But don't worry. At the end of practice, we'll let you catch up." That usually drives the point home.

One punishment that I do not believe in is reducing a player's minutes in a game. If the penalty is worthy of suspension, then the player should miss the whole game. Conversely, if a player dresses for the game, he should be allowed to play as much as he is needed. (This applies to injuries, too, as we'll discuss in the next chapter.)

If you try to punish a player by limiting his minutes, you are getting into murky waters. First of all, the ever-changing conditions in games never really allow you to predict how many minutes a particular player will be playing. A second problem is that you may send the wrong message to the player about his role on the team.

When a player has an unexcused absence or exhibits bad conduct, a good one-on-one talk generally ensures that it will not happen again. Of course, what is said in these talks will vary depending on the circumstances, but one of the main points you want to emphasize to the player is that his behavior reflects what kind of person he is. Ask him, "Is this the person you want to show to the rest of the world?" Tell him that people, including college representatives, will be forming opinions of him based on the image he presents on the court.

In addition, you can remind players that they also represent their families and their school. In these situations, try to appeal to the players' sense of loyalty, pride, and commitment.

People often ask me if kids are as easy to coach and as good today as they were 50 years ago. I think kids today are as good as ever. They need the same things kids needed 50 years ago: discipline, love, and attention. They need adults in their lives who care for them, treat them as human beings, take the time to work with them, and give them constructive criticism. As coaches, we should provide all of these—not only because it's the right thing to do, but also because we want to better our young athletes.

Curfew on Discipline

During the 1989 season, we played against a team on which some of the players had broken curfew. Before the game, their coach announced that those players would not start, and none of them played in the first half while we built a lead. But the coach allowed the curfew violators to play in the second half, and because they did, their team was able to pull out a victory. To me, the only thing this team's coach proved to his players was "We can't win without you." The original intent of the punishment was lost, and the players suffered no negative consequences from their actions.

Good Decisions on Players

One of the best ways to prevent problems from happening is to pick good people for your team. The only way to develop the best team possible is to put good people on it, so choose players who want to come to practice, are unselfish, and are dedicated to their studies. I don't care how talented the player is; a player of lesser ability with a greater attitude will do better in the long run.

Talent is only about seventh or eighth on the list of what I look for in a player. Don't get me wrong, talent is nice. But other things are more important.

When evaluating players, I ask, "What kind of person is he? A good person? Loyal? Dedicated? Does he get along well with people? Is he eager to sacrifice for the good of the team? Will he solve instead of create problems? Is he emotionally balanced? Is he conscientious about schoolwork?"

If the answer to all of these questions is "yes," only then do I start to consider the player's physical talent and basketball skills. By picking good people this way, you'll

One of my most rewarding seasons was the 2000-2001 year. Our backcourt was supposed to be made up of three young men who would later go on to Division I colleges. Because of various circumstances, though, all three were not in school or on our roster when the season began. That meant that three young men who were expecting to be backups all of a sudden became starters. Our motto became "Is this year's story going to be about the guys who left or about the guys who stayed?"

Everyone decided the story should be that those who stayed were champions. And champions they were. That team won our conference regular season, our conference tournament, the Washington, DC, city championship, and the prestigious Alhambra tournament. The team was clearly one of the top teams in the nation.

find that you don't have to worry about punishment. You'll be too busy using your reward system instead!

One example of a young man's character exceeding his basketball talent was Billy Mecca, whom I kept as the 16th player his junior year. The only reason I kept him was because he was a great kid and possessed all the personal qualities I like to see. He could be an inspirational leader for us, I thought; he could improve the team's chemistry with his attitude and his closeness to the rest of the members of the team. But because Billy was only five-foot-five and had limited abilities, I told him he probably would have a tough time making the team as a senior. Billy proved me wrong his senior year (and I was never so happy to be wrong). He became our starting point guard, won a full scholarship to Niagara University, and today is the assistant athletic director at Quinnipiac College in Connecticut.

Invariably, every four or five years, these situations repeat themselves. Some player I'm counting on will fall backward because

he no longer works to improve his game; some other player will improve dramatically, emerge almost out of nowhere, and become an established star. Such disappointments and surprises are not unique to DeMatha. If you'll recall, Michael Jordan once got cut from his high school basketball team.

One way to help minimize these mistakes is to be more concerned with whom you're going to cut than whom you're going to keep, even though it's tempting to take the opposite approach. When you're deciding who will be on your team, make sure you know the name of each player you're thinking of cutting, what he can and can't do, and why you're cutting him. And when you do make cuts, be sure to invite those underclassmen back and let them know they will get a fair shot next year if they work hard to improve—as Billy Mecca did.

Keep an open mind about the potential of your players. The projected starter may not pan out, but the player you put in his place may be the next Michael Jordan!

Chemistry 101

The professional basketball that your players see on TV has unfortunately become a game of individual stars. One thing that hasn't changed, though, is that the teams that play together are still the most successful. The Los Angeles Laker teams of the early 2000s won multiple NBA championships only when Shaquille O'Neal and Kobe Bryant decided to play together and put the team's fortune ahead of their own egos.

Although you may not have a Shaq, a Kobe, or a Jordan, each team has its stars, and you as the coach must help all of your players understand that the success of the team is more important than their individual accomplishments. In other words, you must coach chemistry. Good coaches are also good salesmen, so take every opportunity to remind your players of the value of hard work, commitment, dedication, sacrifice, and teamwork.

A team with strong chemistry will not only play better on the court, it will also be able to better weather any storms that come along. Adversity can tear teams apart, but good chemistry will help keep them together and minimize dissension and finger-pointing. When players start blaming each other, that's when you have problems. By constantly coaching against that, you can help head off potential problems.

THOUGHT FOR THE DAY

For the strength of the pack is the wolf, and the strength of the wolf is the pack.
—Rudyard Kipling

Preserving or improving team chemistry should be always on your mind. You can do something simple such as giving your players the thought for the day at each practice. This is something I've done for years, and it is a great opportunity to instill the values you want in your players. You'll see examples of thoughts for the day scattered throughout the pages of this book. (See chapter 6 for a more detailed explanation of how I incorporate the thought for the day into practice.) Hall of fame coach Pete Newell talks about four guidelines he keeps in mind to instill chemistry:

1. Teach your players to compete hard every day.
2. Maintain great communication between and among players and coaches.
3. Do not fear failure (have an attack frame of mind).
4. Do not allow excuses. Just get it done.

My own two top guidelines for instilling chemistry within a team are as follows: (1) Choose good people, and (2) define players' roles.

Coaching Chemistry

"Coach chemistry every day." At O'Connell, I use this motto with our coaches all the time. You need to coach chemistry in all that you do—by checking on players' grades, by asking how things are going in their lives, by getting in the gym and shooting with them one on one, and so on.

One of the big ways that we do this at O'Connell is through our summer overnight camp for youth players. We ask our players to referee at the camp. They work a long day, lift weights after lunch, have a skill workout after dinner, and pick up at the end of the day. They then stay together in the dorms.

This time brings the group together.

Choose Good People

The first step in coaching chemistry is one that we just talked about: choosing good people. As mentioned, talent is not even near the top of what I look for when deciding which players I want to keep. I've cut players with more than enough talent to make the squad because I knew by their attitudes that they would be bad for team chemistry. And I've kept players who were less talented physically because I knew their attitudes and charisma would be invaluable to team chemistry.

The MVP Who Never Started

In 2000, I had the honor to coach a senior named Tilden Brill. He understood that he wasn't going to play a lot, but his enthusiasm was infectious, and he was easily the most popular player on the team. When we gathered in the locker room before every game, Tilden would lead the chants and get the adrenaline pumping. He was probably the most remarkable leader of that kind that I've ever coached, and we had a tremendously successful year in large part because of him. We won 29 games that year, as well as our league title, the city title, and the prestigious Alhambra tournament.

If you asked me who our MVP was, it was a no-brainer: a guy who never started. At our season-ending banquet that year, we created an award—the Tilden Brill Award—to be given to the top team leaders. He showed how a guy who didn't play a lot could become the heart and soul of a team, and he made us champions. When you're selecting your team, don't get too mesmerized by the stars, and consider making room for the Tilden Brills of the world.

Define Players' Roles

Another important part of coaching chemistry is defining the role that each player will play for the team, and then letting each player know what his role is and how the team will benefit if he performs his role well. Before the season starts, I try to let each player know how I envision him contributing to the team's success.

Your best players will be easiest to identify, and if they are competitors, they will relish taking on a prominent role. You still need to let the rest of the team know how this benefits them. If you have a great post player, you might say something like, "If we're going to be successful, we've got to pound the ball inside to Jim. And the more times he gets the ball, the better we'll all do. The defense will start collapsing on him, and that's going to leave the rest of you open for good shots."

Put a lot of thought into how players who aren't superstars can contribute. I like to have at least one defensive stopper and several

Morgan, here in 1991, knows how to define players' roles so that everyone contributes.

Courtesy of DeMatha Catholic High School

excellent rebounders. To one of these players, I may say, "You may not end up taking a lot of shots, but where you're really going to help us win is in being aggressive and grabbing 10 rebounds a game for us." Every great team needs these blue-collar players. If you want a shiny floor, someone has to polish it. If you want a beautiful garden, someone has to weed it.

Another example is with juniors who may not get a lot of playing time during the season. I might call one in and say, "Right now, it looks like you're not going to be in the top eight, so you're probably not going to get as much playing time as you'd like. But you have to make every practice your season and be ready. A little foul trouble or an injury, bingo, you're in there."

I often follow that up with examples of previous players who were in similar positions. Speaking to that junior, I might bring up Kenny Carr, who didn't play much when he was a junior because Adrian Dantley was in front of him. But he bought into what I said and worked hard every practice. The next year, he was a first-team All-American. He went on to become a three-time All-American at North Carolina State, play 10 years in the NBA, and play on the 1976 Olympic team that won the gold medal in Montreal.

Summary

The following are the most effective ways to motivate your players to become the best they can be on and off the court:

- Be fair in applying rewards and disciplinary actions.
- Praise your players whenever possible, especially for an outstanding effort.
- Emphasize in your speech, actions, and reward system what is important to you. Your players will react to what you emphasize.

- Never discipline to punish; discipline to teach.
- Take the time to talk with your players individually to motivate them and to work out problems.
- Use inspirational poems and clever sayings to motivate players.
- Never announce penalties for rule violations in advance.
- Remember that partial suspensions (reducing playing time as punishment) can send the wrong message to a player.
- Choose good people for your team.
- Coach chemistry at every opportunity, with the goal that your players will be more concerned about the success of the team than their individual accomplishments.

CHAPTER 4

Running a Basketball Program

It's flattering when coaches ask us for advice on how to build or improve their basketball program, but they should not expect a magic formula. There isn't one; at least we haven't found it.

Although top basketball programs achieve a similar level of success, they don't do it the same way. Your efforts to run a top-notch program will bear fruit only if you target them to your particular needs. Although DeMatha and O'Connell basketball are recognized as two of the finest high school programs in the nation, the system we use may not be ideal for you. Instead, look to build your own DeMatha or O'Connell using a variation of our approach that suits your situation best. In this chapter, we provide guidelines for developing and implementing a system that you can tailor to the specifics of your program.

Style of Play

The first and most important step in building a basketball program is developing a system, or a style of play. Your philosophy and knowledge of the game will shape that system. But don't get too set in your ways. Be flexible so you can change your system to best utilize the abilities of your players.

Unlike colleges, at the high school level, we cannot give scholarships to players who we think would look good in our school's uniform. Nor do we have the luxury of keeping the same players for several years as do coaches in the NBA. Therefore, we must be flexible enough to adapt our system each year to maximize the attributes of the players on the team.

In 2004, we had a talented team returning to O'Connell, but in August, our 6-9 center decided to transfer to another school. We went from a team that was going to be strong inside to a team that had good overall height but no players taller than 6-6. We had to adjust our emphasis for that year. A 6-5 player named Ernie Lomax became our starting center. Ernie was not a scorer, but he was a big physical presence who loved to pass. We were able to use our post as our leading assist man, because he was always able to find the open man. The team adjusted great to the new philosophy. We went 30-4, and we won the state, league, and Alhambra championship. If we had tried to bend the players to fit the system that we had anticipated, we would not have been as successful. Instead, coaches need to bend the system to fit their players.

Some coaches do very well with mediocre players but find that their teams struggle when they have more talented athletes. Other coaches seem to excel with a superstar but don't fare as well with a solid all-around team. Those mixed results based on personnel differences reflect the coaches' stubbornness in sticking with the style of play that they like, no matter what. They might try to modify it slightly from year to year, but the same basic style of play emerges because it's the one they are most comfortable with. What these coaches fail to consider or acknowledge is that certain systems are more successful with certain kinds of talent. A coach who stays primarily with one system will only be successful during those years when the talent happens to match the system.

For example, a coach who is married to a zone defense that best suits a taller, slower

A Mismatch

The varsity team was small and quick, and the players excelled in a full-court pressure defense. Our junior varsity, in contrast, was one of the biggest we've ever had. It featured six-foot-seven Kenny Carr, who would later make a name for himself at North Carolina State and with the Portland Trailblazers.

When the junior varsity returned from its first game, I asked the coach how much he'd won by. "We got beat," he replied.

"You got beat? How?"

"Well, we were pressing all over the court," he answered, "and they just kept zipping through us. Our big guys just couldn't stay up with them."

I then understood the problem and its correction. "You don't have a pressing team," I replied. "A team with that size should do no more than just play solid half-court defense because no one will ever get a second shot against you."

The coach of that team, Marty Fletcher, took my advice, and that team never lost another game. Marty is currently the assistant athletic director and head coach of the men's and women's basketball teams at the University of Colorado at Colorado Springs.

team may find himself coaching a team that lacks size but is extremely quick. Instead of playing his favorite zone with such a team, that coach should switch to a pressing defense that would take advantage of players' quickness and create turnovers. But the reverse can also be true, as it was one year at DeMatha.

To be a consistent winner, the coach and the system must be flexible enough to bring out the best in the players as individuals and to capitalize on those strengths for the good of the team. Your coaching philosophy should allow for such flexibility. Although the system that fits that particular team may not be your favorite or the one you know best, it may be the one that gives your team its chance to become the best it can be. Providing that chance is the essence of coaching.

If you bend the system to fit the ability of the players, you can then take it one step further and design a system that will get the ball into the hands of your best players most frequently. Set aside at least one special play to accomplish this purpose. If you're blessed with two or three highly skilled players, then it is wise to have a play for each of them. To keep all the players happy, some coaches have a play isolating each position. Whatever the approach, a coach needs set plays that allow the team to go to its money players in the clutch.

Having advocated flexibility, we must now issue a word of caution: Make sure your system is *intelligently* flexible. Remember, there is no progress without change, but change does not necessarily mean progress. Study your system, and change only when the talent you have makes it beneficial to do so. Your knowledge and perception of players' skills and intangibles will help guide you to the type and extent of change, if any, that will be most beneficial.

THOUGHT FOR THE DAY

We don't need more strength, more ability, or greater opportunity. What we need is to use what we have. –Basil S. Walsh

AP Photo/SJP

Six-foot-seven Kenny Carr enjoyed a long NBA career following his playing days with Morgan.

Coaching Staff

A head coach must surround himself with good people and must use the knowledge and talents of these people as fully and effectively as those of the players. Assistant coaches want to work under a great head coach.

A great head coach is one who nurtures the development of his assistants by giving them both responsibility and guidance. This responsibility and guidance help the assistants reach their goals and help them define their own philosophies in coaching. In addition, a great head coach teaches his assistants

how to compete to win not only the big game in January, but also the summer matchup in July. And finally, a great head coach is one who teaches his assistants the organizational and business side of running a program.

If you're coaching in a program that provides for assistant coaches, hiring and working with your staff are two of the most important things you will do. The old adage "Two heads are better than one" certainly applies to assistant coaches.

When hiring assistants, look first at character and what kind of person a candidate is before evaluating his talent and experience. I believe that successful people share six personality traits, and I look for these in my assistants:

1. Energy
2. Likability
3. Integrity
4. Drive
5. Willingness to sacrifice
6. Ability to see what needs to be done ahead of time

Find young assistants who are willing to do what you ask your players to do: work. Your assistants should be willing to work hard at developing relationships with the community, your feeder programs, and the student body. They should be eager to learn the game.

In addition, you want assistants who believe in your overall coaching philosophy. After all, in many respects they are an extension of you, another set of eyes and ears. However, you don't want clones of yourself or people who are afraid to speak up. Assistants who are free to think independently and encouraged to do so can elevate your program more than you might imagine possible.

Once you've hired your assistants (or accepted the services of volunteers), make sure you put them to work. Don't try to do everything yourself, or you and your program will suffer.

Head Coach's Responsibilities to Assistants

I view my number one responsibility to my assistants as preparing them to be head coaches. Assistants should view you as a teacher, facilitator, role model, and friend—in that order.

Mark McCormack, one of the true pioneers in sport management and marketing, has four rules for treating employees right, and we've come up with additional ideas about how to build a good staff and keep morale high. Here are the highlights of how we recommend maximizing a staff's effectiveness and keeping it happy.

Pay them what they are worth. Unfortunately, many of us are not in a position to reward our assistants with top-dollar salaries. At DeMatha, we've never had a big budget for paying assistants, but there are many more ways to "pay" a person than money. I try to take my assistants to as many clinics as possible. If I have them assist in my demonstration, I'll give them a portion of my stipend for appearing at the clinic. I also try to get my assistants jobs at summer camps, be it mine or others, to help them financially and provide opportunities for their personal and professional growth. Another little thing I like to do is take my assistants out to dinner at a local restaurant called Ledo's after every home game. I pay the bill out of money raised through the basketball clinic I run at DeMatha. We talk about the game and enjoy each other's company, which is important in promoting a sense of togetherness. Be creative in finding ways to "pay" your assistants if you can't afford to give them what they are worth in terms of salary.

Make them feel important. Give your assistants responsibilities and then let them coach. I'll talk more throughout this book about specific ways I work with my assistants. Their responsibilities include helping with planning and scouting, keeping track of fouls and time-outs during games, and taking down comments. The more important your assistants feel, the more creative they will be. Incidentally, I also try to do this with JV coaches and freshman coaches, even though they may not be my direct assistants. I have them scout for us and study films. This lets them know I'm sincerely interested in their development. I also provide jobs for all of them at my summer basketball camp.

Welcome and encourage new ideas. Don't surround yourself with yes-men. Make your assistants think for themselves, and encourage them to give you their thoughts in writing. I always say that if you really want to know what someone thinks, get his opinion in writing. This has two important benefits. First, some people are not as likely to speak up in meetings, so writing may be a more comfortable way for them to express ideas. Second, writing anything down forces you to really think about what you want to say and how you want to say it.

Reward and recognize their efforts in front of the team. For example, at practice the day after a game, I'll go over a list of my comments that an assistant had written down for me during the game. I'll take that opportunity to say, "As usual, Neil did a great job putting down comments," giving Neil a verbal pat on the back. I may also acknowledge an assistant who put together a terrific scouting report for us. Opportunities to recognize staff members are there; make yourself aware of them and take advantage.

Coach your coaches. Less experienced assistants need a lot of teaching and guidance from the head coach. For example, during the off-season, I encourage each of our assistant coaches to review one of our previous games each week and ask himself two questions: (1) What is the other team doing to hurt us? (2) What are we doing that hurts the other team? This helps an assistant become a student of the game. At the end of the season, in a professional manner, you should evaluate your assistants' work. Sit down with them and explain what you thought they did well. Also explain what they can improve on in order to become a better coach and contribute even more to the program.

Assistant Coaches' Duties

Assistant coaches must accept that their primary job is to help the head coach. A good assistant provides suggestions, takes care of tasks, troubleshoots without having to be prompted, and works cooperatively with everyone in the program to help the head coach as much as possible. Assistant coaches can make the head coach's job easier and contribute significantly to the program's success.

From Assistant to Head Coach

When I was an assistant coach for my father at DeMatha, there were times I wished he would implement more of my suggestions. But after I became a head coach, I realized that a head coach has a very different perspective. I encourage all assistant coaches to remain loyal to their head coach, understanding that he has a broader view of the program. At the same time, assistant coaches should remain strong in their own convictions.

I was offered a head coaching job at the age of 23, but I turned it down because I did not believe I was ready. Three years later, I took the head job at O'Connell and was glad I had given myself time to learn and mature before doing so. I had been coached by my father on the things that successful coaches do and, more important, what they do not do. This allowed me to be more prepared when I took the reins at O'Connell. I have, in turn, always coached my coaches so that they can also be prepared when they take the reins of their own program.

I have been fortunate to have several great assistant coaches who have moved closer to achieving their aims in the coaching profession based on their work on our staff. Six of them are currently high school head coaches, one is a head coach at the college level, and three are assistant coaches at colleges. I believe that we helped them to improve each day and prepare for their future, and we let them know that we wanted to see them progress in their careers.

Here are some specific things that an assistant coach can do in order to be most valuable to the program and the boss:

- Make positive things happen! Don't wait to be told.
- Offer alternative suggestions, when appropriate, but don't resist what the head coach wants to do.
- Be patient. Don't rush the process of building knowledge and a resume.
- Demonstrate your value to the program. You do not need to tell people you're good; it will be apparent by your actions and their effects.
- Be honest in assessing your own strengths and weaknesses. Self-awareness and determination to shore up shortcomings are two essential attributes in coaching.
- Know what your aspirations are in coaching. Are you driven to be a head coach or would you rather be an assistant coach at a larger program?

Joe and an assistant coach observe their team from the bench during a game.

Six Rules for Coaching Job Interviews

1. Do your homework.
2. Don't knock your present employer. In fact, don't knock anybody.
3. Be honest.
4. Display confidence.
5. Talk about money last.
6. Demonstrate through your answers that you know how to run a program from A to Z.

With the development of assistants comes the prospect of their moving up the career ladder. Having one of your assistants interview for a head coaching job is a bittersweet experience: On a selfish level, you don't want to lose that coach, but you're also excited for him if it's what he wants to pursue. I view it as part of my job to help prepare my assistants to make the best impression possible, but I tell them, "I can open the door for you [by making an introductory phone call or the like], but you have to get the job."

The first and most important rule in any interview is to be yourself. That's sometimes easier said than done, and it becomes easier if you've prepared thoroughly in advance. List any possible questions you think might come up, and consider how you would respond. Check that your response is genuine—what you truly believe.

One helpful strategy when answering a question is to paraphrase it before responding directly. This does two things: It avoids confusion, and it gives you a few extra seconds (which can be extremely valuable) to formulate your answer. It also never hurts to compliment the interviewer by saying something like, "That's a really good question."

Also be sure to make a list of questions that you want to ask. A job interview is a two-way street—you're interviewing them as much as they are interviewing you. You can find out most of the information you're looking for by letting the other party do most of the talking, but be prepared with your own questions.

I was once asked to talk with the search committee at Georgetown University, which I did, and they encouraged me to apply for the job. They told me what they had in mind and asked if I had any questions. I had a list in my mind, so I asked about assistants and their salaries, the recruiting budget, the scouting budget, an office, and so forth. Times have changed, and most of those details are now already set, but in this particular case the school administrators hadn't given much thought to a lot of these details. For that reason, I didn't apply for the job.

After the interview, it's always a good idea to write a thank-you note to everyone you talked to. You never know when that may help you get the job. If you're lucky enough to receive an offer, make sure you think it through. Know why you want to take the job, what it can lead to in the next three to five years, and how it fits into your total career plan.

Sources of Support

The better your players work together and support one another's efforts on the court, the better your basketball team will be. Similarly, the off-court success of your basketball program depends on the amount of support it receives from various groups, starting with the school's administration.

Administrative Support

Coaches often ask me if a certain coaching job is a "good job." In my opinion, the support of the administration should be the primary factor in a coach's decision on whether or not to take a job. Look for an administration that respects its coaches and takes time to listen to their needs.

Student Support

Nothing beats having a large, loud, and vocal student section cheering the team on at games. We talked in chapter 2 about communicating with the student body, and those same methods can bolster support. We're also fortunate at DeMatha to have a wonderful pep

Al Burch

At O'Connell, I was very fortunate to be hired by and work for a man named Al Burch. Al was a former All-Met player at St. John's (a team in our conference) who had lettered nine times in high school. He was a former coach who had set a national high school record with 42 consecutive victories while leading the O'Connell baseball team. He had moved on to become the principal.

Al understood the value of a strong sports program along with a strong academic program. He also believed strongly in people and the value of the individual. He listened to his coaches, trusted his coaches, and held them to a high standard for how to run their programs. He would often call me into his office and give me advice on coaching. He often said that he learned how to be a leader as both an athlete and as a coach. Al told me to keep him informed, to ask questions, and to take care of the student-athletes. I have tried my best to follow his advice. As a coach, you must keep your leadership informed about your program!

---

band that adds spirit and enthusiasm to all of our games.

Because the basketball team represents the school, players and coaches should know that their peers are behind them 100 percent. This will give players and coaches extra confidence and inspiration. Remind your players to fulfill their responsibility of representing their families, their school, and themselves with dignity and class. Players and coaches should exhibit exemplary behavior that their school's students and faculty can be proud of.

Community Support

Support and enthusiasm from community members can make a big difference in the success of your program. Take the time to meet people, send them schedules and information about your team, and invite them to be your guests at games and practices. As discussed in chapter 2, positive community relations can do much to enhance your basketball program.

Medical Support

The athletic trainer is imperative to the success of your program. Bishop O'Connell has two certified athletic trainers, Don Tillson and Terri Lynn Wootten. Terri Lynn works with the boys' basketball team full time in the winter. She takes care of all of our athletes from day to day to make sure that they are healthy. In addition, she has set up a medical team to make sure that we have the best medical care that is available. We are fortunate to have Chris Annunziata (the Washington Redskins' orthopedic surgeon), Dr. Robert Nirschl (of Nirschl Orthopaedics), and Tony Casolaro (the Washington Redskins' head of internal medicine) as part of that medical team. They are the best in their fields and have all given their time to aid our players at a moment's notice.

Championship Training

Jason Clark, who is a current player at Georgetown University, was the Washington, DC, player of the year when he was at O'Connell. At our postseason banquet, we have a tradition of giving each of the seniors an opportunity to speak. Jason thanked many people who had helped him accomplish all that he had over his four years in high school, but the last person he thanked was Terri Lynn. He said that she got him through the four years because he was always in the training room. He became emotional and gave her a huge hug. This example demonstrates how every member of a coach's staff is of the utmost importance. As a coach, you should give all members of your staff the recognition they deserve.

Having a certified trainer on hand does not free a coach from his responsibility to be well versed in training techniques. I am responsible for the players' physical conditioning on the court, so I make all the decisions with regard to their training. The players themselves are responsible for their conditioning off the court, and I make that very clear to them. The players are also responsible for informing me when they are injured. I don't want them trying to be heroes and then missing even more time by aggravating an injury. We would never play an injured player who could harm his body further, but at times the muscle or joint may be sore but not structurally compromised. In those instances, I speak with both the trainer and the player, and all three of us decide whether the player can go. If there is any doubt, he sits out.

If a player is unable to play in a game because of injury, you should not even have the player in uniform for the game. Conversely, if you have a player who is experiencing pain, soreness, or swelling but is cleared to play by medical staff, you should not be afraid to start him (assuming he's normally a starter). It's a mistake to let him warm up and then sit him down for a quarter before putting him in.

Feeder System

Once you've developed your basketball system and have the school and community fully behind you, you are ready for the final piece of the puzzle in putting together a successful basketball program: implementation. And one of the essential ingredients for establishing and maintaining a high level of performance is the steady flow of well-trained and talented athletes.

Most of the kids who come to DeMatha go to local Catholic grade schools or junior high schools in the Washington, DC, area. My staff and I conduct free clinics for the coaches and players at these schools, and we also work with the local Boys' Clubs. We also invite area coaches and players to attend our clinics at DeMatha, and we frequently include our players in these clinics to demonstrate basketball fundamentals. We talk to the kids about the importance of studying hard and preparing for high school. Obviously, all of the kids we work with at clinics are not going to come to DeMatha, but we believe that the clinics are a nice community gesture and good for everyone involved.

We also invite the local Catholic Youth Organization (CYO) and Boys' Club teams to be our guests at one game each season.

Afterward, we have a little reception and give the youngsters a chance to meet the members of the team. During the holidays, we run the DeMatha Christmas tournament, which includes 32 area Boys' Club and CYO teams. Events like these can help sell your school and your program, and they foster strong community relationships to boot.

If you have a feeder system within your school (freshman and junior varsity teams), you should be sure to spend time with the coaches of these teams. Talk with them about your philosophy, objectives, and the type of basketball you like to emphasize. Treat these coaches as if they are members of your own staff, and always make yourself available to them.

At DeMatha, we have two younger teams that feed into the varsity, a 9th-grade team and a junior varsity (JV) team. The JV team consists mostly of 10th graders and, occasionally, an outstanding freshman. I rarely place juniors on the JV; I would rather have them on the varsity if we think they are going to contribute in any way. However, I have made three exceptions to that rule since I've been coaching at DeMatha. In all three cases, the exceptions were made because the athletes were terrific kids, exhibited potential, and provided us with some size when the program was lacking in big men.

One exception to the rule was a young man named Mike Graybill. Mike played on the JV team as a junior and then made varsity his senior year. He won a basketball scholarship to Boston University, where he continued to get bigger and stronger. While a junior there, he decided for the first time to use his much larger physique on the football field. The next thing I knew, Mike was being drafted as an offensive lineman by the Cleveland Browns. I'm glad we kept him in our program his junior year, and it's a lesson to all of us about what can happen when a young person is given a chance.

I spend a significant amount of time with our JV and freshman coaches. I invite them to sit in on all of our varsity coaching meetings, encourage them to see the team play as much as they can, and ask them for their

As an assistant under his father in the 90s, Joe coaches freshmen at DeMatha.

input whenever possible. By the same token, I make it a point to watch their teams play whenever I get the chance. This is important to those coaches and helps to make them feel like the integral part of the program that they are. Plus, younger players feel special when the varsity coaches show their support and interest.

Team Rules

No basketball program is complete without some sort of structure, the primary component of which is team rules. As mentioned in chapter 3, our players make the rules for the team every year. We believe that if the players truly feel it is their team, they will take better care of it.

Once our team is selected, we take all of our players to a classroom for a meeting on the team rules. They vote on each issue by Australian ballot, meaning the players do not have to sign their names to their votes. At the meeting, I ask the players what the team rules will be on smoking, drug use, drinking, curfew, dress code to and from games, and bringing dates to games.

THOUGHT FOR THE DAY

If you hoot with the owls at night, you cannot soar with the eagles at dawn. –Morgan Wootten

Frequently, while the players are voting on the rules, a new player on the team will ask me what previous teams have done. This is my opportunity to say, "Well, I can tell you what the national championship team with Danny Ferry voted for as its rules." Funny thing, more often than not, the current players will vote the same way.

After the results are tallied, we then call another meeting, and I announce to the players, "These are the rules that you have selected for the season. Because they are your rules, I know there will be absolutely no problems."

Some people may think that it is a problem to have teenagers vote on sensitive issues or that the athletes are not yet responsible enough to determine their own rules. I have not found this to be true. Almost without exception, this is the way our teams vote:

- *No drugs,* because they are illegal. The only dissension to this came in the 1960s when one player voted that using marijuana was okay as long as you were smart in the way you used it. He was voted down.

- *No drinking,* with the possible exception of holiday celebrations at home with the family when a glass of wine might be served with the meal.

- *Seniors should set the curfew.* So, the day before a game when we gather at the end of practice, I'll ask the seniors what the curfew for that night will be. I've found that they're generally tougher with the curfew than I would have been. On a Friday night before a Saturday game, the seniors will frequently announce that it's all right to go watch a local college game, but that everyone must come right home and have the lights out by 11:30 p.m.

- *Players must wear a coat and tie to all games.* The athletes are aware that college coaches and recruiters will be judging their performances before and after the game as well as when they are on the floor. We tell our players in our meetings, "You only have one chance to make a first impression." A coat and tie can help make that first impression a good one.

- *Team members may not drive a date to the game* (unless she has no other way of getting there). However, a player may give his date a ride home afterward. Before the game, the players' focus should be on the forthcoming competition.

It is very rare that we get dissenting votes from a player. And if we do, the player will usually feel compelled to go along with the rules because his peers chose them. The rules weren't just handed down from on high by the coaches. When I ask former players how effective the team rules were, they invariably confirm this impression. The players will say, "Coach, we stuck to them because we knew they were our rules."

But when I ask about the teams we have played, teams for which the coaches made the rules, I usually find that their players rarely obeyed the rules. Their players thought it was not their team, but the coach's team. After all, it's just human nature that people will take better care of their own car than of a rental car. And so it is with players—they will take better care of their team if they truly believe it is their team.

A United Stand

One year when I coached football at DeMatha, we were leading in a championship game 7-0. However, the opposing team had first and goal on our two-yard line, and time was running out. Then one of our linebackers, Ricky Cook, called time-out and had a team meeting right out in the middle of the field. Not one of the players came over to the bench during the entire time-out. When play resumed, we made one of the greatest goal-line stands I've ever seen and won the game, 7-0.

After the game, I asked Ricky why he had called time-out and what had gone on in the huddle. He said he had told the players, "Fellows, for 10 weeks now we have been Spartans. We have worked our butts off. We've gone to parties where people from other teams have been sitting around drinking, but we haven't had a drop. We've sacrificed, and we've given up a lot. These two yards right here in front of us represent our sacrifice. We know these guys coming at us have not made the same sacrifice we have. Now let's find out if our sacrifice has been worth it."

That incident verified for me the truth of a statement made by Vince Lombardi: "Those who have invested the most are the last to surrender."

Although players vote on the rules, I nevertheless have certain expectations. Primarily, I expect the players to act as gentlemen at all times. I tell our players they will never hear profanity from the coaching staff, and we don't expect to hear it from them.

I constantly remind our players whom they are representing—themselves, their families, and the school—and of the responsibilities that accompany that. I also tell them they will always be DeMatha players. For that reason,

I give all of our athletes a letter titled "The DeMatha Player" and share with them a short poem called "Players as Models." These written passages remind the athletes that they are always in the public eye and should therefore conduct themselves in a manner reflecting positively on those they represent.

For the off-season, I don't stress rules so much as individual improvement. In the spring, I hold a meeting to talk about which players will be playing on what summer league teams. At the meeting, I have each player complete a written evaluation of his present skills and what he thinks he needs to work on.

Players as Models

There are little eyes upon you

And they're watching night and day.

There are little ears that quickly

Take in every word you say.

There are little hands all eager

To do anything you do;

And a little boy who's dreaming

Of the day he'll be like you.

You're the little fellow's idol,

You're the wisest of the wise.

In this little mind about you

No suspicions ever rise.

He believes in you devoutly,

Holds all you say and do.

He will say and do, in your way,

When he's grown up just like you.

There's a wide-eyed little fellow

Who believes you're always right;

And his eyes are always opened,

And he watches day and night.

You are setting an example

Every day in all you do

For the little boy who's waiting

To grow up to be like you.

Reprinted by permission of Perry D. Biggerstaff.

Team Pride

Addressing players' physical development is only half the challenge. We must be concerned with their mental and social approach as well. Specifically, a coach must develop team pride and spirit, those intangibles that, unlike the players, can remain with a program through the years.

Intangibles, such as pride and spirit, can be major benefits to your program. The sense of great pride found at DeMatha and O'Connell is a big reason why the basketball programs have thrived over such a long period of time.

Playing Time

One of the biggest threats to team spirit is the selection of a starting lineup. If the selection process is handled improperly, nonstarters may feel dejected, an attitude that can be contagious and harmful to your team. For example, you might say, "Joe, if you beat out Bill, you'll be the starter." In a player's eyes, this is the equivalent to saying, "Joe, you can be the winner and make Bill the loser." Thus, in a player's mind, you have 5 winners and 5 losers among your top 10 players, an obviously unhealthy situation.

But part of being a good teacher-coach is the ability to sell. So, when dealing with the issue of starters and nonstarters, you have to sell your players on the fact that being in the starting lineup or on the bench is not a win–lose situation.

Instead, you can create a win–win atmosphere. To make the previous example a win–win situation, you could say, "Joe, you're doing a great job, and we're going to start you at the guard position." Immediately afterward, take Bill aside, and tell him, "Bill, this team is really going to count on you because you're the kind of guy who can come off the bench and spark us."

I always tell my team, "We can only start 5 players, but we need a lot of finishers. Any one of you may be called on to finish a game because of injuries, foul trouble, or any number of situations that may develop." I think this approach increases nonstarters' appreciation of their role on the team, and thus builds depth. It's a big reason why we often have 8 to 10 players we are comfortable putting on the floor when the game is on the line.

Team depth can also be built during the off-season. At O'Connell, we have two different sets of players start in two separate summer leagues. In this way, we allow all players to experience both starting and coming off the bench.

A Famous Sixth Man

Our 1973 national championship team featured Adrian Dantley as our star player. Also on that team was a young man named Ronnie Satterthwaite, who, although an outstanding player, did not figure to start. Before the start of that season, I had taken Ronnie aside and said, "Ronnie, I don't think you're going to start, but you're going to be our sixth man, and you're going to be the most famous sixth man in America. I'm going to make a rule with you now. If I don't put you in any game in the first quarter, come to me at the end of the quarter, ask me who you should go in for, and I will put you in the game. You can tell your mother, father, grandparents, girlfriend, and everybody to come to the game because you're going to play in every game. And the latest you're going to get in is the second quarter."

Ronnie's face lit up when he heard me say that, and he was happy as could be. He went on to have a terrific season for us and wound up with a scholarship to William and Mary, where he was eventually named Southern Conference Player of the Year. I think this is the perfect example of creating a win–win situation with starters and nonstarters. By taking Ronnie aside and talking to him, I avoided having him sitting on the bench as a disgruntled sixth man who thought he should have been a starter.

Unhappiness and disenchantment can grow like a cancer. Players who are unhappy will practice with less enthusiasm, and that inhibits team development. But by creating win–win situations, you can diffuse some of these situations before they become problems.

Captains

Another method I use to build team unity is to rotate the appointment of two captains—a game captain and a bench captain—for each game. The game captain is chosen from among the five starters, and the bench captain from among the nonstarters.

These two captains have the responsibility of meeting with the other team's captains and the officials before the game. During the game, the game captain takes on the traditional roles associated with a captain, and the bench captain is given the job of keeping the bench full of team spirit. By the end of the year, every player has been a captain several times over. This creates more of an attitude of team unity among the players than would the appointment of one or two captains for the entire year.

At Bishop O'Connell, less focus is put on the captain; the team leader is far more important. Our coaching staff turns to the leader often, working with him on his leadership skills both in front of and away from the team.

Former Players

Whenever one of our former players returns to DeMatha for a visit, I always ask him to talk to the players. This, too, develops team pride. More than 190 of our players have gone on to play at the college level. When these veterans visit the school and communicate their personal experiences and "DeMatha pride," it helps instill that pride in the younger players.

A picture I have on my office wall shows two penguins standing on the ice. One penguin is saying to the other, "I cried because I had no feet, until I met a man who had no class." Above all else, team pride is developed by being positive and by emphasizing that the team must carry itself with class. Any program can take pride in itself, win or lose, when the players and coaches behave with class and give their best effort to get the most out of their abilities.

You can be a model for your players to follow by organizing spirited practices, by being optimistic in what you say and do, by treating your young people as you would want your own child to be treated, and by responding positively to both victory and defeat. Your players will draw on your example and learn from it. If you teach them well, the athletes who graduate from your program will be better players and people than they were when they entered it.

Summary

The keys to creating and maintaining a successful program are

- implementing a sound system or style of play that fits the players you have available;
- developing your assistant coaches and using them effectively;
- setting up and nurturing a feeder system;
- getting administration, student, community, and medical support;
- instituting a structure of roles to which the players are committed; and
- instilling pride in every player who is issued a uniform.

PART II

COACHING PLANS

5 | Season Planning

All of us would rather work on our zone press than press our players to return their insurance forms. Some coaching duties are not fun, but attending to such matters is essential before the basketball season begins. The following areas should be addressed in the weeks and months leading up to the first team meeting:

- Medical services
- Conditioning and strength training
- Summer play
- Team managers
- Equipment
- Tactical plan
- Competitive schedule
- Scouting
- Travel
- College scholarships

Medical Services

Before beginning physical conditioning and practice sessions, make sure that every candidate for the team has passed a complete medical examination and has a physician's

permission to try out. We have a doctor come to the school in early August to give complete physicals at a reasonable rate for athletes on all of our teams.

A related requirement involves insurance coverage for athletes. Because the school insurance on every student is minimal, we have the parents of our candidates complete a form indicating that their child will be covered under the family's medical insurance. This form includes the parents' insurance information, their permission for the child's participation in school athletics, and their authorization for the coaches and qualified medical personnel to make on-the-spot decisions in emergency care situations.

Some type of medical staff should be available for all your practices and games. High schools are limited to some extent in their medical resources, though most are now required to have a certified athletic trainer on staff. However, very few high school coaches are lucky enough to have a doctor at every practice or every game. In most cases, they must rely on a team physician (usually an orthopedist) to whom players can have quick access. And, to improve athletes' chances of returning quickly and safely to competition, coaches should also have a sports medicine specialist in injury rehabilitation available to call when necessary.

You can gain access to competent sports medicine professionals by meeting with local medical experts. Spend time with them, check their backgrounds and references, and select the best and most interested individuals. Then, make them feel like a part of the school's basketball program.

Give them season passes and an open invitation to all games and scrimmages. Most physicians take on such positions simply because they love basketball, not to get rich. So let them watch your team perform as much as they want to. The doctors we have worked with usually accept only the insurance money as compensation for their services, and they do not bill the family for the additional cost.

Athletic trainers are also a big help. Because a physician cannot be present at every game and practice, a regular attending certified athletic trainer or a student trainer should be on hand at all times.

Conditioning and Strength Training

The days of working a team into shape when formal practices get underway in the fall are long over given today's level of competition and emphasis on training. Players must be in top physical condition by the start of the season. Conditioning, therefore, must be a year-round process for athletes. That's why we recommend off-season as well as in-season conditioning programs.

Before the summer leagues start, you should meet with each player individually to discuss his written evaluation and to give him your assessment of his status. Provide details regarding what the player should concentrate on in his off-season workouts. At this time, we issue daily summer workout forms, one for post players (see table 5.1) and one for perimeter players (see table 5.2). These evaluations and suggestions give the players specific ideas for improving their skills.

At the end of the summer, evaluate each player's performance in the summer leagues.

When school starts, you should again meet individually with each varsity candidate and share your thoughts on where he stands and how far he needs to go in the time remaining before varsity tryouts. During the season, practices should be structured to ensure that players remain in top condition.

Strength training is an important element of a basketball player's overall physical conditioning. But it must be a certain kind of training. The weightlifter who is trying to develop bulk and the All-American body may get stares on the street, but he will not be nearly as impressive playing on a basketball court. Instead, players should perform workouts designed to develop the specific muscles that a basketball player uses. The emphasis should be on repetition, not on the amount of weight used in the exercise. This weight program has proven successful for us over the years, both in preventing serious injuries and in boosting players' performance-related strength.

Training to Bond

Fortunately, many schools, including O'Connell, now provide strength classes. As a result, our players can lift on a daily basis throughout the entire year, working on strength, flexibility, explosion, and conditioning.

Yet we still use weight training as another way for our team to bond together. Prior to instituting strength classes, we used to lift after school, but because of the size of our weight room, this was tough. Therefore, we began lifting three days a week at 6:30 a.m. for one hour. When we first began this practice, the players did not want to get up that early, but after staying with the workout for a while, they started to see the added strength that they gained. By lifting in the mornings, players are able to focus on their strength without having to go to practice directly afterward. Plus, the players have said that this gets them going for school and helps them feel more awake. But the best part of this practice is that the players know that their teammates are there each morning, working out beside them.

TABLE 5.1   Summer Workout for Post Players

Big-man drills (10 minutes)	Hook drill Reverse hook drill Right-hand tap drill Left-hand tap drill Six and in Second effort Superman V-cut, catch, chin the ball, look middle and find the defense Foot fight in the post
Warm-up shots	Around the basket within 5 feet (60) • Remember to have your legs bent and your hands ready *before* you catch.
Warzone shots	Catch, turn middle (25) Catch, turn baseline (25) Catch, turn middle, up and under (25) Catch, turn baseline, up and under (25) Catch, turn middle, jump hook (25) Catch, turn baseline, jump hook (25) Catch, ball fake middle, drop step baseline (25) Catch, ball fake baseline, drop step middle (25)
Short corner shots	Jump shot off the point guard's drive on the right baseline (25) Show hands, catch, lunge to the basket on the right baseline (25) Jump shot off the point guard's drive to the left baseline (25) Show hands, catch, lunge to the basket on the left baseline (25)
Midpost shots	Catch, turn middle (25) Catch, turn middle, jump hook (25) Catch, turn baseline, jump hook (25)
High-post jump shots	Catch, turn on left foot, jump shot (25) Catch, turn on right foot, jump shot (25) Catch, turn on right foot, strong-side drive (25) Catch, turn on left foot, strong-side drive (25) Catch, turn on right foot, crossover to basket (25) Catch, turn on left foot, crossover to basket (25)
Plyometrics and conditioning	Forward line jumps over cone, two footed (2 minutes) Ski jumps over cone, one footed (2 minutes; do a set for each foot) Jump rope, two footed (5 minutes) Depth jumps to medicine ball dunks (15 times) Bleacher step-ups, alternating feet (2 minutes) Lateral cone hops (2 minutes) Depth jump to layup (15 times both for the left and for the right)

• Remember to go to the foul line and shoot a one-and-one or a two-shot foul after each set of 25.
• Always demand the ball by getting low and showing your hands.
• After catching the ball, show your chicken wings and find the defense, then make your move.

TABLE 5.2 Summer Workout for Perimeter Players

Ballhandling drills (10 minutes)	Ball slap Ball pinch Waist circles Double-leg circles Single-leg circles Full-body circles Step-outs, side catch Football hike Dribbling figure eight Dribble on left knee (behind the back) Dribble on right knee (behind the back) M dribble The walk (between legs)

Moves on the move (5 minutes)	Between the legs
	Behind the back
	Back dribble and crossover
	Crossover
	Fake crossover
	Stop-and-go
	Fake crossover to crossover
	  • For each move, travel the length of the floor and back.
	  • Remember to make the move then explode by the defender.

Warm-up shots	Move around the basket within 5 feet (60) • Remember to have your legs bent and your hands ready *before* you catch.

Spot shooting	Right baseline (50)
	Right wing (50)
	Middle (50)
	Left wing (50)
	Left baseline (50)
	  • These are the rapid-fire shots that should be done at game speed.
	  • Take one step back after a set of 10.
	  • Double-step into all your shots.

Catch and go, jump stop	Top of the key (20)
	Left wing (20)
	Right wing (20)
	  • Catch and go, alternate between one hard dribble right and one hard dribble left.
	  • Be sure to cover a large amount of ground with each dribble.

Moves to jump shot	Top of the key (20)
	Left wing (20)
	Right wing (20)
	• Use one of your moves on the move to a jump shot.
	• You should make sure you go by your defender by pushing the ball out in front of you after making the move.
Right and left pivot	Catch, turn on right foot, jump shot (25)
	Catch, turn on left foot, jump shot (25)
	Catch, turn on right foot, crossover to the basket (25)
	Catch, turn on left foot, crossover to the basket (25)
	Catch, turn on right foot, strong-side drive to basket (25)
	Catch, turn on left foot, strong-side drive to basket (25)
Shooting off screens	Take defender away, pop out to the wing, jump shot (25)
	Take defender away, curl off the screen (25)
	Take defender away, fade to the corner (25)
Around the world	Three-point shots (two sets of 30)
Plyometrics and conditioning	Forward line jumps over cone, two footed (2 minutes)
	Ski jumps over cone, one footed (2 minutes; do a set for each foot)
	Jump rope, two footed (5 minutes)
	Depth jumps to medicine ball dunks (15 times)
	Bleacher step-ups, alternating feet (2 minutes)
	Stationary rim taps (2 minutes)
	Lateral cone hops (2 minutes)
	Depth jump to layup (15 times both for the left and for the right)

• Shoot a one-and-one or two-shot foul between each set (make up a situation similar to game pressure).
• All shots should be done in rapid fire (game speed).

As a coach, you shouldn't think that you need to be an expert in every area of strength training. Your school may have a strength coach, but if not, do not be afraid to seek out advice from others in order to help your athletes.

THOUGHT FOR THE DAY

Discipline yourself and others won't have to.
–John Wooden

Courtesy of Bishop O'Connell High School/Tommy Orndorff

As a head coach, make sure to coordinate your own summer league with your players' AAU coaches.

Summer Play

Players play games all the time now. In fact, O'Connell varsity players play over 100 games a year. That is an amazing amount of games! They play 30 to 35 games with the school team and over 75 games with their Amateur Athletic Union (AAU) teams.

Coaches should work with AAU programs and coordinate with them regarding team schedules. This provides a great example to the players on how to communicate and work with multiple coaches. We coordinate our summer league and team camp schedules with the AAU coaches. As a coach, you need to recognize that if a player has an opportunity to go to a big tournament with 100 college coaches present, the player should not miss that opportunity. When one of your lead players is away at such an event, this also provides an opportunity for other players to take the lead in a summer game or two.

However, summertime is not just about games. We also want our players to work on their skills throughout the summer. We tell them that they need to balance games with time spent working on their skills. To this end, we give each of our players a notebook with a personalized summer workout. This notebook provides a place to record the number of shots the player makes and takes, along with a weight training schedule, a ballhandling routine, and goals for each week. In addition, the notebook includes motivational messages and thoughts on nutrition. The players keep these notebooks with them all summer long to chart their progress.

We have also created a shot board where we chart the number of shots that each player attempts and makes in the off-season. These are not shots in a game, just workout shots. The shot board encourages two things: competitiveness (trying to win the shot board) and improved shooting skills.

This off-season work allows the players to develop two skills that college coaches are looking for. When evaluating a player, college coaches will often ask what kind of kid and what kind of student he is. Then they will ask, "How well does he shoot it?" and "How well does he handle it?" Players can answer those questions with the skill work that they put in during the off-season.

In addition to improving skills through individual practice in the off-season, players should also get involved in summer camps. Summer basketball camps have grown to the point where they are now essential in the modern era. When Joe Gallagher and I started a day basketball camp back in 1960, we had no idea that camps would become so popular. Over the last 25 years in particular, the majority of high school players and coaches have either attended or worked at camps—or both. In fact, when Duke University assistant coach Steve Wojciechowski came to my camp in 2002 to speak on Duke's man-to-man defense, he mentioned that he had attended my camp when he was 12 years old!

Better Every Day

Ahmad Smith was a great player at O'Connell and is now playing pro ball in the German division I league. When he arrived at O'Connell as a sophomore, not many would have thought that he would be playing basketball for money one day, but he was incredibly determined to improve his skill level. Because of that, Ahmad went from an unknown and unremarkable sophomore to a player who hit winning free throws in big games and was named first-team All-Metro in the Washington, DC, area as a senior.

From there he went to St. Bonaventure and, unfortunately, was there during a scandal that led to the university president's resignation. Most of the players left, but not Ahmad. He stayed and led the Bonnies in scoring, rebounding, and assists as a senior. The fact that he stuck with it when everyone else bailed out speaks volumes about his level of commitment and persistence. And he was not done there. He started in a small pro league in Ireland, and then he moved on to a division III pro league in Spain, a division II league in Germany, and now the division I league.

Ahmad's story is a testament to what can happen when a player devotes himself to developing his skills to the highest possible level. This type of improvement doesn't happen in games. It results from many hours of focused individual practice during the off-season.

Camps have grown for good reason: They can be great settings for helping players develop skills and learn the game. Younger players get a valuable opportunity to be schooled in the fundamentals of basketball that will be so important no matter how far they advance up the competitive ladder. Those who go to overnight camps and spend some time away from home also gain a little maturity and at the same time meet players and coaches from around the state and country and get exposed to good competition.

Several factors need to be considered when recommending camps for players. The first is whether you want them to go to a team camp or an individual camp. If the main goal is for the team to improve as a unit, you may want to consider a team camp, where you get three or four days of good competition against other teams. Players and coaches also get to spend time together and learn more about one another.

Generally though, we prefer camps where players can concentrate on their own individual skills. Players should never lose sight of the team concept, but as we've mentioned earlier, outside of the season is a good time for them to work a little harder on their own games. You'll have plenty of opportunities to focus on the team aspect when practices start.

When selecting an individual camp, make sure it is one that stresses the fundamentals. At a good teaching camp, players can work on basic techniques that they have not mastered and can refine skills that they are adept at. Ideally, a player will leave a camp with a good idea of his strengths and weaknesses, and what he needs to work on to improve those weaknesses. The best way to find good teaching camps in your area is word of mouth. Talk to other coaches and players about the camps they've been to. You can also get a good idea of a camp's quality by how difficult it is to get into.

For rising juniors and seniors, camps provide not only excellent competition but also exposure to college coaches. If you have a particularly promising player, consider recommending one of the all-star camps, where other potential college players often go. A word of caution, though: With the ever-changing recruiting rules, there's no guarantee that your players will get the kind of exposure to college coaches that they may want.

In addition to advising players to attend camps that stress the fundamentals and might get them a look from colleges of interest, steer them toward camps that provide a good dose of fun. Individual contests and games of 3-on-3 and 5-on-5 appeal to most players' competitive side. In short, endorse camps that foster an environment that will increase players' love of the game even more.

Coaches should also take advantage of any opportunity they have to work at a good basketball camp. We always tell the coaches who work with us at camp, "Call yourself a teacher." But if you're not comfortable jumping in that far right away, see if you can attend as an observer. The more you can observe how another coach teaches, the more you can grow as a teacher yourself. We've had many coaches come to our camp and spend the week just watching. They often come back the following year to work the camp. I've also had parents who plan to coach their child's team take a week to either work or be an observer.

High school coaches should work at camps if at all possible. Camps are tremendous opportunities to further your professional development and growth. Many coaches have written to tell me how much basketball they learned at our camp by observing the teaching of fundamentals, exchanging ideas with other coaches, and participating in our popular daily roundtable for coaches. At these roundtables, we exchange ideas and talk about issues facing basketball coaches, and we delve into the Xs and Os. Camps are also great places to network. Many high school coaches have made contacts that led to college jobs.

Running Your Own Camp

If you're interested in running your own basketball camp, you should first work at other good camps to see how it's done. This will help give you an idea of all the things that need to be considered to run an efficient camp and how to organize daily schedules. You should also talk to others who have run successful camps and benefit from their experience and wisdom.

After you've done that, start with a day camp. Both day and overnight camps are huge undertakings, but day camps present fewer logistical challenges. Here is a list of factors to take into account before trying to conduct your own camp:

- Facility
- Staff
- Insurance
- Transportation
- Meals or snacks
- Equipment
- Age level
- Team assignment of campers
- Time devoted to games versus instruction
- Teaching approach (for example, classroom or on-court lectures, instructional and drill stations, and so forth)
- Number of hours and daily schedule
- Guest speakers
- Trainers and medical supplies
- Security, including a camp bank for campers' valuables
- Emergency procedures
- Brochure and application, including medical and parental consent forms
- Advertising and promotion
- Tuition fees
- Registration process
- Administrative tasks (for example, payroll, accounting, processing applications, and so forth)
- Housing and room assignments (overnight camps only)
- Trophies and camp shirts

That's only a partial list, but these are important things to think about before you open your doors for business. I've been doing camps a long time, and they are fun and can be rewarding. Just like anything else, though, they go much more smoothly when you plan properly.

Team Managers

Mature and responsible managers can be an invaluable resource to a coach. They can be given a great deal of responsibility and are well respected by all members of the team. By relieving coaches of burdensome tasks, managers make it possible for us to spend more time coaching.

We carry four managers for our varsity basketball team: One keeps the score book and calls the local media outlets; another keeps statistics; the third, our student trainer, helps out with balls and jackets on the bench; and the fourth manager videotapes all of our games and the occasional practice or drill I want taped. For home games, we add a fifth manager to assist the visiting team in whatever way he can. If we travel to a tournament at the end of the year, we try to take that fifth manager with us.

Those are the more glamorous of a basketball manager's duties. But good managers can also be assigned these tasks:

- Distribute all basketball equipment
- Prepare the gym for practice
- Clean up and lock up after practice
- Make travel arrangements
- Plan team meals when necessary

In selecting managers, try to choose students from different classes and bring them up through the system to maintain continuity, much as you would your players. Any student who is interested is allowed to try out for a manager's position. Most will try out as freshmen and prove themselves with the freshman team, move up to the junior varsity, and then if they are qualified, eventually make it to the varsity team. A few exceptionally talented freshmen have started with the varsity. But I've had fewer freshmen managers than freshmen players at the varsity level.

One young man, Jeff Hathaway, came to me as a freshman and informed me that he wanted to be a manager for our basketball team. I told him that the usual procedure was to start as a manager for the freshman team, and then perhaps work his way up to the varsity. He asked me if he could try out for the varsity anyway as any other freshman is allowed to do, so I told him yes. Jeff became a four-year varsity manager and trainer for us, and he has since moved on to bigger and better things; most recently, he served as chair of the 2012 NCAA tournament selection committee.

Candidates for manager try out in much the same way as players do, and I look for the same qualities in a manager as I do in a player. We evaluate a candidate's abilities by giving him jobs to do and then observing the manner in which they are handled. If I have to take the candidate by the hand and remind him of certain things every day, then that person is not likely to get the job. If, on the other hand, I assign a potential manager a task, and it's done after the first mention, then I know I've found a good one.

Mike Cresson was a four-year varsity manager for us at O'Connell. He was invaluable with all that he did—an assistant coach, of sorts! Mike graduated from Virginia Tech, became a history teacher at O'Connell, and has recently been named the school's admissions director. Based on his motivation and aptitude as a manager in our program, he should have a very bright future.

Equipment

Never underestimate the importance of good equipment. From an economic point of view, it is wise to put everything out on bids. Your athletic director and school administration will appreciate the fact that you are looking for the most reasonable deal. Keep in mind, though, that the lowest price is not always the best buy. Compare quality and cost, then make the right decision.

The overall look of a team can be helpful in providing confidence for the players. You want them to look like basketball players. And if they look good, they'll feel good. And if they feel good, they'll play better. To keep the spending on attractive uniforms in check, we try to stagger purchasing them, so that we are never buying both varsity and freshman team uniforms in the same year. We also try to get four years out of a set of uniforms before passing them down to the junior varsity.

Our players are responsible for their other apparel, including their shoes and socks. I recommend that the team decide on a specific high-top shoe so all the players will be dressed alike, further enhancing that team look. Make sure your team uses shoes of the highest quality that are light, durable, and give great ankle support.

Obviously, you must include the purchase of basketballs in your equipment for the upcoming season. Every year, our league votes on a basketball to be used in league play. In past years, *The Rock* has been the winner. Use the same basketball in practice that you will use in games so the players are used to it. To alter a cliché, familiarity breeds confidence.

The school itself establishes the facilities for the season: the gymnasium and baskets. Yet there are little things that you don't want to overlook, such as good nets on the baskets and proper padding on the backboard (which is a rule in most leagues). The nicer a place is to practice in, the better the practice will be.

Change for the Sake of Change

When I first took over the job at O'Connell, I wanted to show everyone that change was going to take place. We started with the gym. The gym floor was repainted and sealed, new glass backboards were installed on the side, a new sound system was put in, and eventually we raised money to get a scorer's table and team chairs for the two benches. I believe that this signaled to the players that we were going to be a different program.

If you want the students to look like, act like, and think like players, then they must practice like ones. A good practice facility helps distinguish true *players* from their peers on the playgrounds and in rec centers. Not every school is going to have a state-of-the-art gymnasium. But, by being a good salesman and a good planner, you can make the best out of any situation.

Tough Court Cases

The first team I ever coached at St. Joseph's had no gym in which to practice. All we had was an outdoor blacktop playing surface, and a good friend of mine, Johnny Ryall, put up the money to buy two outdoor baskets. When the weather was bad, we would simply shovel the snow off the court. (I hadn't, incidentally, learned quite as much about basketball then and did not plan my practices effectively. We spent one third of our practices shooting layups, but that team sure shot layups better than anybody else around.)

When I moved on to St. John's College High School as the junior varsity coach, I had to wait until 6:00 every evening to practice. However, the ambitious freshman team braved the cold and snow and practiced on outdoor courts instead.

Understandably, everyone wants to have the perfect facility, no matter how impossible that may be. One of the buzzwords in coaching today is "innovation," and you can be innovative with your facility. But whatever kind of facility you have, be positive about it—don't play it down; play it up.

Tactical Plan

Head coaches and their assistants must be on the same page with regard to every aspect of the school's program, and that takes planning. Our coaching staff holds four meetings during the month of October in which we establish our master plan for the entire season (appendix A shows sample agendas from our meetings). This plan includes every tactic that we intend to teach and use during the year:

- Man-to-man offense
- Zone offense
- Pressure offense
- Man-to-man defense (including pressure)
- Zone defense (including trapping)
- Foul shot alignments
- Jump ball alignments
- Out-of-bounds plays
- Fast break scenarios
- Our "time and score" codes
- Coaching in special situations
- Pregame, halftime, and postgame procedures
- Time-out procedures

Once your staff draws up an initial master practice plan (see the sample in figure 5.1), you will find that it changes very little from year to year. Obviously, adjustments must be made when rule changes, such as the three-point shot or a shot clock, are introduced. And specific aspects of your attack might vary slightly depending on the abilities of that year's roster, but the general nature of a master plan allows it to remain fairly consistent over time.

From this master plan, we will then build a monthly, weekly, and finally a daily plan. These planning sessions are often long but are always rewarding, and I encourage you to take the time to plan. Such meetings will help you have everything in place when the season actually starts, will allow you to jump right into the fun part of coaching when practice begins, and will help you avoid running into the unexpected.

One of the favorite sayings of the U.S. Secret Service, well known for protecting presidents and other national and international dignitaries, is "Prior proper planning prevents poor performance." And one of my favorites is "Failing to prepare is preparing to fail." Success and rewards don't come to people just by accident. They come as a result of exhaustive, intelligent, and effective planning.

Sample Master Practice Plan

OFFENSE

1. Team
    a. vs. man-to-man
    b. vs. zone
    c. vs. combination
    d. vs. pressure

DEFENSE

1. Team
    a. Man-to-man
    b. Zone
    c. Combination
    d. Pressure

2. Individual
    a. On the ball
    b. Away from the ball
    c. Pivot or post area

CONDITIONING

1. Physiological
2. Psychological

FUNDAMENTALS

1. Footwork
2. Passing
3. Shooting
4. Dribbling

(continued)

Sample Master Practice Plan *(continued)*

REBOUNDING

1. Offensive
2. Defensive

CONVERSIONS

1. Offense to defense
2. Defense to offense

FREE-THROW SITUATIONS

1. Offensive alignment
2. Defensive alignment

JUMP BALL SITUATIONS

1. Offensive circle
2. Midcourt
3. Defensive circle

OUT-OF-BOUNDS SITUATIONS

1. Defensive end
2. Sidelines
3. Offensive end

TIME AND SCORE SITUATIONS

1. Delay game for lead protection
2. Special blitz offense when trailing
3. Special plays

PLAYER AND TEAM EVALUATION

1. Our team
   a. Charts and stats
   b. Scouting reports
   c. Films
2. Opponents
   a. Stats
   b. Scouting reports
   c. Films

RULES

GAME ORGANIZATION

1. Pregame
2. Strategy
   a. Game plan
   b. Bench
   c. Time-outs
   d. Halftime
3. Postgame

TRIP ORGANIZATION

1. Schedule
2. Players
   a. Rules
   b. Dress code
   c. Curfew
3. Staff
4. Guests
5. Transportation
6. Lodging
7. Meals

PUBLIC RELATIONS

1. Faculty
2. Students
3. Parents
4. Community
5. News media
6. College coaches

FIGURE 5.1 Sample master practice plan.

Competitive Schedule

Another significant part of preparing for a season involves scheduling your team's games. High school schedules, to a large extent, are set by school conference administrators. However, most schools are free to schedule nonconference games on their own. You should have some say in whom and when your team will play. If you work closely with your athletic director, he or she will try to accommodate your preferences.

As the associate athletic director at DeMatha as well as the basketball coach, I am able to set my own schedules for the basketball team. But 99 percent of the time I go along with what my coaches want when making schedules for their sports. Typically, I let the coaches do their own nonleague scheduling and then come to me for final approval.

The object of high school athletics is to compete against schools with similar athletic philosophies and similar operating conditions, including the size of the talent pool from which the schools may draw. For example, our league prohibits us from using five-year players, so we never schedule games against high schools that are allowed to have such players on their rosters. If your school has only 300 students from which the basketball team can be chosen, don't make a habit of playing teams that can select from 1,500 students. In short, schedule games against other schools that are in your school's competitive class.

Keep in mind when scheduling that a program needs successes on which to build. Therefore, do not schedule the most difficult opponents possible for every game. Playing teams you have no chance of beating is not healthy competition, and it can hurt your players' chances of being noticed by colleges. Instead, schedule some games against teams that you have a reasonable chance of defeating.

THOUGHT FOR THE DAY

The will to win is not as important as the will to prepare to win. –Bud Wilkinson

Some coaches prefer to play the toughest nonleague opponents they can in order to toughen their players up and prepare them for competition within their league. I agree that league competition is most important and that playing better opponents can improve a team. However, if you play only the highest-level teams and encounter defeat after defeat before league play, this can undermine players' confidence and set them back in conference games.

I've been told by successful college coaches that more coaches are fired because of overscheduling than for any other reason. This seems to happen more often at smaller colleges where a coach is trying to bring some recognition to a program, but a loss is still a loss. No matter how good the opponent, a team's confidence will erode as the losses pile up. This in turn leads to more losses and, in the end, to the coach's removal.

Beach Balling

The Beach Ball Classic is considered the nation's premier holiday tournament. John Rhodes, the tournament's executive director, and his committee run a first-class event from A to Z. I knew John from my years as my father's assistant, so when I got the O'Connell job, I called him and asked if we could participate. Luckily for us, a team had cancelled on him, and we were able to fill the open spot. This was a huge step up in our schedule, and it was another way of showing a positive change to our players and our community.

In scheduling, strike a healthy balance of tough opponents who will make your team better and opponents against whom you have a reasonable chance of gaining confidence-building victories. Saint Paul's words of wisdom apply here, as they do in all aspects of life: "All things in moderation."

Scouting

Once your schedule is set, you're going to want to know all you can about your upcoming opponents. And that is why you need to determine how and when you will scout.

Coaches have various approaches to scouting. Former UCLA coach John Wooden told me that he preferred to do very little scouting because he found that it either made him scared of the next opponent or lulled him into a feeling of overconfidence. Instead, he wanted to spend most of the time preparing his team to do what it did best. But don't believe for a minute that Coach Wooden didn't know what the other team ran offensively and defensively, or what their strengths and weaknesses were. He did.

I agree with Coach Wooden that you should spend much of your time working on what your team does best. But you need to know your opponents' tendencies, strengths, and weaknesses going into games. Scouting is crucial in having your team as prepared as possible for a game.

To standardize and simplify the scouting process, I have designed a form for scouts to use (see figure 5.2). The form includes everything from offensive and defensive formations to inbounds plays and free-throw-shooting ability. The form also asks for a personal comment from the scout on what he thinks we must do to win the game.

Note that such scouting reports are not given to the players on our teams. Coaches use the reports to determine what we should focus on in practice leading up to an opponent. We always want our players to focus on what our team does, not on what our opponent does.

Travel

One overlooked facet of preparing for the season is determining how to get your team to its games. Players can arrange transportation to home games on their own, but when traveling to away games, it is far better to travel as a team. Supervision is easier when the team travels as a group. Also, a greater camaraderie can develop among the players during those trips. As the coach, you can set the proper mood before the trip and make sure time on the road is used efficiently and productively.

One of the rules that we have established when it comes to travel and team chemistry is the banning of electronics during team dinners and travel. We want players to be able to talk and develop a relationship with each other.

Look for ways to build team spirit when heading to away games. For example, we frequently make the short trip from Hyattsville, Maryland, to play in the northern Virginia suburbs of Washington, DC. If one of our players lives in the northern Virginia area, he'll sometimes have the whole team over for dinner before the game. Or, if we have more than one player who lives there, they may take turns. I can remember our 1990-1991 team that went undefeated. Joe was a senior on that team, and he brought the entire team to our house before every game. That kind of closeness was one reason we went undefeated.

Joe and his teammates celebrate an undefeated season in 1991.

Courtesy of DeMatha Catholic High School

Sample Scouting Report Form

Team scouted: _____   Opponent: _____

Personnel and tendencies (height and weight)

1. _____   6. _____

2. _____   7. _____

3. _____   8. _____

4. _____   9. _____

5. _____   10. _____

First sub, backcourt: _____   First sub, front line: _____

Do they have a player who can take over? _____

Whom do we foul? _____

Pressure offensive set: _____

Half-court man-to-man offensive set: _____

Half-court zone offensive set: _____

Delay game set: _____

Inbounds baseline: _____

Full-court pressure defense: _____

Half-court zone trap: _____

Man-to-man defensive look: _____

Zone defensive look: _____

Defensive look vs. inbounds underneath their basket: _____

Junk defenses (e.g., box-and-one): _____

Matchups

Us   **Opponent**

1. _____   1. _____

2. _____   2. _____

3. _____   3. _____

4. _____   4. _____

5. _____   5. _____

How do they play? _____

What must we do to win? _____

FIGURE 5.2 Sample scouting report form.

From M. Wootten and J. Wootten, 2013, *Coaching basketball successfully, third edition* (Champaign, IL: Human Kinetics).

Today, more high schools than ever are also taking long road trips, particularly during Christmas vacation. End-of-the-year tournaments have become very popular, and some high school teams travel from coast to coast.

My DeMatha team generally takes three trips a year. The first is right before Christmas, the second is at Christmas, and the third is to a postseason tournament. If traveling is done at the right time of the year, only a very small amount of school time is missed by the student-athletes. We never let basketball get ahead of education. Our moderator, Father Damian, who accompanies us on these trips, checks that players are keeping up with their schoolwork and provides tutoring when necessary.

On trips of five hours or less, I recommend traveling by chartered bus. For shorter distances, the bus is quicker than flying because of the time required to get to and from the airport and waiting for luggage. When the trip is more than five hours, though, flying makes more sense. Flying is expensive, and the team may have to raise money to be able to take such a trip. In some cases, tournaments pay a portion of the participating schools' transportation costs, so flying might be an affordable option.

Three such trips a year add to the total educational experience of playing in our program. A basketball road trip might be a young person's first flight or trip out of the area. The players will meet people their own age from other parts of the country, and they will share many experiences together that they will never forget.

Before we make a trip, I emphasize to players that they are representing themselves, their families, and the school. I also tell them that I know their conduct will be exemplary, and I stress that they use common sense with regard to their safety.

We do not have rules or bed checks on the road. The coaches stay in the same hall as the players and are with them throughout the trip. We rely on good supervision and the fact that the players know that we expect them to represent our school, our program, and each other in a classy way.

I also appoint a trip captain from among our seniors. This player is in charge of the entire team on the trip. It's an opportunity to place some additional responsibility on a young adult, and it also reminds the players that it is their team, their trip, and their time to remember. Like everything else in your basketball program, your road trips will be only as successful as the care you take in planning them.

College Scholarships

As mentioned earlier, a coach has equal responsibility to players off the court as on it. And one of the most important high school coaching duties is working with players who want to go to college.

Virtually every high school player dreams of going on to play basketball at the college level. We all know, though, that as the level of competition increases, the chances of making it at that level decrease. Recent figures show that there are nearly 1 million high school basketball players, but only 16,000 players at the college level. That means only 1 out of every 50 high school players will make it in college.

The odds are against most high school players, but the efforts of the coach can help a young athlete get the opportunity to play college ball. You can't fool colleges into taking a player, but you can get the information regarding your seniors into recruiters' hands, then provide any follow-up information they may need.

Great players will have more than enough scholarship offers, and, in that case, your role as coach is to provide guidance in helping them narrow down the choices. Generally, though, it's the average player whom you have to work hard to help, and you can do it. As proof of the dividends that hard work can yield, more than 95 percent of DeMatha's basketball players have been offered a basketball or academic scholarship to college. With few exceptions, these scholarships have been accepted. (Most of the offers that were turned down were done so by young men wanting to go to Ivy League schools, which only award scholarships based on financial need.)

Once the college representatives begin to show up at your games or practices, you must be sure to treat them all equally. Do not give big-name coaches preferential treatment. They are all college coaches with jobs to do, and they should all be treated fairly. College recruiters know when they come to DeMatha that they will have the same opportunity to talk with a player as would a Mike Krzyzewski, Gary Williams, or Tom Izzo. The word is out that every college has the same chance at a DeMatha player, and this is the word you should make sure gets out about your program. Why? Because that coach who comes to recruit your star player may end up offering your sixth man a scholarship.

In the case of the heavily recruited players, we have found it is best to have certain rules by which the college recruiters must abide. These rules are not designed to inconvenience the recruiters, but rather to try to control the distractions and pressures that can often be placed on an 18-year-old who is still in high school. Here are our recruiting rules:

- All contacts must be made through the coach's office, and we will facilitate immediate communication with the young man's parents.

- Any recruiter coming to the school will have the opportunity to meet and talk with any player whom he is interested in.

- If the recruiter sparks an interest in the young man, and the young man wants a school representative to visit his home, then this will be set up at the convenience of both parties.

- If the recruiter wants the young man to visit the school's campus, and the young man wishes to do so, then we will set up the visit through the coach's office and the young man's parents. Unofficial visits to the campus are also encouraged.

- Visits are allowed in the fall until basketball practice starts and can resume after the season. In-season visits are allowed only if there is a legitimate gap during which time the team is not practicing.

All coaches should make efforts to help their players with college placement, particularly if a program is just getting started or if the coach is new to an existing program. Even if none of the players goes on to play in college, the effort is not wasted. The players will appreciate that you are working hard to make

Postage Paid

In my first year at DeMatha, I wrote a letter that included a thumbnail sketch of that year's seniors, a schedule of all our scrimmages and games, and a schedule of all our practices. I sent that letter to over 400 colleges and encouraged each of them to send a representative to see our players in action. I was brief and conservative in my descriptions of players, not wanting to oversell their abilities and lose credibility with the college representatives.

The results of this first letter were almost immediate. In one of our first games that season, our point guard, Johnny Herbert, scored 38 points and played an outstanding game. As we were walking off the floor, a gentleman approached me and said, "I'm Coach Byron Gilbreath from Georgia Tech, and I enjoyed the way your team played. I particularly like the way your point guard played. I would like him to visit Georgia Tech, and I feel pretty confident Coach Hyder will offer him a scholarship."

After Johnny had showered, I introduced him to Coach Gilbreath. They talked for a while, his visit was set up, and Johnny went on to become captain of the Georgia Tech team. He is now a successful businessman in Georgia.

It makes me feel good knowing that the letter I took the time to write may have had something to do with Johnny's successes in athletics and life. I often kid my godson, Steven Morgan Herbert, "Just think, if I hadn't written that letter, there might not be any you." Now, whenever something good happens to the family, Steven just says, "I know. I know. It's the letter."

colleges aware of them. Don't limit yourself to only Division I schools either. There are plenty of Division II and III schools out there whose coaches would love to have a good, hardworking student-athlete.

You may even find yourself assisting players from other teams. I've had many players from other schools call me to help them get into college, saying that their own coaches won't write a letter or lift a finger on their behalf. That always saddens me, and I do whatever I can. I encourage you to do the same.

Although I may offer advice and guidance, I make it our policy to let the players make their own decisions about college. I don't tell our players whom to marry, and I don't tell them where to go to college—they have to be responsible for their own lives. If you tell a player where to go to college, and things do not work out very well, the player may blame it on you. But if he makes his own decision, he is the one who has to make it work.

What College Coaches Look For

If you're fortunate enough to have players who are good enough to draw interest from colleges, the day will come when they have to play in front of college coaches. That's a lot of pressure. Every player wants to look good in that situation, and the resulting nervousness sometimes makes players timid because they're afraid they will make a mistake. With this in mind, I take time to go over with the players a list of factors that college coaches consider when evaluating a player:

1. *Body language.* What is a player's body language after he makes a mistake? How does he react to his coach's constructive criticism? When a substitute comes into the game to take his place? After a foul is called against him that he disagrees with?

2. *Decision making.* Can the player make the right decisions to complete a play, or is he so concerned about trying to be spectacular that he ends up hurting his team?

3. *Ability to play within a system.* Can the player stick with the game plan and make everyone around him a better player, or is he a one-on-one whiz who doesn't help his teammates at all?

4. *Relationship with teammates.* Is the player a pouter when things don't go well? Does he interact well with his teammates?

5. *On-court behavior.* Does the player play with class? A classy player doesn't taunt an opponent after making a good play. A classy player does exhibit good conduct toward others and respect for the game.

6. *Skill level.* How well does the player shoot the ball, how well does he handle the ball, and how well does he pass the ball?

7. *Competitiveness.* Is the player a competitor? Because players now play so many games, some players do not care as much whether they win or lose; it does not always matter to them because they know they will just play again later that day.

8. *Love of the game.* Does the athlete play because he loves the game, or does he play because he loves what the game can give him?

9. *Conduct.* Potential recruits need to know that their conduct is important in every game, and that they are always under scrutiny, even if indirectly. A college recruiter isn't going to just talk to the player and his coach; he's going to talk to opposing coaches as well. Stress to your players that even the impression they make on opposing coaches can affect their future.

10. *Contribution to winning.* Is the player willing to do the little things that help his team win? Is he willing to sacrifice for the good of the team? Does he make the winning play regardless of what the play is?

Summary

The following items are among the many important plans you need to make before the season:

- Make sure that you have complete medical screenings and proof of insurance coverage for each athlete who tries out for your team.

- Develop a relationship with a local doctor and sports medicine staff who can provide treatment for and rehabilitation of injuries.

- Have qualified student trainers on hand at all practices and games to provide immediate preliminary treatment for injuries.

- Structure in-season practices to provide the necessary conditioning, and provide your players with workout plans for the off-season. Being in top physical shape is a year-round process!

- Institute a weight training program that benefits the muscle groups used specifically in basketball and that emphasizes strength development rather than muscle definition and bulk.

- Have players focus on individual skills, not just playing games, in the off-season.

- Make sure that you, your players, and your assistant coaches all try to attend or work at a summer basketball camp. Look for camps that do a good job of teaching the fundamentals.

- Select responsible, mature student managers to help relieve you of some of the necessary noncoaching tasks.

- Put all your equipment purchases out on bids to help you get the most for your dollar.

- Meet with your assistants to develop a master plan that includes all the basketball strategies you wish to employ in the upcoming season.

- Schedule games against teams in your competitive class that you have a reasonable chance of defeating.

- Scout as many of your opponents as possible, using some form of assessment tool to make your analysis more organized if not objective.

- Try to arrange a small number of longer road trips to expand players' horizons and build cohesion among team members.

- Work with seniors who want to go to college by actively pursuing college recruiters and helping blue-chippers narrow their choices of colleges, but do not make any decisions for them.

CHAPTER 6

Practice Planning

Before the date that our practices begin, I divide our season-long master plan into five monthly practice plans. I also examine our monthly plan for November and draw up a daily practice plan detailing what we want to cover in each of the sessions. The monthly plan is, then, a chart of the available practice days in November and what we will be working on in those practices leading up to the opener (see appendix B).

This monthly plan should not be etched in stone. Conditions constantly change, and you must have the flexibility to alter the plan to best suit the circumstances of any given day or week. After every practice, I meet with my assistants and discuss what we need to work on and why. We finalize the plan for the next practice in these meetings. A sample of a practice plan we might develop is shown in table 6.1.

Avoid burning your team out by practicing too much. Err on the side of caution. It is better to underpractice than to overpractice. Two practices a day is too demanding for most players at any time of the year. Two-a-days often result in mental and physical

fatigue—as well as injuries—rather than improved conditioning and performance.

You can avoid overpracticing by planning longer practices at the beginning of the year when the players need the extra work and can handle it better. Before the team is selected, our practices run between 2 and 2 1/2 hours. After that point, I limit the majority of our practices to 2 hours. The day before a game, though, we practice no more than 90 minutes and do not perform any heavy physical work. This helps keep the players rested and sharp for the following day's game.

By January, we are primarily working on fine-tuning various elements of the game, so we may reduce practice time by 10 more minutes. By February, practices are usually shortened by another 5 minutes or so, making the average practice about 1 hour and 45 minutes.

A coach should also give the players at least one day a week off from practicing. Sometimes I will even give the players two days off. Players need this time to rest their bodies and their minds, and they will be fresher and more effective over the course of the season if you provide such breaks.

TABLE 6.1 Sample Practice Plan

Offense	Defense	Other
Half-court man offense Half-court offense vs. zone trap Time-score Shooting	1-on-1 to 2-on-2 Offense-defense vs. wizard Half-court defense (22-Tough individual defense vs. dribbler)	Warm-up Big 3: 5 two-shot fouls 3-on-2, 2-on-1 fast break drills Recognition drill Stations: offensive work Fouls + sprints + 70%

Time (min)	Drill	Emphasis
10	Warm-up	
5	1-on-1 to 2-on-2	Move your feet
5	Offense–defense vs. wizard	See the whole floor
5	Individual defense vs. dribbler	Stay low
10	Half-court offense vs. zone trap	Ball movement
10	Stations: offensive work	Perimeter: shallow cuts
10	Half-court defense (22-Tough)	Post: shooting
15	Big 3: 5 two-shot fouls 3-on-2, 2-on-1 fast break drills Recognition drill	Full speed
20	Half-court man offense	Patience: getting a good shot
5	Time–score	Down 2 with 30 sec to go
5	Shooting drill	Game speed
10	Fouls (5 one-and-ones) + sprints	Reward winner

Comments
1. One more practice before next game
2. Academic slips due on Friday
3. Stay on the books

Conducting Practices

On average, our practices last about 2 hours, with the time broken down into segments of varying length. Each segment is reserved for a specific purpose. I learned long ago to adhere strictly to this schedule, even if my temptation was to stay with a drill until the players were doing it right. Invariably, we would end up spending 20 minutes on the drill instead of the 5 minutes I had allotted for it. What I found was that the longer I stuck with a certain drill, the worse the performance became.

If a certain practice segment goes poorly, I now cut it off after the allotted time anyway. I then call the team together and tell them, "Fellows, the last 10 minutes we really cheated ourselves out of a chance to improve. We didn't do well. But now we have to move on to the next thing, and we have to work hard and work smart because we don't want to cheat ourselves out of any more valuable practice minutes." The players generally pick up the intensity for the next drill, and that higher intensity usually carries over into the remainder of the practice.

At DeMatha, practices officially start every afternoon at 3:30, or about 30 minutes after the school day ends. However, the players are already out on the floor working in special groups several minutes before the official starting time.

From the time school ends, the players have a half hour to put their books away, get changed, get ankles taped if needed, and prepare for practice by stretching on their own. We do not stretch out as a team because we have our bigger players use one set of stretching exercises, and our smaller players a different set. Also, players with minor injuries may want to take this time for other types of stretching or rehabilitation exercises.

Our players are encouraged to have all of their preparation work done by 3:25, at which time the big men work out individually with their coach, while the perimeter players work on their individual skills and moves.

Staying on Schedule

At O'Connell, we are in a different situation than my father because we are a coed school. We expect players to be in the gym 10 minutes after classes end. Classes end at 2:50, so players have to be in the gym at 3 p.m. Players are allowed to see a teacher between these times if necessary, but we do ask them to bring a note from the teacher. This enables players to get the academic help they need but also lets them know that it is not a time to socialize.

When players come in, we try to have 20 minutes of prepractice. This allows us to work with players in a one-on-one setting or spend time shooting as a group or one on one. We will blow the whistle at 3:20 and start practice with 20 minutes of shooting under our belts. We then usually practice from 3:20 to 5:20. Our girls' team follows us with a practice at 5:20, so we need to make sure we stay on schedule.

Courtesy of DeMatha Catholic High School

Morgan and assistant coach Mike Brey, now head coach at Notre Dame, conduct a team practice.

At precisely 3:30, I blow the whistle, and the players sprint to where I am standing. I place particular emphasis on the players sprinting toward me, because I believe that the way you begin anything will have a direct effect on how well you complete it. Players who take their time and walk over to start practice won't have the enthusiasm necessary to make the practice as productive as it could be. By hustling from the beginning, players establish the proper state of mind to accomplish what we want.

If players fail to hustle over to you at the start of practice, here's what I would suggest. Once the team is gathered around you, say this to them: "You all are supposed to be hustling over here, and I see most of you just walking. You're obviously not warmed up yet. Let's see if we can't get you warmed up a little bit."

At this point, line your team up and have them jog up and down the court a couple of times to loosen up. Then have them run 25 to 30 sprints the length of the gym. Once they've caught their wind and walked around a bit, blow the whistle again and see if they don't hustle over to you this time—and, in all likelihood, for the rest of the season. I did this once early in my career, and the players quickly got the message. In subsequent years, the word has gotten out before practices begin, and the players haven't needed any reminders. If you emphasize the importance of hustling at the beginning of practice, your players will do just that. As I said, it's not what you coach, but what you emphasize.

THOUGHT FOR THE DAY

Good, better, best. Never let it rest until the good is better, better than the best.
—Tim Duncan

Another way I emphasize working hard in practice is to ask my players, "How would you feel if a college scout watched you practice today?" This has practical implications beyond just motivating players. It can also affect their chances of playing in college. Coaches move around more today than they used to, and players need to impress *every* coach who is watching, whether the coach is watching that particular player or not.

For example, if a Division III coach comes to watch one of your players, your Division I prospect needs to be just as fired up for a couple of reasons. First, that Division III coach may move up to Division I before you know it, or he could become an Olympic coach. Second, coaches talk to other coaches. Make sure your players know that. That same Division III coach could be approached by a Division I coach who says, "I wasn't able to make it over to that practice, but how did so-and-so look? We're interested in him." You don't want the Division III coach to say, "He really dogged it."

Emphasize to your players that they need to practice hard all of the time, not only because it will make them and the team better, but also because they never know who might be watching. It's your job as a coach to prepare them for these situations.

Once the players have sprinted over to me, I will briefly set the tone for the practice. For example, I might say, "Fellows, we have five practices left before our first ball game. We've got to be ready to make today one of our finest days mentally and physically. Let's make it a good one!"

Before we take the floor, I like to give the players what I call the "thought for the day." (Many of these thoughts appear throughout the book.) Each day I pick a saying with a different meaning; for example, "We are many, but are we much?" (John Wooden). This particular thought helps the players chew on the notion of whether we're developing as well as we should be as a team.

Then, at the end of every practice, we go into a classroom to talk about the practice and the future. We always finish that session discussing the thought for the day. This has become a valued tradition at DeMatha, and the young men seem to thoroughly enjoy giving their interpretations. These can range from very serious to very funny. I remember one year I asked one player for his ideas on the thought, "It wasn't raining when Noah built the ark" (Howard Ruff).

He said, "I don't know. Carry an umbrella?" The whole team had a good laugh, and we were able to have a good discussion about the importance of good preparation.

These thoughts are also good to come back to throughout the season if they help reinforce a point you're trying to make. For example, another thought I use is "The little things make the big things happen" (John Wooden). This can be used if your team is getting sloppy and not executing the little things well. If nobody moves after the ball is slapped on an inbounds play, I can stop practice for a second and refocus the players by reminding them of this thought and our discussion that followed.

I've found the thought for the day to be one of the most positive things we do to develop team unity and great chemistry among our players. Perhaps more important, these thoughts can quietly help the players develop a philosophy of life.

After I've given the players that day's thought, we break into our first drill, which is a full-court passing drill in which the players line up at diagonal ends of the court and hand off and throw various passes to their teammates coming from the other end of the floor. This drill helps loosen the players up even more, promotes good conditioning, and helps improve their ballhandling skills. The fact that we start our practice with this drill emphasizes to the players the importance that we place on good passing and catching.

A typical practice at DeMatha proceeds something like this:

1. Full-court pass drill
2. Full-court layup drill
3. 10 foul shots in a row (If the player makes 9 or 10, he picks up a permission. If he makes 7 or 8, nothing happens. If he makes fewer than 7, he picks up a double separator.)
4. Defensive footwork and individual defensive work
5. Full-court 1-on-1 drills, building to 2-on-2 all the way to 5-on-5
6. Individual station work (We have three baskets in operation, each representing a station at which a different skill is taught and developed. The skills being taught change from practice to practice. The players rotate every 3 minutes, taking 9 minutes for the entire segment.)
7. Team defensive drills
8. Fast break drills
9. Second set of 10 foul shots (Each player shoots 5 two-shot fouls while rotating from basket to basket. Permission and separator rules used in segment 3 apply.)
10. Team offensive drills (These include any teaching that needs to be done and half-court games.)
11. Time and score repertoire (We try to allow 5 minutes at the end of practice to work on special situations. Each practice we work on a different situation—for example, down by two points with 30 seconds left to play.)
12. Third set of foul shots (Each player shoots 5 one-and-one situations. Permissions and separators again apply.)
13. 20 conditioning sprints
14. Balance the ledger on permissions and separators

A typical practice at O'Connell may include the following segments:

1. Prepractice (shooting, 2-on-2 break-down, big-man and guard work)
2. Stretching
3. Thought for the day
4. Warm-up drill
5. 10 straight free throws
6. 1-on-1, 2-on-2, 3-on-3, and 5-on-5
7. Shell drill
8. Half-court defense (change up)
9. Big 3: 5 two-shot fouls
10. Post perimeter, 2-on-2, 3-on-3
11. Teach man offense as a whole
12. 10-point games
13. Time–score
14. Fouls and 20 in 2

Maximizing Practices

The primary purpose of the master plan is to organize your practices from the most general season-long plan all the way down to the most specific daily practice plan. This organization and planning are crucial to making your practices as effective as possible, and they provide the road map to guide your team on its season-long objective of playing up to its potential.

The master plan allows you to combine time management skills with hard-core basketball instruction and coaching. As previously mentioned, in devising your practice schedules, you should make sure that the players never spend too much time on one particular drill. Too much time on one thing can lead to laziness and boredom, which in turn can lead to the development of bad habits—exactly what you don't want to happen in practice. Too little time on a certain drill, however, may not promote maximum skill development. As you gain more experience, you will be better able to determine just how much time to spend on a particular drill. In any event, keep your practices moving! Your players will stay sharper physically and mentally if you do.

THOUGHT FOR THE DAY

We are what we repeatedly do. Excellence, then, is not an act but a habit. –Aristotle

In organizing your practices, also remember to allow for, and even encourage, fun. Never lose sight of the fact that basketball is a game, and that games are supposed to be fun. The players are out there playing for you because they love the game to begin with, so you as the coach must encourage this, especially in practices. The fun in games will take care of itself, but the fun in practices you can control.

A practice cannot be truly effective if it is not fun. The basketball season is a long one, and if players at any point no longer have fun in practice, their enthusiasm and effort will decrease correspondingly. This lack of mental and physical sharpness can spread like a cancer, which may be the reason why some teams are better in the first part of the season than the last. So keep your practices fun all year long.

The system of permissions and separators is one way I keep the fun in our practices at DeMatha. This system helps make practice competitive, and all athletes find fun in competition. Some of our biggest laughs come at the end of practice, when the players with extra permissions and the players with double separators try to negotiate deals with each other.

Inevitably, at some point in the season, your team won't be playing hard enough, competing the way you want them to compete, or playing as physically as they need to in order to be successful. A little trick I use to help shake my team out of the doldrums is something I call "Intensity," and it has been a big help to us through the years.

Intensity is quite simple. I put my top 10 guys out on the floor, throw the ball up, and let them scrimmage for five minutes (running time on the clock). The players just go at it, and the coaches don't call any fouls. If one team isn't hustling, say they don't get back on defense, we'll blow the whistle and make that team run a separator. Then we'll give the ball to the other team and keep on playing.

This is not only a great way to get the competitive juices flowing again, but it also helps physical conditioning. Players will soon learn that you're not going to call fouls, which is the main reason why the intensity picks up. Let me make clear that I don't let the players get overly physical to the point where someone may get injured, but generally speaking I let them go at it.

I also tell the players that if intensity doesn't work, we may have to go to something I call "Duel at Dawn." I've never had to.

Another effective way to keep practices spirited is to have three or four drills that accomplish the same goal or develop the same skill, then rotate those drills to keep them fresh. Also, try to use the clock, a point system, or a double separator to inspire motivation and competition.

At O'Connell, we execute many of our drills versus the clock; for example, in one of our drills, the players have to make 120 points in 3 minutes. If they do not make it, they might have to repeat the drill or do some running. We also use a point system in all of our live action. For example, a rebound is 1 point, an assist is 1 point, a charge is 2 points (for the defense), a dive is 2 points, a deflection is 1 point, a turnover is minus 1 point, a bad shot is minus 1 point, and not sprinting to change ends is minus 1 point. The team with the highest point total after a quarter will get a drink while the team with fewer points will have to run lines based on the difference between their total and the total of the other team.

We also play a controlled scrimmage called a 10-point game in a best-of-three series. The winning team will get a drink, and the losing team will run a double separator. The great thing about the point system is that it enables you to award points for the areas that you want to emphasize as a coach.

Finally, we have an "attitude of the day" award so that we can reward the player who is executing the details that we want emphasized. All of these ideas help bring out the competitive nature of the players in practice.

In addition to fun and intensity, the culture you set in practice is very important. Here's a great piece of advice for coaches: "Set the tone, and the content will follow." If you set a tone, or culture, from the beginning, great things can happen. At O'Connell, we expect the players to be on time, to work hard, to be leaders in school and on the court, to be in great physical shape, and to grow every day. When you create a culture, the expectation of greatness soon comes from the players themselves. They expect great things to happen, they expect to get better, and they have pride in what they are doing and in the school that they represent.

Writing notes to yourself can help you stay focused on maintaining the proper culture. For example, you might write yourself a reminder to talk to a player about his grades in a class, or you might write a reminder that a player owes you extra hill runs because a teacher told you that the player was disruptive in class. You could also write a note reminding yourself that you want the team to spend 10 minutes in the next practice talking about what it means to be a man. A coach has many tasks to juggle, and these small notes can help you focus on your culture every day and not allow something to fall through the cracks. Also, this allows you to be an example for the kids, taking care of the details just as you want the players to take care of the details. A great culture leads to great practices.

Keeping Practices Effective and Fun

Following are some tips for keeping practices both effective and fun:

- Take the time to prepare and organize your practice in advance. Know exactly what you want to do at the start of each practice.

- Keep your drills and various segments short and snappy. The players' ability to concentrate on one topic decreases the longer you spend on it.

- Keep the attitude upbeat and positive by handing out more praise than criticism. Use the sandwich technique described in chapter 2 for constructive criticism.

- Have fun yourself, and take advantage of humorous opportunities. If the players see that you are having fun at practice, they will be more likely to have fun themselves.

- Keep everybody involved. If you are going 5-on-5, assign the remaining players to the two teams and let them reap the rewards or suffer the consequences of how their teammates fare. This gives those not physically involved a stake in what happens and keeps them part of the practice mentally and emotionally.

To reiterate, my primary objective for the team is to have them play hard, play smart, play together, and have fun. That applies to practices as well as games. And the best way to ensure that your team plays that way is for you to be prepared and run a well-organized practice.

Summary

Practices will be only as good as your preparation for them. Keep the ideas from this chapter in mind when planning and conducting practice sessions.

- Schedule practices with the master plan and long-term picture in mind, not just how much you can work players to fatigue.

- Plan every minute of your practices, and stick to the plan.
- Create a winning practice culture at the start of every season.
- Make your players sprint over to you to begin practice on a hustling, enthusiastic note.
- Keep the fun in practices.

PART III

COACHING OFFENSE

CHAPTER 7

Teaching Offensive Positions and Sets

Basketball is unique among sports in that there are fewer specialists or one-dimensional athletes in the game. Each player must be a total player. Football has field-goal kickers, baseball has designated hitters, and soccer and hockey have goalies. But basketball players, although they may excel in certain areas of the game (for example, three-point shooting, rebounding, or defense), must have a wide array of skills.

Multiple skills are essential to play the game effectively. Every basketball player should be able to

- pass and receive the basketball,
- make the transition from offense to defense and from defense to offense,
- rebound offensively and defensively in relation to their position (a point guard, for instance, is not expected to rebound as much as a post player),
- play good defense, and
- work well with the other four players.

But a coach should not expect each player to have equal ability in all of these areas. Therefore, you must help players develop and strengthen their abilities, then blend these attributes into the best possible team structure. First, you must identify the skills that are needed. Next, you need to position the players where they will be most effective.

Traditional Position Skills

Basketball players need to have a variety of skills, but each player has specific strengths that should be cultivated and developed. In addition to the universal skills, all five offensive player positions require somewhat different secondary skills and attributes. The following is a rather simplified description of these five offensive spots:

1. Point guard
2. Shooting guard
3. Small forward
4. Power forward
5. Center

Point Guard Most systems designate a player to run the offense. Often referred to as the point guard or "1 player," this player is usually the best ball handler on the squad. He should be able to lead a fast break that develops out of any situation, whether it be a steal, a rebound, or a basket by the opponent. If the fast break is not there, he must be able to bring the ball up the floor against pressure defense and set up the half-court offense. The point guard does not have to be a big scorer, but he should be able to shoot well enough to force defenses to come out and cover him on the perimeter and not sag back into the middle.

The point guard should also be an excellent passer. His ability to hit the open player is very important, as is his ability to anticipate the way a play might develop and to make the pass that sets up the assist pass. He should have the smarts to go to the player with the hot hand, but also the ability to get everybody involved in the offense. The point guard should have the ability to penetrate, attract the defense, and finish the play. Finishing the play means that he should make sure that the offense gets a good shot, whether it be on a fast break or through penetration. The 1 player should have the intelligence to read the defenses and adjust the offense accordingly. The ideal point guard is, in a lot of ways, an extension of the coach on the floor.

Shooting Guard   The second guard is frequently the bigger of the two guards. The "2 player" is generally one of the best outside shooters and, ideally, is the second-best ball handler on the team. He must be a good receiver because he will frequently get the first pass to start the offense. And, therefore, he must also be a good passer in order to keep the offense moving and take advantage of opportunities to get the ball inside to the post players.

Like the point guard, the 2 player should be able to create and finish the play either on the fast break or by dishing off to an open teammate. The player at the 2 position can also help the team by grabbing offensive rebounds, either by following the shot or by sneaking in from the weak side to get good rebounding position.

Small Forward   Also called the swingman because of the required versatility to play in the post and on the perimeter depending on the situation, the small forward is typically taller than the guards, but perhaps not as quick or as good a ball handler. But the "3 player" should possess many of the same skills as the guards. He should be able to handle the ball well, because he is sometimes called on to help the guards break pressure defenses. The small forward must also pass the ball well. Sometimes this player can be the best passer on the team, because his slight height advantage over the guards opens up more avenues through which to pass the ball. And he should be able to shoot from the outside to help the 1 and 2 players draw a sagging or zone defense away from the lane area.

Where the 3 player differs from the guards is in the area of offensive rebounding. The small forward must be a good offensive rebounder. From the 3 position, a player often has the best shot at an offensive rebound because opponents concentrate on blocking out the power forward and center.

Power Forward   The power forward should be one of the biggest and strongest players on the team; therefore, this player should be one of your dominant rebounders, both offensively and defensively. The "4 player" should be a physical player. Every team needs a physical presence, and because of his size and strength, the power forward can often provide it.

Like the guards and the 3 player, the power forward should be able to handle the ball well and should be a good passer and receiver. This player's size and strength should enable him to post up inside and take the ball to the basket either for an easy shot or to draw a foul.

Center   In many cases, the center will be the heart of the team. Like the power forward, the "5 player" should be either your best or second-best rebounder. Unlike the perimeter players, the center must be able to play with his back to the basket and must be a solid inside scoring threat. Therefore, you must work with your center to develop the fundamental moves that will allow him to score consistently from inside 10 feet.

Because the 5 player often shoots in traffic, he will frequently draw the most fouls. For that reason, the center should be a good free-throw shooter (but then again, all your players should be good free-throw shooters). Shots taken near the basket are the highest percentage shots, so a good part of your offense should be designed to get the ball inside to the center.

Perimeter and Post

Over the years, I have quit designating players by the traditional position designations (that is, point guard, shooting guard, and so forth) just described. However, I still find it useful to designate numbers to certain players for alignment purposes when taking the ball out of bounds or setting up the offense. For example, I may want the 3 player to always inbound the ball, and I may want the 1 player to always try to be the first recipient of the inbounds pass. So I do use numbers for alignment and teaching purposes.

But, overall, I prefer to break the players down into two groups: perimeter players and post players. Perimeter players can be defined as any player who has the ability to play effectively while facing the basket. Post players are defined as those who have the ability to go inside and play with their back to the basket. As we all know, players today are becoming more and more skillful, and you will find that many athletes have the ability to play both the perimeter and the post. And in today's motion offenses, those versatile players are extremely valuable.

With the advent of these multidimensional players, more and more teams are using the entire court to create space for the offense. Many offensive sets incorporate the big man who can shoot the ball, go inside, and shoot off the dribble; these sets also allow offensive players to take advantage of matchups that occur throughout every game.

One thing that all of the great players have in common, besides great ability, is the intelligence to play within their abilities. They do what they can do well, but they do not try to do the things they cannot do well. I'm sure you've heard the old coaching cliché that "a player must play within himself." That means we must help our players learn their strengths. We must remind them to do what they do best. A player shouldn't try to shoot three-point shots if his range is 15 feet. And a player shouldn't try to dunk the ball on the fast break if he can't jump that high.

Teams also must play within their capabilities. A slow team that tries to win with a run-and-gun style will be disappointed. It is up to us, the coaches, to develop a style of play that is within the abilities of our teams.

Emphasizing Player Strengths

A player really needs to know his strength and then must work to make that strength even stronger. Many players end up being solid at many skills, but great at none. A player is often better off becoming great at one move, such as a catch-and-shoot or rip move left or right, instead of being average at a variety of moves. Tell players to pick their favorite move and become great at that move. The defense may know what a player's best move is, but if it is great, they still won't be able to stop it.

Courtesy of Bishop O'Connell High School/Tommy Orndorff

As a coach, teach players to maximize their strengths.

Offensive Sets

Before getting into much detail regarding offensive sets, I want to point out here that my basic offense is the fast break. In theory, I hope we never have to set up an offense. We strive to take at least one third of our shots off of the transition game. My rationale for this approach is this: If a team walks the ball up the floor and plays right into the teeth of the defense with every single possession, then that team is in for a long game. That's basically playing 5-on-5 basketball for four quarters.

In any offense, fast break or half court, you always want to create a numbers advantage. With the fast break, a team can create a numbers advantage and through good passing can find an open player for a high-percentage shot. In a half-court offense, through good movement, passing, and screens, you can often create a quick 2-on-1 or 3-on-2 matchup that can yield a high-percentage shot.

As much as we would like to, we know we can't run a fast break down the court every time, so we have to be prepared to set up an offense. In these situations, there are two basic sets from which to choose; all offensive formations fall into one of two categories, the one-guard front or the two-guard front.

One-Guard Front

The one-guard front is a good offensive set to use when you have two post players who are effective inside. This set features a true point guard directing the offense from the top of the key. That can be a lonely position against a good pressure defense because the 1 guard is running the show by himself.

The 2 guard is generally on the right wing, and the small forward on the left wing. (I define the wing area as the foul line extended.) However, if these players are more comfortable on the left and right wings, respectively, it is wise to play them in those spots instead.

For the post players, you have a few more options. You can use a double low post, with the power forward and the center positioned down low on either side of the basket. Another option is to use a high post and a low post, with the low player down near one block and the high player out near the foul line.

A strength of the one-guard front is that it affords more opportunities to pass the ball inside; the three perimeter players are constantly looking to feed the two post players. By emphasizing the inside game, you can sometimes get the opponent into foul trouble. And because your two best inside players are already stationed near the basket, this formation is often the most effective for offensive rebounding.

Outside shooting ability is the biggest variable in determining whether to play this offensive set. A one-guard front can lose its effectiveness if your perimeter players are not good enough outside shooters to keep the defense honest. Good outside shooters force the defense into making a decision—sag and control the inside game or come out, play

---

Controlling Tempo

At O'Connell, we want to break down the game so that 33 percent of our offense is off our fast break, 33 percent comes from running our half-court offense, 20 percent comes off our defense, and 14 percent comes off offensive boards. If you can get easy points off your fast break, the offensive glass, and your defense, you are going to win a high percentage of games.

If you have to run your half-court offense for 70 percent of the game, then you are letting the other team dictate the tempo. On the flip side, if you think the other team is stronger or more experienced than your ball club, you may want to run your half-court offense more often to slow the game down. The bottom line is that you need to control the tempo so that the pace of the game favors your team. The team that controls the tempo usually wins the game.

THOUGHT FOR THE DAY

Basketball (athletics) not only builds character, it reveals character. –John Wooden

tight on the perimeter players, and deny the outside shot. If your perimeter is not a threat (or, on the opposite end of the spectrum, if your post is not a threat), the defense can overplay the strength of your offense.

Another weakness of the one-guard front is that it can put the offense in poor position to get back on defense to prevent the fast break. If you are playing a one-guard front and your opponent is a good fast-breaking team, you must think long and hard about the most effective way to stop the break. You can designate certain players to drop back into coverage whenever a shot goes up (from any offensive set), you can double-team the rebounder to prevent the outlet pass, or you can apply full-court pressure on the opponent's ball handler to slow him down. Whatever way you choose to halt the break, have it ready if you are playing a one-guard front.

Two-Guard Front

The two-guard front is the formation that many teams will use when the coach thinks the team has only one good inside player to play the post. In this offensive set, both guards are out on either side of the top of the key facing the basket, about 12 to 14 feet apart. The two forwards now become wing players, each stationed on the side where he is most comfortable. The center can set up at the low post (down on the block), medium post (halfway between the block and the foul line), or high post (at the foul line); or the center can rotate among all three spots at various times.

The two-guard offense makes the most sense when you have a good outside shooting team, or if you have only one good post player, and it is in your best interest to spread the defense out. With good screening and ball movement, you should be able to get good outside shots out of the two-guard front. Teams that use this alignment generally will look to the outside shot rather than try to hammer inside. Unlike the one-guard front, the two players out at the top of the key provide excellent coverage against the fast break.

Whereas the one-guard front frees another player to hit the offensive boards, the two-guard front can leave you relatively weak in the rebounding department. In the two-guard alignment, you really have only one player (the center) in good position to go after the rebound.

Court Balance

Many formations can be run out of one-guard and two-guard sets, such as the 1-4, the 1-3-1, the 2-1-2, and so on. But no matter what type of offense your team is running, always try to make sure you have floor balance. To achieve floor balance, the offensive players should distribute themselves evenly across the floor, not cluster in one spot.

The object of maintaining court balance is to spread out the defense. Spreading out the defense will allow you better penetration and better shots. This is the reason football teams put a wide receiver on each side. Some football teams even use four wide receivers, two on each side, to further spread the defense.

Good floor balance is particularly crucial once a shot is taken at the offensive end of the floor. You must have the right mixture of players crashing the boards fighting for the offensive rebound and of others hustling back on defense to prevent the opponent from getting an easy transition basket. I prefer to have three players hitting the boards; but the right mixture of rebounders and defenders depends on your team's capabilities and on your opponent's fast break potential.

Make sure that each player knows what to do in this situation. The one thing you do not want is a player unsure of whether he's supposed to crash the boards or hustle back on defense. When a player is unsure of what he's supposed to do, he often does nothing. And doing nothing is worse than doing the wrong thing. That is why we tell our players to do something, even if it is wrong. We'll correct it later.

Summary

In this chapter, we discussed the attributes and skills required for the various offensive player positions. The chapter also included an overview of the general offensive sets that can be used and their respective strengths and weaknesses. Here are the specific points to remember:

- All players should be able to pass and receive the ball, change ends of the floor, rebound, play good defense, and work well with their teammates.

- The point guard will be your best ball handler and one of your best passers. He leads the offense and the fast break.

- The shooting guard is obviously one of your best outside shooters and often your second-best ball handler.

- The small forward should possess the same skills as the guards but should be big enough to be a more effective rebounder.

- The power forward and the center are your biggest, most physical players. They should be able to rebound aggressively and play inside with their backs to the basket.

- I prefer to designate only two positions to players: perimeter and post. The perimeter players are farther away from the basket and play facing it; the post players are closer to the hoop and play with their backs to it.

- A basic one-guard front offensive set is more effective for getting the ball inside to the two post players. The lack of an outside shooting threat can limit this set's effectiveness by allowing the defense to sag.

- The two-guard front works best if you have only one good post player or excellent outside shooters.

- In any offensive set, players need to maintain floor balance in order to force the defense to spread out to cover them.

Teaching Offensive Skills

The most effective way to develop basketball skills is to repeatedly practice the proper execution of those skills. I call such proper execution of skills the fundamentals of basketball. Skills are given abilities, whereas fundamentals are the execution of those abilities.

I emphasize the fundamentals—the proper execution of skills—at every level of my program, because a coach can build something worthwhile only with a good foundation. It is through learning and repetition of the fundamentals that players will develop their individual skills and, therefore, contribute maximally to the success of a team offense.

I break down the individual skills into two categories: playing with the ball and playing without the ball. An athlete must be able to do both in order to be a complete player.

Playing With the Ball

Individual talent notwithstanding, each player must be a scoring threat while on the court. So the first thing you'll want to teach your players is to square up and face the basket whenever they receive the ball.

Any time a player catches the ball, no matter the location on the court, he should immediately get into the triple-threat position (figure 8.1). The feet should be about shoulder-width apart and the knees bent. If a player is right-handed, the left foot should be slightly ahead of the right foot, with the left foot acting as the pivot foot. Reverse the footwork for players who are left-handed. In either case, the feet and shoulders should be facing the hoop so that any move made will be in the direction of the basket. From this triple-threat position, a player can dribble, pass, or shoot.

The ball should be protected on the back hip (the right hip for right-handed players), not held out in front where the defense has an opportunity to swipe at it. Stress to

FIGURE 8.1 Triple-threat position.

players that they should stay low, a position that allows them to make their moves more quickly and, therefore, gives the defense less time to react.

We teach players to double-step into the catch (described later in the chapter) so that they are in a triple-threat position every time they receive the ball on the perimeter. An offensive player will be most successful if he attacks the defender by moving in a straight line to the basket (see figure 8.2*a*). Discourage your players from taking the "banana cut"—a wide path to avoid the defense (see figure 8.2*b*). This path allows the defensive player to recover, minimizing the effectiveness of the move.

Also, teach your players to "close the gap." In other words, once the dribbler slices by the defender, he should get the defender close to his back, preventing the player from coming between him and the basket. Closing the

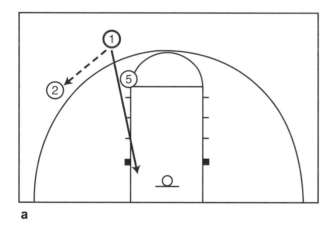

a

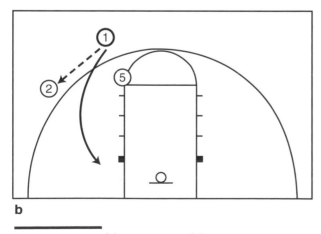

b

FIGURE 8.2 *(a)* Straight line; *(b)* banana cut.

gap in this manner minimizes the defender's chances of recovering and getting back into the play.

Use simple phrases to remind players to close the gap, such as "Clip the hip," meaning the player should attack the defender's hip to go directly at the basket. Other phrases include "Don't dribble in your pocket" or "Explode on your first dribble," meaning the player should push the ball out in front rather than make the first dribble to the side. These are common mistakes that players make.

Stationary Moves

After a player has caught the ball and squared up to the basket in the triple-threat position, he is ready to attack the defender. He can do so by using what I call "stationary moves." I use that term because the player makes the initial move from a stationary triple-threat position, before putting the ball on the floor in a dribble.

Strong-Side Drive

From the triple-threat position, the player executes a jab step. The purpose of the jab step is to get the defense to react. The step should be made with the right foot by right-handed players, and the left foot by left-handed players.

To ensure that the offensive player stays balanced, the jab step should be quick and short (only about 6 inches [15 cm]; figure 8.3*a*). If the defender does not react quickly enough to the jab step, the offensive player should then take a longer step with the same foot, trying to get his head and shoulders by the defender (figure 8.3*b*). The player should then close the gap and explode to the basket with one dribble (figure 8.3*c*).

While teaching stationary moves, emphasize the advantages of using the dribble effectively. Players should try to get to the basket using the fewest dribbles possible. This helps prevent their defender or another defender from getting into the play and possibly stopping the drive. Also emphasize to your players the importance of keeping their head up while

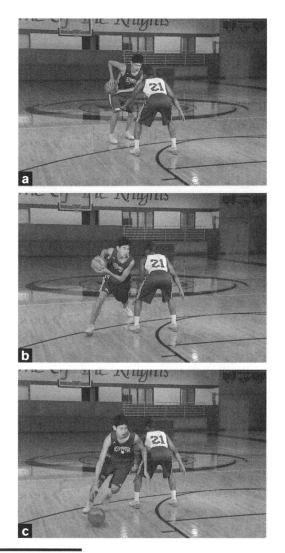

FIGURE 8.3 Strong-side drive.

dribbling. This will give them the court vision to see both help-side defenders and their own teammates to whom they can dish the ball if the defense collapses when they drive.

Crossover Step

If the offensive player executes a jab step, and the defender responds by sliding over in the direction of that step, the offensive player can then go in the opposite direction with a crossover step. First, a right-handed offensive player jabs with the right foot, forcing the defense to react and take away the strong-side drive (figure 8.4*a*). The offensive player then starts to cross the right foot over to the left side (figure 8.4*b*), stepping by the defender's

foot and putting the defender on his right hip. The player should keep the ball as low as possible as he rolls his shoulders through and steps by the defender. The offensive player keeps the defender on the right hip, and he puts the ball down left-handed to protect it from the defense (figure 8.4*c*).

Once again, the offensive player should attack the defender by going in a straight line to the basket, thus limiting the defender's chance to recover. The fundamentals of effective dribbling, closing the gap, and keeping the head up apply to the crossover drive just as they do to the strong-side drive. When executed properly, either of these moves can lead to a jump shot or power layup if the defense reacts to the offensive player's footwork.

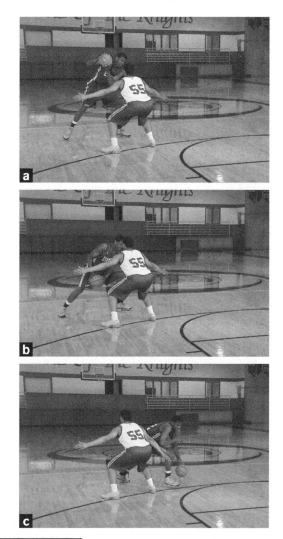

FIGURE 8.4 Crossover step.

Jab Step to the Jumper

The defense will eventually adjust to the jab step by taking a retreat step to prevent the offensive player from slicing to the basket. As the defense retreats, the offensive player now has room to go straight up and shoot the jumper (if within shooting range).

To get the shot off, the offensive player must maintain balance after making the jab step. The player can do so only by keeping the feet shoulder-width apart and staying low. This is why it is important to teach players to keep the jab step short. A jab step that is too long will force the offensive player to reset, and the defense will be able to recover in time to stop the shot.

Moves on the Move

As opposed to stationary moves, "moves on the move" occur when the offensive player is already dribbling the ball and in motion when he reaches his defender. In each of the following moves, the ball handler changes either the speed or direction of the dribble to get the defender off balance and to beat the defender in the open court.

Stop-and-Go

The offensive player begins this move by dribbling hard in one direction, all the while protecting the ball with the off hand. The dribbler then comes to a quick stop, and as soon as the defender stops or becomes off balance, the offensive player then explodes past the defender—pushing the ball out in front of himself, knifing his shoulder by the defender, closing the gap, and keeping the defender behind him.

Once again, the dribbler must stay low for maximum quickness and control of the ball. And, as with the stationary moves, the offensive player must attack and freeze the defender. If the move is made too far from the defender, the defender will have enough time to recover and render the move ineffective.

The dribbler must push the ball out in front to beat the defender. If the dribbler keeps the ball either behind or beside himself, then the defender will have a better opportunity to recover and stop the play.

The complete basketball player will be able to perform the stop-and-go move with the weak hand as well as the strong hand. Encourage players to work at perfecting these moves with their weak hand.

Crossover Dribble

If a dribbler cannot change directions, the defense can force the ball to one side of the court and keep it there. The crossover dribble is an effective way for ball handlers to change direction.

As with the stop-and-go, the offensive player begins the move by dribbling hard in one direction. To execute the crossover, the offensive player plants the front foot and crosses the ball in front of the body to the other hand, away from the planted foot. He then steps with the opposite foot, pushing off with the plant foot, and slices by the defender.

The danger with the crossover is that the offensive player brings the ball in front of the defender. So to help your players avoid losing the ball, teach them to keep the dribble as low as possible, underneath the defender's hands. Once by the defender, the offensive player should keep the defender on the hip, close the gap, and push the ball out in front.

Reverse Dribble

To execute the reverse, the offensive player plants the right foot (if dribbling left-handed) or the left foot (if dribbling right-handed). The ball handler then spins around on the planted foot, protecting the ball by keeping his body between the ball and the defender. As the player brings the ball around on the reverse, he should keep it in the same hand until the defender is beaten. By keeping the ball in the same hand, the offensive player can avoid palming the ball or leaving the ball behind where defenders can reach in and steal it. After the offensive player has put the defender on the hip, the dribbler can change hands to protect the ball, push it out in front, close the gap, and beat the defender.

Again, emphasize to your players that they must be as low as possible when making this move. The low position will make them quicker, keep them under control, and enable them to control the ball better.

The big problem with the reverse is that the offensive player turns his back to the defense and to his own teammates. A ball handler performing a reverse could miss an open player cutting to the basket. Also, ball handlers who turn their back to the defense are susceptible to traps and to offensive charging fouls if a defender is smart enough to get in proper position.

Fake Reverse Dribble

The fake reverse is almost the same move as the reverse, except that it is only half a spin. A player must stay low with this move and push off the back foot with some strength to get by the defender. The dribbler should keep the ball in the same hand the entire time, because he is not changing directions but instead is changing speeds.

The fake reverse allows the offensive player to have better vision of the court, because he doesn't fully turn away from the basket. However, the dribbler must still protect the ball with his body and off hand to be successful with this maneuver.

Additional Dribble Moves

The behind-the-back dribble, between-the-legs dribble, pull-back dribble, and inside-out dribble are all very effective in freeing an offensive player from defensive pressure if the dribbler attacks the defender and moves forward while performing the moves. Teach players to make something happen after they successfully execute one of these moves. The player should experience the satisfaction of finishing the play after going to all that work to beat the defender in the open court.

Dribbling Recap

Key points to teach players about using the dribble to get open:

- Stay low.
- Keep your head up.
- Play under control.
- Attack the defender—don't try to avoid him.
- Go somewhere with your dribble; dribble with a purpose.

- Strengthen the weak hand.
- Keep the defender behind you.
- Close the gap.
- Push the ball out in front.
- Protect the ball with the body and the off hand.
- Change pace and speed.
- Change direction.
- Practice repeatedly in the open court.

Footwork

Footwork is key in helping players to become multidimensional. All players should spend daily practice time working on footwork.

Double Step

We want all of our players to take a double step into every catch. A left-handed player would step with his right foot (figure 8.5*a*) then his left foot (figure 8.5*b*), which would take him into a triple-threat position. A right-handed player would come in left then right. We call this "ball in the air, feet in the air" to

FIGURE 8.5 Double step.

remind the players that they should meet the pass. This enables the players to be ready to make a move or shoot every time they catch the ball. The double step should only be taught once the players have mastered the stationary moves.

Inside Pivot

While the double step is used each time a player catches the ball facing the basket, the inside pivot is used when the player is on the move, such as when coming off a screen or cutting across the lane. Players will always pivot on their inside foot. The player should have all his weight on the inside foot (figure 8.6a), and he should swing the outside foot on the catch (figure 8.6b) so that he can square his shoulders to the basket. We call this the kickstand technique. Think about a bike when the kickstand is down; all the weight of the bike is leaning on the kickstand. Similarly, on the inside pivot, all the weight should be on the inside leg. The player should be able to pivot off either foot depending on the direction he is going. It is not as natural for a left-handed player to pivot on his left foot or for a right-handed player to pivot on his right

foot, so constant work is necessary. Players should also progress to being able to perform the stationary moves (described earlier) off either foot.

Reverse Pivot

When a player's back is to the basket (for example, when the player sprints to the wing to get open), after catching the ball, he must perform a reverse pivot in order to get into a position to face the basket. To perform the reverse pivot, a right-handed player swings his right shoulder open toward the basket (figure 8.7a) and pivots on his left foot (figure 8.7b) to reverse his body so he can square up. We tell our players, "Open the gate; don't close it." This motion will create space between the offensive player and his defender.

FIGURE 8.7 Reverse pivot.

Spin Move

The spin move can be used when a player has his back to the basket and is being pressured by a defender (for example, on the three-point line). The offensive player does not reverse and square up, as described for the reverse pivot. Instead, he simply spins off the physical

FIGURE 8.6 Inside pivot.

pressure to move past his defender. Specifically, he spins off the foot in the direction he is going and uses an explosive dribble to create space and close the gap against his defender. This quick move allows the offensive player to beat his defender without using his dribble until he is by the defender.

Euro Step

This popular footwork move allows players to avoid the charge or avoid a defender in front of them. The offensive player steps with his inside foot and pushes off after he plants the foot, stepping across the defender's body. He then jumps off his opposite foot, which has stepped by the defender, and shoots the ball with his inside hand. The phrase we use to teach this step is "Push off one foot and jump off the other."

Passing

I emphasize passing in every drill that we do, especially the fast break drills. A team that passes well will have fewer turnovers and create more scoring opportunities. In addition, one of the best ways to handle full-court and half-court pressure is through effective passing. In the half-court offense, good, crisp passing can keep the defense on the move and result in an open shot.

Even the best pass accomplishes nothing if it is mishandled. Stress to your players the importance of being good receivers as well as good passers.

The first step in becoming a good receiver is to always be prepared to receive a pass. The hands should always be about shoulder level in anticipation of a pass. Also, players should work hard to get open and make themselves a viable target.

Once the player is open and the pass is thrown to him, he must receive the ball properly. Proper reception of a pass is executed in three phases:

1. The player must catch the ball with the eyes. He should look the ball all the way into the hands.

2. The player must catch the ball with the feet. He should not wait for the ball to come to him; rather, he should move his feet to go get the ball.

3. The player should then catch the ball with both hands.

Passing Dos and Don'ts

Do:

- Make the easy pass—it doesn't have to be an assist.

- Hit the open player.

- Use pass fakes to open up passing lanes. (Don't just move the ball, but actually fake the pass.)

- Use the air pass on the break, not the bounce pass.

- Use the dribble to create better passing angles.

- Feed the post with a bounce pass.

- Step into the defender when making the pass.

- Feed the post from below the foul line extended.

- Follow through on the pass—don't let it float.

- Throw with two hands. One-handed passes are difficult to retrieve and often result in a turnover.

- Throw away from the defender.

- Look at the basket in order to see the entire floor.

Don't:

- Throw to a voice.

- Jump to pass.

- Pass to a player in trouble.

- Pass a player into trouble.

- Make a pass from the middle of the floor—pick a side.

- Overpass—especially on the break.

Passing Drills

Following are some drills specific to passing. Although passing is an often overlooked skill, players must be able to pass effectively in order to create more scoring opportunities and commit fewer turnovers. Good passing helps win ball games!

FIGURE-EIGHT PASSING

Two players, each with a ball, face each other 10 to 12 feet (3.0 to 3.6 m) apart. They begin with the ball in the right hand, complete a figure eight between and around their legs (using both hands), end with the ball in the right hand, and throw an underhand pass to their partner. The partner simultaneously does the same. Start and pass with the left hand during the next repetition.

TURN AND CATCH

Players pair up. One is a passer and one a receiver. The receiver starts with his back to the passer. The passer calls the receiver's name and passes the ball; the receiver turns, finds the ball, and catches it.

BEHIND-THE-BACK PASS

Two passers, each with a ball, face opposite directions with their sides to each other. Both players simultaneously pass behind the back to each other using the same hand.

BIG MAN'S HANDS

This drill is for centers and forwards. A big man dribbles a ball with one hand in the low-post area. As the player is dribbling, a partner or coach throws a tennis ball to his opposite hand. The player must focus on watching and catching the pass while his other hand is active.

TARGET PASSING

Two players face each other; each player has a ball. One player passes high to his partner, and the other player passes low at the same time. This enables players to work on passing, catching, and overall hand-eye coordination.

Players can also put their right foot out and throw to the right side of their teammate's body, then put their left foot out and throw to the left side of the body; or they can pass with two hands but follow through with one.

CONFIDENCE PASS

This is a one-player drill. The player holds the ball above his head with both hands, brings the hands down in front of the body, and bounces the ball hard on the floor between the feet. The player then catches the ball behind the back with both hands.

Ballhandling

All players, regardless of position, must be able to handle the ball well. Whether players are rebounding, dribbling upcourt to improve a passing angle, catching the ball in the post or on the break, playing against pressure defenses, or grabbing loose balls, the players'

Ballhandling Dos and Don'ts

Do:

- Spend time with the ball so that you are comfortable with it.
- Keep your head up at all times.
- Learn to be comfortable dribbling with both hands.
- Dribble with a purpose—for example, as a tool to get open or to get out of trouble.
- Dribble in a straight line.
- Learn to accelerate after making a move past a defender.

Don't:

- Expose the ball to the defense; use your off hand to protect the ball.
- Dribble side to side.
- Play with the ball as a toy.
- Dribble by your foot or in your pocket when making a move past a defender.

hands must be familiar with the ball to be successful in this game.

Ballhandling Drills

Perhaps the best way to increase confidence with the ball is through ballhandling drills. We recommend doing the drills in this order for maximum player development: (1) Start with some basic warm-up drills, (2) move on to one-ball dribbling drills, and (3) end with two-ball dribbling drills.

Have players begin these drills at about half speed and gradually build to full speed. Also, instruct players to keep their heads up as much as possible during the drills to increase their confidence and to condition them to do the same thing in game conditions. Though used for ballhandling, these drills can greatly improve any phase of a player's game, whether it be rebounding, passing, shooting, or playing defense. Because these drills are so important, players should spend 10 to 15 minutes a day on them.

Remind players to concentrate on handling the ball with their finger pads because that part of the hand is used to shoot, dribble, and pass. The finger pads give the player a higher degree of ball control than he would be able to achieve with any other part of the hand.

Warm-Ups

Ballhandling warm-up drills are the first drills we do when we start a workout. These drills accomplish a few things: They help players develop hand-eye coordination, quickness with the ball (which is much more important than natural quickness), and confidence. Players must always be looking up while performing these drills. Encourage them to push the limit until they make a mistake; this will allow players to constantly challenge themselves and improve speed rather than play it safe and therefore limit improvement.

BALL SLAP

Players hold the ball in front of them in one hand and slap it with the other hand. Then they switch hands and repeat.

BALL PINCH

With the hand facing upward, players start with the ball resting on the fingers, just off the palm of the hand. The players then bring the fingers together, pinching the ball and bringing it to the ends of the fingers.

BALL PAT

Players tap the ball back and forth between the fingers of both hands, keeping the ball out in front.

BODY CIRCLES

Using both hands, players move the ball rapidly in circles around different sections of the body. They should perform several circles around the legs, several more around the midsection, and several more circles around the head.

CORKSCREW

This is similar to body circles, but players should circle the legs once, the midsection once, and the head once. Then they repeat in reverse order, going up and down the body.

STEP-OUTS

Players begin with legs together, circling the ball around both legs in a clockwise fashion. Next, they step out with the right leg and circle the ball around the right leg only. They bring their legs back together and circle both legs once more before stepping out with the left leg and circling the left leg. Finally, they bring both legs back together and continue to repeat the cycle as quickly as they can. After performing the drill circling the legs clockwise, players should reverse to counterclockwise and repeat the drill.

SOCKS

Players start with the legs together and the ball held behind the knees. The players drop the ball, clap the hands in front, and catch the ball before it hits the floor. Have the players see how low they can go.

FOOTBALL HIKE

Players put their feet shoulder-width apart and hold the ball in front. They then toss the ball back between the legs and catch it in the back with both hands. Have the players switch from back to front again, repeating the drill to build their quickness. Emphasize to players that they must move the ball and their hands, not their body. Younger players can let the ball bounce one time as they are working to develop their quickness.

SIDE CATCH

With feet shoulder-width apart, players hold the ball between their feet, with the left hand in back of the left leg and the right hand in front. Players then toss the ball up, switch the hands while it is in the air, and catch it before it hits the floor. Have the players repeat the drill, trying to improve their quickness. Emphasize to players that they must move the ball and their hands, not their body. Younger players can let the ball bounce one time as they are working to develop their quickness.

POCKETS

Players start with the ball at the midsection. They drop the ball, slap imaginary front pockets with their hands, and catch the ball before it hits the floor. Have the players repeat the drill to their side and back pockets.

One-Ball Dribbling

The following ballhandling drills require the use of one ball. Players must always be looking up while performing these drills. Again, encourage players to push past their current comfort level.

DRIBBLING FIGURE EIGHT

This drill is a great way to learn the between-the-legs dribble. Players position their feet wider than their shoulders, dribble the ball around the outside of the leg to the back, then push the ball between their legs to the opposite hand. Using the hand that receives the ball, the players then dribble around the front

of the opposite leg until reaching the back; then they once again push the ball through. Pushing the ball through rather than trying to dribble it normally through is important. This helps players control the ball and keep their head up to see the floor.

RIGHT KNEE, LEFT KNEE

In this drill, players work on the behind-the-back dribble. While standing, players dribble the ball behind their back, lifting their left knee up on a right-hand dribble and their right knee up on a left-hand dribble.

M DRIBBLE

Players sit on the ground with legs open. They dribble the ball on the outside of one leg, then between both legs, and finally on the outside of the opposite leg. After one cycle, they repeat this motion.

SIT-UPS

Players dribble with the left or right hand while simultaneously doing sit-ups.

THE WALK

Players walk down the floor dribbling the ball between their legs every time they take a step. Tell the players to push the ball through and to keep their head up.

CRAB RUN

Players bend forward and pass the ball between their legs in a figure-eight fashion as they run as fast as they can down the floor. They then return down the court moving backward.

BUTTERFLY OR SPIDER DRIBBLE

Players start with the ball centered between the legs. They quickly dribble the ball, hitting it with the right and then left hand from the front, then quickly repeating the process from the back. Have the players work front to back and back to front, repeating for quickness.

Two-Ball Dribbling

The following ballhandling drills require the use of two balls. Players must always be looking up while performing these drills. Again, encourage players to push past their current comfort level.

HIGH AND LOW

Players dribble two balls simultaneously, one high and one low. They perform this drill in place initially, and then while moving down the length of the floor, facing forward on the way down and backward on the way back.

EVEN AND ODD

Players first bounce a ball in each hand at the same time and at the same height (even). Next, they bounce a ball in each hand in an alternating fashion (odd). They perform this drill in place initially, and then while moving down the length of the floor, facing forward on the way down and backward on the way back.

WALK THE DOG

While in a kneeling or seated position, players dribble a ball with each hand. They hit each ball with one finger at a time, rotating through all five fingers (like hitting a keyboard).

SIT-UPS

Players dribble one ball in each hand while executing a sit-up.

Shooting

One thing I am probably guilty of more than many coaches is having my team spend too little time practicing shooting. It's natural for coaches to want to work on the team's offensive plays, inbounds situations, defenses, presses, and so forth; however, we have to make sure we don't fall into the trap of worrying too much about those situations and forgetting that our players have to put the ball in the basket.

Travis Garrison was one of the best pure shooting big men I ever coached. When I spoke to him after his freshman year at the University of Maryland, he said, "Coach, one of the best things we ever did at DeMatha was shoot hundreds of shots each day."

In Travis' senior year at DeMatha, we had just lost an important league game on the road for our third defeat of the year. We doubled the amount of shots we took each day, and we became unbeatable, winning our last 18 games in a row, including the league championship and the city title.

The biggest change we made was spending more practice time on shooting. After stretching, we ran 20 minutes of shooting drills (with three or four guys at each basket in the gym) to practice game situation shots—off the pass or off a dribble. Our shooting percentage kept getting better and better (we shot 68 percent in the city title game), and we became deadly

After playing for Morgan, Travis Garrison went on to a successful college career at Maryland.

Mark Goldman/Icon SMI

from three-point range, so much so that teams had to abandon their zone defenses against us.

The time we spent on simple shooting drills at the beginning of each practice turned that whole season around for us. Shooting drills are a fun way for the players to start practice every day, and these drills made the rest of our practice time much more effective. Most important, our players' confidence shot up, and they began to take shots with the expectation that they would make them.

I'm reminded of the time Ben Hogan was fighting for the U.S. Open golf championship on the last hole. He took out his two- or three-iron and knocked a crucial shot about eight inches from the cup. Afterward, everybody was oohing and aahing over the shot—except Hogan. "I don't know what the big deal is," he said. "I hit 200 of those a day in practice. I should be able to get it close." That's confidence.

Many of the drills we use to practice shooting are found in chapter 10 (on half-court offense) and are excellent for getting players to shoot in gamelike conditions.

THOUGHT FOR THE DAY

Inch by inch, life's a cinch. Yard by yard, it's really hard.

Shooting Dos and Don'ts

Do:

- Provide passers a target as a receiver.
- Know your range.
- Know what a good shot is.
- When receiving a pass for a shot, step into the pass to get the shot off more quickly.
- Plant your inside foot when squaring to the basket for the shot.
- Use shot fakes to get by the defense.
- Lift the elbow, follow through, and reach for the peach (basket).
- Get power for the shot from the legs.
- Practice shooting as if you were in a game.

Don't:

- Take giant steps. Don't pass up an open 12-footer to get a contested 8-footer.
- Leave the off hand on the ball too long because it could adversely affect the shot.
- Fade on the shot.
- Follow the flight of the ball—keep your eye on the target.
- Dip or hitch. Catch the ball, get it to the shot area, and shoot.

Playing Without the Ball

Much of our practice time is devoted to instructing and reviewing offensive perimeter and post moves that players use to get open. Players must know how to screen, how to use screens, and how to get open by reading the defense and using the V-cut or L-cut.

A V-cut is a hard step or steps taken in the direction opposite from where a player wants to get open (figure 8.8). Like the jab, the V-cut is used to get a defender off balance or out of position and to thereby give the offensive player the advantage. So instruct your players to use the V-cut to set up a defender for a screen set. And tell players to also use the V-cut when trying to get open on backdoor cuts, basket cuts, or cuts to the perimeter.

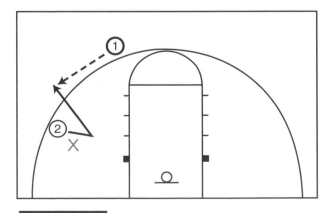

FIGURE 8.8 V-cut.

The L-cut is similar to the V-cut, but in this move the player takes an L-shaped path. The player sprints forward, slows down for a beat to try to relax the defender, then plants the inside foot and sprints directly outward (figure 8.9).

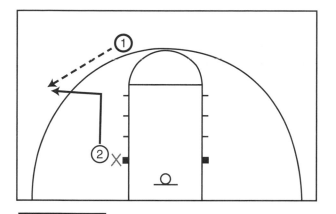

FIGURE 8.9 L-cut.

Backdoor and Perimeter Cuts

A backdoor cut is most effective when an offensive player is being overplayed by the defense. Because the player does not have the ball, proper instruction and execution of the footwork involved are crucial to the success of this move.

1. The offensive player steps with the inside foot (the foot closer to the baseline) into the defender to freeze him and reduce his quickness. The closer a player is to the defender, the better; the defender will have less time to react to the cut.

2. After taking this initial step, the offensive player then takes a hard step toward the perimeter with his outside foot (the foot closer to midcourt).

3. If the defender does not cover this move toward the perimeter, the offensive player will be open for a pass. The player should turn and face the basket immediately after receiving the ball.

4. If the defender stays close on the perimeter move, then the offensive player should pivot and push off the

outside foot, making the backdoor cut to the basket (figure 8.10). The passer should throw the ball out in front to where the cutter will be, not where he currently is.

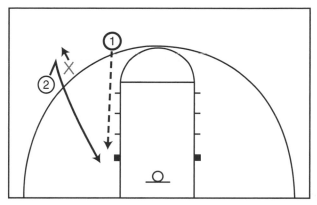

FIGURE 8.10 Backdoor cut.

Reading the defense like this should allow offensive players to get open at virtually any point in the game. Again, the offensive player making the cut must close the gap between himself and the defender, or the defender will have time to react and deny the pass.

If the backdoor pass is prevented by the defense, then the offensive player can turn the backdoor cut into a V-cut or L-cut that will help him get open. He initiates the backdoor cut and, when reading that it is no longer there, makes a V-cut or L-cut and fades to the corner to get open (figure 8.11). The defensive player will probably be so concerned with protecting the basket that the offensive player should be open to receive the ball in the corner or on the wing.

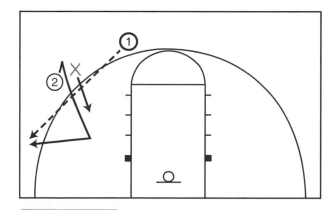

FIGURE 8.11 Perimeter cut.

Inside and Fake Inside Pivots

Pivots are also effective tools when a player is attempting to get open. For the inside pivot, the player starts on the wing, sprints to the block, plants his inside foot, and swings his opposite shoulder open, putting his defender on his back (on the right side of the floor, it would be his left foot and his right shoulder). He then sprints back to the same wing he started from to receive the pass (figure 8.12). Through this move, the offensive player has also created the advantage of using his body to block the passing lane from the defender. He can now use the stationary spin or reverse pivot move previously discussed in this chapter.

If the inside pivot is prevented by the defense, the player can alternatively use the fake inside pivot. In this move, the player sprints to the block, plants his inside foot, opens his opposite shoulder up as a fake, then continues across the lane to the opposite wing for a pass (figure 8.13).

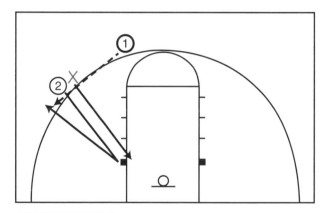

FIGURE 8.12 Inside pivot.

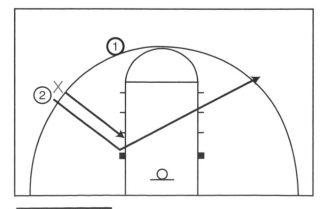

FIGURE 8.13 Fake inside pivot.

Screens

In teaching players how to set and use screens, I have found it helpful to emphasize that both the screener and the player using the screen are potential receivers. Players are more likely to be enthusiastic about setting the screen if they know they have as good a chance of getting the ball as the cutter coming off the screen. Carry this emphasis over into breakdown drills and practices as well.

Setting Screens

Stance and position are the elements that make up an effective screen. The screener should be in a strong, balanced stance with knees bent and feet shoulder-width apart. The arms should be slightly bent, but hanging along the sides; the hands should be protecting the crotch and midsection. It is not necessary to have the elbows any wider than the shoulders when setting a screen. Remember, the screener runs the risk of getting into foul trouble if he uses his arms to screen off defenders. The key to a good screen is proper positioning, not the width of the arms.

The screener should also avoid leaning while setting the pick. Leaning only reduces the strength and balance of the screener; it makes the screen less effective and often results in a foul against the screener. Instead, the player setting the screen should be taught to establish good position and to maintain a strong stance. It is then the cutter's responsibility to use the screen properly to get open.

To help the cutter use the screen effectively, the screener is responsible for setting the screen at an angle that will help the cutter get open (see figure 8.14a). With only one exception, screens should be set with the screener's body between the defensive player and the basket. This is true for all screens except the down screen, in which a player moves down from the foul line extended and screens a defender. The cutter then comes off the screen, getting open by moving out from the baseline.

If the screener can be seen by the defender, he should set himself close enough to the defender that only a piece of paper could slide between them. If the defender is unable to see the screener, the screener must allow the defender enough room to take one step.

The screener needs to have two thirds of his body toward the basket because if he sets the screen either too low or too high, the defense can get over or around the screen without any trouble (see figure 8.14*b*).

When setting a screen on the ball, the screener is looking to do one of three things:

1. **Slip.** If the defender guarding the screener hedges early, the screener slips to the basket (figure 8.15).
2. **Roll.** If the ball handler starts to turn the corner or string his defender out, the screener opens up and rolls all the way to the rim (figure 8.16). Many times the roller will not be open until he gets to the rim.

3. **Sprint away.** If the defender guarding the screener anticipates the roll and moves toward the rim, the screener sprints away from his screen, turns, and faces the basket, ready for a shot (figure 8.17).

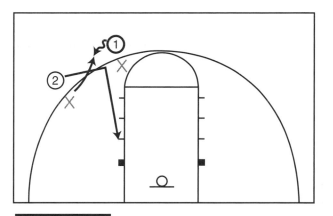

FIGURE 8.15 Slip.

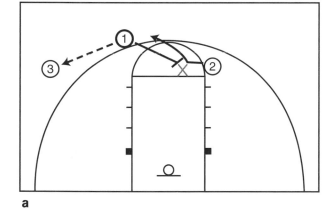

a

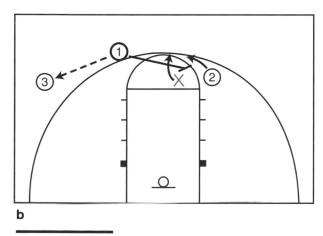

b

FIGURE 8.14 *(a)* Proper screening position; *(b)* improper screening position.

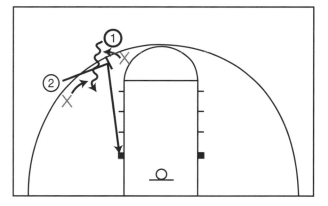

FIGURE 8.16 Roll.

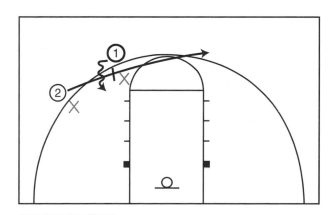

FIGURE 8.17 Sprint away.

Using Screens

After the screen is set, the screener cannot move. It is now up to the cutter to get open. When using a screen, the first rule is that the cutter must read his defender and the defender guarding the screener in order to determine what cut to make off the screen. The cutter must be taught to delay his cut until the screen is set. He must let the screen take place and then read the defense. If he moves too soon, the screen will be ineffective because the defense will be able to get around it. Emphasize to players that they must be patient as cutters.

Players often want to play too fast. They will try to get open immediately and won't wait for the defense to react to the fakes and V-cuts. The cutter should take his defender away from the screen with a V-cut (figure 8.18a), and then rub him off in the screen by going shoulder to shoulder with the screener so the defender cannot get through (figure 8.18b).

FIGURE 8.18 Proper use of a screen.

If the player realizes that his defender is trailing him after the V-cut, he should curl off the screen (figure 8.19). He should come off the screen low, touching his shoulder to the screener's hip so that he is ready to shoot. This also helps ensure that the cutter does not get pushed away from using the screen by a physical defender.

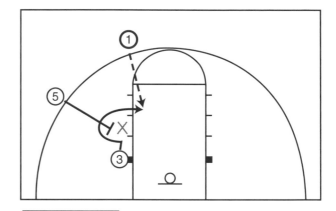

FIGURE 8.19 Curl.

If the defender gets over the top of the screen, then the offensive player should come to the point of the screen and yell, "Fade!" The player should then turn and move away (not backpedal), prepared for the pass (figure 8.20). When the screener hears "Fade!" he should set the screen again, looking for a slip or coming back to the ball.

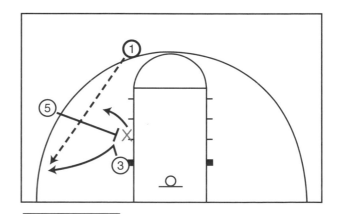

FIGURE 8.20 Fade.

If the defender jumps in front of the screen, the cutter should go backdoor (figure 8.21), using the techniques described earlier in this chapter, while the screener opens up.

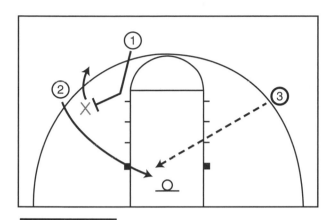

FIGURE 8.21 Backdoor cut.

If the defender fights through the screen, the offensive player can simply come off the screen without curling, popping out for a clean catch (figure 8.22). The screener looks for a slip or sprints away.

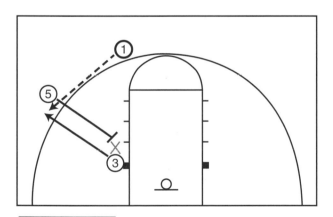

FIGURE 8.22 Pop out.

If the defender overplays the curl cut, the offensive player should perform a reverse curl cut; in this move, the offensive player steps up the lane and then curls toward the sideline for a catch (figure 8.23).

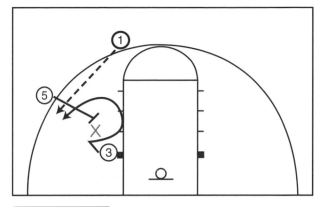

FIGURE 8.23 Reverse curl cut.

If the defender takes away the strong wing cut, the offensive player should cut across the lane toward the opposite wing (figure 8.24).

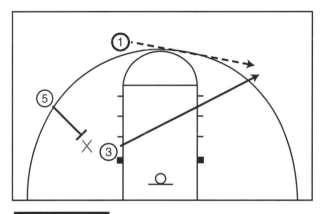

FIGURE 8.24 Cut to opposite wing.

The offense can even fake a pick to get a player open if they have used that player to set a screen earlier. When executed on the perimeter, this is referred to as a slip. In figure 8.25, player 5 has passed to 1 and, because

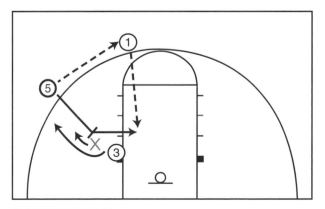

FIGURE 8.25 Slip.

he has screened for 3 so often, his defender anticipates the screen and starts that way immediately after the pass to 1. Player 5 can read this and run the change of pace. After he passes to 1, he can move toward 3's defender to set the screen; but instead of continuing, he slips to the basket. He then cuts between 1 and the helpless defender toward the basket for the pass and the layup.

This maneuver also works in the post area. We call it "duck." For example, in figure 8.26, player 4 has cross-screened for 5 so often that his defensive player anticipates it will happen again and moves over toward the screen. Player 4 begins the cross-screen to fool the defense, reads how the defense reacts, and then flashes back to the ball with his defensive player trailing in the lane.

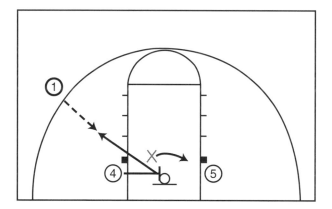

FIGURE 8.26 Duck.

The same move would be effective even if 4 went all the way across and set the screen. He could then flash back to the ball before 5 was able to use the screen. This duck move works well against teams that switch in the post because the player defending 4 will be looking to pick up 5. If 4 flashes back quickly to the ball, the player defending 5 will have no chance to switch and keep up.

Off a ball screen, the dribbler can do one of four things:

1. **Split the screen.** The ball handler dribbles between his defender and the man guarding the screen (figure 8.27). This can be useful if a gap exists between the defender and the screen, which usually occurs if the defender hedges high.

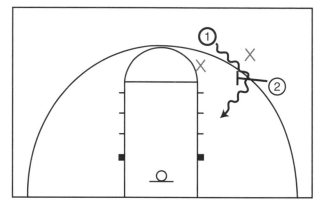

FIGURE 8.27 Split the screen.

2. **Turn the corner.** The ball handler drives hard off the screen toward the basket (figure 8.28). This can be effective if the defender guarding the screener stays close to the screener and does not show.

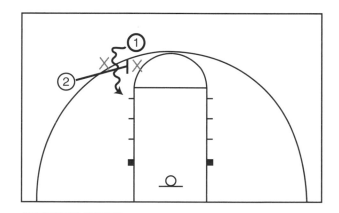

FIGURE 8.28 Turn the corner.

3. **Back dribble, pass, and attack.** The ball handler takes two dribbles back, then dribbles forward to attack one of the defenders (figure 8.29). This can be useful if the ball screen is defended well; it helps give the dribbler time to find the open area.

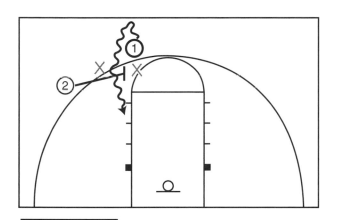

FIGURE 8.29 Back dribble, pass, and attack.

4. **String out the defense.** If the ball handler is trapped, he can dribble directly off the screen in a straight line, creating a pass back to the screener, who has popped or sprinted away (figure 8.30).

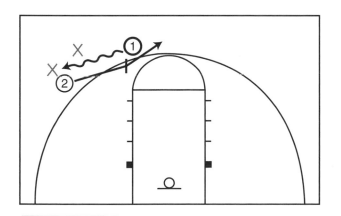

FIGURE 8.30 String out the defense.

On all of these moves, the screener is looking to slip the screen, rescreen, or space out after the player using the screen has made a decision.

Summary

The proper execution of basketball skills is essential for offensive success. Emphasize these fundamentals at all levels of your program:

- A team that handles (dribbles and passes) and shoots the ball well will obviously have a greater chance of being successful. Use drills to teach and improve.
- Playing with the ball includes moves from a stationary position and moves while dribbling, passing, shooting, and ballhandling.
- Playing without the ball includes screening and cutting to get open.
- Moves from a stationary position include the strong-side drive, crossover step, and jab step.
- Moves while dribbling (moves on the move) include the stop-and-go, crossover dribble, reverse dribble, and fake reverse.
- Coaches must ensure that their players practice shooting, preferably while simulating game situations.
- Proper positioning and a strong, balanced stance are the keys to setting an effective screen.
- Players using screens should employ V-cuts, L-cuts, backdoor cuts, and perimeter cuts to get open.

Developing a Quick-Scoring Attack

The fast break is our first option in any offense at any time during the game. Our teams have had great success running the primary break, which is created from steals, rebounds, blocked shots, made field goals, or made free throws.

We've emphasized the running style of play because the break

- is the best way to create easy scoring opportunities and to control the tempo of the game,

- is the first and often the most effective way of beating full- or half-court pressure defenses, and

- works well against a zone defense if your players push the ball up the floor and get a scoring opportunity before the zone has time to set up.

To run a breaking offense effectively, players need to buy into two principles that make a fast break work:

1. **Hit the open man.** If a teammate is ahead on the break, players should pass the ball to him. If the teammate is closer to the basket and open, players should pass it to him. But in emphasizing passing, a coach must make sure that players know what a good pass is. Players should avoid overpassing or passing to a player who is in no position to do anything with the ball.

2. **The more you give it up, the more you get it back.** Emphasize that the pass that leads directly to the score is no more important than the pass that sets up the pass that leads to the score. Players too often focus on making the assist pass that leads directly to the basket, often forcing the ball to teammates who are not open, which leads to turnovers and missed scoring opportunities.

Fast Break Dos and Don'ts

Execution is the key to a successful fast break. Here are some important points to teach players about running the break:

Do:

- Look up and see the whole floor.
- Pass ahead to the open player (until someone has a good scoring opportunity).
- Sprint the floor. (Run! Run! Run!)
- Play under control.
- Let the play make itself.
- Read the numbers; go where you have an advantage.
- Make the defense play you.
- Get wide to fill the lanes.
- Make the easy play.
- When bringing the ball down in the middle, stop at the foul line to make a play.
- Use the chest pass on the break; the bounce pass is too difficult to handle.
- Be a good receiver.
- As the back player (last trailer), delay at half-court to cover the break defensively.
- Communicate!

Don't:

- Have your mind made up about what you want to do.
- Overpass.
- Jump to pass.
- Pass to a player in trouble.
- Take giant steps.
- Try to make a great play; the play will make itself.

Break After an Opponent's Score

Because the fast break is our primary offense, we run it as often as possible, including after an opponent scores. My rationale for doing this is simple. Even if our defense holds the opposing team to 40 percent shooting from the field, that, combined with made free throws, can mean 20 to 35 chances per game to fast break off a made shot.

Obviously, the first thing your team will have to do after an opponent's score is to inbound the ball. Your first decision, then, involves selecting a player who will handle that chore. On made field goals, our 5 player (center) takes the ball out for two reasons: (1) I learned from John Wooden that it is best to have a taller player inbound the ball because of his increased court vision, and (2) the center is often closest to the ball after it comes through the net, so he can get to it and inbound it quicker than most other players.

With the center inbounding, this is how we run our Bingo package after an opponent's score. Our 1 player (point guard) works to get open on the ball side as close to the inbounds player as necessary to provide a passing option, and the 4 player (power forward) posts up at the nearest foul line in case we need him to help relieve any full-court pressure. To get open, the 4 player heads to midcourt, then makes a hard V-cut to come back to the ball (see figure 9.1).

While this is happening, players 2 and 3 sprint to the outside lanes closest to where they were when the opponent's basket was scored. If 2 and 3 find themselves on the same side of the floor when the ball goes through the hoop, whoever sprints to the closest lane first remains there while the other player crosses over to fill the opposite lane. After they take care of their rebounding duties, players 2 and 3 sprint down the court immediately and at every opportunity, especially after made goals. This helps stretch the defense and makes it more difficult for them to set up quick full-court pressure.

Inbounding the ball, the 5 player first looks deep for the two players (3 and 2) sprinting up the court. Next, he looks for a short pass to 4 or 1. If, while reading the defense, 5 sees that an advantage exists deep, then that is where the pass should go. If he does not see an advantage, he should dump it off short.

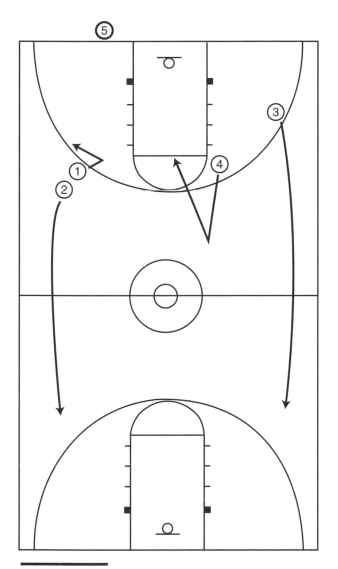

FIGURE 9.1 Bingo.

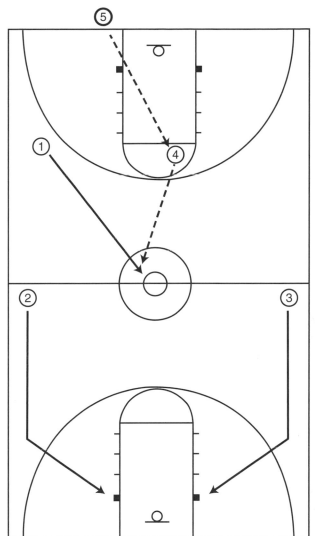

FIGURE 9.2 Bingo: guard in front.

Remind your inbounder to stay out of the foul lane area behind the baseline so that he does not throw the ball against the back of the backboard when passing to a deep receiver. (I call this clearing the backboard.)

If player 1 receives the ball far enough upcourt, he can push the ball up and create a 3-on-2 or 2-on-1 break. If the ball is thrown in to player 4, player 1 runs a diagonal cut down the court looking for the ball to try to create the quick 3-on-2 (see figure 9.2). If the 3-on-2 situation is not available, 1 pushes the ball up the floor and passes ahead to 2 or 3 if either one has gotten open. Player 1 does not need to pass ahead if neither 2 nor 3 will have an advantage over the defense after catching the ball.

Break Against Pressure

Following are specific breaks that can be run against pressure. For example, Bingo can also be used against a zone press, while the two-man and three-man fronts are useful in dead-ball situations.

Bingo Versus Zone Press

Bingo can also be used as a zone press break in live-ball situations. In this press break, player 5 begins with the ball out of bounds. If the deep pass is not open and player 1 receives the ball, player 4 sprints out on the opposite side. Because he is on the weak side, the 2 player rips to the middle. The 3 player floats long on the strong side. This creates the same triangle action that occurs on the two-player front (figure 9.3a).

Player 1 dribble probes up the sideline. Player 5 trails and maintains a 10-foot rope to allow the dribbler to throw back if necessary. Player 1 will continue to look up as he probes. If he throws ahead, the team attacks; we want to make the defense pay for pressing. If 1 reverses to 5, player 2 sprints out and floats long. Player 4 sprints long to the opposite side. Player 3 rips to the middle (figure 9.3b).

Two-Player Front

The two-player front press break can be used against the press in dead-ball situations. In the two-player front, your designated inbounder should take the ball out. Having a designated inbounder allows for consistency. Pick a player with decent size so he can see over the defender on the ball. Player 2 should start opposite the inbounder. Your best athlete (player 3) should be ball side behind half-court. Player 4 should be on or near the half-court line on the opposite side, and player 5 should be deep opposite.

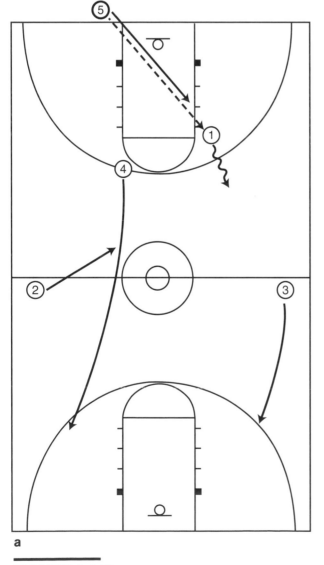

a

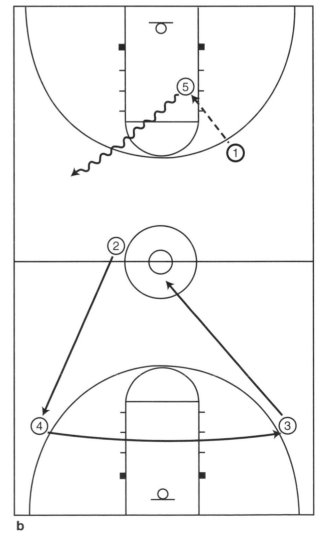

b

FIGURE 9.3 Bingo versus zone press.

On the hit, player 2 works to get open, and 3 bursts to the ball. Player 4 is a late receiver. The reason for the ball slap is that many times the inbounder can throw a quick strike to an open player. This can occur when the defender is face guarding the offensive player. The inbounder should be trained to look up.

When the ball comes in to 2, player 1 should step in behind the ball on a 10-foot rope. The 10-foot rope will allow the ball handler to throw back if he is trapped. Player 3, coming from the opposite side at half-court, rips forward to become a potential receiver. The ball-side player at half-court (player 4) floats

long, stretching the defense. Player 5 sprints deep to the side opposite the ball (figure 9.4a). The 2 player looks up while dribbling up the sideline. If 2 cannot throw ahead, he reverses to 1. Player 3 goes back to ball side and floats long. Player 4 rips middle, while 5 goes opposite long (figure 9.4b).

Player 1 dribble probes up the sideline, looking up. Players 3, 4, and 5 continue to use the triangle principle. As an attack rule, any time the ball is thrown ahead to 3, 4, or 5, the players will attack as if they have a quick fast break. We want to make the opponent pay for pressing us.

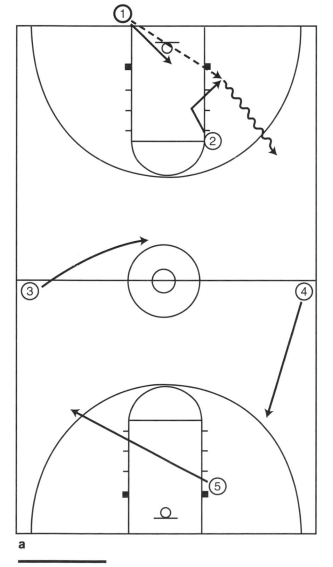

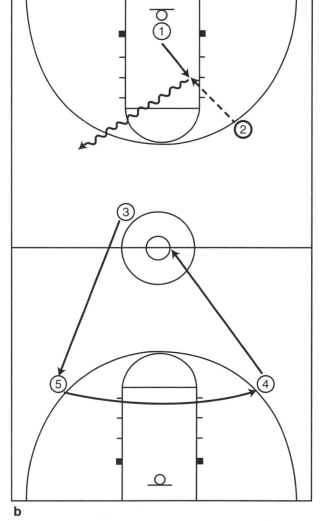

a **b**

FIGURE 9.4 Two-player front.

Three-Player Front

Another option in dead-ball situations is the three-player front. This press break is only used in special circumstances. If a team is applying all-out pressure toward the end of the game, the three-player front is a great home run play. Players 4 and 5 line up at half-court, then rip forward as receivers. Players 2 and 3 line up on the two elbows of the foul line; player 3 sets a screen for 2 and then goes deep (figure 9.5).

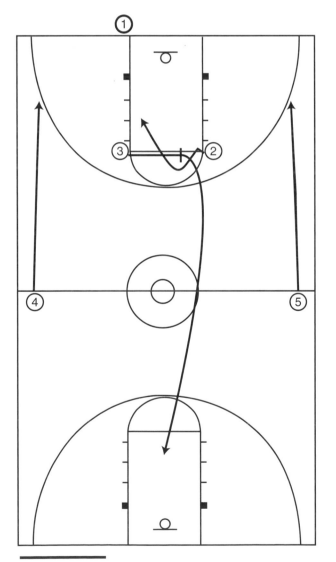

FIGURE 9.5 Three-player front.

Primary Break

When executed properly, the primary fast break should create positive offensive situations that yield one of the following results:

- 1-on-1: layup or foul
- 2-on-1: layup or foul (two passes only)
- 3-on-2: layup or short jumper
- 4-on-2 or 5-on-2: layup or short jumper

When the defense has three or more players back to defend, players should go to the secondary break described later in this chapter.

1-on-1 Situation

This situation should always produce a high-percentage shot, whether it be a layup or a short jumper. When they are on a 1-on-1 breakaway, I encourage my players to attempt a shot for two reasons: (1) Chances are it will be a good shot, and (2) it's human nature that offensive players generally change ends quicker than defensive players, which can result in a rebounding edge as offensive teammates are hustling down the floor in anticipation of a miss.

The best way to get a shot out of the 1-on-1 situation is to have the offensive player read the defender. If the offensive player thinks he can beat the defender on the dribble, he should take it all the way to the basket and look for a driving layup.

If the defender does a good job against the dribble, then the offensive player should pull up for the short jump shot. (Certain time and score conditions may prompt you to tell your players to take only the layup if it's available. If it's not, you may want to have them pull back out and set up the half-court offense.)

2-on-1 Situation

One of the fundamentals you should teach your players about the fast break is that they must get a shot off when they have a numbers advantage. Ideally, the shot will be relatively uncontested and taken from close range. I tell my players that if they are in doubt about what to do in a 2-on-1 (or 3-on-2) situation, they should shoot the ball (given the time and score situation). When a shot is taken, we can either score, rebound the shot if it misses, or at least prevent the defense from fast breaking as a result of our turnover. We must use a numbers advantage as quickly as possible because the remaining defenders are eventually going to get involved in the play.

In a 2-on-1 situation, the offensive players must fill the outside lanes and spread out wide enough to prevent the defender from playing them both at the same time (figure 9.6). As the offensive players enter the scoring area (which I consider to be about one step outside the three-point arc), one of them should take control of the ball. It is now the ball handler's job to

1. make the defensive player guard either him or his teammate,
2. read the defensive player's choice, and
3. create an easy shot opportunity.

The ball handler should always dribble with the inside hand. For example, a player on the right side of the court should dribble with the left hand. By using the inside hand, the ball handler will not have to bring the ball across his body or the defender's body to make a

pass. As a result, he can keep the ball away from the defense and also make the quick pass to his teammate.

To get the defense to commit, the ball handler must look at the basket and be a scoring threat. If the ball handler is not a scoring threat, the defender can anticipate the pass and guard both players successfully.

Most important though, the ball handler must stay under control and read the defense. More primary breaks are destroyed because of mental errors than physical errors. Too often, a player will decide what play he is going to make before reading the defense. Acting too soon, the ball handler may jump to pass, have nowhere to go with the ball, and be forced into a walk; he may charge or rush a shot; or he may try to make a big play that looks good to the crowd but does not get the job done.

In a 2-on-1 break, the ball handler should keep possession of the ball until the defender has decided to either guard the ball handler or drop off and guard the other player. Once the defender commits, the offensive player should respond appropriately with either a dump pass to his teammate for a layup or a strong drive to the basket. If the ball handler keeps these principles in mind, your team should get a good shot in every 2-on-1 situation.

THOUGHT FOR THE DAY

Make haste slowly.

3-on-2 Situation

Many of the same principles just described apply in the 3-on-2 break. Teach your players to maintain proper court spacing. If they spread the court and pass the ball effectively, the defense will not be able to adjust and guard all three players.

In the 3-on-2 situation, the middle player is the key because he is the one who should have the ball when the offensive players enter the scoring area. The middle player should

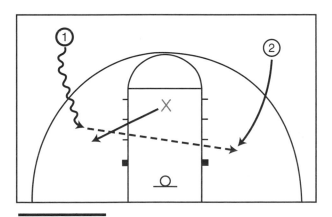

FIGURE 9.6 2-on-1.

never penetrate farther than the foul line, unless the defense opens up and gives him the lane. Too much penetration by the middle player typically results in three-second calls, charging fouls, and missed opportunities.

If the up player in the defense comes out too far to contest the break, the middle player should pass to one of the wings and create a 2-on-1 situation against the back player on defense (see figure 9.7).

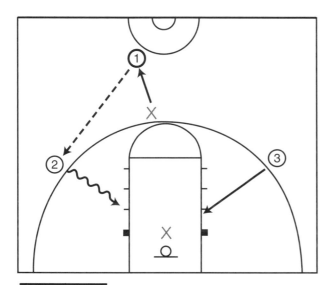

FIGURE 9.7 3-on-2: pass ahead.

If the defense stays back in a 3-on-2 break, the middle player (1) should pass to the open wing, then step toward his pass. If player 1 hits 2 on the wing, 3 must decide whether to cut behind the defense toward the basket or look to get open for the short jumper off a pass from 2. The diagonal pass from 2 to 3 is not automatic, and both the passer and the cutter should read the defense to see if it is available. The defense may have adjusted well, with the bottom player covering the first pass and the top player sinking into the hole to take away the pass from 2 to 3 (see figure 9.8).

If the defense responds in this manner, the middle player will be open at the corner of the foul line for the jumper. This is an acceptable shot for two reasons. First, player 1 is wide open at a reasonable shooting distance. Second, the offense has a distinct rebounding advantage. So even if the shot is missed, the offensive team should be able to get a second or even a third shot.

If player 2 returns a pass to the middle player, player 1 now has the option of attacking the back defender for a quick 2-on-1 with the 3 player. If the back defender commits to 1, then the ball handler should dump a pass to 3 for a layup (see figure 9.9).

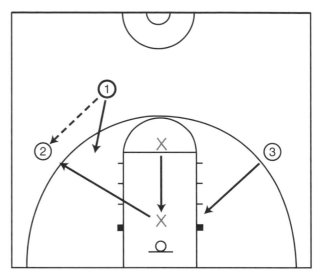

FIGURE 9.8 3-on-2: passer follows pass.

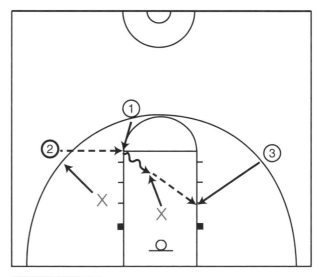

FIGURE 9.9 3-on-2: reversal.

4-on-2 and 5-on-2 Situations

Teams rarely find themselves in 4-on-2 and 5-on-2 situations. It is more common for the 4 and 5 players to become involved in the secondary break (described next). And in fact, in these situations players 4 and 5 behave exactly as they would in the secondary break.

The first three players down the floor operate as they would in a 3-on-2 situation. The fourth player down the court slices through the lane to be a potential receiver or rebounder. The fifth player involved should hold up near midcourt to cover a possible break by the opposition in the event of a quick turnover (figure 9.10).

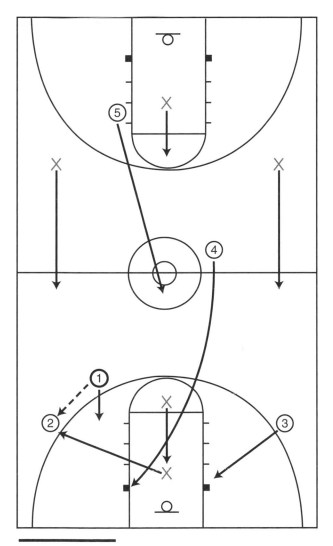

FIGURE 9.10 4-on-2 and 5-on-2.

These fast break scenarios are such an important part of the game that I recommend spending 20 to 25 minutes each practice on fast break drills included at the end of this chapter. It is through repetition that players will grasp the many options available to them off the break and improve their decision making.

Secondary Break

If the primary break does not pan out, the secondary break begins. This will happen when the offense fails to execute the initial break options properly, or when the defense does a good job of stopping a quick strike.

The secondary break is triggered when either the 2 or 3 player takes the ball to the baseline after receiving the pass from 1 (who has followed the pass). The 4 player should enter the scoring area as a trailer on the opposite side of the floor from 1. So, as the ball goes to the baseline, 4 makes a diagonal cut to the ball-side block for a feed from the wing (see figure 9.11). The 5 player delays in the backcourt to cover any quick break by the

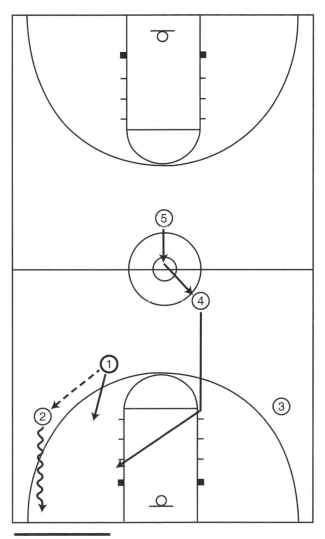

FIGURE 9.11 Secondary break: primary option.

opponent that may result from a turnover or missed shot. He then fills the spot that player 4 vacates when 4 makes the diagonal cut.

Many options can develop out of the secondary break, such as hitting 5 at the foul line for a jumper, reversing the ball to 3 as 5 slides down the lane to the low post, or 4 screening across the lane to help 5 get open. The four options that follow have been particularly successful for us over the last few years.

Option 1

If player 1 has already hit 2, and 2 is unable to get the ball to the first big man down (4), then 2 reverses the ball to 1, who reverses to 5, who passes it to 3 on the opposite wing. While this is going on, the big man down low (4) is following the direction of the ball (figure 9.12a). Once 3 gets possession, 1 and 5 then set a staggered screen for 2, who comes off the screen looking for the pass from 3 and the open jump shot (see figure 9.12b).

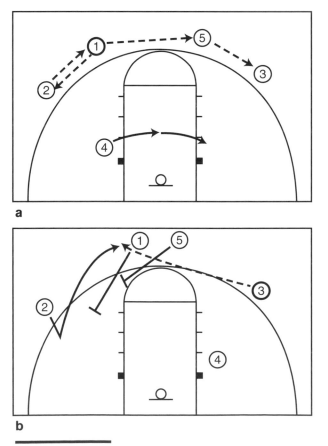

a

b

FIGURE 9.12 Secondary break: option 1.

Option 2

This play begins similar to option 1 but can be run to either side. If the point guard (1) can't get the ball to 2 on the wing, he reverses to 5, who swings it to 3. As with option 1, player 4 is following the ball underneath. After 5 has passed to 3 on the wing, 2 sets a back screen for 5 (figure 9.13a), and we look for the lob from 3 inside to 5. If the lob to 5 is not available, 5 then sets up on the low post opposite 4, while the perimeter players reverse the ball from 3 to 2 to 1, who looks to score off the dribble while the defense is still getting set (see figure 9.13b). The offense can begin its regular rotation if no shot is taken off the secondary break.

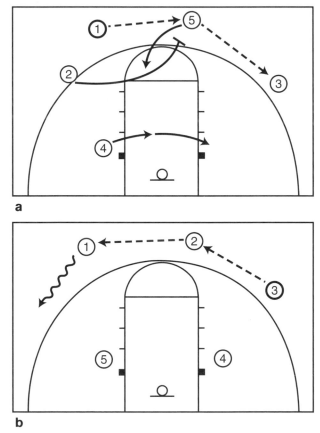

a

b

FIGURE 9.13 Secondary break: option 2.

Option 3

If player 1 cannot pass to either 2 on the wing or 5 at the high post, then 5 sets a screen for 1, who drives hard off the screen over to the left wing. While that's taking place, 4 and 3 get in position to set screens for 2 as he circles under the basket from the opposite wing. After setting the screen up top, 5 then rotates down to join 3 in setting a double screen. As 2 comes off the double screen, 1 looks to hit 2 for the short jump shot (see figure 9.14). This can be run to either side and can also occur after the ball has come back to 1 from the wing.

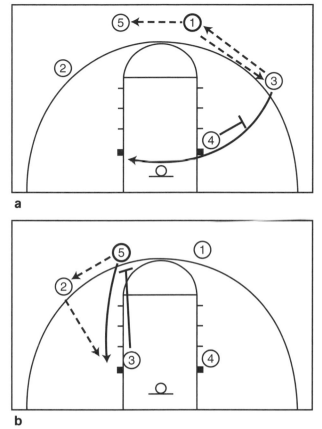

a

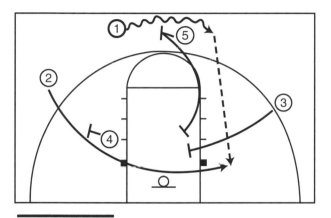

FIGURE 9.14 Secondary break: option 3.

Option 4

The point guard (1) can also dribble to the opposite side of the court to begin the play. In option 4, he passes ahead to the left wing (3), who looks down low to 4 for the post-up. If 4 is not open, 3 reverses direction by passing back to 1, who swings it to 5. After 3 makes the pass back to 1, 4 steps out to set the screen for 3, who then cuts off 4 to the opposite low post (figure 9.15a). The high post (5) looks for 3 coming off the screen down low. If 3 is not open, 5 passes to the right wing (2). After 5 makes the pass, 3 jumps up to set a back screen for 5, who cuts to the basket looking for the pass from 2 (figure 9.15b).

Fast Break Drills

Fast break drills should improve your players' conditioning and reinforce proper fundamentals. After a season of performing these drills, your players should learn the good habits of sprinting the floor, looking up at all

b

FIGURE 9.15 Secondary break: option 4.

times, passing ahead, clearing the basket after scores, inbounding the ball quickly, being good receivers, and communicating on the break.

FULL-COURT LAYUPS

Have one of your players line up at half-court with a ball, and place the remaining players along the right sideline. Player 1 dribbles to the foul line as if he is running the middle position on the fast break. When he reaches the foul line, he should jump stop and pass to 2, who has filled the right lane for the layup.

When 2 gets his own rebound (he only gets one shot), he must inbound the ball as after a made field goal. Player 1, who has moved across the court to become the outlet receiver, should then sprint the outside lane up the court. Player 2 will hit 1 with a baseball pass for the layup (see figure 9.16).

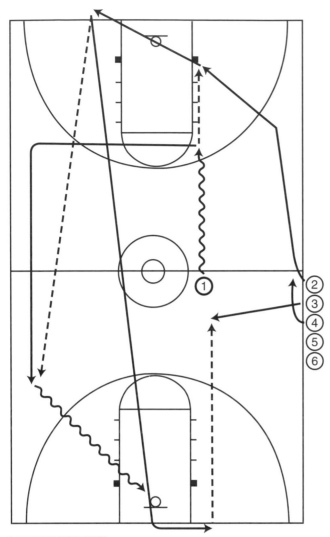

FIGURE 9.16 Full-court layups.

stay in their lanes, passing the ball to each other as they move down the court.

As they approach the scoring area, the middle player (1) takes control of the ball, dribbles to one of the corners of the foul line, and hits 2 or 3 for a layup. As 2 and 3 approach the scoring area and reach the foul line extended, they cut at about a 45-degree angle to the basket to receive the pass. As 1 makes the pass to the wing, he should step toward the pass, as on any fast break situation (see figure 9.17).

After the made basket, the players must communicate and decide what lanes to fill on the return trip down the court. As they score their second layup, the next group of three players starts down the floor.

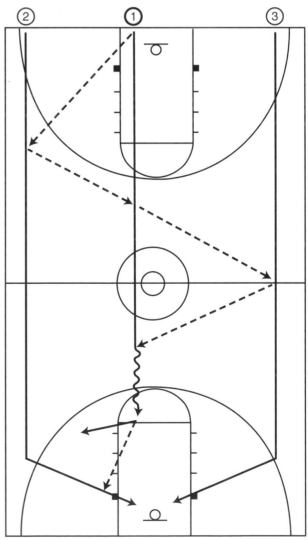

FIGURE 9.17 Three lines straight.

After making the pass, 2 should hustle down the court to rebound so that the ball never hits the floor. If 1 makes the layup, 2 takes the ball out of bounds, clears the backboard, and hits the new player (3) stepping out of line at midcourt. But if 1 misses the shot, 2 should rebound the miss, pivot, and outlet the ball to the next player (3) stepping out of line. The process then starts over again with 3 and 4 assuming the roles of 1 and 2. The drill can be run on either the right or left side.

THREE LINES STRAIGHT

Players get in three lines evenly spaced along the baseline. Every player in the middle line has a ball. The first player in each line runs straight down the floor. These three players

THREE-PLAYER WEAVE

This drill sets up the same as "three lines straight," with the players lined up in three lines along the baseline and the player in the middle holding the ball. The difference in this drill is that each player runs behind the teammate whom he passes to. In doing this, the players will weave their way down the court. As the ball enters the scoring area, the player in the middle (at that point) takes control of the ball, jump stops at the foul line, and makes a scoring pass to one of the wide players sprinting toward the basket.

The players should sprint the floor, always looking to pass ahead. At the same time, they should stay wide and not crowd each other. Players must never pass behind them to keep the drill going. If one player gets ahead of the others, he should drive to the basket for the layup. After the basket is made, the players communicate to each other about what lane they will fill, then return in the same fashion to the other basket.

FIVE-PLAYER WEAVE

This is a variation of the three-player weave that gets more of your players involved. Put your players in five lines along the baseline. The player in the middle lane passes the ball to his closest teammate and then cuts behind two players to the side of the pass. This process continues to the basket for a layup, followed by reorganization and sprinting-weaving-passing for a layup at the opposite end of the court.

Two Players Full Court

Following is a series of full-court, two-player drills. Each one has the same general organization and will develop various fast break skills. The drills can be done simultaneously on opposite sides of the floor.

Have one of the two players positioned as a rebounder and the other as an outlet receiver. The rebounder throws the ball off the backboard, gets his own rebound, pivots, and throws the outlet pass to his partner, who is getting open on the ball-side wing.

The rebounder must protect the ball while pivoting, keeping in mind where the defense might be playing.

The outlet receiver catches the ball and takes it to the middle of the floor. The rebounder fills the outside lane, staying wide and keeping good spacing between himself and the middle player.

LAYUP

The middle player takes the ball hard to the foul line with a high-speed dribble and jump stops. The sprinter, once in the scoring area, makes a 45-degree-angle cut to the basket to receive the pass and score the layup (see figure 9.18). The two players then reverse roles and return to the opposite end of the floor.

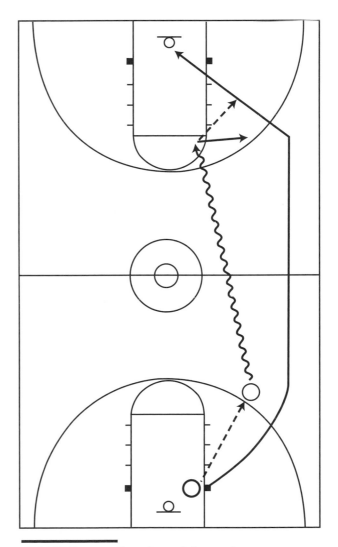

FIGURE 9.18 Two players full court: layup.

JUMP SHOT

In this drill, the middle player hits the sprint player for a short jumper from the wing off the fast break. Emphasize to your players how important it is for the shooter to be under control when preparing to shoot. The shooter should get his feet squared up to the basket and directly underneath the shoulders. He should take short, quick steps to catch the ball in a balanced position for his shot. After the shot, the players reverse roles and return to the opposite end.

Another variation of this is to have the outlet player dribble to the middle of the floor and shoot a jumper from the foul line. The sprint player needs to enter the scoring area under control, ready for the rebound. If the player sprints out of control, he runs the risk of burying himself under the basket and being out of rebounding position. The shooter must also enter the scoring area under control, with head up, good balance, and proper footwork on the shot.

V-CUT FOR JUMPER

The outlet player receives the pass from the rebounder and pushes the ball downcourt to the foul line. The middle player hits the sprint player on the wing as he enters the scoring area (see figure 9.19). The sprint player then squares up to the basket and fakes the shot. While this is happening, the middle player makes a V-cut away from the ball and comes back toward the ball for the short jumper. When coming back to the ball, the player should have his hands up and his inside foot planted so that he can get the shot off as quickly as possible. The two players then reverse roles and return to the other end.

FADE

Players must use their imagination for this drill to be truly effective. As the sprint player approaches the scoring area, he makes a hard cut to the basket to prepare for the pass from his partner. Now, however, the sprint player must imagine that the defender is back and

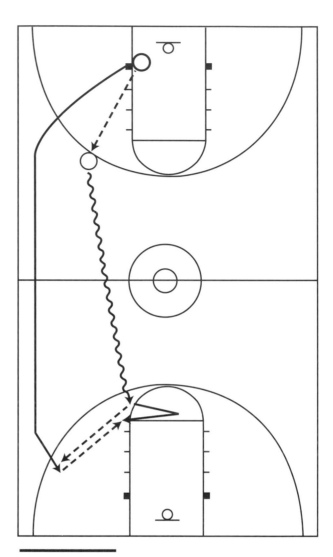

FIGURE 9.19 Two players full court: V-cut for jumper.

has recovered to prevent the pass. The sprint player then reads the defense and, instead of cutting through the lane, makes a quick V-cut and fades to the corner for the jumper off the pass from the middle player (figure 9.20).

CHASE

The rebounder hits the outlet receiver, who then uses a high-speed dribble to get to the other end of the court for a layup. As the dribbler pushes the ball ahead, the rebounder attempts to chase him down from behind and either tip the ball, block the shot (without fouling), or create enough noise to distract the player into missing the shot.

the ball's penetration, drops to cover the basket. The back defender (X5), who went out to the wing on the first pass, must go out under control to contain the ball. The ball defender (X4), who had dropped to the hole, must split the other two offensive players. If the ball is returned to the middle player, then the defensive players recover their original positions.

When the offensive players score or a turnover occurs, the two defensive players become the offensive players, and the drill enters the 2-on-1 phase. The middle player in the initial 3-on-2 situation (now X1) sprints to cover his basket defensively against the two

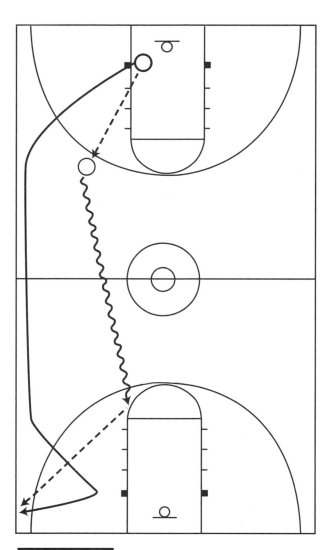

FIGURE 9.20 Fade.

3-ON-2, 2-ON-1

As shown in figure 9.21a, this drill begins with three offensive players (1, 2, 3) at one basket and two defensive players (X4, X5) at midcourt. The drill starts when one of the offensive players rebounds a missed shot and outlets the ball. The three offensive players then fill the right, left, and middle lanes. At this time, the two defensive players sprint back to defend their basket, communicating to each other about who will stop the ball and who will take the hole to protect the basket.

The defender protecting the basket (X5) picks up the wing who receives the first pass. The ball defender (X4), who initially stopped

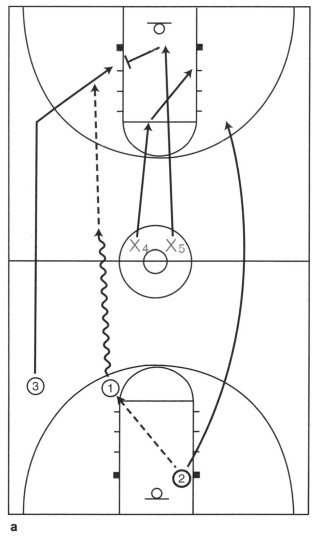

a

FIGURE 9.21 3-on-2, 2-on-1: *(a)* initial set.

(continued)

new offensive players (4, 5). The other two players (X2, X3) step out of bounds to become the defensive players in the next 3-on-2 situation (figure 9.21*b*).

If the middle player was the shooter in the 3-on-2, the lowest numbered player on offense should sprint to defend the basket. This allows the shooter to concentrate on the shot and not worry about being responsible for covering the break. Emphasize to the defensive player in the 2-on-1 situation that he must recover in time to avoid giving up a layup.

On a score or turnover in the 2-on-1 situation, the defensive player (X1) switches back to offense (1), outlets to one of two new players (6, 7) coming onto the court from the starting baseline, then becomes the sprinter down one side of the court for the 3-on-2 at the other end (figure 9.21*c*). To keep the drill going, you need to keep two offensive lines at one end and two defenders at the other.

RECOGNITION

This drill starts with a five-player offensive team at one basket, ready to run the break. The coach stands along a sideline at the other end of the court with three or more players standing on the sideline who will play defense when called on.

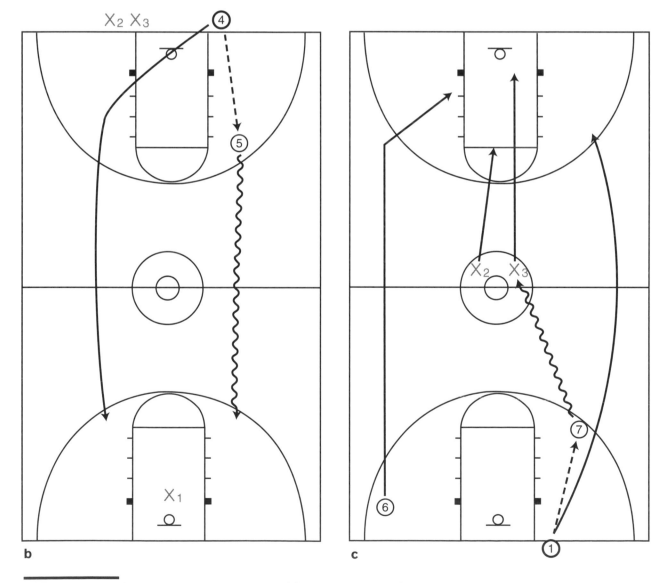

FIGURE 9.21 (continued) 3-on-2, 2-on-1: *(b)* secondary phase; *(c)* 3-on-2 after 2-on-1.

Have a manager shoot the ball to get the drill started. As the offensive team starts upcourt, send a certain number of players from the sideline to play defense against them (figure 9.22). The offensive players are responsible for recognizing the defense and playing accordingly, scoring on either the primary or secondary break.

You can vary the number of defensive players and give them special instructions to see if the offense can read the defense and recognize what is available. For example, you might tell the defense to play tight on the perimeter players to see if the offensive team can find the open post player. Or you might tell the defense to sag into the lane to see if the offense can find the player for the open jumper. And in some instances, you might tell

one player to jump the outlet pass to make sure the offense is not becoming casual with the ball when they begin the break. Whether they score or commit a turnover, the same five players stay on offense and return in the same fashion to the other basket, where defenders along the other sideline are waiting.

4-ON-4 TRANSITION

Start with four defensive players spread along the foul line, one near each corner of the foul line and one on each wing. Have four offensive players line up along the baseline opposite the four defenders (figure 9.23). The drill begins when you throw the ball to one of the offensive players and call the name of a defensive player. The player whose name you call must run,

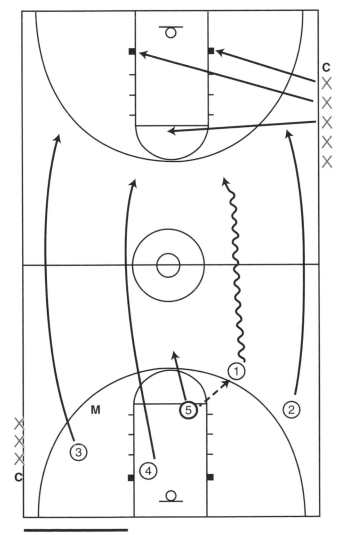

FIGURE 9.22   Recognition.

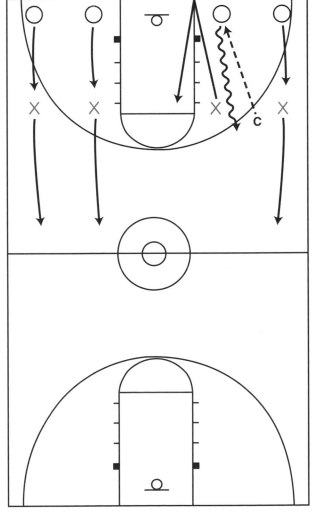

FIGURE 9.23   4-on-4 transition.

touch the baseline, and then sprint to help the other three defensive players, who are retreating and defending the opposite basket.

The offensive players run the primary and secondary break (if necessary) while the defensive players communicate and help each other until the fourth defensive player recovers. (The offense is typically forced into the secondary break because the defense should have enough players back by then to shut down the primary break.)

This drill can be done with any number of players, from 2-on-2 through 5-on-5. The drill ends when the offensive team scores or turns the ball over, or when the defense rebounds a miss.

CHANGE

I recommend this drill if your team is not changing from offense to defense quickly enough, or if they are not challenging the opponent's fast break. Start with 5-on-5 in the half-court area. On your whistle, the offensive team gives up possession of the ball and sprints back to defend its basket. The defensive players switch to offense and break for the score. Give the new offensive team an opportunity to score off the break or out of your half-court offense before resetting.

If your team still has difficulty changing ends, stop the drill and have them do some sprint work. As I've said, I don't use sprints as a form of punishment, but as conditioning. If the players are not changing ends well, it must be because they are not in shape and need to work on sprints. Sprint work will also help develop the mental toughness that allows players to continue to play their game even if fatigue sets in.

HIP DRILL

Have players form one line on the right wing. Each player attacks the basket using a high-speed dribble, as if he is about to score a layup off the break. As the player drives, you have two options. You can yell, "Hip," which is a signal to the player to stop quickly and pull

up for the jumper. Or you can say nothing and allow him to score on the layup.

The purpose of this drill is to simulate a defensive player stepping in front of the dribbler in an effort to take the charge. This drill should condition your players to play under control while preparing for—and even anticipating—the unexpected.

I also have our teams run this drill when our players are trying to create too much instead of just getting good shots. This drill helps keep the players from playing too fast and helps them stay under control when driving to the basket.

RECOVERY

Position a coach or manager at each end of the court; five offensive players are at one end of the court. Those players will rebound a shot (taken by the coach or manager at that end) and run the break against a defense. Designate a different number of defenders each time to see how your players read the situation. Tell your players before the drill begins whether to score out of the primary break or out of the secondary break. On some occasions, you might have them enter into your half-court offense.

After the coach or manager has taken the shot to begin the drill, your offensive team rebounds, runs the break designated by you, and scores. As the offensive team is scoring, the coach or manager at that end of the court throws a ball down the court to the other coach or manager (who took the initial shot), where five new offensive players have taken the court. The players who just ran your break must then sprint back on defense, trying to beat the ball down the floor and prevent an easy layup by the new offensive team.

This drill will emphasize to your team the importance of changing ends of the floor, and it will improve their quickness in doing so. Plus, your point player (whoever that is when the shot is taken) will learn to cover the break instead of watching the play.

CHAPTER 10 | Man-to-Man Offense

As previously discussed, we prefer to run the fast break as the primary offense, and we try to score off the fast break as often as possible. However, opponents will sometimes force us to set up the half-court offense. When that happens, we must be prepared with a designed offense that will be effective against either a man-to-man or zone defense.

Motion Offense

Our man-to-man motion offense is designed to take advantage of our players' individual offensive fundamentals and their ability to work as a unit to get good shots. Movement in the offense is based on the fundamental basketball concepts of reading the defense, setting and using screens, cutting, and identifying and taking advantage of 2-on-2 or 3-on-3 situations as they present themselves.

The most effective way to teach players the motion offense is to break it down into perimeter and post movement. Playing 2-on-2 and 3-on-3 can benefit the players because it helps them learn how to play in an open motion. Focus on constant repetition of the individual and position fundamentals used within this offense, eventually working your way up to 5-on-5 play. Building up to 5-on-5 helps the players learn the responsibilities of each position first, before integrating those responsibilities with those of the remaining positions. This building process promotes greater understanding of the overall offense as well as of each player's role in that offense.

In a motion offense, the screener is just as important as the player coming off the screen; the cutter who does not receive the pass is as important as the cutter who does; the pass that leads to the assist is as important as the assist; and the passer is as important as the scorer because all the players are working together toward the same goal—a good shot.

This does not mean that every player has the same role. Rather, it means that when your team has the ball, each and every player on the floor can do something to help get a good shot, whether it's setting a screen, maintaining balance in the post, reversing the ball, or catching the ball and facing the basket. If a player cannot consistently hit the 15-foot jumper, then it is not in his or the team's best interest to work to get him a shot from that range. One of the strengths of the motion offense is that it allows you to adjust to your personnel and provides the flexibility for different players with different skills to contribute to the offense at appropriate times during a game.

Fundamentals of the Motion Offense

Here are the fundamentals of the motion offense:

- Keep good spacing, using the three-point arc to help.
- Read the defense.
- Remember that screeners are often good receivers.
- Pass and move; don't stand still.
- Reverse the ball—take advantage of shifts in the defense.
- Feed the post from below the foul line extended.
- Don't play fast—let the play make itself.
- Be greedy receivers—come to the ball.
- Use V-cuts to get open.
- Catch, turn, and face the basket—be a threat.
- Communicate on backdoor cuts and screens.
- Dribble with a purpose: to attack the basket, to get out of trouble, to improve a passing angle, or to advance the ball upcourt.
- Pass away from the defense.
- Move with a purpose.
- Be prepared to set screens and receive screens—read your teammates.
- Be patient as a screener, cutter, and passer.
- When passing, wait for screens to be completed—let the possibilities develop.

Motion Offense Breakdown Drills

Before getting into the specifics of the man-to-man motion offense, let's discuss some breakdown drills that can be used to teach players the motion offense. Because the offense allows for individual moves and a great deal of two-player and three-player basketball, you should develop players' skills for these situations. Break the offense down so that players learn how to work as individuals and as part of a smaller unit before learning how to work as a five-player team.

We use a number of perimeter and post drills to teach our players to read the defense, to understand motion principles (such as spacing and balance), and to anticipate situations that they can take advantage of. These drills enable perimeter players to become familiar with the proper movement in 3-on-3 situations, and they enable the post players to become familiar with the proper movement in 2-on-2 situations, before the two groups are combined for a five-player offense. At this point, the screens discussed in chapter 8 become critical to the success of the motion offense. If players do not know how to read what cuts they should make, the offense will become stagnant and predictable.

When we first bring the perimeter and post players together for a five-player team, we run drills with no defense so the offensive players can learn the movement, balance, and spacing that are needed to execute the offense successfully. Then players work against a defense that is playing at half speed, which helps build the offense's confidence and informs players how the defense will react to their movement. Finally, we go full speed against a live defense, with players using the movements they have learned and repeated in the drills.

Perimeter Player Development Drills

As mentioned, these drills familiarize perimeter players with the proper movement in 3-on-3 situations. In these perimeter drills, players also learn spacing, balance, and other motion principles, as well as how to read their defenders and to anticipate the movements of other players.

SHALLOW-CUT SERIES

Getting the ball to the wing is a key to starting our motion offense. This can be done through the dribble or the pass. A shallow cut is one way to accomplish this using the dribble. In a shallow cut, a player dribbles from one offensive position to another, and the player in the position now occupied by the dribbler rotates to fill the spot vacated by the dribbler.

For example, a point guard may dribble from the point to the right wing; the player on the right wing then rotates to fill the spot at the point. Sometimes a shallow cut is necessary to get the ball to the wing when a perimeter player is being overplayed, or to relieve pressure on the point guard's dribble by getting him to the wing where he has more options.

STEP 1

Player 1 dribbles over and shallows 2 off the right wing. Player 2 relocates to the top of the key, using the three-point arc to help with balance and spacing. Player 1 shoots the jumper from the wing (see figure 10.1).

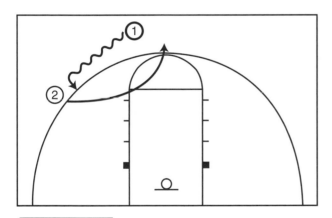

FIGURE 10.1 Shallow cut, step 1: relocate to top of key.

STEP 2

Player 1 again dribbles over to the right wing. The 2 player relocates to the top and steps up for the return pass from 1 and the shot (see figure 10.2).

STEP 3

Player 1 dribbles over to the right wing; 2 relocates to the top for the pass from 1 (as shown in step 2). Player 2 comes to meet the pass, catches it, faces the basket, fakes the

shot, then drives into the elbow and draws 1's defender. Player 1 steps up for the shot after receiving the pass from 2 (see figure 10.3).

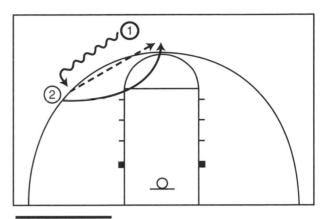

FIGURE 10.2 Shallow cut, step 2: return pass.

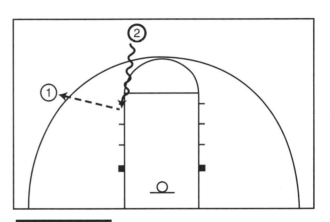

FIGURE 10.3 Shallow cut, step 3: drive and pitch.

STEP 4

Player 2 dribbles to the top, and 1 relocates to the wing, receives the return pass from 2, and takes the shot (see figure 10.4).

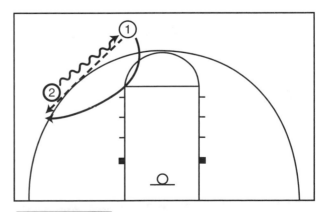

FIGURE 10.4 Shallow cut, step 4: relocate to wing.

STEP 5

Player 1 dribbles at 2 as if he is going to shallow him out. Player 2 begins to relocate, but instead V-cuts and fades to the corner for the pass from 1 and the jumper (see figure 10.5).

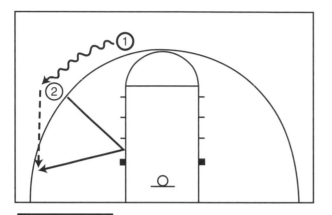

FIGURE 10.5 Shallow cut, step 5: fade.

STEP 6

Player 1 dribbles at 2, who instead of shallowing to the top, continues through the lane to the opposite wing. Player 1 skip passes (throws a crosscourt pass) over the defense to 2, who steps up for the jumper (see figure 10.6).

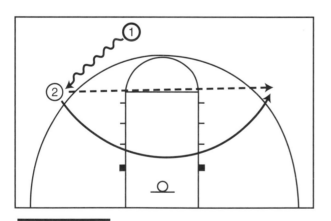

FIGURE 10.6 Shallow cut, step 6: circle and skip pass.

STEP 7

Player 1 passes to 2 and then V-cuts away. Player 1 can then either cut to the basket for a layup or replace himself at the top for the jumper (see figure 10.7).

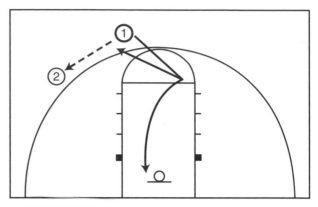

FIGURE 10.7 Shallow cut, step 7: V-cut for shot.

STEP 8

Player 1 shallows 2 off the wing and then reverses the ball to 2 at the top (see figure 10.8a). Player 2 dribbles toward the opposite wing while 1 fakes a cut to the basket (to put the defense on its heels) and then V-cuts back to the ball for the jumper (see figure 10.8b).

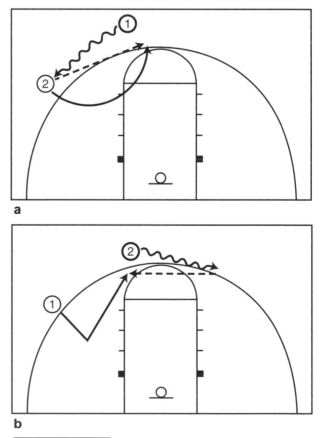

FIGURE 10.8 Shallow cut, step 8: V-cut from wing.

STEP 9

Player 2 starts at the block, receives an imaginary down screen, V-cuts, and gets open on the wing. Player 1 takes a short dribble and passes to 2, who squares and shoots (see figure 10.9).

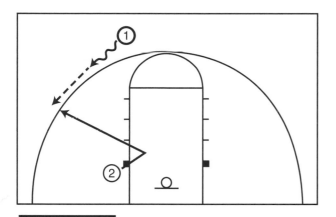

FIGURE 10.9 Shallow cut, step 9: V-cut to wing.

STEP 10

Player 1 shallows 2 off the wing and feeds the post with a bounce pass to the target hand presented by the coach. After the pass to the post, 1 and 2 relocate and look to step up for the jumper (see figure 10.10). The coach passes to either one, and the other fades back to cover the break.

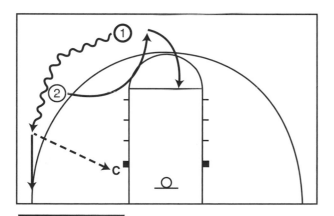

FIGURE 10.10 Shallow cut, step 10: relocation.

THREE-PLAYER PERIMETER SERIES

The next step in building to a 5-on-5 offense is to add your third perimeter player to the perimeter drills. The addition of the third player adds the final dimension to the perimeter portion of the offense. Once these drills are successfully executed, the perimeter players should have a good understanding of their roles both individually and collectively in the offense.

STEP 1

Player 1 passes to 2 and then screens away for 3. Player 3 can make one of three cuts off the screen: (a) V-cut for the jumper from the top (as shown in figure 10.11), (b) V-cut and go backdoor, or (c) V-cut and fade to the corner. Player 2 passes to 3 for the score.

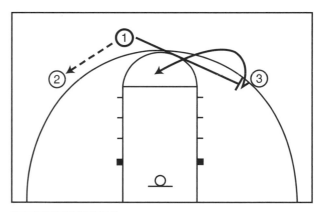

FIGURE 10.11 Three-player perimeter, step 1: screen away.

STEP 2

Player 1 passes to 2 and then receives a back screen from 3. Player 1 V-cuts and uses the screen to get open on the opposite wing (as shown in figure 10.12). Player 2 has two options: (a) skip pass over the top to 1 for the jumper, or (b) pass to 3, who opens back up to the ball as a receiver.

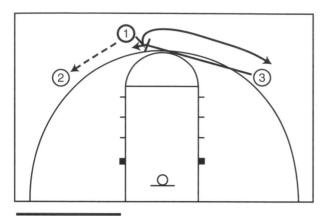

FIGURE 10.12 Three-player perimeter, step 2: back screen.

STEP 3

Player 1 passes to 2 and receives a back screen from 3. Player 1 begins to use the screen but cuts to the basket instead, as shown in figure 10.13. Player 2 can make one of two plays: (a) hit 1 on the cut, or (b) hit 3, who opens up to the ball after the screen.

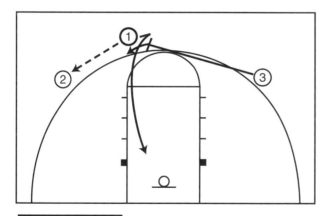

FIGURE 10.13 Three-player perimeter, step 3: basket cut.

STEP 4

Player 1 passes to 2 and receives a back screen from 3 (as shown in step 2). Player 2 reverses the ball to 3, now at the point, who passes to 1, now on the left wing. Player 3 then receives a back screen from 2 and a skip pass from 1 for the shot on the right wing (see figure 10.14). Use this drill if your players get in the habit of setting only one perimeter screen per possession.

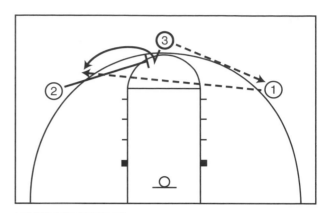

FIGURE 10.14 Three-player perimeter, step 4: reverse, back screen, and skip.

STEP 5

Player 1 shallows 2 off the wing. Player 2 receives a back screen from 3 as he relocates to the top and uses the screen to get open on the opposite wing. Player 3 opens back up to the ball (see figure 10.15). Player 1 can (a) skip pass to 2, or (b) hit 3 shaping up to the ball.

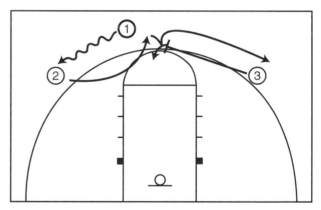

FIGURE 10.15 Three-player perimeter, step 5: shallow to back screen.

STEP 6

Player 1 passes to 2 and receives a back screen from 3, using it to get open on the far wing (as shown in step 2). Player 3 opens up to the ball. Player 2 swings the ball to 3, who uses a shot fake to get by the defender. Player 3 penetrates and passes back to 2, who is stepping up for the shot (see figure 10.16).

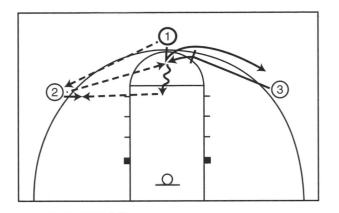

FIGURE 10.16 Three-player perimeter, step 6: back screen, penetrate, and feed.

STEP 7

Player 1 shallows out 3, who then receives a back screen from 2 (see figure 10.17a). Player 2 opens up after setting the screen and receives the pass from 1. Player 2 starts toward 3, who makes a hard cut to the basket and then fades to the corner for the pass from 2 and the jumper (see figure 10.17b).

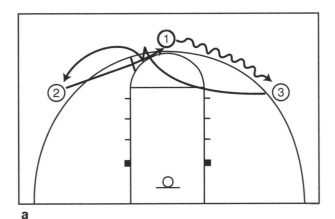

a

b

FIGURE 10.17 Three-player perimeter, step 7: (a) drive and (b) fade.

After working 2-on-0 and 3-on-0, you can introduce defensive players into the drills and play 2-on-2 and 3-on-3. At times, you may want to limit the number of dribbles the offensive players can take, or you may specify a minimum number of passes that they must make before a shot is attempted (other than a layup). This will help the offense play under control and at a speed that will make the players read the defense and move with a purpose. Remember, your toughest task will be slowing them down so they do not miss scoring opportunities.

Post Player Development Drills

Post play in the motion offense usually involves two players. On occasion, we will go with four perimeter players and one post player to help open up the middle and to create more room for the players to operate offensively.

Balance and spacing are as important in the post as they are on the perimeter. When we play with two post players, we usually maintain balance by having one player in the high post and one in the low post, with each on a different side of the lane. This stretches the defense and gives the post players plenty of room, which will help the two as they work together to get open.

TWO-PLAYER POST SERIES

These are the drills we use to get our two post players to work together as a unit. Note that a coach (C) serves as the perimeter passer in each of these drills.

STEP 1

Player 4 starts in the high post and downscreens diagonally for 5, who V-cuts and flashes to the high post for the pass from the perimeter. Player 4 opens back up to the ball and seals his imaginary defender for the feed from 5 (see figure 10.18).

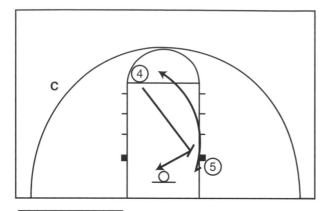

FIGURE 10.18 Two-player post, step 1: down screen, cut high.

STEP 2

Player 4 screens diagonally for 5, who V-cuts high and flashes into the low post. Player 4 opens up to the ball and slides high in order to maintain balance in the post. Player 4 may flash to catch the ball at the foul line for the jumper. The coach passes to either one for the shot (see figure 10.19).

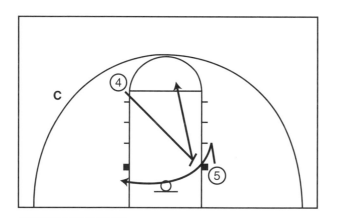

FIGURE 10.19 Two-player post, step 2: down screen, cut low.

STEP 3

Player 4 screens diagonally for 5, who V-cuts and flashes high. Player 4 runs "duck" because the imaginary defensive post players have switched, and he rolls back to the ball in the low post (see figure 10.20). If the pass is not made into the post, the two players maintain balance and spacing, continuing to screen to get open.

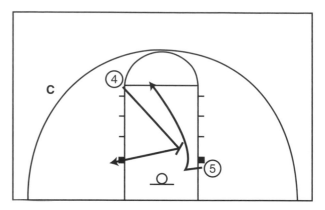

FIGURE 10.20 Two-player post, step 3: screener back to ball.

STEP 4

Player 4 begins to screen for 5 but immediately flashes back to the ball because the defense is anticipating the screen. Player 5 flashes to the opposite high post looking for the jumper (see figure 10.21).

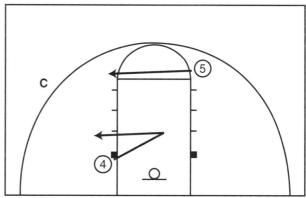

FIGURE 10.21 Two-player post, step 4: fake screen.

STEP 5

Player 5 starts high and slides down to the low post. Player 4 maintains balance by starting low and flashing high (see figure 10.22). The coach may pass to either player or may wait for a screen to take place.

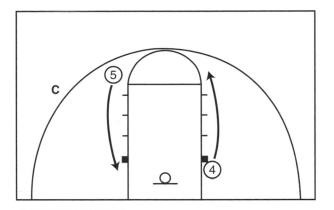

FIGURE 10.22 Two-player post, step 5: balance the post.

STEP 6

Player 5 back-screens for 4 in the high post (see figure 10.23*a*), then opens up to the pass from the perimeter for the foul line jumper. Player 4 hooks in and seals his imaginary defender for the feed from 5 (see figure 10.23*b*).

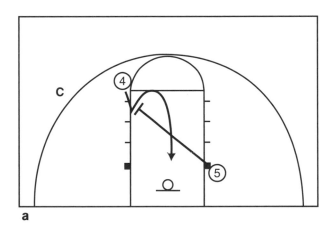

a

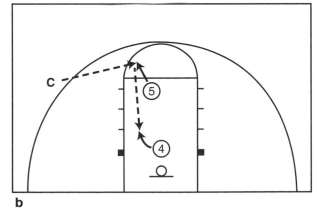

b

FIGURE 10.23 Two-player post, step 6: *(a)* back screen and *(b)* feed.

Each of these post drills can also be initiated with an up screen as well as a down screen. Remind the cutters and the screeners that they must go to either the high post or the low post to maintain balance. If they flash into the midpost area, this reduces the offensive options that the two post players have. For example, in step 3, if 4 screens for 5, and 5 cuts to the midpost, 4 cannot come back to the ball because there is no room for him to occupy either the high or low post without getting in 5's way.

Run the post options with only offensive players first, and then add two defensive players. Your next step after working the perimeter and post players separately is to have one unguarded perimeter player involved in the post drills, and one unguarded post player in the perimeter drills. This exposes the post players to what the perimeter players are doing, and vice versa, which allows greater understanding of the roles in the offense and will help the players to function better when you combine all five players.

The final step before going live 5-on-5 is to run a five-player offense with no defense, concentrating on the basics emphasized in the breakdown drills and the principles listed earlier in the chapter. Tell the players to take their time as they adjust to playing with one another and get a feel for how to read the defense and their teammates' offensive movements. Patience and repetition are the keys to learning and executing any motion offense.

The 5 Game Motion Offense

The 5 Game is our main motion offense, and it is primarily a way of providing some initial structure. This structure will help your players develop good habits such as spacing, balance, and timing. It also gives the players a basic set to return to if they begin to play without regard to the principles that you emphasize in the motion offense.

The standard 5 Game involves three perimeter and two post players, but many variations and options are available to players in this offense. What you should emphasize to your players is that each option and variation they employ must include the basic elements of a motion offense—cutting and screening.

Start your motion offense in a 1-2-2 set, with wing players positioned wide and high on the perimeter, and a post player occupying each block. The point player should pick a side and stay out of the middle of the floor so the defenders guarding the wing players cannot steal the entry pass.

To begin the offense, the point player passes to one of the wings. After 1 passes to 2, he can cut through the middle and look for the ball on the way to the basket, or he can screen away for 3, who will then replace 1 at the top.

When the ball gets to the wing, the post player on the ball side (4) screens away for the opposite player (5), as shown in figure 10.24. Player 5 waits for the screen, makes a V-cut to get his defender moving in one direction, and uses the screen effectively to get open coming across the lane.

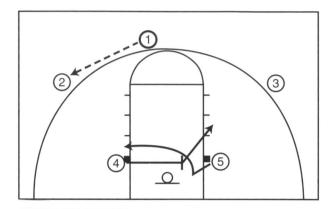

FIGURE 10.24 5 Game: cross-screen.

Do not allow 5 to simply flash across the lane when he sees the wing catch the ball. Not only will he probably be covered, but he will take 4 out of the play by preventing him from screening and then possibly rolling open to the ball as a receiver.

If the defense switches in the post, the offensive post players should run "duck." In this play, the screener comes back to the ball while keeping the new defender on his back (figure 10.25). Player 5 stays on the weak side. Again, this is effective only if 4 and 5 are working together.

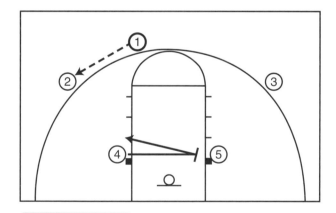

FIGURE 10.25 5 Game: duck.

If the wing player passes to the post player, the wing should either exchange with the player at the top of the key or relocate to an open spot on the perimeter as his defensive player digs in the post. By reading his defender's movement in the post, the wing player can get open for the jumper. Teach him

---

5 Game Guidelines

Have your players follow these basic principles when running the motion offense, but emphasize to them the necessity of reading the defense before each movement:

- As the point player, pass to one wing and exchange with the other by using the screen or the basket cut. Or, the point can use the dribble (shallow cut) to exchange with a wing.

- As a wing player, down-screen on any pass back to the point.

- As a post player, after a count of one, screen for the opposite post any time a pass is made to the wing on your side.

Remind your players that being ready to receive a screen is just as important as being ready to screen. They owe it to their teammates to move effectively when one of them tries to help another get open.

to key on the direction his defender's back is facing—that's the direction he wants to go to get the jumper.

For example, if his defender's back is to the baseline, the wing player (2) should move to the baseline for the open jumper (figure 10.26). This makes it difficult for the defender to recover and defend the jump shot because he must swing open to the ball instead of just taking an advance step to cover 2.

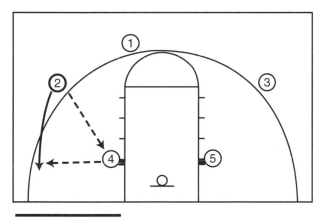

FIGURE 10.26 5 Game: relocate.

If the wing passes the ball back to the point, the wing should then screen down for the post player (see figure 10.27), or the post player should set a back screen for the wing player. If the wing player (2) screens down for the post player, the 2 player should open back up to the ball after the screen. By reading where his defender is in relation to the screen and using the screen effectively, your post player (5) should be able to get open.

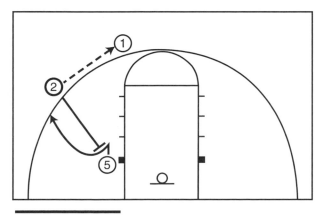

FIGURE 10.27 5 Game: down screen from wing.

If the post player's (5) defender fights over 2's down screen, 5 should fade to the corner and create space between him and the defender for the shot. If the defender plays behind the post player on the screen, 5 should curl around the screen for the feed from the top and the layup (see figure 10.28). If the wing (2) does down-screen after he passes the ball to the top, and the ball is reversed, 2 becomes the post receiver on the off-ball side while the post player heads to the wing (see figure 10.29).

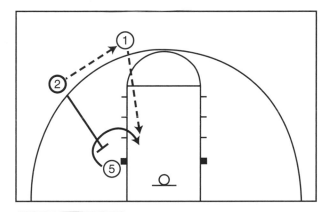

FIGURE 10.28 5 Game: peel cut.

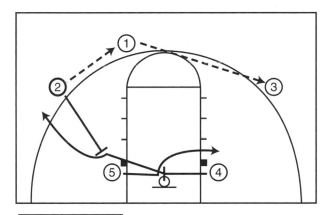

FIGURE 10.29 5 Game: movement.

This type of movement is what makes the 5 Game motion offense so difficult to defend. It will allow you to take advantage of the particular skills that your players have (for example, posting up perimeter players or having post players on the perimeter), and it will put your players in positions to exploit the defense in game situations. The movement has guidelines, but it is unpredictable and allows enough freedom that the defense cannot expect the same pattern each time.

Special 5 Game Plays

Although the basic movement in the 5 Game is triggered by players reading the defense, we do implement designed plays that are choreographed to give the defense different looks and to take advantage of adjustments the defense may make. These designed plays can add to your offense's effectiveness. We call these options "specials" out of the 5 Game.

Circle

Circle is a play that takes advantage of teams whose defensive post players switch. Player 1 uses the dribble to enter the ball to the wing. As player 1 does this, 4 flashes high to the elbow looking for the ball, and 3 circles through to screen for 5 (see figure 10.30). If the defense is switching, an immediate mismatch is created between 5's and 3's defensive players. The same can be done on the other side with 2 screening for 4.

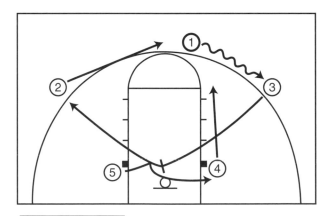

FIGURE 10.30 Circle.

Orange

Orange is another special out of the 5 Game. Player 3 begins the play by screening for 5 and then shaping up to the ball. Player 5 becomes a perimeter player and receives the pass from

1. If 3 cannot get the post feed from 5, he moves across the lane to the opposite block, as 4 moves up the lane slightly to make room for him (see figure 10.31a). Meanwhile, 2 walks his defender down to a position where he (2) can use the double screen set by 3 and 4. As he comes off the double screen, 2 then looks for the pass from 5 (see figure 10.31b).

If 5 does not pass to 2 coming off the double, he hits 1, who has made a V-cut and

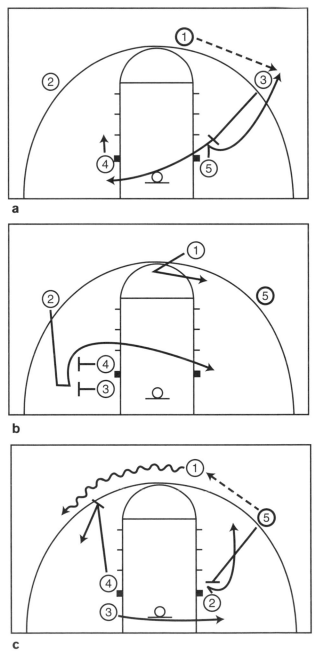

a

b

c

FIGURE 10.31 Orange.

returned to the point. Player 5 then sets a down screen for 2 at the block, helping him to get open for the shot. At the same time, 3 moves back across the lane and establishes position on the low side of 5 to allow 4 and 1 to work a two-player game on the right side if 2 is not open. Player 4 flashes up the lane and sets a screen at the top of the circle for 1, who looks for the drive or the quick jumper off the screen. After 1 uses the screen, 4 rolls in the direction of the ball, looking to seal his defender for the feed from 1 (see figure 10.31c). If 1 shoots the ball, you have two players (3 and 5) rebounding from the weak side and 2 covering the break defensively.

40

40 is a motion offense that is similar to the 5 Game. The major difference is that 40 uses four perimeter players and one post player, whereas the 5 Game uses three perimeter players and two post players. These offenses have many similarities, the major one being the use of screening. Many of the screens used in the 5 Game will also be used in 40. To determine which motion offense is best for your team, you need to evaluate your personnel.

In 40, the 2 and 3 players are positioned on the foul line extended. The point guard (1) is located in the slot (the lane line extended), and the 4 player is located in the slot on the opposite side. The 5 player can be on the ball-side block or the weak-side block. This is a true motion offense in that there is not a specific continuity, but rather options for the players to use, along with a strong emphasis on spacing. For this offense to be successful, players must understand spacing, how to set and use screens, how to use rim cuts, and how to react to drives.

The four players on the perimeter are all interchangeable in this offense. When a pass is made, perimeter players without the ball should do one of the following:

1. Relocate.
2. Set or use a screen (figure 10.32a).
3. Execute a rim cut (that is, cut to the basket; see figure 10.32b).

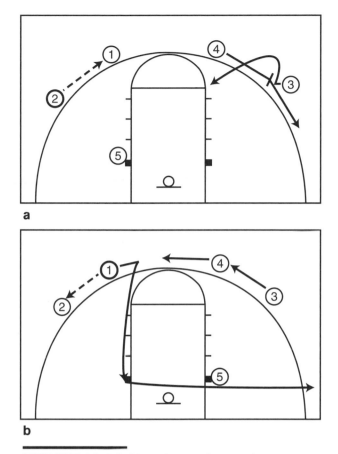

FIGURE 10.32 40: perimeter player options.

When a pass is made, the post player has several options as well. He should do one of the following:

1. Post up.
2. Duck in (figure 10.33a).
3. Set a screen (ball screen or back screen; see figure 10.33b).

As a coach, you must know the strengths of your personnel in order to determine what players should do when a post player sets a back screen. You may want the post player to set the back screen, step out to be a receiver, and then dive back to the block. But you may also have a player on the perimeter who is an effective player on the block. In this case, when the post player back-screens for him, he might stay down low while the post takes his place on the perimeter.

When using 40, stress to your players that they need to space out and space up. Players must space out, away from the lane, after

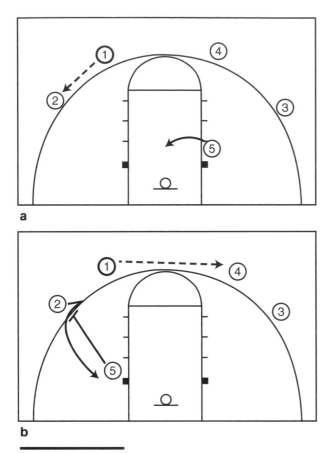

a

b

FIGURE 10.33 40: post player options.

making a cut or using a screen, and then they must space up, back to the perimeter. Spacing up allows backdoor opportunities. Players have a tendency to enter into the lane to make a cut or use a screen and then stay there. You must constantly stress the need to space out and space up. In addition, when a drive is made, all players must react to it as it occurs, not after it is finished.

Set Plays

Every offense needs a way to get the ball to the right player at the right time. That's what set plays are for, so you must have these to run against both a man-to-man defense and a zone (which we'll cover in chapter 11). The following four set plays have enabled us to get the ball to the player we wanted to. They can be valuable throughout the game but are especially helpful when the game is on the line.

Power

The point guard (1) passes to the wing (2) and then screens for the opposite post (5). The wing (2) then looks to hit 5, who uses the screen to flash to the high post and possibly an open shot (see figure 10.34a).

If 5 is not open, he then continues to the high post where he receives the pass from 2. While this is taking place, 3 screens for 1

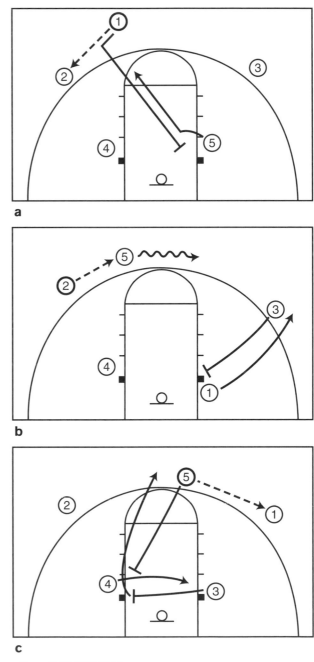

a

b

c

FIGURE 10.34 Power.

(who has just finished setting the screen for 5 to flash to the high post), and 1 breaks out to the wing looking to shoot off the pass from 5 (see figure 10.34b).

If the shot is not there for 1, 3 heads to the opposite low post to screen for 4, who cuts into the lane looking for the pass from 1. After 4 has made his cut, 5 rotates to the low post to screen for 3, who flashes to the lane looking for the pass from 1 and the shot. If the shot isn't there, 3 continues to the point, and the offense is back in position to run its regular rotation, with 4 and 5 in the low-post positions and 1, 3, and 2 out on the perimeter (see figure 10.34c).

Cross

The point guard (1) passes to the wing (3) and then cuts down and through the lane after making the pass. The 2 player cuts through the key right off 5 and on the heels of 1. The wing (3) can pass to 1 or 2 if either is open on the cut. If not, 3 then passes to 5, who steps to the ball (see figure 10.35a).

After 3 hits 5 stepping to the high post, 3 proceeds to set a screen for 2, who comes off the screen out to the wing spot just vacated by 3. On the opposite side of the floor, 4 is setting the same screen for 1, who comes off the screen out to the wing position. The 5 player can then hit 1 or 2 on the wing (see figure 10.35b).

Entry

Entry also begins on the pass from the point (1) to the wing (2). After making the pass, 1 cuts down and off 5 and proceeds to the low post. On the opposite side of the lane, 4 walks his defender down to the low post. The 5 player then pops out to the top of the key to receive the pass from 2 (see figure 10.36a).

After 2 hits the 5 player, 4 shapes up in the lane looking for the pass from 5. If the pass is not there, 5 then swings the ball to 3 on the opposite wing (see figure 10.36b). After hitting 3, 5 can dive (head to the vacant low post) or set a screen for 3 to use to get open for the jumper.

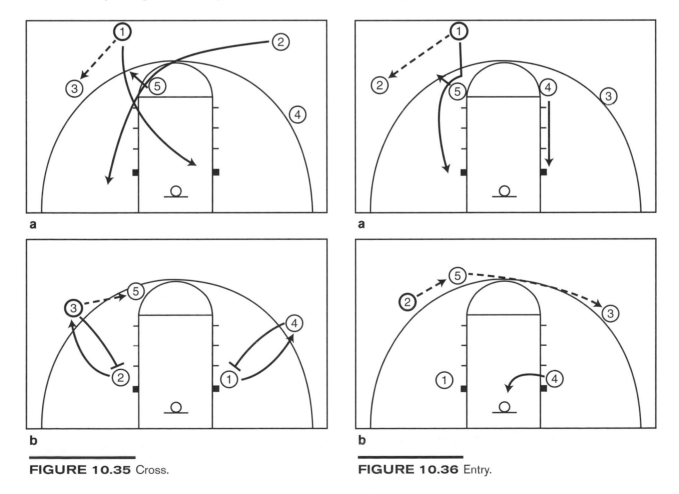

a

b

FIGURE 10.35 Cross.

a

b

FIGURE 10.36 Entry.

New York

This play starts a little differently than the others. The point (1) dribbles hard off the screen set by 2 above the top of the key. The 2 player pops out farther and prepares to receive the pass from 1. Meanwhile, 3 goes from the wing to underneath the basket and off the double screen set by 5 and 4 at the low post (see figure 10.37a).

After driving off the screen, 1 then reverses the ball to 2 at the top. If 2 is not open for the jumper, he swings it to 3, who is on the wing after coming off the double screen set by 4 and 5. Players 5 and 4 then split, and the offense goes into the regular five-player rotation (see figure 10.37b).

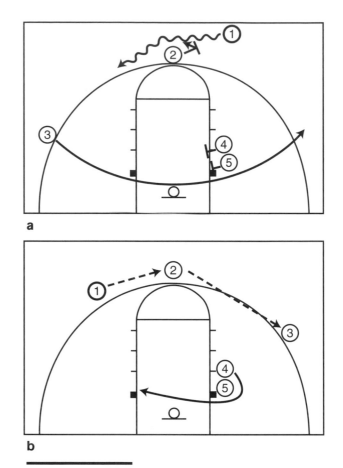

a

b

FIGURE 10.37 New York.

To attack a zone defense, use a formation that is most effective against the alignment you are facing. Attack an even-front (two players) zone with an odd front (one player), and vice versa. This will allow your offensive perimeter players to get into the gaps of the defense where they can create offensive opportunities for themselves and their teammates.

Zone Offensive Sets

The offensive sets shown in figure 11.1, *a* through *d,* will give players the freedom to move. And these sets will help your players stay organized and properly spread out to attack each of these types of zones.

Fundamentals of Zone Offense

Here are some fundamentals pertaining to zone offense:

- Fast break; attack before they can set the defense.
- Attack the zone; don't play passively.
- Take good shots.
- Play with patience and poise. Teams use a zone to make you shoot quickly.

- Gap and split the zone. Make two defenders play one offensive player.
- Keep good post timing and movement.
- Find open areas and step up for the jumper.
- Screen the defenders in the zone.
- Maintain good rebounding position. Hit the offensive boards.
- Drive the zone. Use the dribble to freeze the defense, create 2-on-1 opportunities, or improve passing angles.
- Make the defense work by reversing the ball.
- Make someone in the zone play you (particularly perimeter players).
- Use the skip pass.
- Look to the basket. Be offensive minded.
- Use pass fakes and shot fakes to move the defense.
- Dribble away from an area, and then fill the area with another player (vacuum principle).
- Take the defender as far as you can, stretching the defense to create gaps and help with reversal.

(continued)

- Communicate. Call a teammate's name if you want to screen.
- Use shallow cuts to move the ball and the zone.
- Play out of sets.
- Balance the floor.
- Keep good spacing. Perimeter players should use the three-point arc.

Although the sets themselves are important to ensure balance, spacing, and organization, even more important are the principles you teach your players to use when attacking any zone defense. As with the motion offense, you must teach your players several fundamental skills that pertain specifically to playing against zone defenses.

Not all of the zone defenses that you face will be exactly alike; however, the principles of playing a zone and playing against a zone are universal. So a fundamentally sound offense should work well against a zone defense.

Drift Offense

We call our basic zone offense "Drift" because it's designed to get the players to drift into the open spaces and seams in the zone they are playing against. We like this offense against a zone for two reasons: (1) It gives us two post players, which helps us attack the zone from the inside; and (2) it assigns basic movements but at the same time allows for a great deal of freedom for players to apply basic zone offense principles (such as stepping into an opening).

Start Drift in a two-guard front, and have player 3 always come to the ball-side wing. As 1 passes to 2, 3 moves through the lane behind the zone. Player 2 swings the ball to 3, then drifts to the open area on the wing opposite 3 (see figure 11.2). Player 4, who is in the low post on the ball side, stays for a two-second count, then backs out after 3 has received the ball on the wing and looked into the post. Player 5 then slides down into the medium post, and the offense is now in a 1-2-2 set.

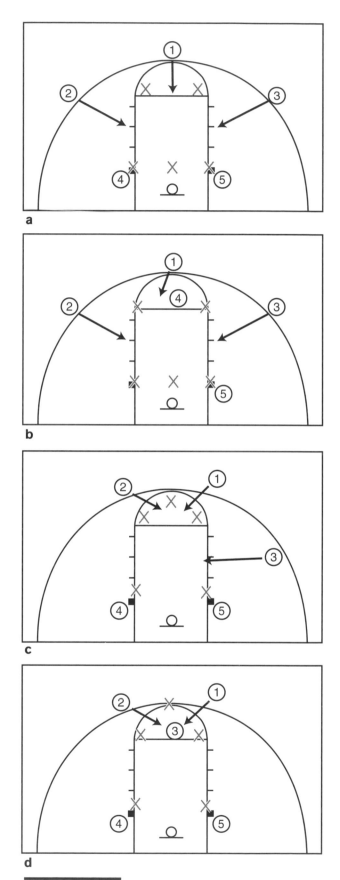

FIGURE 11.1 *(a)* 1-2-2 set, *(b)* 1-3-1 set, *(c)* 2-3 set, and *(d)* 2-1-2 set.

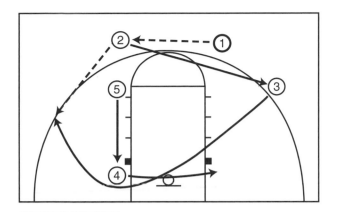

FIGURE 11.2 Drift: drift to open area.

When the ball is reversed (from 3 to 1 to 2), the post on the ball side (4) stays for the two count and then backs out to the other side. The opposite post (5) moves across the lane high toward the ball (see figure 11.3), flashing into the gap from behind the defense, while keeping his feet active and looking for the pass from the wing.

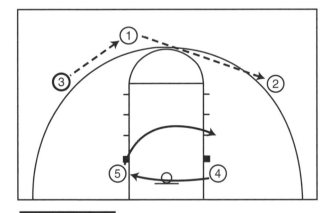

FIGURE 11.3 Drift: reversal.

Sell your players on the fact that they must move the zone in order to get a good shot. One of the most effective ways to move the zone is by using the skip pass, a crosscourt pass that goes across the zone. To receive the skip pass, the perimeter player must (a) find a gap and not hide behind a defender or get buried along the baseline, and (b) stay behind the three-point arc to create three-point opportunities and to stretch the defense in order to open up the post players.

Another way to move the zone is by using the dribble. After 1 catches the ball on the reversal from 3, he attacks the outside shoulder of the opposite guard in the zone and creates a shot for himself or for 2 (see figure 11.4). If the bottom player in the zone comes out to play 2 on the wing, 5 steps up the lane for the feed from 1. Player 5 could also screen (using the same screening techniques as in a man-to-man offense) the bottom player in the zone to help 2 get open for the jumper.

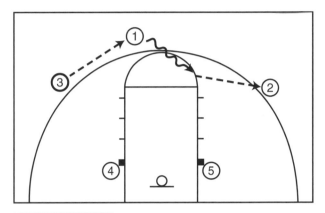

FIGURE 11.4 Drift: dribble penetration.

From the original two-guard alignment, player 1 can also pass to 3, while 4 and 5 X-cut, and 2 drifts to the wing opposite 3 as shown in figure 11.5. Player 5 then backs out, 4 slides into the low post, and the offense is back in the 1-2-2 Drift set.

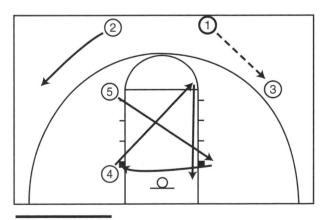

FIGURE 11.5 Drift: X-cut entry.

You can also reverse the post movement and have the low post come to the ball from behind the zone. The advantage of having your players flash to the ball from behind is that they can read and seal off the defender before the defender is even aware of their presence. Additionally, attacking from behind allows the post player to reverse pivot and gain an inside rebounding position if he is denied the cut and a shot is taken.

Remind the players flashing to the open post that they are passers as well as shooters. For example, with the defense drawn in to play the post, 4 can pitch the ball back out to a perimeter player stepping up for the jumper. Often, player 4's best option is to pass the ball to a weak-side perimeter player stepping up into a gap for the shot (see figure 11.6).

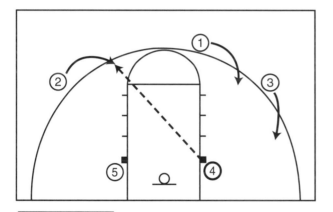

FIGURE 11.6 Drift: skip pass.

The Drift offense offers the kind of versatility you need to take advantage of your talent in a given year or a hot hand on a given night. It also affords several alternatives that you can run when facing tough zone defenses that take away the basic options of the offense. These additional options give the defense a different look and force it to adjust. Options can also be used to disguise plays and thereby confuse the defense. For example, you can give the defense the same look as one play when you are actually executing another.

Shallow Cut

Player 1 dribbles to 2 on the wing, and 2 shallow cuts up to the top to replace 1. As he cuts, player 2 could also screen the top guard in the zone to give 1 more room on the wing. As the ball moves to the wing, 4 backs out, and 5 slides into the low post (see figure 11.7).

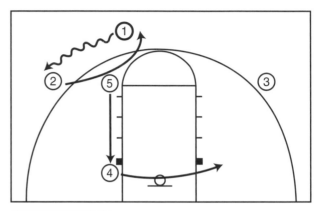

FIGURE 11.7 Drift: shallow cut.

Baseline Step-Out

Player 4 steps out to the low baseline on the ball side and receives the ball from player 2. Player 5 then slides from the high post to the low post and looks for the ball. Player 3 finds the open area on the opposite wing and reads the high-post defense to see if he (3) can flash into the open gap (see figure 11.8).

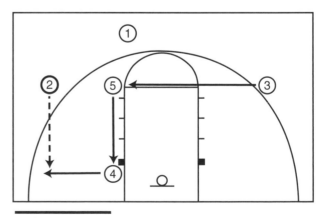

FIGURE 11.8 Drift: baseline step-out.

Release

Player 5 releases and steps off the high post to be a receiver on the perimeter for 2. He (5) can then look inside for 4 stepping in and sealing the low-post defender; or he can look to the weak side for 3, who should be finding the gap on the weak side (see figure 11.9). If the pass goes to 3, 4 flashes low to the ball side from behind the defense, and 5 reenters the post. Player 4 then backs out of the post, and 5 flashes in to create the regular Drift movement.

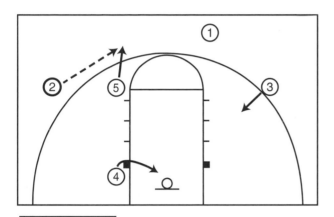

FIGURE 11.9 Drift: release.

Circle

The perimeter movement in the circle option is as effective against a zone as it is against a man-to-man defense. Player 1 dribbles at either wing player and circles him through to the opposite wing. The weak-side wing then replaces the point (see figure 11.10). This has been very successful for us in getting shots for the right players.

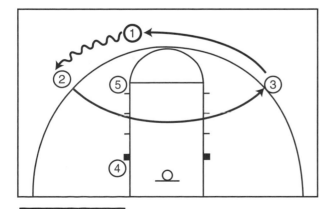

FIGURE 11.10 Drift: circle.

Chase

Player 1 dribbles at the wing player as if he is going to circle him through to the other side. When 2 gets behind the zone, he V-cuts back out to the corner, as shown in figure 11.11. Player 1 ball fakes to 3 to convince the zone that 2 is moving through the lane.

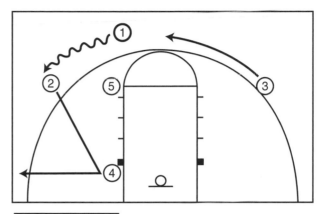

FIGURE 11.11 Drift: chase.

Hold

After 1 enters into the Drift movement with a pass to 2, 2 passes back to 1, who is looking for the gap in the top of the zone. Player 2 moves through the lane underneath and behind the opposite low post to the far corner, while 4 sets a screen on the low defender to help 2 get open coming off the baseline. Player 1 passes to 3, who looks for 2 coming off the screen (see figure 11.12). Timing is very important.

If 2 is not open, 3 can hit 4 stepping up the lane if the zone shifts and denies the pass to 2. Player 3 should also look for 5 flashing to the middle for the short jumper.

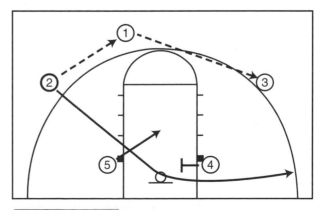

FIGURE 11.12 Drift: hold.

If 3 cannot hit either receiver, he throws back to 1. Player 2 then moves back to the other side behind the zone, and everyone is back in the Drift set.

Double Screen

This option starts with 4 and 5 stacked on the right block; player 3 is positioned on the left block. Player 1 dribbles right, and 2 shallow cuts to the top. Player 3 uses the double screen by 4 and 5 to get open in the right corner. As the ball goes to 3, 4 peels off 5 and looks for the pass (see figure 11.13). After screening, 5 opens up to the ball and looks for the post feed.

If nothing is available, 3 reverses to 1 and runs the baseline, using 4 and 5 to help him get open on the opposite side.

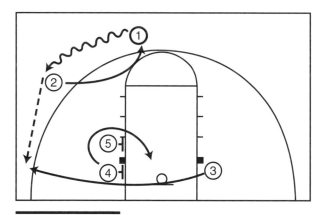

FIGURE 11.13 Drift: double screen.

3 Set

This option starts with 2 and 4 stacked on the strong-side elbow and 3 and 5 stacked on the weak-side block. Player 1 dribbles to the right wing as 2 breaks to fill the gap at the top vacated by 1. Player 4 can help 2 or 1 get open by screening the top defender in the zone. Player 5 sets a screen on the low defender to get 3 open on the perimeter and then opens up to the ball (see figure 11.14).

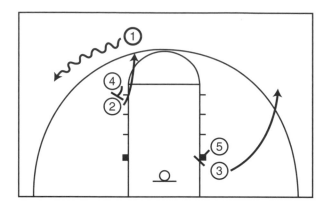

FIGURE 11.14 Drift: 3 set.

2 Set

This option starts with 2 and 4 stacked on one block and 3 and 5 stacked on the other. Player 1 picks a side, allowing the perimeter player in the stack on the ball side (in this case, 2) to make the middle cut and become the top player in the zone offense. Players 4 and 5 look to screen the bottom players in the post to help free the perimeter players (see figure 11.15). After screening, 4 and 5 should look to seal and step up the lane for the post feed.

The 3 set and 2 set options are particularly useful in attacking a zone defense because they force the defense to adjust to the set and thereby change the defensive alignment. If the

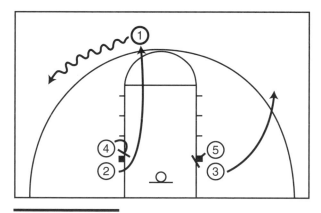

FIGURE 11.15 Drift: 2 set.

defense does not adjust, some players will be left unguarded for easy scoring opportunities.

Playing out of these sets also creates overload situations for your team and creates confusion for the zone. Finally, these sets allow your post players to attack the zone from behind, flashing into open gaps in the lane and screening the zone to help produce shots for your perimeter players.

Versus an Odd Front

Drift can be used to attack a 1-2-2 zone by making one adjustment to your perimeter players. Player 1 picks a side, pushing the wing toward the corner. The opposite wing (3) then "tilts" the offense to create a two-guard front. He stays behind 1 to create a good passing angle so that the defense can't steal the ball through the passing lane (see figure 11.16). By moving the zone and overloading the wing, you have essentially changed the defense to a 2-2-1 zone.

Your players should now follow the fundamental zone principles to attack the defense. On the reversal, 3 dribbles hard to the corner, 1 follows, and 2 tilts to stay behind the ball. Post movement continues as in Drift, but you can have the opposite post flash to give you the overload.

Other Zone Offenses

All of the zone offenses below follow the same zone principles discussed at the beginning of the chapter. They provide different options when an opponent has caught on to the movements in your standard zone offense.

Hold

Hold is a continuity offense that we have used as an option instead of Drift. In this offense, 1 starts up top and picks a side. Players 2 and 3 set up on the wings. Player 5 is at the high post, and 4 is in the short corner. The 1 player makes someone play him, then passes the ball off to a wing. If 3 receives the ball, 5 rolls to the strong-side block (called the war zone), where he must be a greedy receiver. Player 4 stays on the strong side (if 1 chooses the side opposite of 4, 4 must run to get to the strong side), while 2 flashes to the high post (figure 11.17).

Player 3 drives into the zone as 1 fills in behind him. If 3 is stopped on the drive, he first looks for 4 and 5 down low. Note that 5 does not have to be a scorer, but he must post up strong; we use the term *post depth*. This will open up driving lanes for others. Some of our best passers have been posts.

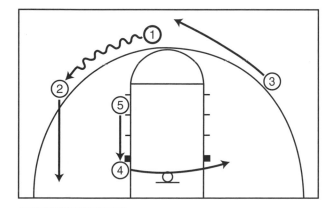

FIGURE 11.16 Drift: versus an odd front.

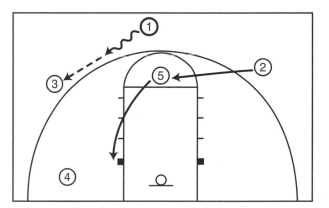

FIGURE 11.17 Hold: roll and flash.

If 3 cannot pass low, he reverses the ball to 1. When 1 catches the ball, he first looks for a pass to the 5 player, who is sealing off his opponent in the low post. If 5 is not open, 1 dribbles opposite and passes to 2 as 5 continues to the strong-side block and 4 runs the baseline or a wrinkle cut. If 4 is denied the ball on a wrinkle cut, 2 quickly reverses to 1, who then uses 4 as a ball screen (figure 11.18). Player 1 can pull up and shoot, kick to 3, or dump down to 5.

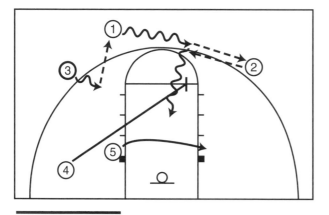

FIGURE 11.18 Hold: dribble penetration and reverse.

As a release against an odd front (for example, a 1-2-2 or 3-2), player 1 begins this offense by dribbling strongly away from 5. Player 5 then steps out to receive the pass. Player 5 first looks for a pass down low to 4, who is sealing off his defender for a lob. If that is not open, 5 makes a quick reversal to 3. If this occurs, 5 dives to the war zone, and the normal Hold pattern continues, with 4 releasing on a wrinkle cut or short corner cut (figure 11.19).

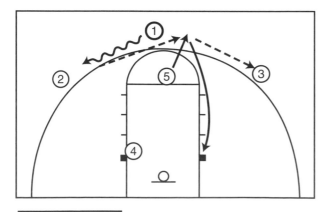

FIGURE 11.19 Hold: release against odd front.

Tight 4

In the Tight 4 offense, player 1 attacks the outside defender in the zone, making someone play him. Player 5 pops out to the short corner after 1 attacks, while 2 remains about 10 feet away from 1 for the reversal. Player 3 rolls to the block as 4 rips to the open area at the high post. As 1 passes to 5 in the corner, 2 shifts back to the opposite wing. Player 5 reverses to 1, and 1 dribbles toward 2 and reverses the ball (figure 11.20). The same motion is then repeated on the opposite side.

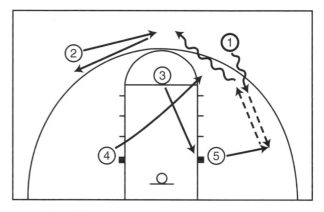

FIGURE 11.20 Tight 4.

Emphasize to players that they should make someone play them. Receivers should be greedy, wanting the ball and bursting toward it on the pass. Remind the post to pop out late, after the guard attacks.

Shield

This continuity offense is best suited for a team that has two players who can both post up and face up. Player 1 picks a side and makes a defender play him before passing to 2 on the wing. The weak-side post (5) will wrinkle to the high-post area. The strong-side post (4) can stay in the short corner or duck in to the low post. On the reversal from 2 to 1, 5 sprints to the short corner. Player 4 looks for a high-low pass. If it isn't there, he continues to flash to the high post (figure 11.21). This crossing action will move the back of the zone and allow for driving lanes.

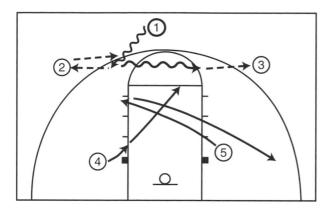

FIGURE 11.21 Shield.

Cutters

This zone offense is best when your 2, 3, and 4 players are all similar in their skill levels. In addition, player 1 should be a good shooter. The Cutters offense uses the same initial setup as Hold (described earlier). Player 1 starts up top and picks a side. Players 2 and 3 set up on the wings. Player 5 is at the high post, and 4 is in the short corner. Player 5 rolls to the low block as 1 drives to a side, hitting 2. Player 4 stays on the strong side (if the 1 player goes to the opposite side of 4, 4 must run to get to the strong side). Player 2 looks inside and reverses to 1 or skips to 3. Player 2 then cuts in front of 5 (the coach should emphasize this point, because most players want to cut behind), looking for the ball (figure 11.22a). If 2 is not open, 1 looks to 5, who is sealing, and 4 replaces 2. If the skip pass was made to player 3, he looks to feed the post, dump down to 2, or drive. If he reverses the ball, he cuts over top of the war zone to the short corner as 5 looks to seal off his defender, and 2 replaces 3 (figure 11.22b).

Zone Set Plays

As mentioned in chapter 10, you also want to have set plays in your repertoire in addition to the regular offensive rotation. The set plays can help free up a specific player for a shot. Here are some plays that we've used extensively in recent years.

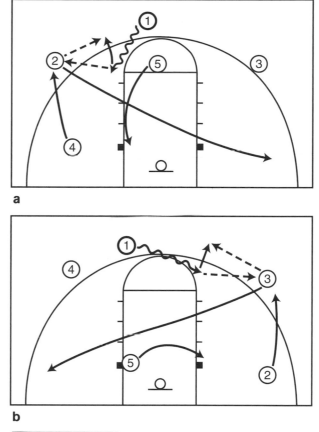

FIGURE 11.22 Cutters.

63

This play begins in a common zone offense formation, with a point guard (1), two wings (2 and 3), one post player at the foul line (5), and the other post player at the low post (4). The point guard begins the play by going to the side of the intended shooter, who should be on the weak side. In this case, it is 2. When 2 receives the pass, 5 dives down on 2's side (see figure 11.23a).

If there are no options, 2 swings the ball back out top to 1, who takes it to the opposite side and passes to 3. After 2 has passed back to 1, player 2 then drops to the baseline and prepares to cut. The two post players, meanwhile, cut to the opposite side toward the ball (see figure 11.23b).

Once 3 receives the pass from 1, he looks inside. Again, if there are no options, he swings it back to 1. This is where the new wrinkle comes in. The point guard dribbles hard to the opposite side, while 3 screens the top side of the zone, and 4 screens the bottom. Player 5 cuts toward the opposite side. Player 2 comes under the basket and off the screen, and 1 skips a pass to 2 for the open jumper (see figure 11.23c).

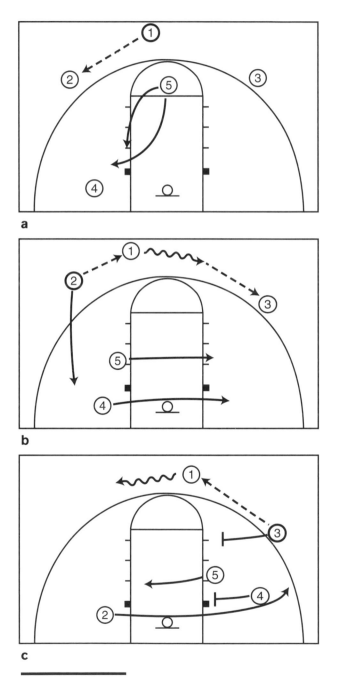

a

b

c

FIGURE 11.23 63.

Wheel

Wheel starts with the point guard going to the strong-side wing (the same side where your low post, 4, has set up). The 1 player dribbles over to the wing spot, while 2 cuts through the lane to set up in the opposite corner, and 3 moves out top to the point position (figure 11.24a). The ball is then swung back out top to 3, while 5 screens the defensive player playing the top position in the zone. The 3 player attacks off the screen, looking for the shot. If no shot is available, player 3 can continue past 4, who sets a second screen against the defense (figure 11.24b).

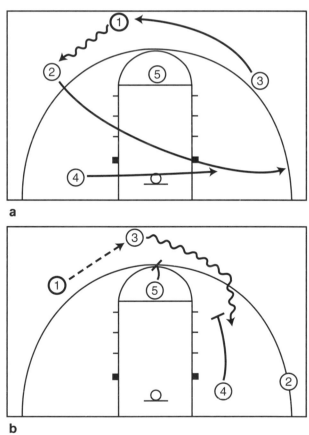

a

b

FIGURE 11.24 Wheel.

Wheel 2

The Wheel offense can also be run from a two-guard front. This is a very simple offense that can be useful for a team that has limited practice time. It can also be used against man-to-man defenses.

Player 1 hits 3 and then makes a rim cut (sprints to the basket) as 2 replaces 1. Once 1 is midway through his cut, 4 cuts to the rim. Player 1 fills in the location that 2 has left (figure 11.25a). Player 5 cuts to the open area after 4 reaches the rim. Player 5 goes to the block if he does not receive the ball sooner, and 4 returns to his original spot (figure 11.25b). Player 3 can look to drive at any time. Emphasize to players that all cuts should come right after one another (the vacuum principle).

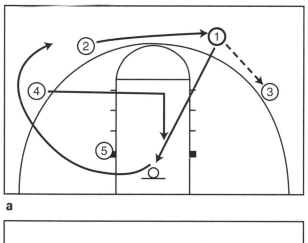

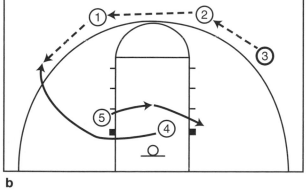

FIGURE 11.25 Wheel 2.

Wheel 3

In this version of Wheel, player 3 reverses the ball to 2, and 2 reverses the ball to 1. The motion is then repeated.

Wheel With UCLA Option

In the Wheel with UCLA option, 1 hits 3 and then makes a rim cut. Player 4 cuts after 1, and 2 replaces 1 (figure 11.26a). After 5 cuts, he sets a screen for 2 (figure 11.26b). Player 5 then steps out to receive a pass from 3 (figure 11.26c). If 5 does not have any scoring options, 5 passes back out, and the motion begins again.

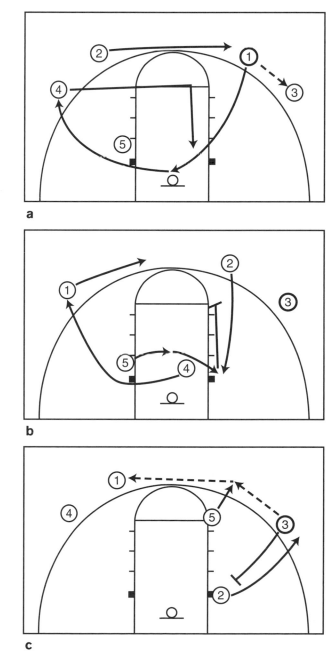

FIGURE 11.26 Wheel with UCLA option.

Wheel With UCLA Option 2

In the second Wheel with UCLA option, 3 hits 2 if 2 is open, or he hits 5 if 2 is not open. Player 3 down-screens for 2, and 5 hits 2 off the screen or 3 on a duck-in. If neither 2 nor 3 is open, 5 reverses to 1, and the Wheel motion begins again.

Counter

When using Counter, the players start in the usual formation with three guards, a high post, and a low post. The point guard starts by going to the weak side, driving hard toward 3 on the wing. The 2 player replaces 1 at the point of the offense, shading toward the ball side. As 1 is dribbling to the wing position, 3 starts to cut through the middle of the zone (see figure 11.27a).

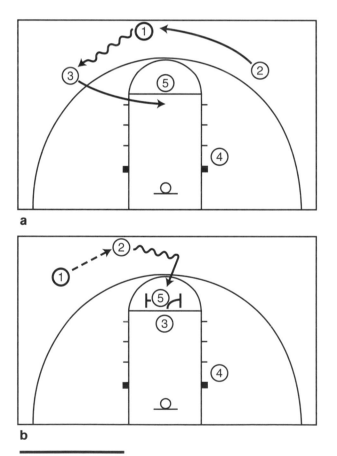

a

b

FIGURE 11.27 Counter.

The 1 player then swings the ball back to 2. When 2 catches the ball, the high post (5) screens the inside top of the zone. At the same time, 3 comes up (instead of going all the way through to the opposite wing) and screens the inside of the zone opposite 5. The 2 player starts to drive wide as if he is going to the opposite wing. He then changes direction and goes between the two screens for a jumper right around the foul line (see figure 11.27b).

Wrinkle

Wrinkle is actually a rotation designed to force the zone to move, which inevitably results in openings for passes, shots, or drives. The play starts in the same formation as Counter. The 5 player at the high post should be the player you want as the permanent post, whereas the 4 player at the low post should have more flexibility to face the basket and play like another wing if necessary. In this play, the low post can start either in the usual position or in the short corner, which is several feet away from the lane toward the corner of the court.

The point (1) starts the play by dribbling to the strong side and passing to 2 on the wing. If 4 wasn't in the short corner to begin with, he should fill it now and face the wing (2). The high post (5) rolls low and posts up above the block. The 2 player on the wing looks to see if the pass is available into the post (see figure 11.28a).

If the pass is not available, 2 swings the ball back to 1, who drives to the opposite side of the zone. Immediately after passing back to the point, 2 cuts through the zone to the opposite corner. The 5 player cuts directly behind 2 and flashes to the ball, looking for the pass from 1. If 1 can't pass to 5 in the lane, he looks to 3 on the wing. As 1 passes to 3, 5 posts above the block on that side of the lane, while 4 fills the wing spot on the weak side vacated by 2 when he cut through the zone (see figure 11.28b).

If 3 is unable to penetrate or pass to 5 at the post, he swings the ball back to 1, and the play again rotates in the other direction. The 1 player drives to the opposite side of the zone, while 3 cuts through to the opposite corner after passing the ball. Meanwhile, 5 is flashing into the lane looking for the pass from 1, then posting above the block as 1 passes

to the wing, which is now occupied by 4. The 2 player then pops up to the weak-side wing in case the play comes back that way (see figure 11.28c).

The key to making this play work is continuous ball movement, making the zone adjust. Moving the ball and continuing the rotation should give you plenty of options for penetrating drives or passes for open shots.

Thru

In this set, player 1 passes to 2 and then cuts strong side, where 1 receives the ball back from 2. Player 5 rolls to the block and sets a screen. Player 1, a good shooter, forces the lower player on the outside of the zone to come out and guard him. Player 4 moves to the baseline or above the screen for a shot. Player 3 flashes to the foul line (figure 11.29).

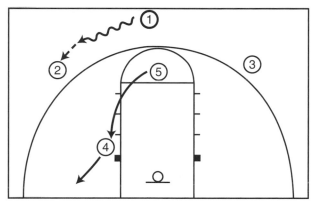

a

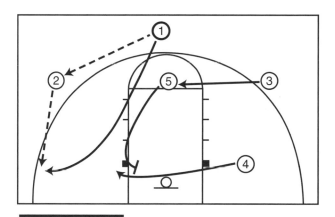

FIGURE 11.29 Thru.

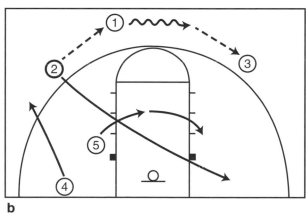

b

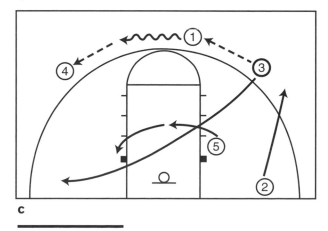

c

FIGURE 11.28 Wrinkle.

Power

In this set, player 1 hits player 4 at the wing and goes to the opposite side. Player 5 sets a screen for 2 near the top of the key; 2 must use the screen as he cuts to the opposite corner. After the screen, 5 rolls to the strong-side low block, while 3 cuts to the weak-side block. As 5 rolls to the block, 3 flashes high, and 4 looks

for 5 on the post-up. If it isn't available and 3, now at the elbow, receives the ball (figure 11.30*a*), he looks for the high-low to 5 or a quick backdoor to 1. If 1 does not receive the pass by the time he gets to the block, he replaces the strong-side wing. After 4 screens for 2, player 4 receives a flex screen from 5 (figure 11.30*b*). Player 3 looks for 4 coming across the lane for an easy basket.

If 4 isn't open, 3 passes to 1 and then steps into the slot. Player 5 proceeds to the strong-side block as 2 cuts to the weak-side block; 2 then flashes to the strong-side elbow (figure 11.30*c*). Player 1 looks for 5 down low or 2 at the elbow. If 2 receives the pass, he looks high-low for 5 and for 3, who back cuts. If 2 has no available options, the pattern is repeated.

In the Power set, the offense can use various entries to show the defense a different look. In the stack high entry (figure 11.31), player 1 has the ball up top, players 4 and 5 are stacked on the strong-side elbow, and players 2 and 3 are stacked on the weak-side elbow. On the signal, player 4 breaks out to the strong-side wing, 5 breaks to the free-throw line, 2 breaks high, and 3 breaks to the opposite-side wing.

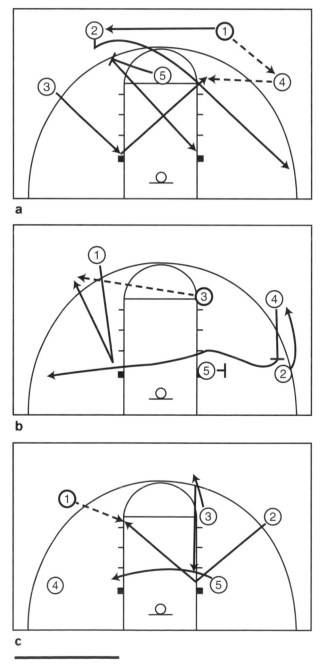

FIGURE 11.30 Power.

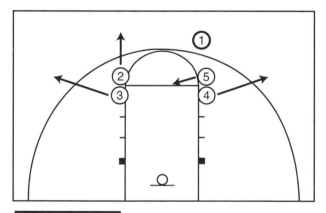

FIGURE 11.31 Power: stack high entry.

In the stack high cross entry (figure 11.32), players set up the same way as in the stack high entry. While 5 again moves to the free-throw line and 2 breaks high, players 4 and 3 switch, with 3 moving to the strong-side wing and 4 moving to the weak-side wing.

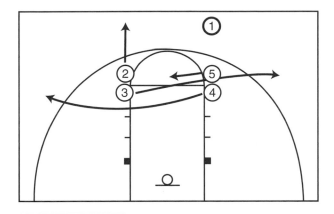

FIGURE 11.32 Power: stack high cross entry.

Finally, in the staggered entry (figure 11.33), player 1 again begins with the ball up top, and his teammates are staggered; 4 and 5 are stacked on the strong-side block, and 2 and 3 are stacked on the weak-side elbow. From here, 4 pops to the strong-side wing, 5 stays on the block, 3 flashes to the high post, and 2 cuts to the corner. Player 1 passes to 4 on the wing, then goes to the opposite side.

Each of these entries takes your team directly into the Power set.

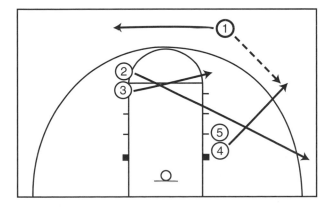

FIGURE 11.33 Power: staggered entry.

Zone Offense Drills

We prefer to have our team use the same principles out of different sets rather than run a different offense for each zone we face. To do this, the players must know the zone principles outlined in the previous several pages. After you teach the principles of the zone offense, the best way to work on them is to have players apply them in zone situations. Again, we suggest breaking things down into post, perimeter, and team play.

Post Drill Station

The first area we break down is the proper movement of the post players against a zone. Proper post movement is crucial because a zone defense often clutters the post area. We work our post players against two basic zone sets.

TWO POSTS VERSUS BACK OF 2-3 OR 2-1-2 ZONE

Starting from the positions illustrated, the offensive players work on screening for each other, flashing to open areas (preferably in the lane), stepping out on the baseline and facing the basket, and sealing defenders (figure 11.34). They should look to work as a two-player team. A coach and two managers simulate perimeter passes.

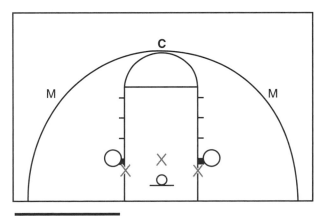

FIGURE 11.34 Post zone station: two on blocks.

THREE BASELINE PLAYERS VERSUS BACK OF 3-2 OR 1-2-2 ZONE

Setting up along the baseline (see figure 11.35), post players work on the same principles as in the previous drill.

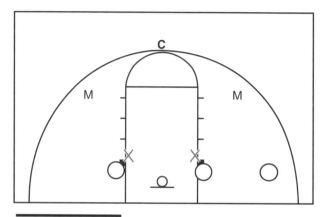

FIGURE 11.35 Post zone station: three on baseline.

Perimeter Drill Station

In their drills, perimeter players should focus on using the dribble to penetrate; splitting the gaps between defenders and looking for the short jump shot; trying to absorb two defenders, and then passing to a teammate in an open area; throwing the skip pass across the zone; and screening the perimeter defenders in the zone.

TWO PERIMETER PLAYERS VERSUS TOP OF 3-2 OR 1-2-2 ZONE

Offensive players work on driving gaps, stepping up for the shot (off-guard), tilting (overloading the zone), shot fakes, and pass fakes. Managers in the corners simulate the baseline pass (see figure 11.36).

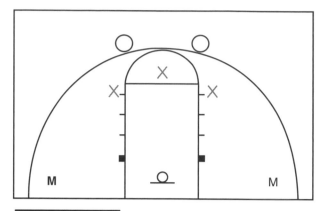

FIGURE 11.36 Perimeter zone station: two-guard front.

THREE PERIMETER PLAYERS VERSUS TOP OF 2-3 OR 2-1-2 ZONE

From the positions indicated in figure 11.37, offensive players work on skip passing, driving the gaps, and looking for the step-up jumpers.

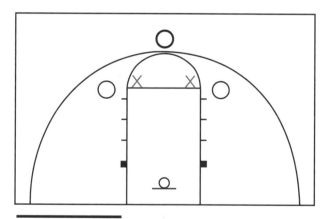

FIGURE 11.37 Perimeter zone station: one-guard front.

INDIVIDUAL ZONE JUMP-SHOT WORK

Move players around to different spots on the court. The player starts with the ball, throws to a coach or teammate, and then steps up for the return pass for the shot (see figure 11.38).

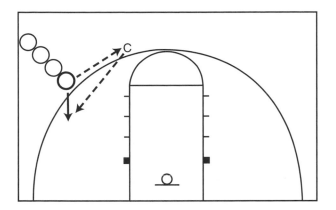

FIGURE 11.38 Perimeter zone station: return for shot.

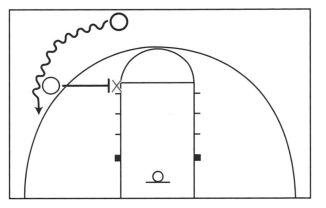

FIGURE 11.40 Perimeter zone station: screen and shoot.

ZONE PENETRATION AND DISH-OFF WORK

The offensive player drives at the outside shoulder of the defender and passes to the wing for the shot, as shown in figure 11.39.

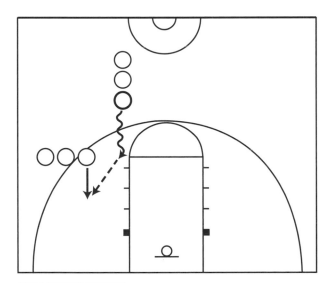

FIGURE 11.39 Perimeter zone station: drive and pitch.

PERIMETER SCREENING WORK

The wing player screens the guard in the zone, allowing for penetration and a shot by the point (see figure 11.40).

PROPER FOOTWORK FOR JUMP SHOTS

Have perimeter players shape up out of the 2 set and 3 set described earlier in the chapter, practicing the correct footwork for getting their shots off. You can work both sides of the court at the same time (figure 11.41).

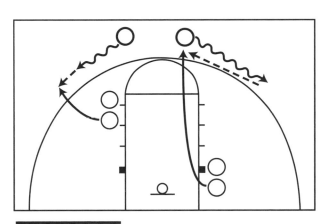

FIGURE 11.41 Perimeter zone station: 2 and 3 sets.

Team Drill Station

Once players learn and execute the zone offense principles in post and perimeter drills, they can move on to team drills.

MOTION BREAKDOWN DRILLS FOR BOTH POST AND PERIMETER PLAYERS

Work on the skip pass and the shallow cut, circle, and chase options described in the Drift offense section earlier in the chapter.

BOX OFFENSE VERSUS DIAMOND DEFENSE 4-ON-4

Work on all zone principles from the set illustrated in figure 11.42.

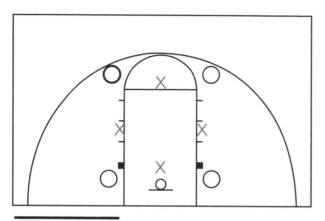

FIGURE 11.42 Box versus diamond.

DIAMOND OFFENSE VERSUS BOX DEFENSE 4-ON-4

Emphasize getting into the seams and other zone principles from the set shown in figure 11.43.

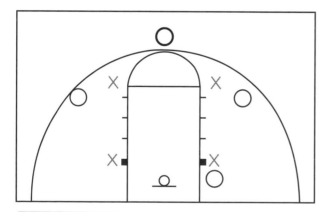

FIGURE 11.43 Diamond versus box.

FOUR OFFENSIVE PLAYERS VERSUS 2-3 ZONE

Advantage is given to the defense so the offense is forced to work extra hard. Good ball and player movement is required.

Improving Offensive Teamwork

Whether you run a man-to-man or zone offense, teamwork is the key to success. And much of the responsibility for developing offensive teamwork falls on the coach. We've got to sell our players on the importance of playing together. We've got to convince the players that the team will accomplish far more if no one is concerned with who gets the credit. To do this, we must sell the players on the fact that if the team does well, everybody goes uptown together. But if only a few individuals do well, the team goes nowhere.

So many times at clinics coaches come up to me and ask for the secret offense, the magic defense, or the trick out-of-bounds play. I tell them I don't think there is any such thing; rather, I advise them to work on developing their players' teamwork and their execution of offensive and defensive fundamentals. These things are far more important than any brilliant coaching tactic.

The tactical side of the game is important, but it is beyond the Xs and Os that champions are developed. It is by having the one-on-one meeting with a player, by recognizing problems in advance and heading them off, by convincing your players that the team comes first, by holding team meetings, by finding motivational poems that stress teamwork and character, by monitoring academics, by working hard to help players get college scholarships, by emphasizing off-season workouts, and by doing all the little things that help build a special relationship between the players and you—their coach.

Vic Bubas, the former coach at Duke University, told me that when the Atlantic Coast Conference tournament approached, he used to get as positive as he could to get the players in a confident, positive frame of mind. He would tell his players, "Gee, you're looking good. I've never seen you stronger. You're rebounding well." That his players believed in him is evident in the fine record Vic established in ACC tourney play. If you show confidence in your players, you'll be amazed at how much the players' self-confidence increases and what kind of payoff it can bring.

Clock and Inbounds Situations

We've covered the fast break and half-court man-to-man and zone offenses. One or all of these three strategies will make up the bulk of your offensive attack throughout any given game. The remainder of your offense will consist of how you handle special situations, such as possessions when the clock is a factor and inbounds plays.

Time and Score Tactics

How a team performs during the closing minutes of games will be a big factor in determining the success of the team. Any time your team is in the last three minutes of a game, your players should follow the rules below to help them control the situation.

- Maintain constant mental concentration and poise. Good players get it done under pressure.
- Stay in your offensive pattern and continue to move and work for a good shot (movement is vital to stir the defense).
- Read the defensive player on every pass, anticipating a gamble by the defense.
- Go inside more than normal for the high-percentage shots.

- Get to the foul line by keeping constant basket pressure on the defense. Foul shots are money in the bank.
- Be active on the offensive boards. Second and third shots are most critical at this point.
- Save three time-outs for the very end of the game.

These rules work only if your players are in excellent physical condition and if you have spent time working on these various situations in practice.

Keeping a Lead

If your team is ahead in the last three minutes of the game, have your players look for either layups or foul shots. Even though it may seem best to simply spread it out and run out the clock, you should never completely take away the thought of scoring on offense. I have seen too many games that were lost when the offensive team tried to freeze the ball and, in effect, played not to lose rather than to win. In those situations, the offense played so cautiously that the defense actually had the advantage. Always have your players attack the defense and look to score. In the final three minutes, though, players should patiently look for only the very high-percentage shots that will result in an easy basket or getting fouled.

Playing Defense With the Lead

If you are on defense and ahead by three or more points during the closing seconds, force your opponents to drive by running at the dribblers and thus not allowing any three-point attempts. Under these conditions, you want your players to get beaten on the dribble because this will force the offensive players inside the three-point arc. At the very least, it will force the offense into making more passes to get the shot off. If you are successful in forcing the offense to drive with the ball, you must also make sure your perimeter players do not rotate off their players to stop the penetration. Otherwise, the players they are guarding will be able to spot up around the arc for the three-point shot.

You can also disrupt the offense's structure and timing in the last seconds by pressing or double-teaming to create turnovers or rushed shots. For example, your players could run at and double-team the opponent's best outside shooter while rotating to pick off the passes in the perimeter area, leaving the post players open for only a two-point shot.

If there is more time on the clock, ask your team to focus on getting three straight stops on defense in order to extend your lead. Remind your players that when a team is down, they may abandon their offense and just start taking deep threes, which can lead to long rebounds. Also remind your players to continue to play at their own pace; scattered play by an opponent can lead to scattered play by your own team.

(For complete information regarding defensive skills and strategies, see chapters 13 to 16.)

Coming From Behind

If you are behind in the closing seconds and have the ball, the strategy is much the same as if you were ahead. Your team should look for a layup or perhaps a six-footer, but it is best to draw a foul in this situation. By going to the line, your team can set up defensively, save valuable time, and score while doing so!

If you are down by more than two points, the defense will be extended to prevent the three-point shot. In this situation, you must read the time and score situation to determine whether you want to take the two-point basket or attempt the three-point shot. If you are behind by four or five points, you will still need two possessions to tie or win the game, so it may be advisable to get two points if they can be scored quickly. Other factors in your decision will include

- the amount of time left in the game,
- the number of time-outs you have remaining,
- the personal foul situation,
- how well the opponent is shooting from the foul line,
- who is shooting well for you, and
- whether you are making a run at them defensively.

I caution you against going to the three-point shot too early. I have seen teams shoot their way out of a game because they forced difficult three-point shots in an attempt to get all of the points back at once. You won't get all of the points back at once, so you'll need some help from your defense.

Defending When Behind

Your defense will have to do a great deal more for you than will your offense in this situation. The offensive team will likely spread out and move away from the basket, which means your defense is more likely to get layups off steals. If your team is down, your players will need to play hard-nosed defense and allow the opponent only one scoring opportunity per possession. Inside of 30 seconds, another good catch-up tactic is to foul opposing players who have poor shooting percentages from the free-throw line. Obviously, the best way to handle the closing minutes of a game is to take control of the game early in the fourth quarter.

Last-Minute Plays

We have three time-and-score plays that our teams use quite often in the closing moments of a game. We call the plays Victory, UCLA, and 4-C. They are effective against either a man-to-man or zone defense.

All factors being equal, we recommend choosing the play that your team executes best and feels the most comfortable with. Other factors, such as the opponent's defensive alignment, should also be considered. On occasion we will call a play, see the defense we're facing, call another time-out, and change to another play.

Victory

"Victory" begins in a 1-4 alignment with players 5, 4, 3, and 2 located along the baseline and with player 1 (or another designated player) taking his defender 1-on-1 from the top of the key. As 1 penetrates, he should be ready to either take the shot or to dump off when the other defensive players help out. Two options can be run out of this set to create shots for the offensive players.

In the first option, as 1 looks to penetrate, your post players screen for the guards to get them open going to the corners. If one of them is open, 1 then hits that player with a pass (see figure 12.1), and the player squares up and shoots. After 4 and 5 have screened, they should open back up to the wing to see if they

can receive the post feed from the guard in the corner or catch the pass off 1's penetration.

In the second option, player 1 dribbles right, and 5 pops out to create a two-player front. As 5 goes to the guard position, 2 and 4 set a double screen on the ball-side block, and 3 uses the double screen to get open in the right corner. Player 1 should look to feed 3 for the shot (see figure 12.2). As 3 comes off the screen, 4 can roll and be a post-up player; 2 can back out to the opposite wing and look for the skip pass from 1 in case the defense shifts entirely to the right.

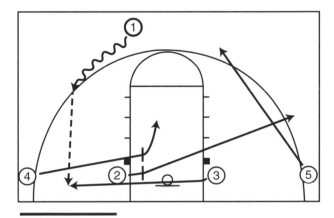

FIGURE 12.2 Victory: option 2.

UCLA

The second play is called UCLA. I put it in our playbook after seeing it executed with such great success by John Wooden's UCLA teams.

This play begins with a two-player front, with 1 driving hard at 2, and 2 shallow cutting to replace 1. As this is happening, 3 flashes to the wing to be a receiver, and 4 flashes into the high post from behind, clearing the left side of the floor. Player 1 hits 4, who then looks for 2 sneaking in the backdoor (see figure 12.3). If 2 is not open, he fades to the corner, and 1 and 3 balance the floor.

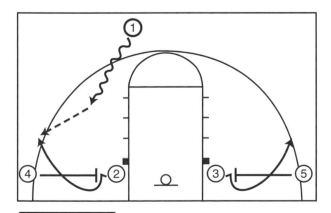

FIGURE 12.1 Victory: option 1.

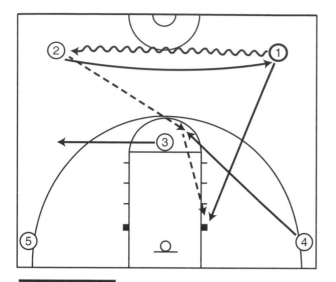

FIGURE 12.3 UCLA.

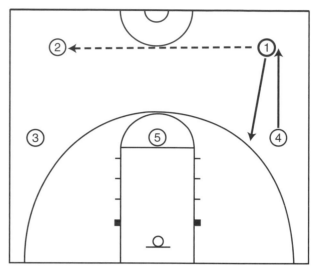

FIGURE 12.5 4-C: exchange.

4-C

This play, 4-C, allows for plenty of movement by the players and keeps them working to be receivers and looking to score. The initial alignment is like a 2-3, with a two-player front, a high post, and two wing players.

Whenever a player in one of the guard positions passes to the wing, he should cut to the basket. As this happens, the off-guard replaces him, and the off-wing fills the guard spot (see figure 12.4). If you keep the offense high (out above the foul line), it will eliminate help-side defense and create backdoor

opportunities for the wings when the guards have the ball.

On a guard-to-guard pass, the guard who passed the ball exchanges with the wing on his side (see figure 12.5). This occupies the off-side help and can create more backdoor opportunities for the players on the other side of the floor. Again, remind your off-ball players to never stop moving and your ball handlers to constantly look for cutters.

If there is any difficulty because a player has picked up his dribble and is under pressure, the high-post player must release, find the open area, and be a receiver (see figure 12.6).

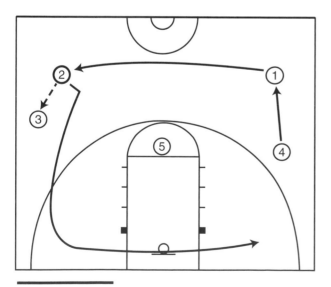

FIGURE 12.4 4-C: guard through.

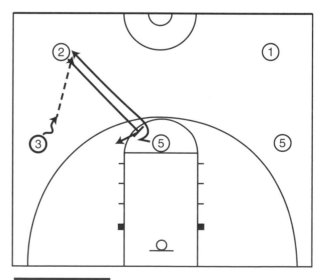

FIGURE 12.6 4-C: screen post.

If either wing picked up his dribble and is in any trouble, then the ball-side guard screens for the high post to make him a receiver. The screener (2) then shapes up to the ball to be a receiver after the screen.

Now 5 is a guard, and 2 is in the high post. This may be a situation you want to create if you have a mismatch you can take advantage of late in the game. If 5 is in the middle, he is your safety valve if a receiver is needed. He can also create the backdoor for himself by coming out high and reading the defense if he is overplayed. Movement such as this is critical to an offense in time and score situations.

Last-Second Plays

When a team scores a field goal and goes ahead of us with less than 10 but more than 3 seconds to go, my preference is not to call a time-out, but to quickly pass the ball inbounds and attempt to score with our quick break. If properly prepared, your team should be capable of getting a shot off from 12 feet and out within 3 seconds or a layup in 4 seconds. That being the case, I would rather surprise our opponents before they can set up the defense.

Many games are lost because the team that scores relaxes for just a second to celebrate their "win," only to have a well-drilled team strike back quickly for the real win. Surprise is an essential element here, but control is just as important. Our quick break must be well organized if it is to be effectively executed.

If the other team scores, and the clock runs down to 3 seconds or less, I always want a time-out while the ball is in the net. If you are unable to create a quick dead-ball situation here, the running clock might kill any opportunity at a shot before your team even inbounds the ball. In this situation, you need a full-court play that gives you the opportunity to score with very little time left.

Ladder

This full-court play can be used from either the baseline or the sideline. The inbounder

should be your best long-distance passer (usually the 1 player). Make sure that the inbounder knows whether he can run the baseline or whether he must remain at a designated spot.

When the inbounder slaps the ball, 4 back-screens for 5, who reads the defense and makes his cut. Player 4 then flashes to an open area. After a one count (following the ball slap), 3 sets a back screen for 2, who reads the defense and makes his cut. Player 3, after screening, looks for the open area in which to flash (see figure 12.7).

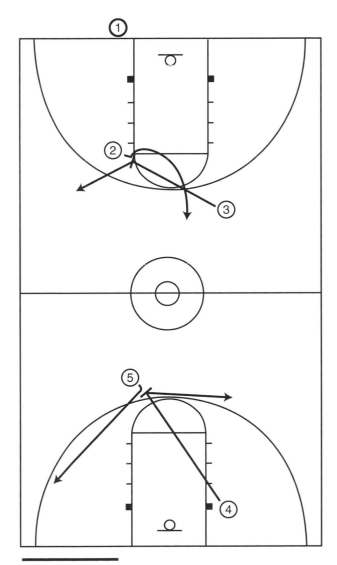

FIGURE 12.7 Ladder.

Tell your inbounder to look for the deep pass first because the deep screen will take place first. In addition, your receivers should break open at different times so your inbounder will have other options to go to if the first receiver is covered.

If this play is run from the sideline with the same screens (as it can be), your players will open up in different areas of the court, depending on where the ball is taken out of bounds.

Deep

In this full-court play, 2 takes the ball out, and 1 and 3 position themselves at each elbow of the foul line. Players 4 and 5 are outside the three-point arc and very close to the hash marks. On the ball slap, 4 and 5 begin downcourt and then come back (V-cut) to set screens. Player 4 screens for 1, and 5 screens for 3. Players 1 and 3 use the screens and sprint wide, looking for the deep pass over the top of the defense. Both 4 and 5 come back to the ball to be receivers after having set the screens, as shown in figure 12.8.

Again, tell your inbounder to look deep first; the short pass is the second option. Depending on the situation, you may need a deep pass for the score, or you may just need the short pass for the possession of the ball. If there is trouble, 1 and 3 can sprint back to the ball to be receivers. The sprint players must look over their inside shoulders so they can see the entire floor, stay balanced, and keep themselves from running out of bounds. You can also invert player positions so that your best ball handlers are in the 4 and 5 slots, coming back to the ball for the short pass.

Screen

If you have very little time left on the clock, a play called Screen is one more option you can employ to get a shot off. This play is possible only after an opponent has scored and your inbounder is allowed to run the baseline.

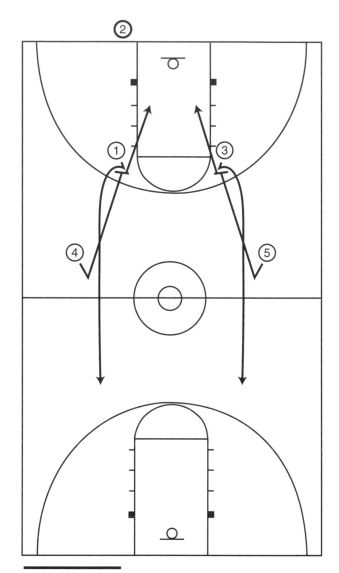

FIGURE 12.8 Deep.

Player 1 sets a screen on the player defending the inbounds pass and looks to take the charge. When the screen is set, 3 runs the baseline. Player 4 looks to be a receiver in an open area, while 5 sets a screen for 2 under the basket at the opposite end of the floor. Player 2 moves to get open in the corner, and 5 cuts back to the ball after the screen. The inbounder (3) should throw long to an open area for the last shot, as shown in figure 12.9.

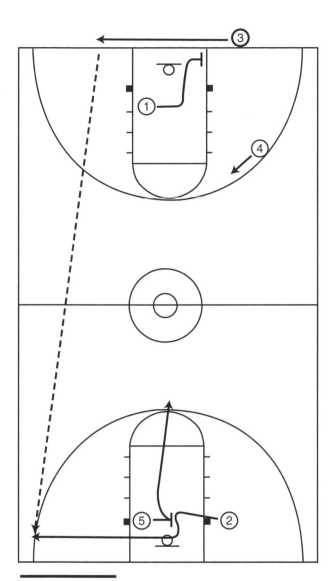

FIGURE 12.9 Screen.

Inbounds Plays

We are presenting here many of the inbounds plays that our teams have used over the years. We tell our players that our number one priority with these plays is to gain possession of the ball, not to create a shot opportunity.

We never have all of these plays in our playbook during any one season. Instead, we select the ones that we think that year's personnel will be able to execute most effectively. We like to have a primary out-of-bounds play

to use against a man-to-man defense and a primary one to use against a zone. Once our team executes the primary plays well, we then add two secondary out-of-bounds plays (one each for man-to-man and zone defenses).

THOUGHT FOR THE DAY

To those who are given much, much is expected. –John F. Kennedy

Because each play has several options, proper execution should ensure that at least one of those options will be open. Therefore, you really only need one or two plays that your team executes well against man-to-man or zone defenses. It is better to be able to execute a few plays very well than to run a dozen or so plays in which the execution leaves something to be desired. Never give your players more than they can handle.

In game situations, I frequently let the inbounder call the play that he thinks is appropriate. I trust players' instincts when it comes to having the feel of the game. They are the ones who have been playing against the opponent's defenses, and they often have a good idea of what is and isn't working. Therefore, I believe players are capable of calling good plays.

There are times, though, when I want to call the play. I communicate the plays using a combination of words and hand signals. I call the formation verbally and follow that with a hand signal indicating the option number I want them to use. For example, I will yell out "Box!" which tells my players to line up in the Box formation; then I will signal the number one with my hand, telling them to run the first option of Box.

The inbounder is often the key to all of these plays. He should have steady balance and a good, firm grip on the ball that enables him to throw a crisp pass. Additionally, taller players often make the best inbounders because they can see over the defense and have a better chance of spotting an open receiver.

Inbounds Plays Versus Man-to-Man Defense

Against man-to-man defenses, we like to use the Box formation. A team can run many plays out of this formation, once again using the principles of screening and cutting. All of these plays can be used when inbounding under the basket or along the sideline against a man-to-man defense. (Some inbounds plays, as described later in this chapter, can be run only from the sideline.)

Players must be sure to wait for the inbounder to hit the ball on any inbounds play. Why? Because the defense may leave someone unguarded near the basket. If so, the inbounder should forget about slapping the ball and pass it immediately to the open player. Once the ball is inbounded, the passer should almost always enter the opposite side of the court from where the receiver caught the ball.

You can stagger the formation in your out-of-bounds plays to give your players more room to get open under the basket. The spacing of the Box formation should be determined by you and your players as you read the defense. You can run the Box spread very wide, or you can run it in tight. In our Box formations, the players in the lane are frequently in line with the basket, and the outside players are about two steps off the lane.

Box 1

On the ball slap by 2, player 5 screens across for 4, who uses a V-cut to get open. After a one-second count (to stagger the times at which the receivers get open), 1 screens for 3. Both screeners come back to the ball to be receivers (see figure 12.10).

Box 2

On the hit, 5 up-screens for 1, and, after a one-second count, 4 up-screens for 3. Again, both screeners come back to the ball. Having your screeners come back to the ball is important so that your inbounder has as many receivers to throw to as possible (see figure 12.11). Your cutters must wait for the screens and read the defense to get open. And again, the

inbounder enters opposite the pass and gets to the point to cover the break in case of a turnover or a quick shot.

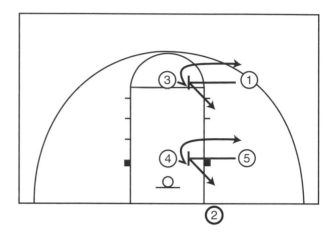

FIGURE 12.10 Box 1.

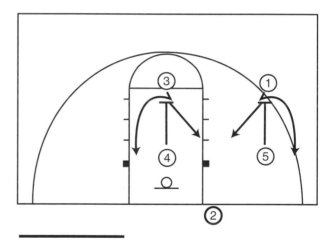

FIGURE 12.11 Box 2.

Box 3

On this option, the Box shifts over a few feet so that the two posts are on the blocks and two perimeter players are on the opposite ends of the free-throw line (see figure 12.12). On the hit, 3 cuts across the lane and screens for 4, who cuts off the screen toward the basket looking for the pass from 2. The 5 player counts to one after the slap and then does a little loop up to set a screen for 3. (With the little deceptive loop in there, I call it a banana screen.) The 3 player comes off the screen looking for the pass in from 2 and the shot. After inbounding the ball, 2 steps in and heads to the opposite wing.

If the shot is not there, the offense is ready to roll. The point (1) is the safety and looks for the inbounds pass as a last resort or the pass from 3 to start the offense.

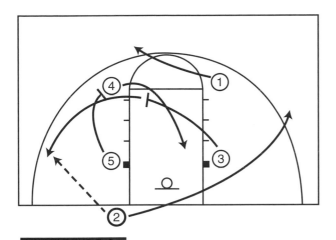

FIGURE 12.12 Box 3.

Box 4

On the slap, 5 steps out hard to his right, stops, and then cuts back looking for a lob at the front of the rim from 2. The 4 player simply cuts to the wing to get open. On the other side, 3 screens for 1, who fades and looks for the three-pointer (see figure 12.13).

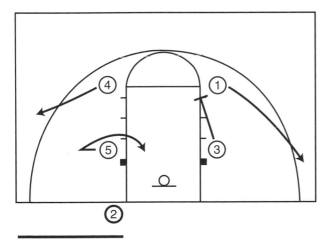

FIGURE 12.13 Box 4.

Box Out

On the hit, 5 cuts to the ball-side corner, and 4 slides across the lane looking for the ball. Player 3 screens for 1, who uses the screen and cuts to the opposite block. Player 4 is trying to get open in the area around the ball-side block, and 3 releases to the top to

look for the lob over the defense as well as to cover the break defensively (see figure 12.14).

The ideal pass is to 1 for the layup. However, if 2 sees that someone else is open before 1, he should pass the ball to that player. (Remember, the purpose of the play is to gain possession, not get a shot.) Once again, after 2 passes the ball in, he enters the court opposite the pass.

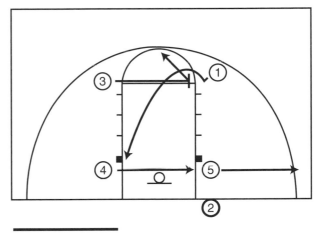
FIGURE 12.14 Box Out.

"T"

This play sets up a little differently, with 4 and 5 stacked in the lane right in front of the basket. On the hit, 4 spins around and cuts off 5 to the right corner of the free-throw line. The 2 player can inbound the ball directly to 4, or get it to 3, who hits 4 (see figure 12.15). (Once again, 1 is the safety on the play.) Once 4 has the ball, 5 shapes up in the lane looking for the feed at the post from 4.

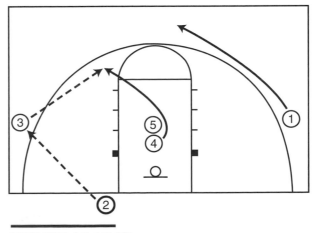
FIGURE 12.15 "T."

Special

This play revolves around the offensive players' ability to read the defense and take advantage of one of several options. The offense, on the hit, reads the defense. The first option is 5 setting an up screen for 4 and then coming back to the ball, as shown in figure 12.16. If 3 has a quick cut to the ball, he can make that cut while the screen is taking place. He may be able to slide in as his defensive player helps with the inside screen. Player 1 works on his own to get open. Player 1 is responsible for covering the fast break unless he receives the ball. In that case, break coverage falls to 3. Out of this set, any movement in which the offense reacts to the defense can be effective in getting a player open. For example, 5 could screen for 4 and then receive a screen from 1 that would have 5 coming to the ball-side block to get open.

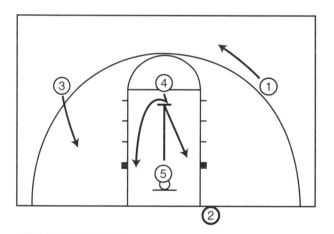

FIGURE 12.16 Special.

Special 2

Start from the same positions as Box Out. On the slap, 5 takes one step toward the rim, reverses direction, and pops to the corner looking for the inbounds pass from 2. After the pass, 2 steps under the rim. The 3 player, meanwhile, is moving to the opposite side of the free-throw line to screen for 1, who comes off the screen and receives the pass from 5 (see figure 12.17a). After setting the screen for 1, the 3 player can then join 4 to set a

double screen for 2, who comes off a single screen from 5 or double screen from 3 and 4 looking for the pass from 1 and the shot (see figure 12.17b).

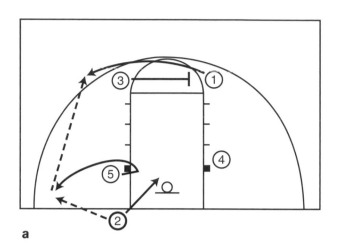

a

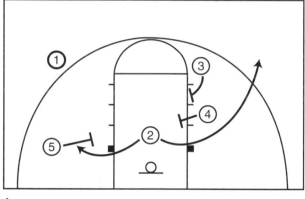

b

FIGURE 12.17 Special 2.

Box Double

Players start from the same positions as for Box Out. Player 1 pops to the corner to receive the pass from 2. Players 5 and 4 slide to the middle of the lane and set a double screen for 3, who rubs off the screen looking for the ball from 1 (see figure 12.18).

If 1 is overplayed and not open for the inbounds pass, then 3 should look for the lob pass from 2. After setting the screen, 4 and 5 must be ready to break out of the double and find open areas to become potential receivers. They may have to flash hard to the ball to help get it inbounds, or they could split into a high and low post. If 4's or 5's defender helps on 3 coming off the screen, then that unguarded post player should flash to the ball and seal any defenders for the feed from 1 or 2.

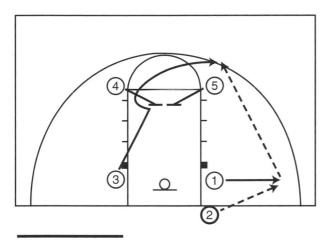

FIGURE 12.18 Box Double.

Box Option

In this option, the players run Box 2, but the screeners do not come back to the ball. Instead, after 1 receives the ball from 2 in the corner, 2 steps inbounds to see if he can get the immediate post feed from 1 (see figure 12.19). If the pass is not there, 2 screens across for 3, who comes hard across the lane looking for the ball from 1. Keep in mind that you can make changes to put specific players in specific roles to take advantage of their abilities (such as posting up 2 in this play).

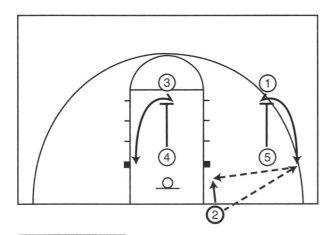

FIGURE 12.19 Box Option.

Line

You can see where this play gets its name. All of the players form a single line directly in front of the inbounds player (2). On the slap, 1 and 3 split, with 1 darting to the corner and 3 cutting across the lane to the opposite low post (see figure 12.20). At the same time, 5 turns around to set a screen for 4 to break into the clear.

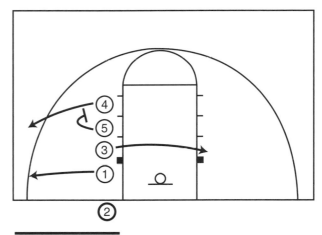

FIGURE 12.20 Line.

Inbounds Plays Versus Zone Defense

When inbounding against a zone, your players need to keep all of the principles of playing against a zone in mind. Remind them to look for gaps and to flash to be receivers. As with the man-to-man plays, these can also be run from anywhere on the court when you are facing a zone defense.

Wide

Player 5 seals one of the low players in the zone, and 1 and 2 dive into available open areas from behind the zone. Player 2 can also start higher on the wing and fade to the corner behind the zone. If 4 has problems getting the ball in, 3 screens the outside defender of the zone, and 5 pops out to the corner (see figure 12.21). Player 3 shapes up under the basket, looking for the feed from 5.

Another play, which we call Wide Option, uses the same formation but stacks 3 and 5 on the ball side. On the ball slap, 5 uses 3 to get open.

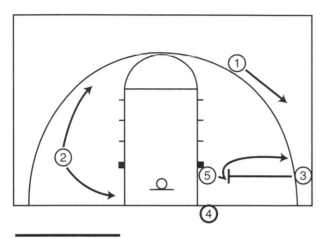

FIGURE 12.21 Wide.

Line

On the hit, 2 breaks to the corner and then fades to the top. Player 4 steps into the lane as if he is going to receive the lob from 1. Instead, 4 screens the middle defender of the zone; 5 slides in behind 4 and times the lob from 1 (see figure 12.22). Player 4 can even jump for the ball, but he must realize that the pass is intended for 5. Player 3 should look for open areas outside the lane.

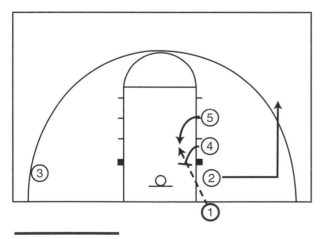

FIGURE 12.22 Line.

Stack

On the hit, the ball-side post (5) screens the middle defender in the zone, which allows the opposite post player (4) to come across the lane looking for the ball. Player 3 breaks to the ball-side corner, and 1 breaks to the opposite corner (see figure 12.23). This gives you a 1-4 set, which spreads the zone along the baseline. This alignment makes it difficult for the defense to take away every option.

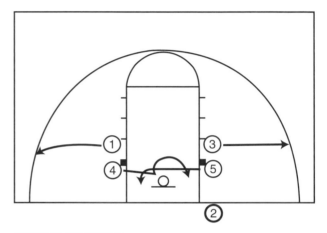

FIGURE 12.23 Stack.

Stack: Color Option

We trigger this option by calling for "Stack" and then yelling any color after that. On the ball slap, the ball-side post (5) sets the same screen as in regular Stack, but now 4 uses it to go high and be a receiver over the top of the zone. Players 5, 3, and 1 all have the same movement as in the original Stack (see figure 12.24). This option gives you a player (4) at

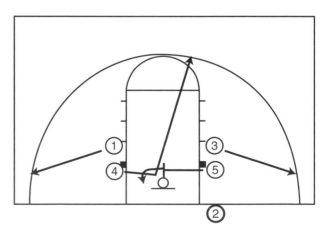

FIGURE 12.24 Stack: color option.

the point to cover the break if there is a turnover or a quick shot. Player 4 also serves as a receiver on the perimeter in case the zone decides to trap in the corners.

High Stack

This play sets up in the same alignment as regular Stack, but we move it back to the free-throw line to spread the defense out a little more. On the slap, 3 cuts to the corner. As with the other Stack plays, 5 screens for 4, who cuts off the screen toward 2 (see figure 12.25). The 1 player floats back out top as the safety valve to set up the offense if necessary and to prevent the other team from getting a fast break.

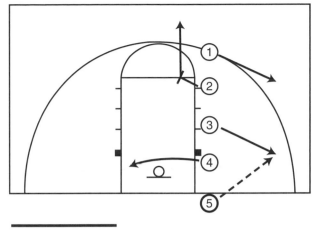

FIGURE 12.26 Load.

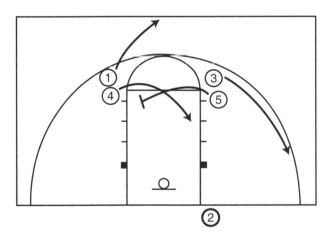

FIGURE 12.25 High Stack.

Load

On the hit, 4 clears away from the ball across the lane, and 3 breaks to the corner. Player 2 screens the top player in the zone so 1 can cut to the wing, then 2 clears to the top of the zone (see figure 12.26). This play gives you plenty of options to gain safe possession of the ball, which is the main priority in any out-of-bounds play. After 5 inbounds the ball to 3, 5 can get into quick post-up position in the area vacated by 4. If the ball is passed to 3 or 2, 4 can flash to the ball-side high post and create an immediate overload. If the defense attempts to trap the corner, you have three receivers, with 4 and 5 in scoring position.

Maryland

Begin in a 1-4 alignment. On the hit, 5 screens the ball-side guard in the zone or the low defender on the ball side of the zone. Player 1 uses the screen to find the gap in the zone. Player 4 then screens the top defender in the zone away from the ball, and 3 uses it to get open at the point or down on the baseline. Players 4 and 5, after the screen, flash into the open gaps looking for the ball (see figure 12.27). Player 2 passes in and enters opposite. The purpose of this play is to stretch the zone and create gaps into which your players can flash. With a quick reversal, you could get 2 the jump shot as he comes inbounds from behind the zone.

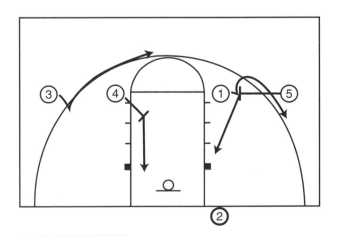

FIGURE 12.27 Maryland.

"L"

We call this play "L" because that's the alignment that the players begin in; 5 and 4 are on the same side as the inbounder (2), and 3 and 1 are stationed across the top. When 2 slaps the ball, 5 and 4 both set screens on their side of the zone. The 3 player uses the screens to get open and receive the pass from 2. He also takes the shot if he's open (see figure 12.28). The 1 player is again the safety valve.

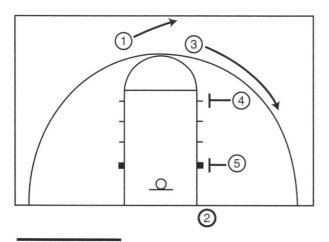

FIGURE 12.28 "L."

Sideline Inbounds Plays

All of the plays just described can be run from the sideline as well as under the basket. However, some other plays are effective only when inbounding from the sidelines. Universal inbounding principles—such as having a tall, firmly balanced inbounder and looking first for safe possession of the ball—still apply.

Box 3: Sideline

This is a different play than the Box 3 run from under the basket. On the hit, player 3 screens for 1 and then comes back to the ball to be a receiver. Player 5 back-screens for 4, who goes to the opposite wing. Player 5 then continues to the open area in the corner, as shown in figure 12.29.

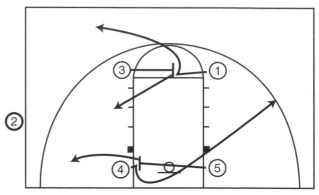

FIGURE 12.29 Box 3: Sideline.

Player 2 may be able to throw over the top of the defense to 4 for the jumper. If he is not able to do so, he still has three strong receivers coming to the ball. Player 2 could hit 1, who then looks for 4 coming off of 5's screen. Player 5 could then shape up on the ball-side block for the feed from 4 instead of continuing through to the corner.

Box 4: Sideline

This is also a different play than the Box 4 run from under the basket. On the hit, 3 screens for 1 and comes back to the ball. Player 5 uses 4's screen and clears through to the corner. The offense again has three receivers coming to the ball. Unlike in the Box 3 option, player 4 attempts to seal off his defender for the lob from 2, rather than cut to the opposite wing (figure 12.30). This pass should not be forced, however; the priority is safe possession of the ball.

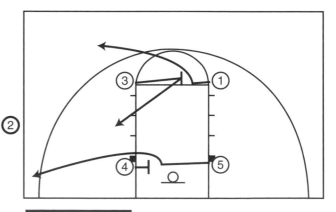

FIGURE 12.30 Box 4: Sideline.

Box Read

From the same initial alignment as Box 3 and Box 4, your offensive players read the defense to get open. Player 3 or 4 could flash straight to the ball, or these players could screen for each other. This option can be used against zone or man-to-man defenses to guarantee safe possession of the ball.

Rub

On the hit, 2 back-screens for 5. At the same time, 3 sets a screen for 4, then flashes back to the ball. After rubbing off 3's screen, 4 proceeds to the foul line, where he sets a screen for 5. Player 1 looks for the lob to 5 going to the basket or looks to hit 2 or 3 coming to the ball. Player 4 flashes to the open area after setting the screen for 5 so that he (4) can also be a receiver (see figure 12.31).

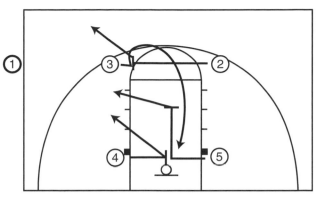

FIGURE 12.32 Rub Tight.

Triple

You can run this play anywhere along the sideline. On the hit, 2 screens for 3, who gets open in the backcourt (see figure 12.33). After

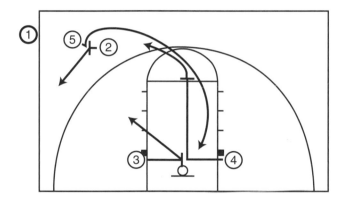

FIGURE 12.31 Rub.

Rub Tight

Start in a Box set and adjust your personnel to take advantage of their specific abilities. On the hit, 4 begins to screen for 5, and 2 back-screens for 3. Both screeners come back to the ball after setting their screens. Player 5 floats up to the foul line after the screen from 4, and then sets a second screen for 3 (see figure 12.32). Player 1 looks to lob the ball to 3 or to pass the ball in to any of the other players flashing to the ball.

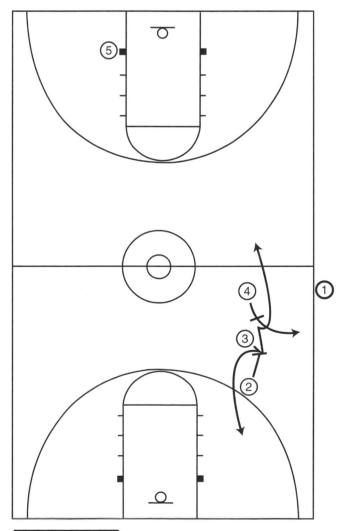

FIGURE 12.33 Triple.

setting the screen for 3, 2 then receives a screen from 4 and gets open going toward the basket. Player 4 comes back to the ball to be a receiver. Player 5 starts on the opposite block and is ready to flash to the ball as a receiver if he is needed. The triple stack should be positioned well off the sideline to allow the players plenty of room to get open and flash back to the ball.

Wide Box

On the hit, 2 screens for 1 and holds. Player 4 flashes to the ball, and 5 breaks to the sideline looking for the ball. The inbounder (3) can pass to 1, 4, or 5 for safe possession of the ball. If the pass goes to 4, he looks for 2 sneaking backdoor, as shown in figure 12.34. This option is often available because 5 has cleared the weak side to become a potential receiver. The backdoor can also work by inbounding the ball to 1, who passes to 4 flashing high, who then hits 2 for the layup.

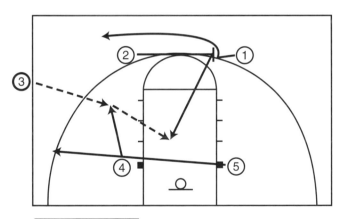

FIGURE 12.34 Wide Box.

Line: Sideline

Like Triple, you can use this play anywhere along the sideline. Player 2 calls "Line" and follows it with either the number "1" or "3." The number called specifies who will be the screener and who will be the cutter. For example, if "1" is called, player 1 (on the hit) sets the screen for 3 and then comes back to the ball. Player 5 sets a back screen for 4, who cuts to the basket looking for the deep pass. Player 5 shapes up to the ball after the screen, leaving three receivers moving toward the sideline (see figure 12.35). Player 4 keeps any center fielder busy and prevents double teams off the inbounds pass because the defense must concern themselves with protecting the basket.

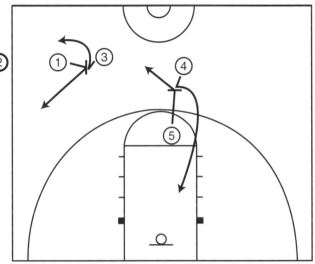

FIGURE 12.35 Line: Sideline (with a "1" call).

8 Play

I like to use this play in time and score situations. I call it the "8 Play" because it takes about eight seconds to run through each of the three options. On the hit, 4 diagonally screens for 5, who comes out as high as he needs to in order to catch the ball. Player 1 works on his own to get open, and 3 flashes hard to the ball. Everything starts when the ball gets to 5. Player 2 inbounds to 5 and then runs a hard backdoor cut with the help of a screen from 3, as shown in figure 12.36. The first scoring option is for 5 to hit 2 on the backdoor.

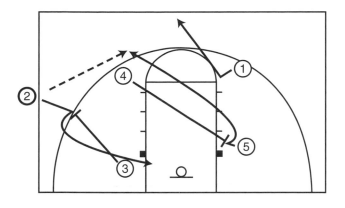

FIGURE 12.36 8 Play: option 1.

If that option is not available, player 3 circles around 5 looking for the handoff and playing two-player basketball with 5 (figure 12.37). This screen and roll is the second scoring option. If 5 cannot get the ball to 3, the entire right side of the floor is cleared out for 5 to take his defender one on one.

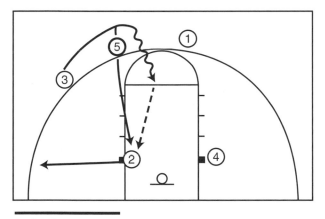

FIGURE 12.37 8 Play: option 2.

If there is no opportunity for the two-player game, 3 takes the handoff from 5 and penetrates to the opposite side of the floor. Player 3 looks for 2 coming off a double screen set by 4 and 1, who slid to the opposite block when 5 received the pass (see figure 12.38). The shot by 2 off the double screen is the third scoring option. If there is nothing available, the players enter into the half-court offense.

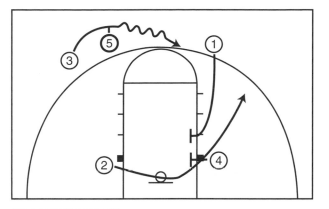

FIGURE 12.38 8 Play: option 3.

8 Play: Zone Options

The 8 Play can also be effective from the sideline against a zone in time and score situations. The primary difference is that you are likely to end up with a jump shot rather than an inside shot.

On the hit, 1 flashes across the top of the key to receive the pass from 2. After the pass, 2 cuts through the zone to the opposite side. Player 4 sets a screen on the low defender in the zone to help free 2 for the shot. The first option is to have 1 dribble, penetrate, and pass to 2 coming off the baseline screen (see figure 12.39).

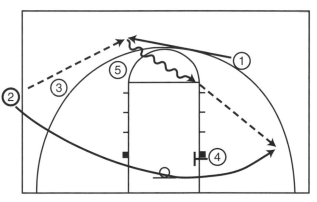

FIGURE 12.39 8 Play: zone option 1.

If nothing is available, 2 steps up to the wing so that 3 can cut through the zone into the corner. As 3 cuts through, 5 trails him into the post area and then flashes high to the ball side, giving you an overload. The second option is to hit 3 for the jumper from the corner on the ball side (see figure 12.40).

After 1 swings the ball to 2, 1 floats to the open area on the opposite side of the court and looks for the skip pass. So if the second option is not available, 2 can pass to 1 for the jump shot, or 1 can feed 4 or 5 as they follow the ball after the skip pass.

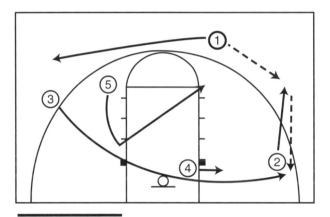

FIGURE 12.40 8 Play: zone option 2.

Color

On the hit, 5 screens for 3, and 1 screens for 2. Player 4 hits 2 and makes a hard cut to the basket, looking for the backdoor pass (see figure 12.41). If 4 does not receive the pass, he positions himself on the ball-side block.

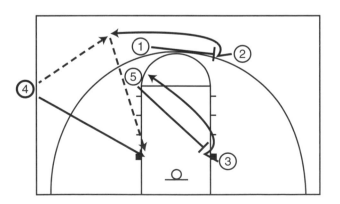

FIGURE 12.41 Color: option 1.

If the first option is not open, 2 reverses the ball to 1, who dribbles to penetrate the left wing. Player 5 sets the cross-screen for 4, who looks for the feed from 1. If 4 makes a curl cut, 1 may hit 5 as the defense recovers to defend 4 (see figure 12.42). Player 1 may also reverse the ball back to 2 to start the offense.

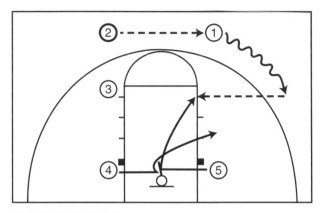

FIGURE 12.42 Color: option 2.

Color Quick

We also have a play in our Color series that we call Quick Option for situations in which only one or two seconds remain in the period. The play begins as regular Color does, but in this case, 4 can hit 5 on the curl in the lane after 5 has set the screen for 3 (see figure 12.43).

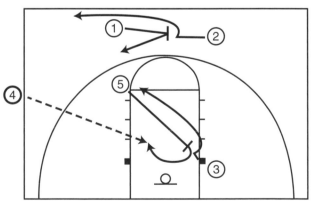

FIGURE 12.43 Color Quick.

PART IV

COACHING DEFENSE

CHAPTER 13 Teaching Defensive Positions and Sets

In previous chapters, I mentioned that I emphasize defense and rebounding to my players. Here's why: Over time, the teams with the best records are the teams that defend and rebound the best. Consequently, I believe that every player must be able to play good defense, no matter what the position.

In professional baseball's American League, each team is allowed to use a designated hitter—a player whose only job is to provide offensive punch and help the team score runs. That player does not have to play defense. But no such position exists in basketball. Every player on the court must be able to play smart defense and must be willing to give the all-out effort that often separates an average defensive player from a great defensive player.

For coaches who may not be blessed with an abundance of talent in a given year, defense can be a great neutralizer. A team of average talent can become a better-than-average team if it creates turnovers, forces the opposition's offense to work for everything it gets, and does not allow easy shots. But that won't happen unless every member of your team knows and executes proper defensive techniques and tactics.

As a coach, you should work with your players and motivate them to develop the desire to be great defensive players. This is where

you will earn your paycheck. You'll have to counteract the fact that in all sports offense gets the most glamour. And the only way to do that is to provide more attention and praise to the great defensive players on the team and constantly emphasize the benefits of a good team defense.

Position Skills

All players must be willing to work at defense and to develop good footwork, which should minimize the number of times they are out of position. Ideally, you look for quickness in all of your players. However, defenders must be able to match up against the size and skills of the players they are guarding. Here's a look at the most common attributes and responsibilities of each defensive position (these descriptions focus on man-to-man defense, but similar characteristics are required for playing zone).

Point Guard Often, the point guard (1) is the quickest player on your team and is therefore assigned to guard the quickest player on the opposing team. The 1 player is frequently one of the more knowledgeable players on the team and is often asked to be the team's leader on defense as well as offense. His feel for the game should enable him to take the proper defensive angles to slow down a fast break or prevent penetration.

When playing pressure defense, the point player is often the one who forces the opposing ball handler into the trap that the defense is trying to set up. He will also call the defensive signals, relaying messages and instructions from the bench to his teammates on the floor. In short, as on offense, the point guard is an extension of the coach on the court.

Shooting Guard   The 2 player (off-guard) is often assigned to the opposing team's best outside shooter. Therefore, he must be a good perimeter defensive player. This means that the 2 player must be mobile enough to follow his player around as he tries to free himself. In addition, the 2 player must be determined enough to work through or around picks that the opposing offense sets to get the ball into their shooter's hands.

The off-guard should also be more of a rebounder than the point guard for two reasons: (a) The player he's defending will often be playing closer to the basket; and (b) the player he's defending will shoot more often, thus the 2 player will have more blockout responsibilities, which should lead to more rebounding opportunities.

Small Forward   If the off-guard is not defending the other team's best shooter, that responsibility will most likely fall to the small forward (3). He, too, must be a good, mobile perimeter defensive player with enough quickness to stay with good outside shooters.

Occasionally, you are blessed with a small forward who can defend both the perimeter and the post effectively. It is not unusual for us to have a 3 who is a perimeter player at the offensive end of the court, but who is assigned to a post player on defense. Because the small forward is often juggling between post and perimeter, he must be intelligent enough to make the necessary adjustments. Also, because of his frequent post duties, the small forward should be a good defensive rebounder.

Power Forward   The power forward (4) is usually one of your bigger and more physical players. This is true on defense as well as offense. The 4 player should be able to play tough post defense on the opposing team's inside players. But, because he may also be forced to guard a forward who likes to play outside, the 4 should have the versatility to go out to the perimeter and play good defense. And, at times, he may be forced to switch to a guard if the other team executes a pick successfully.

As for inside play, the 4 player must be able to prevent easy inside buckets by sliding off his own player and stopping opposing players who have penetrated the lane. Finally, he must be an excellent rebounder who can crash the defensive boards whenever a shot goes up, then get the ball out to a guard to start the fast break.

Center   The 5 player should be your best inside defensive player and, along with the power forward, one of your top two defensive rebounders. The center must be strong and physical to prevent his player from getting a good inside position that could lead to an easy basket. He must be strong enough to block out effectively for rebounding purposes. The center should also be able to provide help defense on any perimeter players who have penetrated the lane; he should be a good enough shot blocker to give the offensive players something to think about when they take the ball inside. Like the power forward, your center should also be a good outlet passer who can start the break after pulling down a defensive rebound.

Types of Defenses

A coach can use countless varieties of defenses. But I recommend choosing the defense that best fits your team's abilities as your primary defense. Then identify two or three secondary defenses that will allow you to adjust to the many different situations that will arise during games.

Basic Man-to-Man

The most conventional defense used in basketball is the straight man-to-man defense in which each defender positions himself between the offensive player to whom he is assigned and the basket (see figure 13.1). In this defense, the weak-side players are sinking and jamming the middle to prevent defensive penetration with the ball and to make the offense take lower-percentage outside shots.

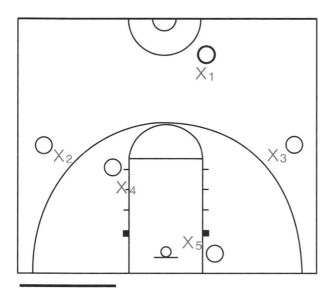

FIGURE 13.1 Basic man-to-man.

This basic defense is most effective against teams that do not have good outside shooters. It also gets the job done against teams that don't have the patience to run sound offenses and work for the open shot. Against teams that are patient, this defense can force them into longer possessions and therefore take some time off the clock. This may be an advantage if your team has the lead or a disadvantage if you are trailing.

The biggest weakness of this defense is that it does not create many turnovers. Also, this defense does not force the offense to make many adjustments; it does not dictate anything to the offense, other than stopping up the middle. It allows the opposition to run their offense, which is the main reason I do not like this defense. I also believe that the game has changed and rendered this basic

defense somewhat obsolete; players today are shooting the basketball too well for defenses to allow outside shots, and the addition of the three-point line has made those shots more costly to give up.

Pressure Man-to-Man

A defense I prefer instead of the straight man-to-man is the half-court pressure man-to-man, which has been made famous by teams such as North Carolina, Duke, and Indiana. I have been using this defense at DeMatha since the 1950s, and my team uses some form of it more than 90 percent of the time. O'Connell also primarily uses pressure man-to-man as its defense.

The only time I take our team out of the pressure man-to-man is when we

- want to use up the clock,
- face a team that plays poorly against a zone, or
- want to give the offense a different look.

From this defense, you can keep the offense off balance just by varying the intensity of the pressure in the man-to-man. You can turn the pressure up by playing the defense full court, or you can turn it down by picking up the offense at three-quarter court or half-court.

Sometimes I'll call for a traditional sagging man-to-man on defense one time, then the next time down the court I'll have the players pick right back up with the pressure man-to-man. We also use an entry defense in which our players let the offense bring the ball upcourt and successfully complete the first pass before turning on the pressure. You don't want to give the offense the same look every time down the floor. Stick with what's working well, but keep the opposition guessing.

The pressure man-to-man defense is similar to the regular man-to-man, the biggest difference being that we place extreme pressure on the ball and contest every single pass. Players position themselves between their opponent and the ball, but only when the player they are guarding is one pass away—receiving distance—from the ball. If the player they are guarding is more than one pass away, they should be clogging the middle (see figure 13.2).

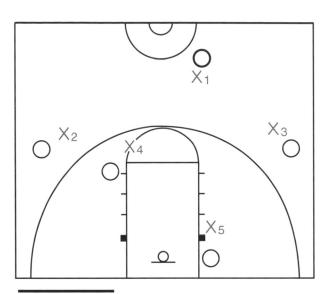

FIGURE 13.2 Pressure man-to-man.

What I like about this defense is the pressure element. It is designed to create turnovers and to drive teams almost completely out of their offense, forcing them to freelance. The defenders are on the attack at all times, always looking to create opportunities rather than reacting to what the offense is running.

Great pressure defense teams do not have to spend much time working against the opponent's offense in practice; the pressure will force the opponent out of that offense anyway. Great pressure can break most offenses and force teams into individual play.

The pressure man-to-man is extremely effective against teams that

- have suspect ballhandling,
- prefer to run a conservative offense and don't like to fast break,
- aren't as talented and quick as your team, and
- are not organized and disciplined offensively.

One of the risks with running a high-intensity pressure defense is that you are occasionally going to give up some easy shots, and even layups. Teams with excellent ball handlers can present problems for this defense, especially if those ball handlers are taller than your defenders and have a good view of passing lanes.

However, I believe the turnovers that result from this defense should outweigh the number of easy baskets you may give up in return. I generally figure that possession of the ball is worth about one point. So if you give away one layup but get three turnovers, you are still ahead of the game.

Another risk is that you stretch your defense over a wider area of the floor. If you are not careful, this can result in a rebounding disadvantage. On the other hand, if the defense is farther away from the basket, so is the offense. This helps neutralize any offensive rebounding advantage.

Finally, note that if your team is not in good condition, this defense will quickly tire your players.

Variations in the Man-to-Man Defense

Out of the man-to-man defense, you can add variations. From the pressure man-to-man defense, you can trap, play a switching man-to-man, or employ the run-and-jump. The run-and-jump is like a switching man-to-man, in which the defender nearest the ball runs toward the offensive player with the ball. The player guarding the ball then jumps over to the player left open by the defender. Unlike in the conventional switching man-to-man, the defenders switch before the offensive players can screen or crisscross. You can try this with a few individuals or with the entire team. You can also extend the pressure man-to-man defense three-quarter court or full court by using all of the same basic principles.

In addition, you can extend the straight man-to-man full court. Again, this probably will not result in any turnovers. But the advantage here is that it can slow the other team down, which can be helpful when trying to use up the clock or when playing a fast-breaking team.

Zone Defenses

Another type of team defense assigns all five defenders a particular area or zone to defend (see figure 13.3) rather than a particular offensive player. This defensive strategy can be implemented through various player alignments, the most popular being the 2-1-2, 2-3, 1-2-2, 1-3-1, and 3-2.

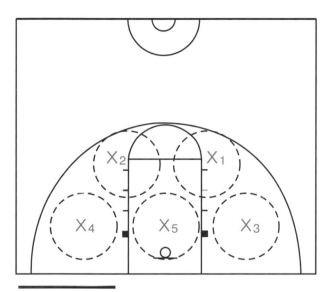

FIGURE 13.3 2-3 zone defense.

The biggest advantage to a zone defense is that it puts your defensive players exactly where you want them, regardless of where the offense puts its players. The offense does not dictate the floor position of the defenders. For example, a zone can ensure that your big players will always be near the bucket, even if the opposition's big players decide to go outside. In this particular case, the zone team would have the rebounding advantage with its big players always in position. And once the rebound is controlled, the zone alignment provides quick outlets for the fast break.

Zone defenses are often effective against teams with good inside players or poor outside shooters because most of the shots over the zone will come from the outside. Zones are also good for slowing teams down and taking time off the clock because the offense may have to take more time to get a good shot. Consequently, a zone can work quite well against a relatively impatient team that likes to make one or two quick passes and then shoot the basketball.

Some teams just do not like to play against a zone defense. In fact, the reason I first installed a zone at DeMatha was because several teams in our league hated to go against it. So I made sure those teams saw a zone. After all, one of the objectives of coaching is to force the other team to do things they do not work on in practice.

Zones lend themselves very well to trapping. Some of the best defenses today are half-court zone traps (see figure 13.4). Zone traps, or any of the other zones, can also be stretched from quarter-court to full court with the principles remaining intact.

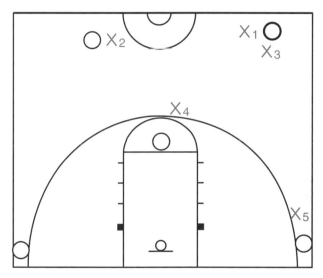

FIGURE 13.4 Half-court zone trap.

Zone defenses are susceptible against good outside shooting teams. The quickest way to bring a team out of a zone is to start hitting bombs right over it. The three-point line has stretched zones out even farther because no team can afford to give up uncontested three-pointers if the other team can make those shots.

THOUGHT FOR THE DAY

There is no glory in defense, just victory.

Even if the outside shots are missed, there is another potential problem. Although zones put defensive players in excellent rebounding position, there are no exact blockout responsibilities because the players are defending an area and not a player. This can leave a pathway for a slicing offensive player to slip through and grab an offensive rebound.

A somewhat less tangible weakness of a zone is that it does not present the individual challenge presented by a man-to-man. For example, a great man-to-man defender approaches every game thinking to himself, *I'm going to shut my player down tonight.* But the defender's feeling of individual responsibility is not as strong when an offensive player scores against a zone. The defender can think, *He didn't score against me. I wasn't guarding him.*

Also, if your team does not change ends of the floor very well, a zone can be vulnerable to a fast break. When playing a zone, the defenders must hustle back and set the zone up before the opposition's offense goes to work. If the offense gets there first or even at the same time, the zone is in trouble and will probably face a numbers disadvantage until a shot goes up or a foul is called.

Combination Defenses

Although 99 percent of all defenses are man-to-man or zone, there is a third category to consider: combination defenses. Because of their unorthodox principles, such defenses are often referred to as junk defenses.

One of the most popular combination defenses is the Box-and-One, shown in figure 13.5. In this defense, four of the players play a 2-2 zone (box) around the lane while the fifth player plays man-to-man on the opposition's best player.

The Diamond-and-Two has three players playing a zone in a triangular shape; the other two defenders are assigned to the opponent's best offensive players. And another combination defense, the 1-3-1 Chaser, has the point player chasing the ball all over the floor while the other players remain in their zones.

The biggest advantage to a junk defense is that it may catch the other team unprepared.

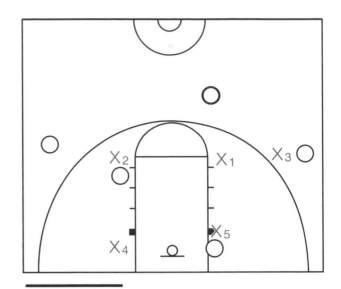

FIGURE 13.5 Box-and-One defense.

You may be able to disrupt their offense by showing them something that they have not seen or worked against in practice. Also, if a junk defense has been successful against that team before, you may take them out of the game mentally because they've had previous trouble with that particular defense. For example, the other team's best player may hate to play against the Box-and-One. Advance scouting should give you this kind of information.

The main weakness of junk defenses is lack of preparation. Chances are a junk defense is not going to be your primary defense; therefore, you may not get to spend much time perfecting it. If your players feel slightly unprepared with the junk defense, they will be less confident, which takes away the mental edge that the junk defense is supposed to provide. A well-prepared and patient offensive team may be able to work against the unfamiliar defense and still come away with a good shot.

My teams have faced many junk defenses over the years. One year, Gonzaga High School played a Box-and-One against our player John Gwynn. John scored 48 points against them, and we never saw another junk defense that season. (John, incidentally, went on to a great career at the University of Connecticut.)

AP Photo/Gerald Herbert

John Gwynn drives to the basket in a game against Syracuse in 1990.

Summary

How well your team plays defensively will determine its success. Great teams are always good defensive teams. This chapter included the following points to help you be a better coach of defensive techniques and tactics:

- All players should be able to play defense.

- The defensive point guard is usually your quickest player, is assigned to the opponent's quickest player, and is usually the floor leader on defense.

- The off-guard on defense is often assigned to the other team's best outside shooter.

- The small forward ideally can play both perimeter and post defense, and he can potentially be assigned to the other team's best outside shooter.

- The power forward should be a big, strong, inside defensive player who is a good rebounder.

- The center should be a strong defensive player in the post and should also be a ferocious rebounder.

- The conventional man-to-man defense effectively clogs the middle and forces outside shots, but it reacts to the offense instead of forcing the offense to react to it.

- The pressure man-to-man defense aims to force the opposing team out of its offense by applying continuous pressure on the player with the ball and on anyone who is one pass away from the ball.

- You can implement variations out of man-to-man defenses such as a full-court press, a switching man-to-man, or the run-and-jump.

- Zone defenses allow you to place defensive players in areas of your choosing, but these defenses are vulnerable to patient teams with good outside shooters.

- Blockout responsibilities are sometimes confusing in a zone.

- Some defenses are a combination of zone and man-to-man. These junk defenses can be useful in select situations, but they are not usually effective as primary defenses.

Teaching Defensive Skills

The best way to teach team defense to players is through a step-by-step process. Begin by concentrating on individual techniques. A team defense will be only as good as the individual defensive skills of the players on the team. That's why you should have your players constantly work on their individual defensive fundamentals.

Stance

The most basic defensive fundamental is the proper stance, and this is where you should begin your instruction. Teach your players to slightly stagger their feet, with one foot slightly ahead of the other (like a boxer's stance). Their feet should be at least shoulder-width apart, and their weight equally distributed on both feet (which will help them maintain their balance during the game). The knees should be bent, with the thighs at about a 45-degree angle to the floor.

Players must learn to stay low while in the defensive stance. This will make them quicker, stronger, and more explosive. A player's back should be fairly straight, and his head should be up and directly over the shoulders. This will also help with balance, which is the key to a good defensive stance. Anything that takes away from a player's balance detracts from his defensive ability.

Finally, players should keep their hands in front of their body with their palms up (figure 14.1). This gives the dribbler something to worry about. Players should not attempt to reach in and steal the ball because doing so destroys their balance and, thereby, their ability to contain the ball.

FIGURE 14.1 Defensive stance.

Steps

Once your players have the proper stance, you should next teach them the steps necessary to contain and pressure the ball handler.

Players will need to be able to perform these basic steps to fulfill their defensive duties: retreat step, advance step, and swing step.

Retreat Step

The first defensive footwork skill that players need to learn is the retreat step. This move is essential for defending a player who makes a right or left move toward the basket.

The player should begin in the proper defensive stance with one foot slightly in front of the other. The player then executes the retreat step by pushing off his front foot and taking a step backward with the rear foot (figure 14.2a), then sliding the front foot back to reestablish position and balance (figure 14.2b). A defender must stay low while taking the retreat step and should never bring the feet any closer together than shoulder width. While retreating, the player should not do anything to destroy his balance, such as bringing his feet together, rising out of his stance, or hopping instead of sliding the feet.

Advance Step

The advance step can make your players actors instead of reactors on defense. If properly taught, this move will allow your players to control and dictate what the offense does. The offensive players will be too concerned about reacting to the defense to initiate any moves against your defensive players.

After receiving the ball, a good offensive player will get in the triple-threat position with the opportunity to drive, shoot, or pass. I want my players to eliminate as many offensive possibilities as they can by forcing the offensive player to immediately put the ball on the floor. This is the object of the advance step.

The advance step is, simply, the opposite of the retreat step. It is performed by pushing off the back foot while stepping forward with the front foot (figure 14.3a), then sliding the back foot forward (figure 14.3b). Again, players should keep their feet shoulder-width apart to maintain good balance.

FIGURE 14.2 Retreat step.

FIGURE 14.3 Advance step.

When taking the advance step, a player must also be prepared to immediately execute the retreat step to stay between the dribbler and the basket. Both the retreat step and advance step are based on two simple movements: step and then slide.

By taking the advance step, the defensive player will force the offensive player to dribble the ball. Depending on how he decides to play him, the defender could then force the offensive player into a number of other situations. For example, the defender could take a retreat step. The offensive player, having used his dribble on the initial advance step, will probably be forced to shoot with the defender staying off him and giving him the shot; or the defender could decide to keep the pressure on the offensive player and force him to drive. In both instances, the defensive player is initiating, and the offensive player is reacting to him.

Emphasize to your players that you want them to use defensive footwork to control, rather than just stay with, their player. You want them to force the opponent's offense to play a certain way—a way that makes it less effective. Proper execution of the advance and retreat steps increases your players' chances of shutting down the opposition.

Swing Step

Most offensive players are instructed to drive in the direction of the defensive player's front foot. The swing step is a defensive maneuver to counter this attack and also counter an offensive player's change of direction. This move will help defenders avoid getting beat by an offensive player slicing to the basket.

Players execute the swing step by pivoting on their back foot (figure 14.4a) while swinging their opposite elbow and front foot in the direction taken by the offensive player (figure 14.4b). From this action, the defensive player regains offense-defense-basket position and continues to stay ahead of the offensive player. Teach your players to stay low while executing the swing step. If they come up and out of their stance, they will be slower to react and more likely to be beaten by the offensive player.

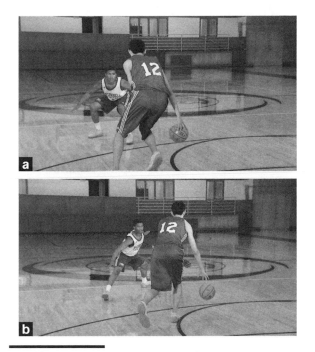

FIGURE 14.4 Swing step.

Defense on the Ball

We have one rule for the player guarding the ball: Don't get beat. Although we emphasize ball containment, defenders must apply "intelligent" pressure on the ball. This means that players should not defend offensive players so loosely that they can pass or shoot as they please, nor so tightly that the defenders cannot prevent drives to the hoop.

However, if one of your players gets beaten on defense, he is by no means out of the play. Tell him to get out of his defensive stance, pick out a point on the floor that he can get to before the offensive player, and run to that spot. Otherwise, if the player stays in his defensive stance, he will never recover. The offensive player will use his body to close the gap and keep the defensive player on his back. But if the defender has run to the point ahead of the offensive player and then gotten into the defensive stance, he can regain control of the situation. So an on-ball defensive player who has been beaten should first get in front of the dribbler (figure 14.5a), then reestablish position and stance to contain him (figure 14.5b), and finally force the ball handler in a particular direction by using the proper footwork (figure 14.5c).

FIGURE 14.5 Recovery after getting beat.

Footwork Drills

Defense is played with the mind, heart, and feet. The mind tells you what to do, the heart gives you the desire to do it, and the feet put you in the proper position to execute it. The most important physical skill in good defense is footwork. Therefore, a coach must have a series of drills designed to familiarize players with the proper footwork to develop quickness of foot.

SLIDE

We begin every year with this drill to review the importance of defensive footwork and to eliminate any bad habits that the players may have picked up over the summer.

**Defending a Player
With the Ball**

These are the main points to emphasize to your players about individual defense:

- Stay low.
- Stay balanced, with your feet staggered, shoulder-width apart.
- Move your feet in a step and slide sequence.
- Pressure and contain the ball.
- Dictate and control the moves of the ball handler. The left foot forward forces the dribbler left; the right foot forward forces the dribbler right.
- Keep your chest open to the offensive player.
- Keep your head up.

The coach stands under the basket, facing the team; the players are spread out across the floor in several lines. Each player begins with the left foot forward. After players get in their defensive stance, the coach gives them one of three instructions: advance, retreat, or swing. On hearing the coach's instruction, the players execute either one advance step, one retreat step, or one swing step. After they have completed one step, the players stay in their defensive stance and await the next instruction.

After players have become skillful at these steps, you or one of your coaches should take a ball and dribble slowly down the court. Carefully observe your players to see if they react to your dribble with the proper defensive step. Remind them that on any offensive attack step, such as the jab step, they should take a retreat step so that they don't give the offensive player an opening. Also remind them to keep their chest open to the ball and to stay low as they advance, retreat, and swing. As you dribble downcourt, change directions to work the players on their swing step, and use the pull-back dribble to work on their advance step.

DIRECTIONAL DRILL

To help players develop the ability to change direction quickly, this drill forces the players to rapidly execute a series of defensive steps.

Line your players up as you did in the slide drill and have them assume the defensive stance. The drill begins on your whistle. You face the players and point either left, right, front, or back. Your players must then keep moving in the direction you point until you point in a different direction. If you point at them, they retreat; if you point over your shoulder, they advance; if you point left or right, they slide laterally in that direction. (Remind players that they should point their lead foot in the direction they are moving in order to avoid ankle injuries if they have to stop quickly.)

Once again, the players should stay low, keep their feet shoulder-width apart, and keep their head up to see your instructions.

HEY!

This is one of my favorite drills and one that the team also enjoys. It combines into one drill all of the basic steps of defensive footwork. Players get to work on the advance step, retreat step, and swing step—while having some fun.

Stand on the baseline under the basket and have your players facing you in three lines across the floor. The players should assume the defensive stance, each player with the same foot forward. When you blow your whistle, the team responds quickly by executing an advance step while simultaneously yelling, "Hey!" to get in the habit of challenging the shooter. The players follow the advance step with a retreat step, a swing step, and then two retreat steps, each on your whistle. When they have completed these five steps, they are still in a good defensive stance, and the opposite foot is now their front foot. They are prepared to begin the process again on your whistle. Repeat until the team has traveled the length of the floor.

Again, observe players to see that they are properly executing each step. Remind play-

ers to keep their head up, stay low, maintain balance, and point their toes in the direction they are headed.

Quickness Drills

Basketball is fast becoming a game of quickness (no pun intended). Although being a good defensive player depends greatly on other factors as well (hard work, desire, and determination), becoming quicker can only make your players better defensive players. Contrary to what some may think, quickness can be improved. Here are a number of drills that will enhance your players' quickness.

THOUGHT FOR THE DAY

Be careful of the choices you make because the choices you make, make you.
–Joe Wootten

MACHINE GUN

You can do this with an individual or with the whole team spread out in several lines across the floor. The players assume a good defensive stance. At the sound of your whistle, the players move their legs up and down as rapidly as possible. The sound of each foot alternately tapping the floor is similar to the rapid fire of a machine gun.

Remind players to get their knees up high for maximum benefit from this drill. See how many times a player's right foot can hit the floor in 15 seconds, then double the figure to get the total number of times both feet hit the floor. Use these numbers to chart improved quickness. Repeat as needed.

DIRECTIONAL MACHINE GUN

The players start by performing the machine gun drill. You then point either left or right; the players follow your signal, turn in that direction, and turn back to you as quickly as they can. Remember that the players should continuously do the machine gun throughout the drill.

LINE JUMPS

Have your players pick out one of the lines on the floor and stand next to it. Making sure they keep their feet together, see how many times players can jump back and forth over the line in 15 seconds. Begin by having players jump side to side, followed by front to back.

LANE SLIDES

Position players on one side of the lane in a defensive stance. You can run this drill simultaneously at both ends of the court with as many players as you prefer. Players slide from one side of the lane to the other while in a defensive stance. When their lead foot touches the line on the opposite side of the lane, they stop and start back across.

TRIANGLE

With an assistant helping, you can do this drill simultaneously at both ends of the court. Line up three players on the foul line, facing the basket with their left foot forward. We have found that using more than three players at each station generally crowds the players involved.

On your whistle, the players take two retreat steps, a swing step, two lateral steps to the left, then two advance steps back to the foul line extended. Their right foot should now be the lead foot. Repeat three times. After the third time, the players should turn and sprint to the far foul line to repeat the drill there. Have another group of three fill their spots on the original end.

CROSS

Put your players in one single-file line under the basket along the baseline. On your whistle, the players advance step and slide to half-court, staying in a defensive stance with their right foot forward. Once they touch the midcourt line, they take one slide to the right and retreat step to the foul line. They then swing open and slide to the sideline on their right, keeping their lead (right) foot pointed in the direction they're headed. After they touch the sideline, they take a retreat step,

then they slide laterally across the court to the other sideline (see figure 14.6). After they have completed the circuit, they turn and jog back to the baseline.

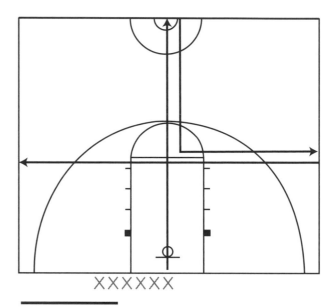

FIGURE 14.6 Cross.

Keep your players well spaced in this drill. As one player reaches the foul line, the next player can begin sliding forward. Anywhere from 6 to 10 players can be involved in the drill at one time. They must talk and communicate to each other to avoid running into one another at the crossing point. Communication is an important part of any successful team defense, and this drill helps you to emphasize this to your players.

FULL-COURT 1-ON-1

This is the most effective drill for developing your players' individual defensive skills. Position all of your players behind the baseline and have them divide themselves into pairs. Each pair will get one ball.

One player stands behind the baseline, turns and faces the defender, and attacks out of the triple-threat position. The defensive player's objective is to pressure and contain the dribbler, keeping his hands active in case of a free ball, and not allowing the dribbler to advance the ball upcourt without trying to dictate the pace of the dribble. The defensive player turns the dribbler, forcing him to change directions as many times as possible on the trip upcourt. You want the trip to be as long and difficult as possible for the dribbler—one he won't likely forget the next time his team has the ball.

The next pair does not begin until the previous group passes the opposite foul line. When the entire team has reached the opposite baseline, the players switch roles (offense to defense and vice versa) and repeat the drill in the other direction.

Do not allow the same players to face each other every day. Variety makes for stiffer competition, and it gives each player an opportunity to play against varying levels of quickness.

Also, when running this drill, you should emphasize the following points to the players:

- Be one arm's length away from the offensive player.
- Stay ahead of the ball (dictate and dominate).
- Constantly put pressure on with the hands (without losing balance), and keep the feet moving by sliding.
- Play the ball from the floor up, with palms up and fingers jabbing at the ball.
- Turn the dribbler by sliding in front of his intended path.
- Do not cross your feet or bring them together; you'll lose your balance.

- Do not turn your head or your back to the ball.
- Turn the dribbler, forcing him to change or reverse his direction (a basic rule in our trapping defense).
- If you get beat, pick out a point ahead of the offensive player, run to that point, then pick up the dribbler.

In teaching this drill, you are beginning to build your half-court and full-court team defenses. It all starts here, because every player must be able to contain the opposing offensive player if your team defenses are to be effective.

Summary

The proper execution of individual techniques is essential for defensive success. Emphasize these fundamentals at all levels of your program:

- The most basic defensive fundamental is a proper stance.
- Steps used to contain and pressure the ball handler include the retreat step, advance step, and swing step.
- Defenders must apply "intelligent" pressure on the ball to avoid getting beat.
- When it comes to playing good defense, footwork and quickness are essential.

Once players have grasped the individual defensive principles and skills presented in chapters 13 and 14, you'll need to show them how to apply those principles and skills as part of a five-player unit. Find a convenient method of identifying your defenses so that every player clearly understands exactly what you have in mind.

A numerical system suits our purposes best. In this system, a double-digit number is associated with a particular half-court defense. A code beginning with 2 indicates a man-to-man defense; a 3 identifies a trapping zone defense; a 4 identifies a straight zone defensive series; a 5 indicates a trapping man-to-man defense; and a 6 identifies a switching man-to-man defense. For example, this is the numbering system for man-to-man defenses:

- 22-Regular = standard man-to-man
- 22-Tough = pressure man-to-man
- 23 = regular trap
- 25 = Blitz Trap
- 26 = Blitz Switch

In addition, we divide the court into four areas to identify where players are to pick up the offensive team (see figure 15.1). If I call for the defense to guard in the 4 area, the players pick up full court; in the 3 area, they pick up at three-quarter court; in the 2 area, they pick up at half-court; and in the 1 area, they pick up at the top of the three-point arc. So, 22-Regular in the 2 area signals a half-court, man-to-man defense.

In this system, 25 is our Blitz Trap, and 26 is our Blitz Switch. When playing against a team that plays out of a 1-4 set, you may want to use the Entry defense, which allows the offense to complete the first penetrating pass. These defenses and others will be covered in more depth later in this chapter.

This defensive coding system is very effective because it can cover not only everything you might use defensively, but also everything you are likely to encounter in games throughout the season.

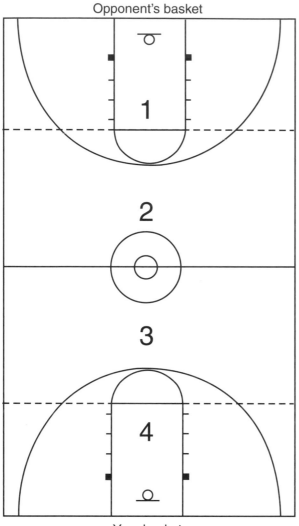

Opponent's basket

Your basket

FIGURE 15.1 Defensive court areas.

Xs and Os of Man-to-Man Defense

Our primary defense is 22-Tough, a pressure man-to-man deny defense with help-side rotation. This defense makes offensive players work to get the ball and, ideally, denies them the ball as we overplay the passing lanes. Good defensive players force their opponents to work very hard for everything they get.

One objective of the 22-Tough defense is to invite the backdoor pass. Such a pass often appears available to the offense because defenders position themselves in passing lanes and off their player (figure 15.2). However, with proper weak-side positioning,

the defense should be able to pick off most backdoor passes. And, by preventing passes to cutters, 22-Tough places even more pressure on offensive players to get open on the perimeter. To extend this overplay full court, we simply call for 22-Tough in the 4 area (see chapter 16). The same pressure man-to-man principles apply, except that the players now deny passes all over the court.

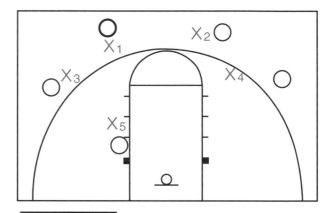

FIGURE 15.2 22-Tough.

In 22-Regular, defenders play man-to-man but position themselves between the offensive players and the basket instead of between offensive players and the ball, as is done in 22-Tough (figure 15.3). The 22-Regular allows offensive players to catch the ball, but defenders should never get beaten by the dribble or the backdoor cut. The basic rule of this defense is for the defenders to keep everything in front of them.

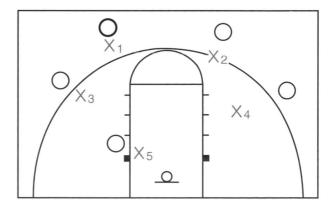

FIGURE 15.3 22-Regular.

Two of the best variations on the 22-Tough are the Blitz Switch (26) and the Blitz Trap (25). These are most effective when you want to

- create turnovers,
- control tempo,
- make strong offensive players give up the ball,
- disrupt the offensive team's patterns and timing,
- wear down the offensive players so they will not be as strong at the end of the game, and
- force weaker offensive players to handle or shoot the ball more.

When your team is in 22-Tough, the player guarding the ball as it crosses midcourt should force the ball to one side and keep the dribbler on that side. This establishes which defenders should be denying the ball to their player and which defenders should be off their player and on the help side. Forcing the ball to one side also creates opportunities for you to execute the Blitz Switch and Blitz Trap.

Blitz Trap—25

Let's look at an example of how a team can execute Blitz Trap. X1 plays on the dribbler's left side as he crosses midcourt. This overplay pressure forces the ball handler to the right, where X2 is prepared to trap him. When the dribbler is three strides away from X2, X2 runs at him under control and in a defensive stance to complete the trap. As he leaves his player, X2 should begin to yell loudly to signal to his teammates that the trap is on and the rotation should begin. This also helps to unnerve the dribbler to the point where he will sometimes pick up the dribble, thereby putting himself in an even more difficult situation.

After X1 and X2 have contained the dribbler within a certain area, they close the trap, remaining balanced and staying low to keep the ball handler within the trap. The trap should form a V with the open side away from the scoring area (see figure 15.4). Remind your players that they can maintain the trap by moving their feet, not by pushing or holding the offensive player with their hands or arms.

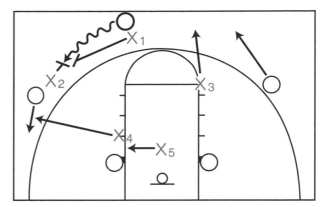

FIGURE 15.4 Blitz Trap.

When the offensive player picks up the dribble, the defenders close the trap even more, keeping their feet active and cutting off the passing lanes. They keep both of their hands together (following the movement of the ball) and avoid the temptation to reach in and try to make a steal. Reaching would cause them to lose their balance, giving the offensive player open passing lanes. Reaching in can also be called a foul and thus can let the offensive player off the hook.

Patience by the two players trapping the ball allows the rotation to take place. Turnovers will occur when the trap forces a hurried decision or a bad pass; the rotating players will be moving through the passing lanes to steal the ball. The defense may also force the offensive player into a violation (travel, double dribble, five-second call) or a charge.

The defenders begin their rotation as soon as they see X2 leave his player to trap the dribbler. Player X4 leaves to intercept the pass to X2's player, X5 rotates over to take the ball-side post, and X3 anticipates the off-wing going to the ball and denies him the pass.

Note that this rotation leaves open the farthest offensive player away from the trap. That's the risk you run in using the Blitz Trap defense. We take the chance that with enough pressure on the passer he will not be able to pick out the open player. If he does spot him, then your players must adjust as best as they can. Note that only a high-post defender does not get involved in the rotation.

Let your players know that because this is a gambling defense, the offense will score occasionally. However, your players should also force enough turnovers to make up for the points they allow.

If the trap is broken with the pass or the dribble, then the defensive players must play help and recover until the defense has readjusted and every offensive player is being guarded. The defenders must talk and move to get back to their players as quickly as possible.

Blitz Switch—26

The Blitz Switch differs from the Blitz Trap in two major ways. First, the Blitz Switch involves only two players. The other players do not rotate to the next available receiver, although a player is encouraged to anticipate and make a steal through a passing lane if he has the angle to do so. Second, X1, instead of forming a trap with X2, will break off from the player he is guarding and pick up X2's player (see figure 15.5).

Aside from these two principles, the Blitz Trap and the Blitz Switch are executed similarly. X1 overplays one of the dribbler's sides to direct the ball toward a teammate. Caution the point defender not to play so far to one side of the ball handler that he gets sliced to

the basket. He still must contain the ball. If the offensive point guard insists on going to the side of the overplay, X1 will simply run the switch with the defensive player on that side of the floor.

When the dribbler is three strides away from X2, X2 runs at him and executes the Blitz Switch. Again, he should begin to yell as he leaves his player to signal that the Blitz Switch is on. As X2 runs at the ball handler, he should come in under control and in a defensive stance so that he does not overrun him. If he does not contain him, the purpose of the Blitz Switch is defeated.

When X2 reaches the dribbler, X1 switches off and runs through to pick up X2's player. This is very effective after the Blitz Trap has been run a few times. Because the dribbler sees X2 release from his player to execute the blitz, the dribbler will attempt to dish the pass off quickly. If X1 is alert, he may be able to pick off that pass. Also, if the offensive team is beating your Blitz Trap by passing off before your players complete their rotation, the Blitz Switch can be an effective way of controlling the tempo of the game without leaving players open to be receivers.

Entry

Entry is used against a 1-4 offensive set that is trying to take advantage of your defense by spreading it out, taking away the help side, and setting up backdoor opportunities. The purpose of the Entry defense is to eliminate the offensive team's ability to turn backdoor passes into layups; instead, it allows the completion of the first penetrating pass to the wing or high post. The completion of the pass to the wing also establishes the ball side and help side of the court so the defense can adjust accordingly. As soon as the first pass has been made, your team can shift back to 22-Tough or whatever other defense you call.

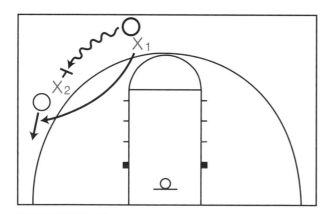

FIGURE 15.5 Blitz Switch.

Fist and Fingers

This defense seeks to trap either the pass or the dribble as the ball is entered into the half-court offense. (The full-court version of Fist and Fingers is discussed in chapter 16.) At times you may want your players to trap only the pass, or at other times only the dribble. Both options are possible from this defense. You can also call for your team to only trap in specific places (corners, midcourt line, below the foul line extended).

To create the trap off the pass, I often have my team play our Entry defense, which allows the completion of the first pass so the trap can take place. The rotation is the same as when running a 25 (Blitz Trap). Timing is critical if a turnover is to be created. The rotation must start as the ball is leaving the passer's hands and the nearest defensive players are beginning their attack and double team on the receiver (see figure 15.6).

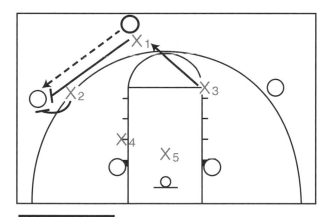

FIGURE 15.6 Fist and Fingers: half-court trap off the pass.

Players should only trap off the dribble if they are at least three running strides away from the ball.

Essentials of Pressure Team Defense

Emphasize these principles to players as you prepare them to perform as a defensive unit:

- Be in excellent physical condition.
- Concentrate!
- Talk to each other on defense.
- Be ready to play; don't need to get ready to play.
- Pressure the ball. This will cut the ball handler's vision in half.
- Stop penetrating passes.
- Dig (sag) to help if the ball enters the post.
- Help and recover.
- Stop the offense from reversing the ball.
- Force the ball outside.
- Move when the ball moves.
- Play aggressively and with enthusiasm.
- Don't allow the offense to play in straight lines.
- Stop moves to the basket.
- See the ball and the offensive player.

Pressure Defense Positioning

Being in the proper position and knowing the responsibilities associated with that position are crucial to good team defense. A player in correct position has an excellent chance of making the right play. Conversely, a player who is even a half step out of position is prone to committing a foul or surrendering a basket.

THOUGHT FOR THE DAY

Ninety percent talk about what they are going to do; ten percent go out and do it.
—Henry Ford

For a pressure man-to-man defense to be successful, each defensive player on the court must know and be able to execute various responsibilities. These responsibilities are constantly changing, depending on the offensive player being guarded and his position in relation to the ball's position.

Defending the Ball

The player guarding the ball should put intelligent pressure on the ball handler in an effort to stop the dribble. The defender should attempt to make the player put the ball on the floor, and then force him to pick it right back up for a "dribble used." See chapter 14 for the steps necessary to contain and pressure the ball handler.

Defending One Pass Away

The defender whose offensive player is one pass away from the ball should be positioned between that player and the ball. The defender should also be slightly off the offensive player. From this position, the defender decreases the offensive player's quickness and gives himself more time to recover and contest the backdoor cut. The defender's chest should face the offensive player, and his back foot should be positioned so that it cuts the offensive player in half. The defender's front foot, outside arm, and hand should be in the passing lane (figure 15.7).

Denied the ball this way, the offensive player is forced to go backdoor, where the help-side defense is positioned. This overplay position also allows the defense to continue to dictate and control the tempo of the game. But to do so, defenders must always see both the ball and their player while they are in the overplay position.

FIGURE 15.7 Defending one pass away.

This type of defense makes it difficult for offensive players to get open. An offensive player can take two or three full steps toward the basket before his defender is required to take a step to contest the pass. Not having to react to every single step of the offensive player also allows the defender to shut down the pass to his player off a V-cut, which many offenses rely on to get started.

Defending Two Passes Away

The defender whose offensive player is two passes away from the ball should have one foot in the foul lane. He should position himself to see both his player and the ball. This puts the defender in position to either stop the penetration on the ball side of the court or to react to the lob pass to his player.

Defending Three Passes Away

When a defender is guarding an offensive player who is three passes away from the ball, the defender should position himself in the lane. From this location, the defender is in the best possible spot to stop the ball-side drive.

Rotation

Following are the most important rules for players to remember when they are forced to rotate in the pressure defense:

1. The high post never gets involved in the rotation (if he did, no one would be left to pick up his man).

2. The low post, off-forward, and off-guard rotate one offensive player closer to the ball.

3. If the ball goes into the post, defenders who are one pass away collapse and dig in, then retreat to their correct positions once the ball is back on the perimeter.

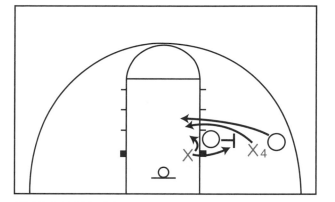

FIGURE 15.8 Getting over the top of a screen.

Rules of Man-to-Man Pressure Team Defense

Here are some important rules when playing man-to-man pressure team defense:

- Do not let offensive players catch the ball. If they do catch the ball, put aggressive but intelligent pressure on the ball.

- Get the dribbler to pick up his dribble and close up on him.

- Completely overplay the first receiver. Get off the player and toward the ball with one hand in the passing lane.

- When the offensive player is not an immediate receiver (two or more passes away), be well off the player and in position to help or deny the flash.

Defense Against the Screen

Any time an offensive player sets a screen, the defensive players must talk to one another. A lack of communication results in confusion and missed assignments, which means uncontested shots for the offense.

When defending screens, players must follow two rules:

1. If the screen is attempted inside the scoring area (three-point line), get over the top of it (figure 15.8).

2. If the screen is attempted outside the scoring area, get through the screen by having the defender guarding the screener take a step off his player to let his teammate through (figure 15.9).

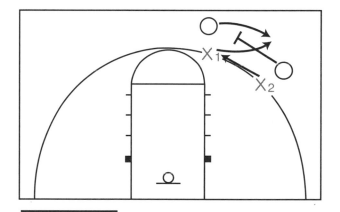

FIGURE 15.9 Getting through a screen.

Defensive players will not always be able to follow these rules, and that is when communication becomes especially important. At times, you may have to tell them to get over the screens even outside the scoring area if the offense is screening for a hot three-point shooter. Obviously, you can't allow a good three-point shooter to have a lot of room to get off his shot.

Team Defense Drills

Although teams may have off nights offensively, with hustle and hard work, team defense can always be consistent. Team defensive drills are important for establishing communication and cohesion among team members. The following drills are ones we've found to be successful in our practices.

HORSESHOE

This drill teaches your players their basic responsibilities in the 22-Tough defense. Designate two offensive guards, two defensive guards, two offensive wings, and two defensive wings. In the early stages of practice, your players will get a better picture of the defensive rotation if you do not include the post players. Make all of your players participate in the drill to become familiar with the rotation, because even your post players may be forced to guard a wing in some situations. Position your offensive players as shown in figure 15.10, with the two guards and two forwards above the foul line.

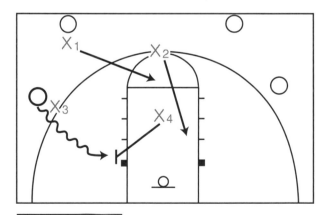

FIGURE 15.10 Horseshoe: drive by wing.

Initially, have the offensive players remain stationary as the defensive players adjust to where the ball is on the court. This allows your players to learn how to play position and help-side defense, and it makes it possible for you to teach as the drill is being run. Because this is a teaching drill, your defensive players should allow the passes to be completed to the offensive players.

Tell the offensive team to pass the ball around the perimeter until they hear the whistle, at which time whoever has possession of the ball holds on to it. The defense is allowed to continue to move after the whistle to gain proper defensive position. Now, you can examine the defense to make certain that each defensive player has adjusted his position with respect to the location of the ball. On your command, the offensive team once again moves the ball, and the process is repeated.

After you are certain that each player on the team knows the position he should be in with respect to the ball, it is then time to show how the defense rotates when a backdoor cut is attempted. On your command, the wing should drive to the basket.

The defender guarding the ball (X3) allows the wing to drive. The help-side forward (X4) sprints across the lane to stop the drive. Then X4 yells as loudly as he can as he approaches the dribbler. This yell serves two purposes: (a) It distracts the dribbler, which may cause him to pick up his dribble or even commit a turnover; and (b) it alerts the other defenders that the rotation is on.

X4 should stop the offensive player outside the lane. If the dribbler is allowed into the lane, too many problems are created for the defense. To keep the drill going, the offensive player should not shoot unless he has an uncontested layup. If he is stopped along the baseline, the ball is reversed.

When X4 challenges the drive, X2 rotates down the lane to seal off X4's offensive player—the weak-side wing. X1 moves toward the foul line to protect against an open player in this dangerous scoring area.

If the offensive player shoots, the blockout assignments correspond with the position of the players after rotation. X4 blocks out the shooter; X2 blocks out the weak-side wing; X1 blocks out the nearest guard. After correcting any errors, have the players reset and begin passing the ball around the perimeter once again.

Rotation from the guard position is slightly different. If X1's player drives to the outside, X3 must stop the dribbler (see figure 15.11). If X3 cannot get there in time to stop the drive, then X4 must come across the lane to stop the ball handler, and X2 then seals off the wing area.

If the dribbler takes an inside route, X2 should stop him before he penetrates the scoring area. If X2 cannot get there in time to stop the drive, he should seal off the ball-side wing area, and X4 should stop the dribbler.

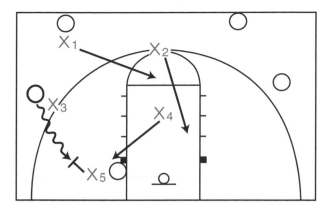

FIGURE 15.12 Horseshoe with the post.

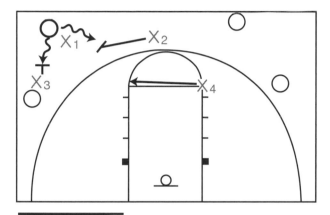

FIGURE 15.11 Horseshoe: drive by guard.

HORSESHOE WITH THE POST

This drill teaches players to rotate and defend against a low post. As the season progresses, run the Horseshoe drill with either a high-post or low-post player. If the post is high, the player guarding him is not involved in the rotation and is one pass away no matter where the ball is on the court. If there is a low-post player, there is a slight change in defensive assignments, but the principles remain the same.

On the drive, the player defending the low post (X5) rotates to pick up the dribbler. X4 rotates down to cover the offensive low post. The off-guard, X2, seals off the off-wing, and X1 slides toward the foul line and stays alert for the pass (see figure 15.12).

HORSESHOE WITH A ONE-PLAYER FRONT

In this drill, the offense sets up in a one-player front. In this case, the rotation rules described in the rotation section of this chapter apply, whether the offensive players are stationary or driving to the basket. Again, X5 rotates to stop the drive, X3 picks up the low-post offensive player, and the defensive point player must rotate and pick up the weak-side wing. The high post, following the rule, is not involved in the rotation (see figure 15.13).

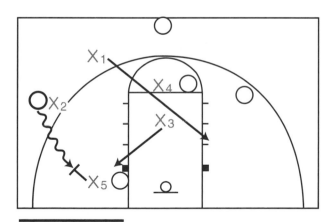

FIGURE 15.13 Horseshoe with a one-player front.

FOGLER

This drill confronts players with every defensive situation they could face in a game: guarding the ball, guarding the cutter, guarding the player one pass away from the ball, and guarding the player two or more passes away from the ball.

Begin with two guards and two forwards as you did in the Horseshoe drill. In this drill, the offensive and defensive players will be active. X2's player starts with the ball, with the defensive players defending as shown in figure 15.14. Because this drill is used to teach defensive positioning and responsibilities, the defense allows the offense to complete their passes, and the offensive players do not break from the established pattern. Let's follow one defensive player through the rotation of the drill.

When the ball is passed to the wing, X2's role changes from guarding the ball to guarding the player one pass away from the ball. X2 must take an advance step into the passing lane to deny the return pass.

After passing the ball, X2's player cuts to the basket, attempting to get between X2 and the ball. X2 must deny him this position, and this is why it is so important that X2 slides in the direction of any pass his player makes. As the passer cuts toward the basket, the player who received the pass holds the ball until you tell him to reverse the ball. The offensive

players rotate as the cutter moves through the lane and then positions himself where the off-wing originally started. When the offense shifts, X2 stops in the lane, because his player is now more than two passes away from the ball. He now becomes the help-side defense.

On your command, the offense now reverses the ball, leaving X2 two passes away. X2 should take a step or two up the lane to get into the passing lane once the ball is reversed to the off-guard. This position on the court allows him to deny his player the ball if he were to flash across the lane to the ball. If the ball handler passes to the off-guard, X2 is one pass away and should be up in the passing lane denying his player the ball (see figure 15.15).

Offensively, on any guard-to-guard pass, the passer and the wing on his side exchange with each other (see figure 15.16). This helps

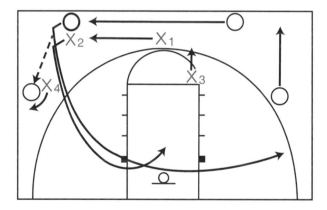

FIGURE 15.14 Fogler: on-ball to help-side defense.

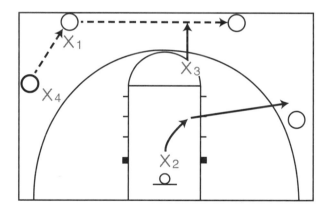

FIGURE 15.15 Fogler: denying wing pass on reversal.

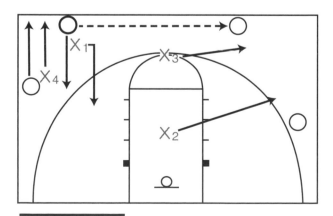

FIGURE 15.16 Fogler: passer and wing exchange.

to work the help-side defensive player on adjusting from one pass away to two passes away. It also gets defenders in the habit of talking to each other.

X3's player then passes to the wing, making all the defenders adjust and placing X2 on the ball (figure 15.17). On the pass to the wing, X3 slides in the direction of the pass, denying the passer the basket cut; X4 steps into the passing lane and denies his player the pass. X1 steps up to the lane to deny the off-guard reversal pass, and X3 replaces X1 as the weak-side defender in the lane (compare figure 15.17 to figure 15.14).

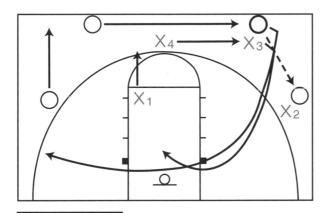

FIGURE 15.17 Fogler: on-ball to help-side defense.

The drill continues as before until players are back at their original positions. Remind your players that they must see both the ball and their player on defense, especially as players adjust from being one pass away to two or three passes away from the ball.

All players must be able to play each of the defensive positions in the Horseshoe and Fogler drills if they are to contribute to a pressure team defense. These two drills require all of the necessary defensive skills.

GUARD OVERPLAY

When we want individuals on the team to improve in a particular defensive skill, we have them perform breakdown drills (in which we break down plays into smaller steps). The guard overplay drill builds the skills and confidence of players in denying the ball from the players they are guarding.

The offensive player starts at the wing position, anticipating a pass from the coach nearest him in the guard position. X1 assumes the defensive overplay position. Begin the drill by having X1's player work to get open while X1 contests the ball by staying between his player and the ball. Player 1 works to receive the ball on the wing or farther back near midcourt. Attempt to throw the ball to the offensive player. Occasionally, intentionally allow the defense to be successful in intercepting or deflecting your pass to the offensive receiver. This helps build the confidence of the defensive player and makes him believe he can force his player to go without the ball. If the defender is overplaying correctly, he should intercept the ball with no problem.

When you call the offensive player's name, he will make a hard backdoor cut to the basket. X1 denies the backdoor pass by pushing off the front foot, turning his head so that he can continue to see both the ball and his player, and closing the gap between himself and his player's path to the basket. He keeps his arm up to deflect the pass and to create a psychological barrier to the passer.

As the offensive player approaches the lane, X1 will open toward the ball and front his player sliding across the free-throw lane. The cutter moves to the opposite wing, looking for a pass from you as you dribble the ball to this side of the court. X1 remains in the deny or overplay position on this side of the court, but this time he has his opposite hand in the passing lane and the corresponding foot forward. He should still be looking straight ahead, splitting the distance between his player and the ball so he can see them both (see figure 15.18).

One problem you may encounter is that as X1 closes to deny his player the ball on the wing, he will get too close to the offensive player. Doing this makes the offensive player quicker and will create problems for the defender. He should continue to be one arm's length away.

Teach players to ignore the offensive player's first step to the basket. If they are continually reacting to the first step, the offensive player can take a quick step back

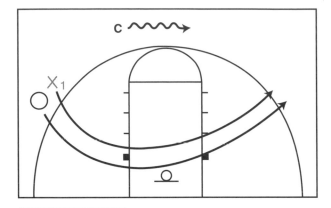

FIGURE 15.18 Guard overplay.

and receive the ball on the perimeter. Also, your players must not open up to the ball too soon or too late. They should open up as soon as the offensive player is in the lane or as soon as they see the pass being attempted.

Constantly remind players that in game situations there will be pressure on the ball and a defender on the weak side, which will make the backdoor extremely difficult to complete. The rule of 22-Tough defense is to not let the player have the ball. He must be made to play without it. No player has ever scored without the basketball.

HALF-COURT 1-ON-1

The half-court 1-on-1 drill enables players to practice executing all of the defensive steps and principles while guarding a player in game conditions. Designate one offensive player and one defensive player. Players begin on the point, on the wing, in the short corner, or in the post; vary the starting position to keep the drill fresh. You run this drill at both ends of the floor, with half of the team at each basket.

Instruct the offensive player to slice the defender to the basket. The defender should force him to either the baseline or the middle of the court; the defender must try to cut off the offensive player's drive before he gets to the basket. Play until the offensive player scores or the defensive player has rebounded or otherwise gained possession of the ball.

2-ON-2 PERIMETER

In this drill, players work on applying perimeter man-to-man defensive principles and footwork—particularly defending the ball and defending one pass away—under gamelike conditions.

Begin with two offensive guards and two defensive guards. Have them play in a live situation using the entire half-court area. Have the defenders play 22-Tough, and tell them to keep all of their defensive principles in mind.

2-ON-2 POST

In this drill, players work on applying post man-to-man defensive principles and footwork under gamelike conditions.

Begin with two offensive players in the post, corresponding defensive players, and a coach on each wing who will look to feed the post players as they get open. Have the defenders work to deny the post player the ball from the baseline side (while the ball is inside the free-throw line extended) and to be active defenders on the help side. The coaches can drive to the basket whenever they want, at which time the post defenders must help and recover to stop the ball (see figure 15.19).

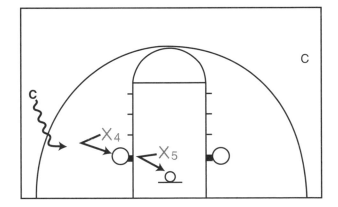

FIGURE 15.19 2-on-2 post.

POST DEFENSE

Post defenders are constantly changing their position in relation to the ball. This drill teaches post defenders how to continually move to maintain proper position between the ball and the offensive player.

Begin with a post offensive player, a post defensive player, a coach, and two managers. The post defender should be positioned behind the offensive player. The coach is at the point, the managers on the wings. The defensive player must react to your pass to either wing and gain defensive position on the post (see figure 15.20). At the beginning of the drill, have the offensive player play at half speed to allow the defender to get the footwork down. When the defender is confident with the footwork, you can then play it live.

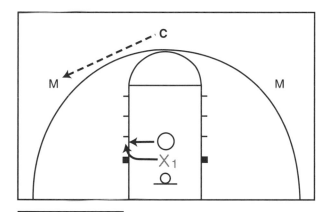

FIGURE 15.20 Post defense.

2-ON-2 ONE SIDE

This drill teaches perimeter defensive players to "dig in" on passes to the post and adjust on passes back to the perimeter. This drill also works the post defensive player on denying the pass to his player. Additionally, the offensive players are working on feeding the post and relocating for a possible jump shot.

This drill consists of one post and one perimeter offensive player, along with a corresponding defensive player guarding each. The offense must work on one side of the court. The perimeter offensive player looks to feed the post and relocate after the pass. The post offensive player must work to get open, then move effectively for the shot. Defensively, the post player should move his feet to deny the pass into the post, and the perimeter defender should contain and pressure the ball but not get beat on the dribble. If the ball is passed into the post, the perimeter defender should dig into the post, keeping his backside to the baseline so that he can see the entire court. If the ball is passed back to the perimeter, the defender must adjust to pick up his open player.

2-ON-2 WINGS

This drill helps to expose perimeter players to situations they will likely face in games when guarding the ball, when one pass away from the ball, and when more than one pass away from the ball.

Start with an offensive player on each wing and a corresponding defender on each of them. Position yourself at the top of the key with the ball. Begin the drill by dribbling to one side of the key. The two defensive players should work at denying their player the ball when they are one pass away, playing on the help side when the ball is two passes away, and playing help and recover if the ball is driven to the basket on their side (see figure 15.21).

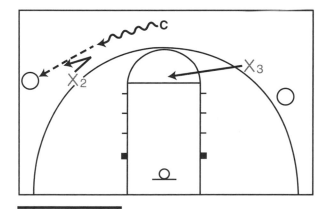

FIGURE 15.21 2-on-2 wings.

Eventually, you can make the drill 3-on-3, with the defense playing 22-Tough and the offense working to get open against pressure.

PERIMETER-TO-POST

This drill teaches your players each of the positions they could play while being part of a team that plays pressure defense. Start with one offensive player and one defensive player. The offensive player starts on the wing. Position yourself at the guard spot with the ball.

The defensive player (X2) begins by overplaying the wing. The offensive player should work to get open from the free-throw line extended up to the hash mark. When you call the offensive player's name, he cuts backdoor, and the defender turns his head and denies the backdoor pass. As the cutter is going through the lane, dribble from the guard position down to the wing that was just vacated (see figure 15.22).

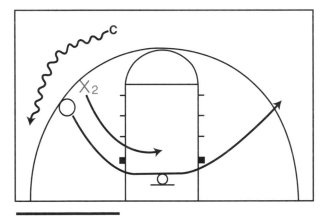

FIGURE 15.22 Perimeter-to-post: deny the backdoor.

Because the defender is now more than two passes away, X2 should have both feet in the lane, seeing both the ball and his player. You can drive at any time to make sure that X2 is in position to help and recover should there be penetration when he is on the weak side.

Next, signal the offensive player to flash across the lane to the ball. As the offensive player flashes, the defender should step up the lane and deny him the ball and the position. After the offensive player flashes, he

V-cuts to the ball-side block and posts up (see figure 15.23). The defensive player now denies the pass into the post from the wing by playing on the baseline side of the offensive player. The players then rotate from offense to defense and from defense to the end of the line.

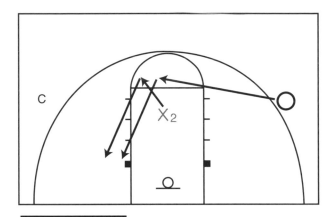

FIGURE 15.23 Perimeter-to-post: deny the flash.

Because this drill is run 1-on-1, you can focus all of your attention on the individual and his development as a fundamentally sound defensive player.

OVERMATCH

This drill is designed to teach quick and proper movement within the defense. Making the defense play with one or two fewer players than the offense forces all of the defensive players to react quickly and correctly. Defensive players must move on the pass, rather than after the pass has been received. It's amazing how much quicker your defense will get when playing with a numbers disadvantage. This will improve defenders' help and recovery skills, as well as their reaction time.

Have six offensive players face four defensive players in the half-court area (6-on-4), placing two offensive players at the baseline on each side of the basket. You can also run this with a 5-on-4 overmatch.

The offense moves the ball, eventually working it down to the baseline. When the baseline player gets the ball, he drives at the back of the defense. Proper rotation should take place as the defensive players help and recover to prevent the score (see figure 15.24).

Don't let defenders get in the habit of guarding an area. Instead, make them work as a unit, talking and helping as they play against the five or six offensive players.

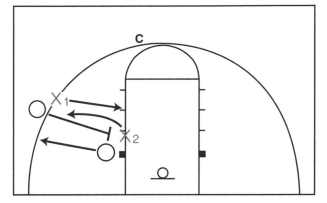

FIGURE 15.25 Defense versus down screen: going over the top.

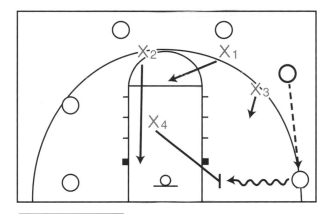

FIGURE 15.24 Overmatch (6-on-4).

DEFENSE VERSUS DOWN SCREEN

This drill helps players practice communication and defensive principles against a down screen, which frequently takes place from perimeter to post. Begin with one offensive wing, one offensive low post, and corresponding defenders. Also, place yourself (or another coach) at the point guard spot with the ball.

As the wing down-screens X2 to get the low-post player open on the wing, X1 should step off his player and toward the ball to give X2 room to slide through the screen. By communicating and giving each other room to move, defenders are able to work successfully against the screen (see figure 15.25).

Another example of how to guard the down screen is shown in the exchange that takes place between the weak-side guard and wing after the ball has been passed to the other side of the court. X2 and X1 must talk to each other to avoid running into each other

while continuing to execute their defensive responsibilities on the weak side. Because X2 is coming up the lane and can see the entire court, he should be telling X1 what to do. X2 must move straight up the lane and into the passing lane to deny the ball (because he is now one pass away). X1 (who is now two passes away) should take a step off his player in the direction of the ball so he can take care of the weak-side defense (see figure 15.26). The defender should never be more than one pass away from the player he is guarding.

Defenders should avoid switching against the screen whenever possible. Encourage players to stick with the offensive player they are guarding by helping and recovering.

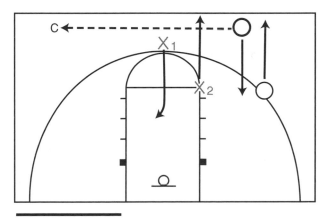

FIGURE 15.26 Defense versus down screen: creating room.

DEFENSE VERSUS CROSS-SCREEN

This drill helps players practice communication and defensive principles against the cross-screen, which frequently takes place between two post players. Begin with two low-post offensive players, corresponding defenders, and a coach on the wing with the ball. The post defender on the strong side should be denying his player the ball. As I've said, your players must be able to play defense in the post as well as on the perimeter, and screens take place in the post. In defending the cross-screen, your players must communicate with each other to be successful. One post player cross-screens for the other post; X5 tells X4 what to expect.

When X4 is screened, he takes one step up the lane and toward the ball to take away the high cut, and X5 defends against the low cut (see figure 15.27). If the offensive player coming off the screen cuts high, X4 is in position to deny the pass. If he cuts low, X5 delays his cut to allow X4 to get around the screen. Player X4 must step up the lane and toward the ball to ensure that the screener does not flash back to the ball to be a receiver as X5 is denying the other post player the cut. As X4 recovers, X5 slides into the lane and becomes the weak-side post defender.

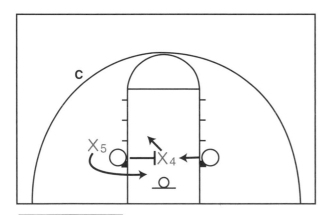

FIGURE 15.27 Defense versus cross-screen.

Remind players that the ball-side defender takes the low cut, and the help-side defender takes the high cut.

DEFENSE VERSUS SCREEN ON THE BALL

This drill helps players work on communication and defensive principles against a screen involving the player with the ball. Begin with a point guard with the ball, a wing, and corresponding defenders.

If the screen occurs on the ball, the player (X3) guarding the screener should step out and hedge to stop the dribbler's penetration (see figure 15.28a). This will give the defender being screened (X1) time to fight over the screen and get back in front of the offensive player he is guarding (see figure 15.28b).

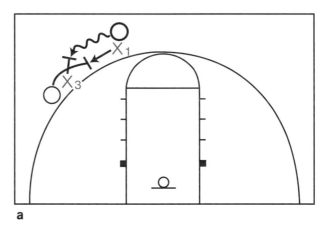

a

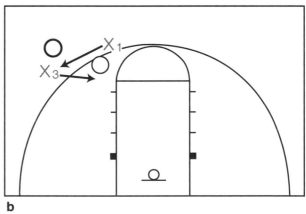

b

FIGURE 15.28 Defense versus screen on the ball.

Remind the defender who is hedging to step back off the player he is guarding and into the path of the dribbler. He should stay low while stepping out so that he can delay the dribbler and contain the ball while his teammate gets over the screen.

5 SPOTS

This drill allows players to work on multiple ways of guarding the ball. Begin with one player on defense and one on offense; a coach is at the top of the key with a ball. At each of the spots shown in figure 15.29, ask the defender to do the following:

1. At spot 1, with the coach at the top of the key, the defender plays denial or gap defense on the wing. The offensive player runs to the opposite wing as the defender stays help side.

2. At spot 2, the coach passes to the offensive player on the weak side. The defender then closes out on the offensive player.

3. At spot 3, the defender guards the offensive player as he flashes through the lane.

4. At spot 4, the defender fronts the post and works as the ball moves from the top of the key to the baseline.

5. At spot 5, the defender plays behind the post and works on only giving up one shot.

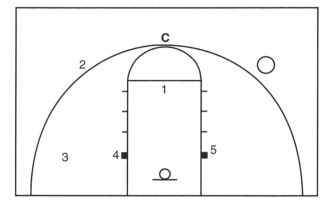

FIGURE 15.29 5 spots.

SWITCH, CHANGE, TOUCH

Players begin this drill playing 5-on-5. When the coach yells "Switch," the defenders have to switch to guarding someone different from whom they are currently guarding. This requires the defense to talk. When the coach yells "Change," the offensive players must drop the ball and sprint back on defense. This simulates a turnover. Finally, when the coach yells "Touch," whoever has the ball must drop it and run to touch the baseline as his four teammates sprint back to play defense. This forces the defense to play in a situation where they have a numbers disadvantage.

CHAPTER 16

Full-Court Team Defense

After teaching the essentials of individual and team defense, and establishing your half-court defense, you should prepare to unleash a full-court pressure team defense. Every team needs a full-court defense for those games when they are trailing in the closing moments and need to force a turnover. Full-court defenses can work to your advantage in other areas as well. They can

- control the tempo of the game to your liking,
- force the opponent to play the length of the floor when on offense,
- take advantage of your team's superior quickness, and
- take advantage of a team that may not handle the ball well.

22-Tough

As described in chapter 15, the alignment that we use most often for our full-court defense is called 22-Tough (see figure 16.1). In this

alignment, X1 takes the inbounder, while X2 positions himself between his player, who is on the elbow working to get open, and the ball. X3 and X4, who are guarding players on either side of the half-court line, also position themselves away from their players and toward the ball. X5 must play well off the low-post player to ensure that he does not break open for a pass upcourt and to prevent the offensive players positioned at midcourt from catching the lob from the inbounder.

Three basic variations of 22-Tough in the 4 area have been effective for us through the years. Each is simple and gives the standard 22-Tough in the 4 area many useful options without drastically changing assignments for most of the defensive players. Also, by giving your defense a "new look," you can keep your opponents off balance.

We labeled these three variations with baseball terms because this seems to help players remember what the defenses are designed to do. They can be adapted to your opponent's pressure offense and style of play.

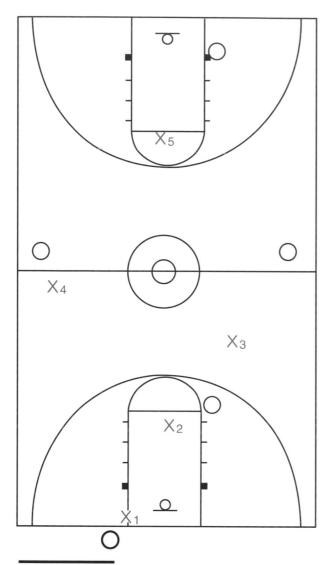

FIGURE 16.1 22-Tough in the 4 area.

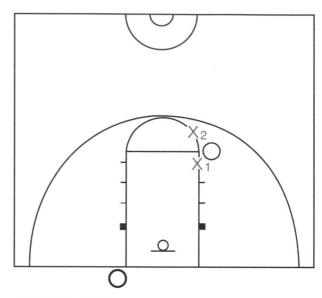

FIGURE 16.2 Shortstop.

Shortstop

In this variation, X1, who usually guards the player inbounding the ball, plays between the ball and the receiver. X2 moves behind and on the ball side of the potential receiver, creating what is in effect a double team (see figure 16.2).

If the offense gets the ball inbounds, X1 should recover to guard the inbounder. The defense would then play a normal 22-Tough in the 4 area.

This defense is particularly effective against a team with only one good ball handler or a team with an exceptional guard to whom you would like to deny the ball. This simple tactic is also very successful against a well-patterned ball club that depends on a single point player to initiate the offense.

When the primary receiver is double-teamed, the offense has a tendency to forgo its patterned style and play in a more haphazard way. In effect, you neutralize their offensive strength.

Center Field

This variation is designed to prevent the lob pass. The player (X1) usually guarding the inbounder plays at the head of the circle. It is X1's responsibility to pick off any medium lob. This is particularly effective when a team uses backcourt screens to break full-court pressure (see figure 16.3). Initially, the center fielder should cheat to the ball side because the backboard will prevent the inbounder from attempting the lob to the weak side.

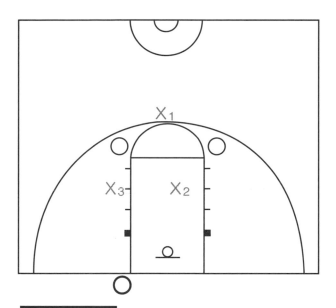

FIGURE 16.3 Center Field.

The center fielder gives 22-Tough a zone look, which often causes the offensive team to make needless and dangerous adjustments to break the press. X2 and X3 can now be even more determined about overplaying because the lob is covered.

Left Field

The purpose of this defensive alignment is to stop the offensive team from successfully completing the full-court pass. X1 moves to the opposite end of the court, into the middle of the 2 area (see figure 16.4). This puts added pressure on the other four defensive players; if the pass is completed to one of their players, the press is broken by a throw back to the uncovered inbounder. Defenders can be assured, however, that they can fully overplay without worrying that the player they are guarding will break downcourt for the long lob.

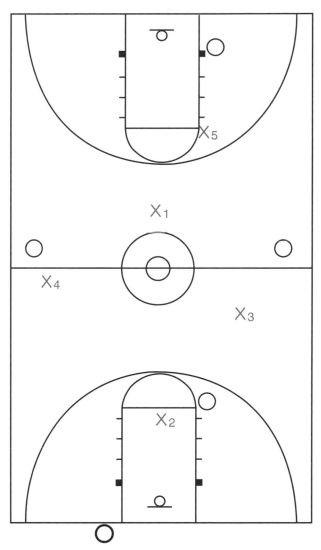

FIGURE 16.4 Left Field.

2-2-1 Wizard

The 2-2-1 Wizard is a safe zone press that can eat up the clock. In this 2-2-1 alignment, X1 and X2 set up on the free-throw line elbows, X4 and X5 begin on either side of half-court, and X3 starts as the safety near the opposite top of the key.

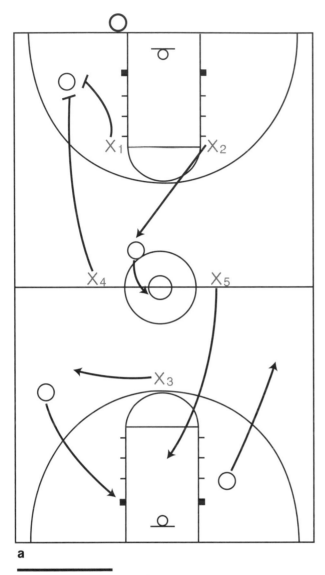

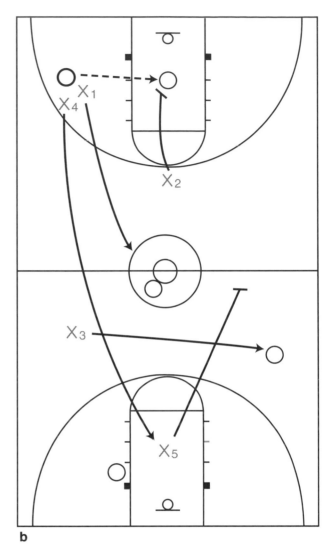

FIGURE 16.5 2-2-1 Wizard.

When the ball is inbounded, X1 forces the ball to the sideline while X2 takes away the middle (figure 16.5*a*). X4 looks for the sideline trap, and X3 takes away the sideline. X5 has the hole. Once the ball is passed back to the middle, X2 forces the opponent to the opposite sideline, while X1 takes away the middle; X4 takes the hole, and X3 sprints to the opposite sideline (figure 16.5*b*). X5 is a late trapper.

Full-Court Switching and Trapping

As previously stated, you never want to give the offense the same look time after time. In addition to the basic variations of 22-Tough,

you can also employ full-court blitzing and switching to disrupt the offense.

Blitz Switch—26

The Blitz Switch (26) can be easily executed in the 4 area. Refer to chapter 15 for a description of this technique. Because this is a two-player defensive tactic, there is no adjustment to be made if you apply it in the backcourt.

Blitz Trap—25

Let's look at what adjustments need to be made when running Blitz Trap (25) (see chapter 15) in the 4 area. If the ball is passed to the nearest offensive player, and your team is in Blitz Trap, X2 will have two options. He can force the ball handler to the sideline for the Fan Trap or force him to the middle for the Funnel Trap.

Fan Trap

X2 forces the player who received the pass to the sideline. X3 releases from his player when the ball handler is three strides away and completes the trap with X2. X5 rotates up to pick up X3's player at the midcourt line and takes an angle that runs through the passing lane for a potential steal. X1 takes away the pass back to the inbounder, and X4 drops to play between the two deep offensive players (see figure 16.6). X4 must remain active, read the trap, judge which receiver is most dangerous, and cheat toward that direction.

Funnel Trap

X2 forces the inbounds receiver to the middle and into the trap with X1. X4 rotates up to look for a steal, moving through the passing lane between the ball handler and the inbounder. X3 stays with his player, and X5 rotates up and plays between the two deep offensive players, just as X4 did in the Fan Trap (see figure 16.7). The deep pass is left unguarded (as the defensive player cheats toward the closer receiver), but this is an extremely difficult pass to complete, especially when the passer is in the middle of an aggressive trap.

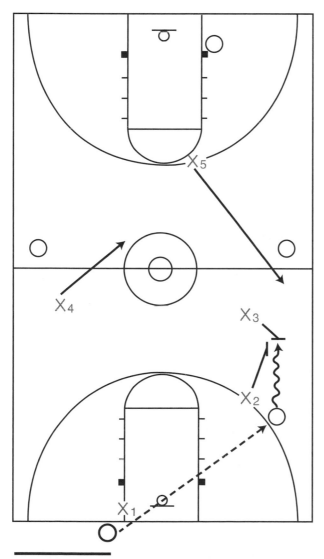

FIGURE 16.6 Fan Trap.

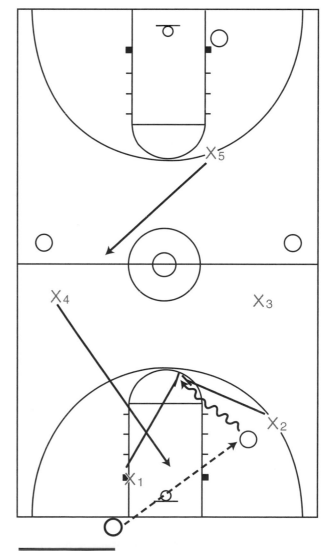

FIGURE 16.7 Funnel Trap.

Fist and Fingers

Fist and Fingers (see chapter 15) can also be used as a full-court defense with only a few adjustments. This defense is similar to the Funnel Trap, except in this case the trap is triggered by the pass or the dribble, not just by the dribble. On the inbounds pass to the nearest receiver, X1 leaves the inbounder (or the center field position he may be in) to trap the ball handler with X2. X4 rotates again, and X5 splits the two deep offensive players while reading the trap (see figure 16.8).

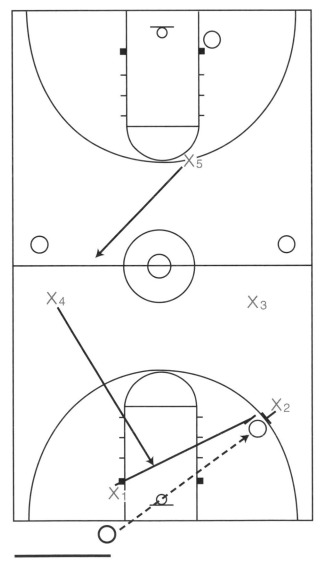

FIGURE 16.8 Fist and Fingers: full court.

23

23 is a safe zone press that helps eat away at the clock. We commonly run it as a half-court press, but it can be extended to the 3 area as a three-quarter press. The defense sets up in a 1-2-2 alignment, with X1 at the point, X2 and X3 at the wings, and X4 and X5 on either side of the basket.

Regardless of whether the defense sets up at three-quarter court or half-court, X1 begins the press by harassing the ball handler, while X2 stunts at the ball handler for a potential trap (figure 16.9a). At the same time, X3 takes away the middle, X4 takes away the sideline, and X5 has the hole.

On a ball reversal, X1 moves to guard the ball, while X2 moves to the middle (figure 16.9b). X3 steps up to trap with X1. X4 has the hole, and X5 takes away the sideline.

Emphasizing Defensive Teamwork

One potential obstacle to developing a strong team defense is getting all players to commit their attention and energy to it. As we've seen in this chapter, one weak link in the chain of five defenders will allow even an average offense to break it down. You, as a coach, can make a difference by selling your players on the value of good individual and team defensive play.

It all goes back to what I've said before: It's not what you coach; it's what you emphasize. I probably emphasize the team defense more than any other phase of basketball. I tell my players that the best defensive player will always start. It may not be the most poetic statement ever uttered, but I tell them this: "No defense, no play."

An occasional good-natured needle can also get a point across to a player or the team about the importance of good defense. A former assistant coach, Pat Smith, also played for me at DeMatha. He claimed that I used to really get to him if he got beat, when

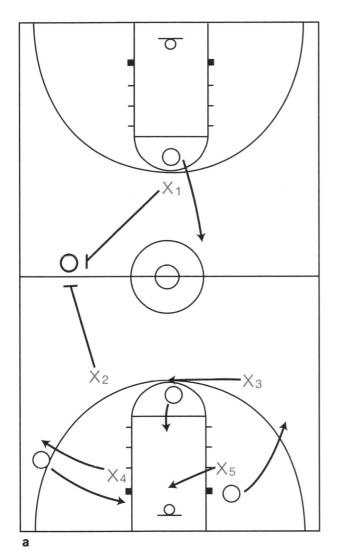 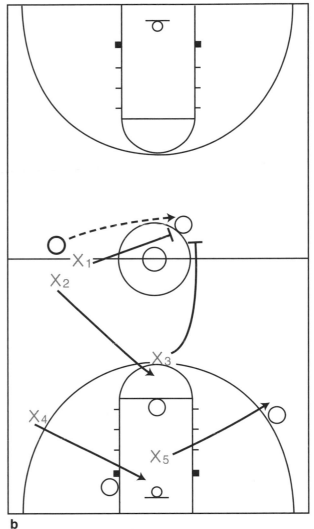

a   b

FIGURE 16.9 23.

I would say something like, "Don't worry, Pat. He's obviously a little too quick for you. But I thought you had the intelligence to be able to take better angles and cut off the quicker players." I want to stress here that such needles can be used to get a point across, but they should always be good-natured. Never use them to embarrass a player.

THOUGHT FOR THE DAY

Our chief want in life is somebody who shall make us do what we can.
—Ralph Waldo Emerson

My emphasis on defense does not necessarily translate into spending more time on it than any other facet of the game. In fact, I recommend spending more practice time on offense than defense.

That reminds me of a clinic I attended where UCLA's John Wooden was the featured speaker. Coach Wooden asked those in attendance if they spent more time on offense or defense. About 95 percent of the coaches said, "Defense."

Coach Wooden said that was fine if that was what they thought was right. But he told the group that he spent more time on offense.

Why? Because offense is more difficult to teach, and the skills are more difficult to develop. If you've coached for long, I'm sure you'll agree.

Almost all basketball players can become good defensive players, but not everyone has the tools to be great on offense. Also, keep in mind that when your players practice offense, half your team is playing defense. So keep an eye on the team without the ball during live practice situations. And instruct and correct players on defense as much or more than the offense they are working against.

Full-Court Defense Drills

When teaching full-court team defense, it is wise to once again use the breakdown method described in chapter 15 and concentrate on a specific phase of the defense. Do not concentrate on too much at a time. I've already described the 1-on-1 full-court drill (see chapter 14), and that is the first phase of building such a defense. The next step in the drill sequence begins with the 2-on-2 drill.

2-ON-2

This drill teaches players to apply full-court pressure defensive tactics and contest the inbounds pass. Use three groups of players in this drill with four players in each group, two players on defense and two on offense. Use only one ball through the entire drill. When the first two offensive players have completed their trip up the court (play stops after a score, a defensive rebound, or a turnover), they switch roles with the defensive unit they just faced, and they return downcourt. Each group must be ready to go as soon as the group in front of it has finished. You can also divide your team in half and have one group work at each basket to get more players involved (stopping the drill at half-court).

In this drill, one offensive player is positioned to inbound the ball, and the other is positioned at least as far back as the elbow of the foul line on the opposite side of the court.

This alignment gives the offensive players the maximum amount of room to maneuver to get the ball inbounds, thus putting pressure on the defensive players to deny the inbounds pass.

X1 lines up just off the baseline. His responsibility is to make the inbounds pass as difficult as possible by yelling, jumping up and down, moving his arms, and staying in the passing lane. X2 should be positioned away from his player and toward the ball. He must keep one hand in the passing lane. This position allows X2 to see both the ball and his player, which is a necessity in this defensive approach. X2 should not let his player flash across the lane. Instead, he should dictate and force him to the baseline. This is a very difficult pass to complete because of the angle and the pressure on both the ball and the receiver.

When the inbounder slaps the ball, the other offensive player makes his move to receive the pass. We do not allow the offensive team to lob the ball inbounds. In live action, there would be help in stealing these lobs. In addition, it does not help the defensive players improve if the offensive team takes the easy way out and does not force the defense to work.

X2 attempts to deny the inbounds pass. However, if the pass is successful, the inbounder clears the area by cutting in front of the player with the ball and looking for the return pass (see figure 16.10). If the pass is not thrown, X2 then plays the ball handler 1-on-1 up the court to the scoring area at the opposite end. Play then continues as 2-on-2 basketball until a defensive rebound or an offensive score or turnover occurs.

Emphasize putting great pressure on the inbounds pass. Once the ball is in play, the defensive player should continue to pressure the ball by keeping his head facing the ball (as was done in the 1-on-1 drill). The dribbler should be turned as many times as possible and ultimately stopped as the defensive player closes on him. Meanwhile, the other defender should not allow his player to catch the ball.

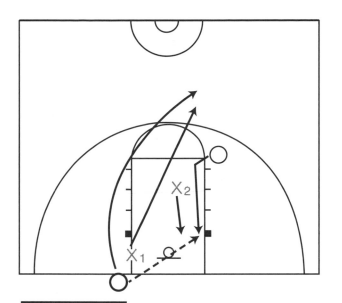

FIGURE 16.10 2-on-2.

3-ON-3

This drill teaches full-court defensive pressure against teams that attack with two immediate receivers. Use groups of six, each group containing three offensive players and three defensive players. Use one ball, and have the groups change roles when one group reaches the end of the court. You can also have players involved at both ends of the court (provided they stop at midcourt to avoid collisions).

The offensive unit starts with an inbounder and two players stacked at the middle of the foul line. X1 takes the inbounder, while X2 and X3 position themselves away from their players and toward the ball. The offensive player farthest from the ball breaks first, using his teammate as a screener if possible. If the first cutter cannot receive the ball, then the other offensive player should cut in the opposite direction and look to receive the inbounds pass.

X1 has the same responsibility as he did in the 2-on-2 drill. X2 and X3 should try to prevent their players from catching the ball and try to stay in proper one-pass-away position. If a screen takes place, the defenders must talk over the screen and play their players. Again, we discourage the lob pass to get the

ball inbounds; the defense will not improve if the offense simply goes over the top.

If the pass is completed, the inbounder steps in and, along with the offensive player not receiving the ball, clears the area by running a defender in front. The defenders must work on staying between their players and the ball, as shown in figure 16.11.

The defender guarding the ball should put aggressive pressure on the ball while turning the offensive player as often as possible. If the ball gets across half-court, the players play 3-on-3 basketball.

Do not allow defenders to switch at any time during this drill. This is essential because you never want anything coming between your defenders and the ball. To make this drill effective, work the defense against as many different alignments as you can think of.

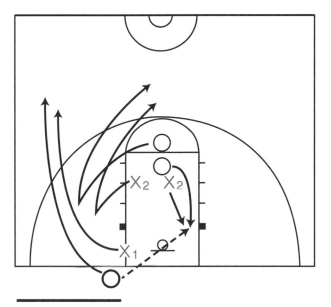

FIGURE 16.11 3-on-3.

4-ON-4

This drill builds one step closer to the complete full-court defense. Use three groups of four offensive and four defensive players; the groups should alternate their assignments frequently. The inbounder and the offensive player nearest to him line up using the same rules as in the full-court 2-on-2 drill. The other two offensive players line up behind the midcourt line as receivers, ready to bring the ball up. Each defender gets into proper position (see figure 16.12).

In this drill, X2's player is the primary receiver, and it is X2's responsibility to deny him the ball. The secondary receivers can move to receive the ball if their teammate needs help. The inbounder can attempt the lob pass in this drill to see how X3 and X4

react to the pass. There is more pressure on the defense here than in regular 5-on-5 situations because there is no defensive post player to help on the long pass.

If the pass is completed short to the player nearest the ball, the inbounder clears the area, looking for a return pass. X2 must put good aggressive pressure on the ball handler as he comes upcourt. When the ball crosses the midcourt line, the drill becomes a game of 4-on-4 basketball.

I like this drill because it puts so much pressure on X3 and X4. They must be able to react up or back to keep the ball away from their players. They should also play off their players toward the ball as if they are two passes away. In addition, they should play with their back to the sideline so they can see the entire court, including the player and the ball. This way they can deny their player the cut to the ball if he is trying to help get the ball inbounds, and they can help pick off the lob pass to the player guarded by X2 if it is attempted.

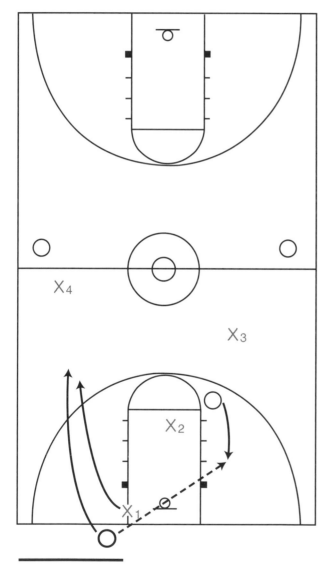

FIGURE 16.12 4-on-4.

5-ON-5

This drill combines all of the elements of a full-court pressure defense; it is basically our 22-Tough defense in the 4 area (described at the beginning of this chapter). You can set up the offense in various alignments, depending on what type of front your opponent presents when breaking full-court man-to-man pressure. The lineup is the same as in the 4-on-4 drill, except you add the two post players (X5 and his player) downcourt.

The responsibilities for X1, X2, X3, and X4 are the same as in the 4-on-4 drill. X5 must play well off the low-post player to ensure that he does not break open for a pass upcourt and to prevent the offensive players positioned at midcourt from catching the lob from the inbounder.

When the ball crosses the midcourt line, the drill becomes a game of 5-on-5 basketball.

PART V

COACHING GAMES

CHAPTER 17

Preparing for Games

The most successful basketball coaches are the ones who are best at preparing their team for each game. Players on a well-prepared team will be confident that they have every chance to win that game as long as they play hard, play smart, play together, and have fun. The bulk of this preparation is done on the practice floor by working on what your team does best and by preparing for what the opposition does best.

Scouting Reports

Scouting is an important part of preparing your team to face your next opponent. Notice I said an important part, not the most important part. Our emphasis in preparation for a game is always on our own strengths, on working even harder and getting even better at what we do best. We are more concerned with what we do offensively, defensively, and in special situations than with what our opponents do.

As mentioned in chapter 5, John Wooden always said that he did not like to do much scouting because he thought that knowing the opponent too well made him either over-confident or petrified. And he believed that his players could sense his feelings about an upcoming game. But you can bet that the

greatest coach who ever lived knew plenty about the opponent when his team took the floor.

Because I believe that scouting is an important part of preparation, a rule at DeMatha is that we want to see every league opponent at least twice—and three times if possible. For nonleague opponents, we want to see them at least once, but preferably twice.

Courtesy of Bishop O'Connell High School/Tommy Orndorff

Scouting your opponent can help better prepare your team come game time.

Before the season begins, we sit down and draw up a master scouting schedule, which tells every member of our staff whom, where, and when they will be scouting. The amount of time spent on scouting is obviously dependent on the number of assistant coaches you have available to scout. If you are coaching alone, you should recruit an interested fan or faculty member to help you with the scouting.

This is a valuable opportunity to give your assistants more input into the program. And scouting will benefit them in many ways. It will give them a chance to observe what is happening in a game and help them develop that "feel" for the game that we noted in the Red Auerbach story earlier in the book (chapter 2). Scouting also exposes the assistants to many different offenses and defenses, which will make them more knowledgeable and enable them to make recommendations concerning the tactics of your own team. Through scouting, your assistants will learn to see specific plays, player tendencies, and team strengths and weaknesses that can be used to your team's advantage.

When the scouts return to practice with all of this information, they can share it with the team and play a significant role in whatever success you have against that opponent. You can make it easier on the people scouting by having a form already prepared that details the information you are looking for about the upcoming opponent. Our scouting form, included in chapter 5, asks for the following information:

- Individual personnel (including height and weight) and their tendencies
- First sub in the backcourt
- First sub along the front line
- The best player to foul
- Offensive set against pressure defense
- Offensive set against half-court man-to-man defense
- Offensive set against half-court zone defense
- Delay game set

- Inbounds plays along the baseline
- Inbounds plays along the sideline
- Full-court pressure defense
- Half-court zone trap
- Man-to-man defensive looks
- Zone defensive looks
- Defensive look versus inbounds underneath their basket
- Junk defenses (box-and-one, and so forth)
- Whether they have a player who can take over
- Matchups that can work to our advantage or disadvantage
- What their style of play is
- What we must do to win

This information provides us with a thorough glimpse of opponents, their strengths, and their weaknesses. In short, the scouting report tells us what we must do to win. Here's the real question you want to answer with all of this information: What does the other team like to do best? Then, you want to keep them from doing that during the game. You want to break the other team's practice habits, getting them away from what they are used to and forcing them to do things they don't practice.

Scouting information can come from various sources. The best scouting approach is having the head coach or assistant coach actually view the game. This is the option to select when time and cost are not prohibitive. You can pick up more things in person than you can through other means.

A second method of obtaining scouting information is through the exchange of videotapes. Many high school basketball programs videotape all of their games. You can call opposing coaches before the season to see if an exchange of these tapes can be worked out. Sometimes, because of their replay potential, videotapes can help you learn even more tactical information about your opposition than attending their games would.

If you are unable to go see a particular opponent and unable to get a tape of one of

Belief in the Scouting Report

In 2005, O'Connell returned a strong team from the previous year (in fact, the team had won the Washington Catholic Athletic Conference regular-season and tournament championships, the Virginia Independent Championship, and the Alhambra Catholic Invitational Tournament). We had a strong senior class that included Marcus Ginyard (who went on to start for 4 years at UNC), Dave Neal (team MVP for Maryland his senior year), and Bryant Majors (who went on to play at Marymount University and now coaches with me). DeMatha had a strong team that year as well. They beat us in our one matchup in the regular season and also beat us in the league championship. We faced them a few weeks later in the Alhambra Catholic Invitational Tournament, the nation's top postseason tournament for Catholic schools.

This time we changed the game plan. We told our players that we were going to play zone (we are primarily a man-to-man team). We also decided that we would spread the floor and make their big center come out and guard Neal, a very versatile player. We did not spend a lot of time on this in practice. We simply explained to our players why we were taking this approach.

O'Connell ran the game plan to perfection, and we won the tournament, finishing 31-3 for the year. The plan was successful because the players believed in what we said. Players will have more confidence in a game plan if you explain to them the reason why an approach is taken. I have always believed in the importance of letting the players know why we do what we do.

its games, you then must rely on the third scouting tactic: telephone calls to other coaches who have seen or played against that team. These coaches can give you some idea of what to expect. Obviously, it is better for you or your staff to actually watch a game, but telephone calls at least give you some information to help in your preparation.

Another little trick you might use is to have someone scout your team for you a few times during the year. It always helps to have a different perspective from someone who's not involved in the day-to-day operation of your program, and you get a great idea of what your opponents' scouts are telling their coaches. You can accomplish this either formally or informally. If you have a friend in coaching whom you respect and trust, you might ask him to prepare a real scouting report on your team. Or, if there are college coaches watching your team, or a former player comes back to see a game, take a few minutes to talk with them and get their impressions. They just might see something that helps you out the rest of the way.

I would like to emphasize once again that scouting is only one phase—and not even the most important phase—of preparing for your next opponent. It pales in comparison to season-long preparation of your team's strengths. If you adjust offenses and defenses from game to game to fit the opponent, your team may be able to do a lot of things—but none of them very well. Find a primary offense and defense that best suit your team's talents and work to perfect those. That is the best way to prepare for any opponent.

THOUGHT FOR THE DAY

Our judgment is only as good as our information.

The Pregame Practice

Knowing what your opponents like to do will have some influence on your practice sessions leading up to that game. Here are a few examples:

- If you know that the opposing team likes to press a lot, you will spend a bit more time on your press offense.
- If you know that the upcoming opponent likes to fast break, you may want to spend some time on sprinting back on defense or jumping to the rebounders to prevent the outlet pass.

- If the team you're preparing for is an up-tempo team that loves to run, you may want to work on slowing down your offense to try to break their rhythm.

- If your next opponent is a great half-court pressure team, you may want to work on a special pressure entry such as a 1-4 set to break the pressure down.

- If the opponent's point guard is also one of their leading scorers, as is often the case, you may want to work on pressuring him full court to try to wear him down and take away some of his offensive efficiency when he enters the scoring zone. (If your point guard is one of your leading scorers, and your opponent tries to press him full court, consider practicing with one of your other players bringing the ball up the floor and then getting it to your point guard to begin the offense.)

- If you know the preferred coaching strategies of coaches in your conference, you can prepare to counter those attacks with the proper tactics. For instance, to prepare for a coach who likes to run the flex, practice the shell drill to teach your players how to get through screens and how to jump to the pass. As a result, your team will be more capable of stopping the strategy when they face it.

As you can see, your points of emphasis may shift to a degree, depending on what your scouting report has told you. I make these changes in practice subtle ones, and I do not tell the players why we are working on certain things. If I think we need to spend a little more time working against a full-court press, I don't tell the players it's because our next opponent is very good at applying full-court pressure. We just do it, and I tell the players we are working on it because it's something we must be able to do to be a good basketball team.

Telling the players why you are working on certain phases of the game often leads to mistaken perceptions. In other words, you run the risk of building the opponent up too much or not enough. If I inform the team that

we are going to face some tough full-court pressure, I could be intimidating my players into thinking that team is better than it is. They may think, *Well, if the coach says they're good and we need to work on it in practice, they might be tougher than we thought. What if we can't get the ball up the court against them?* Such doubts and negative thoughts can lead to poor performance.

The opposite is also true. If I tell the team that our opponent does not handle pressure very well, and that we are going to try to take advantage of that, our players may think they are facing a weak team when that may not be the case.

So you and your staff should withhold from players your reasons for structuring your practices a certain way. It's the coaches' job to worry about why. The players have enough to worry about regarding execution.

We seldom mention anything specific about our next opponent until the day of the game. However, the drills we run in practice are designed to sharpen the strengths that we think will be a factor in the upcoming game.

We also seldom practice our defense against an opponent's offense because our theory is that our pressure is going to force them out of their offense anyway. Sometimes, however, we must prepare for situations in which the offense will be difficult to gain command over. For example, some teams are precise enough to run an effective flex offense, which has become very popular in recent years.

The flex is a baseline, screening offense that emphasizes player and ball movement. But when we have our defense work against the flex in practices, we present it only as a good defensive drill to help in fighting over screens and giving weak-side help. Our players then view this as a drill designed to help our defense, rather than as a preparation for a team that runs the flex offense. (In fact, we have worked on this drill to such an extent that our offense has also become quite adept at running the flex, and we have occasionally used it ourselves in games.)

The example of the flex also indicates what you should keep in mind when you devise your master practice plan at the beginning of the year. In the preseason, you should be assessing the opponents your team will be facing when the season begins in order to get a good idea of the kinds of offenses and defenses you might encounter. This enables you to begin working on the offensive and defensive options that should be most successful against the opposition your team will face throughout the season.

Plan and structure your pregame practices so that you are working on the skills that you think will benefit the team the most in the upcoming game. But sell it to the players as regular practice work designed to improve your team.

Generally, I like to make the heaviest work day the practice two days before a game. The day before a game, I like to keep practice fairly short so we can have fresh legs the following day. I tell the kids, "We're not going to go long, but we're going to go strong." Observe the team closely, and evaluate how the players are responding. Sometimes a short practice can be more beneficial than a long one.

At practice the day before a game, we call the team together and take only about five minutes to go over the opposing team and its tendencies. This is when the assistant who scouted the opposing team should give an overview of what the opponent likes to do. He'll cover what they like to do offensively and defensively and also give our players a brief overview of the opponent's personnel. During this talk, the coach should be extremely careful not to oversell the team we are about to face. At the end of that overview, I usually step in and remind players that although it's important to know what an opponent might do, the most important thing is to focus on what we do.

Pregame Motivation

Before a DeMatha game, I always hold a brief team meeting, either in the locker room when we play on the road or in a classroom when we play at home. I will walk into that room 25 minutes before the game, speak for about 5 minutes, and then leave 20 minutes for the

Carr Team Brainwashed

It was the year that Kenny Carr—who later became an All-American at North Carolina State, a member of the 1976 gold medal Olympic team, and a fine NBA performer with the Portland Trailblazers—was a senior at DeMatha. We were to play in the city championship game against a great team from Eastern High School.

Before the game, I spent about 25 minutes in front of the team talking about Eastern—how great a team they were and how awesome each and every player was. My emphasis was misguided; I placed more importance on how good they were and on what they could do than on what we could do. We got our brains beat out. I learned my lesson well.

players to loosen up. During the 5-minute session, I take the game plan out of my jacket pocket and quickly go over what we are going to do offensively and defensively, what our alignments will be in various situations, and what the matchups will be.

At every O'Connell game, similar to my father, I try to cover a simple game plan 25 minutes before tip-off. I note what the players should watch for—typically the opposition's two favorite tendencies. For example, I might point out that they like to ball screen and that they really pound the boards. So I'll then emphasize that we need to be ready to trap off the screens and to rebound with great energy. We then cover four keys to the game, such as the following:

- Be ready to defend individually and as a team.
- Win the war on the backboards.
- Look for Bingo (a fast break option; see chapter 9) to be available.
- Move the ball and work to get open for great shots in the half-court.

After we cover the four keys, we then get into matchups. Finally, before we take the court, we emphasize the common theme for each game: Play hard, play smart, play together, and have fun!

Readying the Charges for Power

In one of the greatest high school basketball games ever played, we went up against Lew Alcindor (now Kareem Abdul-Jabbar) and Power Memorial High School. Alcindor was undefeated in his high school career. Power Memorial had won 71 games in a row, but they had beaten us by only three points the year before.

Under these conditions, my players needed simple direction, not further motivation. So, on this particular night, I walked into the locker room at the University of Maryland's Cole Field House, called the team together, and gave the following talk:

"Gentlemen, let's all get together. Offensively tonight, against their man-to-man, we're going to run the box. If they go zone, we'll go with our 1-4 set. Any kind of pressure, it will be a two-man front.

"Defensively, we're going to start with a 22-Tough, quarterbacking Feruggio to try to make the other guard handle the ball. Jump balls, we'll use our green alignment. Out of bounds, we're going to run the line. Free throws, it'll be our Maryland alignment. Time and score, we'll go to four corners to score.

"Matchups: Whitmore—you have Alcindor, number 33. Williams—you have Toddman, number 14. Catlett—you have Brown, number 21. Wiles—you have Feruggio, number 22. Austin—you have Haughton, number 11.

"Game captain. Whose turn is it to be captain? All right, Wiles. Bench captain, Petrini.

"Okay, men. Real simple. We have to do a big job on both boards. We've gone over it enough. Total front on Alcindor. Any time he catches the ball, it's got to be on lobs over our heads. We're going to get the pressure up like we've never gotten it up before.

"Great crowd. Great occasion. Two great teams. Let's just make sure of one thing—that we play as hard and as smart as we can, but I want to see us have more fun than they do.

"Let's go."

Morgan talks to his team courtside during DeMatha's historic win over Power Memorial in 1965.

Courtesy of DeMatha Catholic High School

Underdog Versus Favorite

Unfortunately, there are always going to be fans and media people who will want to label your team as an underdog, favorite, or even match to your opponent. But I never look at it this way. I approach each game with the mind-set that we need to do certain things to be successful, no matter who we are playing.

I tell the team, "We have worked hard to get ready for this game. We are well prepared. We are in excellent shape, physically and mentally. And we are going to go out and play as hard and as smart as we can for the next 32 minutes, and we're going to have some fun."

I try to keep the approach low key to prevent the players from falling into the trap of either thinking they must win or playing not to lose.

If the upcoming opponent is one that I know our team thinks it can easily defeat, I try to become more motivational in my approach. I think a coach has to be honest with his team. If you previously beat the team you're playing by 25 points that year, your team is not going to believe you if you try to convince them they're facing a great team. The players will see right through that.

I fear the games when we play a team we are supposed to beat handily the most because of the possibility of a letdown, a lack of intensity. You have to remind the players that they still have to prove themselves on the court, and that they didn't previously win just by showing up. This is when you have to tell the team, "I know we beat these guys by 25 points last time. They've improved a lot, and all they want is to see you come out loafing just a little bit or with the attitude that you've already got this game won. If you do, you're going to find yourselves in a real dogfight."

THOUGHT FOR THE DAY

Every saint has a past and every sinner has a future. –Oscar Wilde

I would much rather play an opponent who is evenly matched with us or even slightly better. In these cases, I know that the players will be mentally sharp and play with intensity. It's when you are the heavy favorites that you really have to get the team's attention and remind everybody that they still have a game to play.

Big Games

When playing a crucial game for a championship or against an arch rival, I make minor adjustments in my pregame message to the players. In these cases, where a big crowd is expected and the motivation is already built in, I try to relax the players a little bit. I think the worst thing coaches can do before a big game is to overemphasize its importance, practice too much, and get their players too tight. The players will be wound up enough anyway from the nature of the game and what is at stake. In this situation, it is the coach's job to unwind the players and send them out on the floor in a confident frame of mind.

A perfect example of this was our game against Power Memorial. We were playing in front of 12,500 people at the University of Maryland, the first sellout at Cole Field House. The players didn't need a Knute Rockne kind of speech to get pumped up. So I merely went over the game plan in a confident manner and told them to go out and enjoy the occasion.

Summary

You cannot work miracles before a game to ready your team. The best approach is to continually work to improve individual and team performance in practice. However, your team will be more set to enter its next game if you apply these points of advice:

- Remember that scouting is an important element of preparation, but not the most important part. Know your opponent's tendencies, but always work more on your strengths.

- In preparing your game plan, make sure the objective is to break the other team's practice habits and get them doing something they aren't used to doing.

- If you have limited scouting resources, try to recruit an interested faculty member or fan to assist you.

- If you are not able to see a game of an upcoming opponent, try to obtain the pertinent information through the exchange of videotapes or through phone calls to other coaches.

- Plan your practices to work on the specific strengths of your team that you think will be most important in the next game.

- Do not spend too much time talking about your opponent because you run the risk of overselling or underselling that team's abilities. Keep the focus on your own team.

• If possible, keep the final workout before the game short so the players will have fresh legs.

• Adjust your pregame talk to fit the circumstances. If you're playing a poor team, gear your talk to avoid a letdown. If you're involved in a big game, try to relax the players.

CHAPTER 18 Handling Game Situations

I've had coaches tell me, "Once the game starts, I stop worrying because I've done everything I can." That is the wrong attitude. Sure, preparation is important to a team's success. But you must also fulfill many responsibilities once the game is under way. It makes no difference whether your team is the favorite or underdog, playing at home or on the road, going for the league title or a .500 season. To paraphrase Gertrude Stein, "A game is a game is a game." And you've got to be ready to handle it.

Starting the Game

Once the game plan has been installed and fine-tuned in practice, your final decisions before the game will involve your starting five and the matchups that will occur.

The Starting Five

I do not emphasize the role of starters as much as many coaches do. As I've mentioned before, I tell players, "It is not important who starts; what we really need is a lot of finishers." However, I do like to maintain as much continuity as possible in our starting five.

I never like to change my starting five after a loss because it may appear that I'm blaming the previous loss on the player who is no longer starting. So whenever I change my starting lineup, I try to do so after a victory. Also, I never make a change without calling the players involved into my office. I tell the player who will not be starting the reasons why I think he can be more effective coming off the bench, and I try to keep his attitude positive and enthusiastic. I want him to understand that we are just adjusting our strategy. I never want to create a win–lose situation with personnel changes, only win–win situations.

Explain to the player whom you are removing from the starting lineup that your decision may not be the right one—that you just believe it is after much consideration. And despite all the knowledge and all the planning in the world, sometimes decisions just come down to gut feelings or instincts.

Learn to develop and trust your instincts regarding personnel decisions. They can sometimes mislead you, but you'll likely find that your instincts are right more often than they are wrong.

"I Had a Feeling . . . "

I remember one important league game we were playing back in the 1960s against Mackin High School. We were losing by 6 points with about two minutes left to go when one of our starting forwards went down with a knee injury. While I was out on the floor trying to determine how injured the player was, my assistant, Frank Fuqua, was getting our top sub at forward ready to come into the game.

After we had attended to our injured player and helped him off the floor, Frank was ready to send in that sub. I told Frank to hold up, turned to the bench, and said, "Billy Hite, get in there." Although Billy was one of the finest all-around athletes we've ever had at DeMatha and a great competitor and clutch performer, he was only 5-11. And here I was, putting him in a forward spot in a crucial ball game.

Well, we ended up taking the game into overtime—Billy Hite made the tying basket. And in that overtime, we pulled away to win easily. In a time span of about eight minutes, Billy Hite scored 13 points.

With less than a minute to go and the game wrapped up, I turned to Frank Fuqua and said, "I just kind of felt he might be the better guy in that situation."

Frank laughed and, with a big grin on his face, said, "Oh, be quiet."

Matchups

Perhaps the most critical personnel decision for a game involves deciding on your matchups, especially if your team plays any form of man-to-man defense. Again, I have several rules that I take into consideration when making matchup decisions.

Leading Scorer's Defensive Assignments

First, if possible, I would rather not place my leading scorer on one of the high-powered offensive players for the other team. If one player is supposed to lead the way offensively for your team and also shut down the opposing team's leading scorer, then you are expecting him to control the entire game at both ends of the floor. This can make a player think that the entire game rests on his shoulders. Even if your leading scorer is a great defensive player, outstanding play and effort at both ends are a lot to ask.

Another consideration is that you do not want your leading scorer to get into early foul trouble because he's guarding the other team's ace. Think about potential foul trouble when assigning matchups. You may have to decide who the most expendable players are, and then go ahead and match them up with some of the best offensive players on the other team.

So, if you can, try to slide your leading scorer onto one of the opponent's lesser scorers. However, if your leading scorer also happens to be your best defensive player, you may want to change this strategy if you are at an important point in a game or if it's crunch time in the closing minutes. I did this many times throughout the years. For example, Keith Bogans, who went on to star at the University of Kentucky, was one of our leading scorers and also our best perimeter defensive player. Most of the time, I would not have him take on the other team's top scorer. But if the situation warranted it, I would change his defensive assignment to try to improve our advantage at crucial times that may have decided the game's outcome.

Guarding the Opposition's Ball Handler

Another critical matchup is the defensive player you assign to guard the other team's ball handler. There is a possibility that whoever guards the primary ball handler will get into foul trouble because he will be around the ball more than the other players, and the officials are always watching the ball. So you may not want your leading scorer or your leading ball handler guarding the other team's best ball handler.

Defending Kenny

I had tough decisions to make when we played Archbishop Molloy High School from New York, featuring the great Kenny Anderson. Kenny was one of the greatest guards to ever play high school basketball, and he later led Georgia Tech to the Final Four as a freshman. We faced him twice, and both times I decided not to put our best ball handler on Kenny in an attempt to avoid getting our man in foul trouble. We thought that Kenny was also such a great defensive player that we needed our best ball handler in there at all times.

The strategy paid off. We won both games against Molloy. In the first game, John Gwynn (who later played at the University of Connecticut) made a jump shot at the buzzer (right after a basket by Anderson), and we won by one point. In the second game, we made two foul shots with about four seconds to go and won by two. We did not lose any players to fouls in either game, and we were able to have our best ball handler in the game at all times.

Taking Away the Opponent's Strengths

Remember that you want good team defense. You may want to try to shut down a great player by using different defenses, rather than spending the whole game trying to find a single player who can contain him.

Against Lew Alcindor, we knew that one man would not be effective. So our team defensive strategy was to try to deny him the ball. We had one guy in front of him and one guy behind him at all times. He caught the ball only 11 times during that game. It was a risk on our part because we were leaving one of their players open at all times. But our thinking was and is in line with this philosophy: "Don't let their best player beat you. Make one of their lesser players beat you."

When deciding on matchups, pay close attention to your scouting reports and try to identify the strengths of each of the players on the opposing team. Then, try to decide on the matchup that best takes away that strength. If one guy on their team is an awesome rebounder, try to take that away with your matchup. If another guy is a great outside shooter but doesn't penetrate well, try to take that away with your matchup.

Having an Alternate Plan

As you determine your matchups, make sure you decide on an alternate plan. If, for example, the other team's leading scorer gets red hot early, you will be forced into a defensive switch. It may only be an individual switch, putting another player on the other team's scorer, but this can sometimes have a psychological effect on the other team. Their big scorer may think, *Uh-oh. I've been hot. Now they're putting their defensive stopper on me.* If this happens, the defensive strategy has already been successful because you've disrupted the offensive player's focus on scoring points.

Sometimes you will have to adjust your whole defense. You may want to start trapping the player who's scoring all the points for the other team. Or you may want to try to deny him the ball and totally overplay him.

You will never be able to take everything away from a good offensive player. What you're looking to take away is what he does best. That's why I'm often heard telling a player, "Make him beat you left-handed." The primary purpose of a matchup is to take away a player's best weapon. Try to get your players to take away the oppositions' aces; then, if your players get good enough, go to work on the oppositions' kings.

Morgan watches his team from the sidelines in 1999.

© Edward Potskowski

During the Game

A coach's job is only half over once the game begins. Ideally, you've prepared your team as well as possible. Now, you must assist your players in the execution of the game plan and provide guidance in the various circumstances that arise during game competition. You must consider

- your conduct,
- the opposing coach's conduct,
- game plan adjustments,
- personnel decisions,
- time-outs, and
- halftime.

Your Conduct

A coach's conduct in game circumstances must be beyond reproach, not only because you represent yourself, your family, and your school, but also because you are the leader of the team. You are the focal point, and your players will look to you and follow your example. If you lose your cool, your composure, or your temper, then your team will do the same. Also, the behavior of a coach can influence the behavior of the crowd.

I try to conduct myself as a gentleman at all times. Basketball, however, is an emotional sport, and there are times when those emotions will be intense. I have had a few technicals, but only a few. In 46 years of coaching, I would guess that I have yet to reach double figures in technicals. This does not mean that I'm a saint. It means that I work hard at keeping my composure, staying focused on the game, and setting the proper example for my players.

Of the technicals that have been called on me, most have been called by relatively inexperienced officials. You will find that the good, experienced officials rarely have to call a technical foul to maintain control of the game. They may simply come over to you and say, "Coach, sit down and relax and worry about coaching." It is wise to heed such advice from an official.

Generally, rookie officials are a bit nervous and insecure, and they may be quicker to resort to a technical to establish control of a game. But this is not an indictment of beginning officials. We all have to start some place, and I remember what the first year of my 10-year officiating career was like. I have the greatest respect for officials and for the hard work and professionalism they bring to our sport. However, you should try to find out who your officials are before each game and what their reputations are. Such knowledge may help you in determining how much you can talk to an official and when it is time to leave him alone.

Only on very rare occasions should you think that an official or officiating crew influenced a game's outcome. As a coach, you need to accept responsibility, not place it elsewhere. But even in those rare cases where the officiating might have made a difference, you cannot use that as an excuse either in talking with your players or publicly, especially not to the media. If you blame officials even once for a loss, you've opened the door for players to do the same rather than hold themselves accountable for their performance. Also, if officials see you've called them out when they read the sports section the next day, how favorable do you think they'll be toward your team the next time they work one of your games? So keep whatever negative thoughts you might have about the officiating to yourself and you will be better for it.

Thoughts When Dealing With Officials

Here are some tips to remember when dealing with officials during games:

1. Ask officials questions, such as "Was there any contact on that play?" or "Can you watch their big man in the lane for 3 seconds?"

2. Try to engage in conversation with officials rather than yell. This helps you to keep your composure and to develop a relationship with the official.

3. Keep in mind that officials are trying to call the game fairly. They do not become officials for the pay or to help one team win over the other.

4. Tell an official when he has made a good call that goes against your club if it truly is a good call. He will respect that you are trying to be fair as well.

5. Never blame officials for a loss. If you blame the officials, your players will start to do the same.

Opposing Coach's Conduct

It is wise not to overlook your counterpart's state of mind as the game progresses. As you know, coaches can get pretty upset, either at the way their team is playing or at the way the game is being called by the officials. Sometimes, you can use this to your advantage.

So you must stay in control of yourself. And watch to see if you can pick up an advantage because the opposing coach is getting out of control. It may help to call a time-out and let the opposing coach pick up a technical or scream at his team.

Sometimes It's What You Don't Say . . .

Early in my coaching career, we were playing one of our top conference rivals, and we could not seem to get any closer than four points. In the fourth quarter, we were playing about as well as we could, but we just couldn't cut any further into the lead.

I called a time-out, told the players how well they were playing, and encouraged them to keep on hustling. The head of our English department, Dr. Charles "Buck" Offutt, was standing behind the bench during that time-out. We tied the game in regulation and won it in overtime, thanks in part to a technical foul on the other team.

The next day at school, Dr. Offutt, a member of the football coaching staff, came up to me and said, "Morgan, I can't believe you called that time-out. You were never playing better when you took it, and then you didn't really have anything to say to the team during the time-out."

I said, "Buck, I took the time-out to allow the other coach to talk to his team because I knew he was emotional at that point, and that he might hurt his team rather than help it. I also figured he might pick up a technical, which he did."

Game Plan Adjustments

I place a great deal of importance on going into each game with a comprehensive game plan that specifies the goals we want to accomplish and how to best accomplish those goals in every conceivable situation, from inbounds plays to foul shot alignments. However, I do not feel obligated to stay with that game plan no matter what. The adjustments you make during the course of a game, although they may seem to be minor ones at the time, could determine the outcome of that game.

As I've said, your basketball coaching philosophy should allow you to be flexible enough to adjust your system to fit the talents of your players. And that flexibility should carry over to actual games. You should be able to adjust your game plan to fit the circumstances of each particular game as it develops.

Minor adjustments that help fine-tune the game plan can pay large dividends. A defensive switch or a critical substitution in a tight game may be just what it takes to put your team in the win column.

As part of the game plan, you should also have some general guidelines that dictate how you prefer to play certain situations. For example, what play do you like to run in a tie game when going for the last shot? And, at what point do you consider a player in foul trouble? When would you like to take him out, and when would you like to put him back in?

Going With the Hot Hand

Our O'Connell team was playing conference opponent St. John's in early December of 2002, and we were up by three points in the third quarter. Our point guard, Ahmad Smith, came down and hit a three-point shot. We went down and got a defensive stop, and Ahmad came back and hit another three-pointer. After another defensive stop, he hit a third three-pointer. This series changed the game.

As coaches, the lesson we can learn from this is that we can have the greatest offensive sets and motion, but having players make the open shots is critical to success. That game seemed to propel us on to a 30-win season and the state championship that year.

Once again, the guidelines you set are not written in stone. The game may dictate that you have to put someone who is in foul trouble back into the game earlier than you would like to. But it is smart to have these general rules to aid you in making decisions.

Wholesale changes in a game plan are not beneficial. If you are forced to throw out an entire game plan and replace it with something else, then one of two things has happened: (1) Your initial preparation was flawed, or (2) something extremely unusual has happened. It is best to stay within your arsenal and to focus on what you have worked on in practices.

I've heard stories of coaches who try to implement a brand-new offense at halftime, one that their teams have never worked on in practice. By trying to change everything in the middle of the game, you are sending the message to your players that you are panicking. So don't be surprised if they begin to panic and question their ability as well.

THOUGHT FOR THE DAY

Fatigue makes cowards of us all.
–Vince Lombardi

Staying on Top

One of the greatest lessons that my good friend Red Auerbach taught me came in a summer league game back in the early 1960s when DeMatha was playing all-stars from the Washington, DC, public schools. They were loaded with talent (12 All-Metropolitan, or All-Met, players!), and we were fortunate to have an excellent team, so this was the most anticipated game of the summer.

It was played outside, and every high school player in the city must have been there. They were on roofs of buildings, hanging on fences and from telephone poles, coming from every imaginable angle trying to see this game.

Red Auerbach was among those in attendance to see the incredibly exciting game. It went to three overtimes, and we ended up losing by a couple of points right at the end.

The next day I saw Red at my summer day camp. He never brought up the thriller from the night before, so I asked him, "What did you think of the game last night?"

"Well," he said, "it's too bad you cost your team the game." Red always tells it like it is.

I said, "What do you mean?"

"You totally lost the feel of the game. I was listening to you during the time-outs. Late in the game, you're talking to your team about what you're going to do on offense when all of your problems were on defense. You weren't blocking out well enough, and the other team was getting second and third chances. That's ultimately what beat you. If you had known what was going on out there, you would have won that game, but you got caught up in it emotionally."

I've never forgotten that lesson, and to this day I have procedures in place to make sure I don't lose sight of anything that's going on out on the court. I rely heavily on my two assistants to do that. I assign one to watch all of the inside play, and the other watches our perimeter players, both offensively and defensively.

I concentrate on trying to get the total feel of the game, more of the big picture. I have somebody who sits next to me and jots down comments during the game. These comments are like an instant photograph of the game for me, and I refer to them often, especially during time-outs and at halftime. I also have someone keep track of how many time-outs both teams have left, as well as the foul situation of both teams. I want to know if the other team's leading rebounder has just picked up his third foul, or if one of their players is getting more points than he normally does. I don't want to be four minutes into the game before I find out that my leading rebounder doesn't have a rebound yet. I've got to be able to call him aside and say, "We're three minutes into the game and you don't have a rebound yet, and there have been seven in the game. We need you to get going."

If you work hard to stay on top of what's going on, you can help keep your players focused. It is human nature for players to take a play off now and then, but by keeping track of everything that's going on, you can quickly identify a weakness when it occurs and refocus your player or make any necessary adjustments.

I'm still grateful to Red Auerbach for teaching me how important it is to not lose the feel of the game—in basketball or in life.

The Vic Bubas Rule

Vic Bubas, a highly successful former coach at Duke, had a simple method for reminding coaches about their place in the game. He would tell coaches to do this: Take a legal pad, draw a line down the middle of it, and write "player" on one side of the line and "coach" on the other side. Then, with this paper in hand, watch the game film. Every time a player scores because of your "coaching genius," put a check mark in the column for the coach. Every time a player makes a good play or makes a shot because he is a good player, put a check mark in the column for the players. When it's over, where will the majority of the check marks be? They will be in the player column. The lesson here is that players make the plays, so the coach should not try to overcontrol them. Let them play. I have also used this method to help players who think too much and are too worried when they play. They need to just go play the game!

Personnel Decisions

Going into any game, I always have a good idea of how I want to handle my personnel in various situations. For example, if a player picks up his second foul in the first half, I will usually take him out of the game. If we can keep the game reasonably close, I prefer not to bring him back into the game until the start of the second half. Then, the player would have three fouls to commit in the second half before disqualification. On occasion, I have swayed from this rule because of particular circumstances. For example, intelligent players learn how to play when they are in foul trouble, so you can sometimes gamble and leave those players in the game a little longer. Plus, if the player involved hardly ever fouls

Courtesy of Bishop O'Connell High School/Tommy Orndorff

Joe instructs players during a recent game.

out of a game, I may put him back into the game earlier than I would otherwise.

Therefore, although your guidelines for juggling personnel should be established in your mind, they must be flexible enough to vary from game to game and opponent to opponent. For example, you should have a good idea of who your first substitute in the backcourt will be, as well as who your first sub in the frontcourt will be. I always have a good idea of who I think those first subs will be, but sometimes the circumstances of the game may cause that to change.

That's why I keep such personnel plans private among the coaches. We do not tell a player, "Hey, Joe, you're the first sub in the backcourt tonight." If you have already told a certain player he will be that sub, and game conditions force a change, then you will have discontented players on the bench. So I suggest that you be discreet about your personnel plans for each game; inform the other coaches, but not the players.

An often overlooked part of coaching is the art of substituting one player for another.

You need to be positive with both players involved. When you send a player in, let him know exactly what you're expecting from him, and then send him in with a pat on the back and a word of encouragement. For the player coming out, never make him look bad by starting to correct him while he's still coming off the court. I always pat him on the back as he's leaving the floor and then have him sit next to me on the bench, where I quietly discuss with him why I took him out. It might be, "You're playing great. I just want to give you a little rest." Or, "I think you're pressing a little bit too hard. We need to see you relax a little bit out there." Or it could be even more specific, like, "We need you to hit the boards harder. You're standing around taking too many plays off."

By staying upbeat with both players involved in the substitution, you get high-quality minutes out of the player you're sending in, and the one you're taking out should be more prepared to reenter the game when you want him to.

The Untested Sophomore

In the late 1970s, we were in Lake Charles, Louisiana, playing in the Pepsi-Cola Classic. We were matched up against Wheatley High from Houston, Texas, a highly talented team with great athletes. But we had some great athletes of our own in Sidney Lowe and Dereck Whittenburg, who would together go on to North Carolina State and form one of the nation's finest backcourts.

Early in the second quarter, we were enjoying a 12-point lead when Whittenburg went down heavily on his ankle. I knew there was no way Whittenburg was going to return to the game. We would discover later that he had broken a bone in his foot, and he ended up missing a big part of the season. (A few years later at North Carolina State, he broke the same bone in his other foot but came back to lead the Wolfpack to the 1983 NCAA championship.) But I never told the team that night that Dereck would not be back. Instead, I told the team, "Let's see if we can keep it close until Dereck gets his foot together."

Pictured here during their historic run to the 1983 NCAA National Championship title with Jim Valvano's Wolfpack, Sidney Lowe and Dereck Whittenburg were previously teammates under Morgan at DeMatha.

AP Photo/Koz

I replaced Whittenburg with an untested sophomore named Bobby Ferry, who was playing in the first varsity game of his life. Before the game, I had been contemplating sending Bobby back to the junior varsity for more seasoning.

The game—one of the greatest I've ever been a part of—went into five overtimes. By the end of the fourth overtime, I had told the team about everything I could possibly think of. So during the break between the fourth and fifth overtime periods, I found myself quoting Churchill: "Gentlemen," I said, "We will stay here all night long until one of two things happens. Either we win, or they lose. We will never give in. We are going to outlast them. We will never, ever, ever give in."

Fortunately, we finished them off in that fifth overtime, the longest game I've ever coached. To this day, I don't know what I would have said if we had gone to a sixth overtime.

By the way, the sophomore I put in for Whittenburg, Bobby Ferry, scored 25 points and missed only three shots in his varsity debut. (He had a younger brother by the name of Danny, who, fortunately, would also decide to play at DeMatha.)

Time-Outs

I always like to save as many of our time-outs as possible for the end of the game. This is important for stopping the clock and setting strategy down the stretch in tight ball games. Unfortunately, though, there are instances in which you are forced to spend a time-out before you would like to.

You may want to call a time-out to

- correct problems in your team's execution,
- review a special play for the last shot,
- freeze an opposing free-throw shooter,
- review a special last-possession defense,
- restore order in the midst of confusion,
- give the opposing team's coach more time to make a mistake, or
- rest your players without substituting.

Coaches who use time-outs effectively have an edge over those who do not. And because of the limited time available during these breaks, you must be well organized to get your message to the team as effectively and efficiently as possible. It is during these breaks that you can communicate to your team what they are doing right, what needs to be improved, and what adjustments you may have decided to make.

Because time-outs are so important, I have a ritual that we follow every time one is called.

1. All of the players on the floor sprint over to our bench. At this point, all of the players not in the game get up off the bench so the five coming off the floor can sit down and get water and towels.

2. While this is going on, I am formulating what I want to say to the team. I am also checking with my assistants to see what they have noticed. By the time I've talked with the assistants and the players have gotten their water, there are only about 20 seconds left in the time-out.

3. I crouch down in front of the players and quickly tell them what we are going to do. I do not spend time telling them what they are not doing. I try to keep the talks during time-outs as upbeat and positive as circumstances allow. I may say, "We've got to get on the offensive boards with more intensity," or "We've got to make sure we do a great job of blocking out. And then once we've gotten the rebound, we want to really look to run. We've got to look up and get the ball down the floor."

Long before our first game, I tell the players that during the time-out their eyes belong to me. I want them looking directly at me. If a player is not looking directly at me, this is an indication to me that he is tired, and I will put a substitute in the game so that player will get some needed rest. Because the players know this, they always look right at me. And if they're looking at me, there's a good chance they're paying attention to what I'm saying.

I've seen some time-out situations that were not organized at all. During one game, a player from the other team actually went up into the stands and talked to his girlfriend during the time-out! This is a complete waste of an opportunity to communicate with your players. Establish a time-out ritual for your players, and demand their full attention. That way, you will take full advantage of time-out opportunities.

Halftime

Halftimes are generally 10 minutes long in high school. Once the buzzer sounds, the players head to the locker room. I leave them there to talk among themselves for the first 3 or 4 minutes. During this time, I am outside the locker room talking to my assistants and quickly going over the key statistics. I am primarily interested in how the rebounding battle is going and if any players on the other team are scoring at an unusually high level.

When I walk into the locker room, every player's eyes turn and focus on me. No matter how the game is going, I will begin my talk by making some positive comment to get their attention. As during time-outs, I do not waste my time focusing on negatives or telling the players what we are not doing. Instead, I concentrate on what we need to do in the second half to get the job done.

Approaches to Halftime Situations

If we're behind, I may say something like, "Here's what we need to do in the second half. We don't want to try to catch up all at once. We don't want to attempt to make up the 12-point deficit in the first two minutes. We're going to hack away at it with sound defense and good execution of our offense." Then I will get into specifics.

If it is a close battle at halftime, I will use this approach: "We're in a tight game. And the way we're going to break away from them is to do it gradually by playing sound defense, hitting the boards a little harder, and working the break."

And if we find ourselves winning at the half, I emphasize going after it even harder. So I may tell the team, "We're just going to tighten the screws, play a little better, and pull away a little bit more. What we need to do is come out real strong in the third quarter and . . . "

By using a good, positive approach at halftime, you can help ensure that your players are ready to take the floor for the second half with a good idea of what they need to do. And this approach will also help them have the confidence needed to do it.

Halftime Organization

Organization at halftime is crucial in communicating effectively with your team. I've been amazed at how casually some teams approach the half. I remember one time when we came out of the locker room a little earlier than usual and saw two of the opposing players already out on the floor. One was eating a hot dog, and the other was eating an ice-cream cone!

As mentioned, I leave the players alone for the first 3 or 4 minutes while I talk to my assistants and formulate my thoughts. I then spend the next 3 to 4 minutes talking with the team. Finally, I try to allow about 3 minutes for players to get their thoughts together and warm up (if they want to) before the second half starts.

Postgame Procedures

I handle postgame in the locker room in much the same way as I handle halftime. I let the players have a few minutes to themselves after the game while I meet with my assistants. I will then go in and talk to the team, always beginning my talk with a positive remark, whether we won or lost.

You may also want to read over the stats that you want to emphasize—for example, most rebounds, steals, charges, blocks, and assists. You can also comment on the team free-throw percentage if it is particularly high. It's usually better not to mention the leading scorer, however, because this player will receive recognition from the outside.

In the postgame, the coach needs to keep everything positive. And in some ways it is even more important to be positive after a loss, even though the temptation may be to let out your frustrations. Remember this: Your leadership and guidance will have much more of an impact on your team after a loss than after a victory.

Winning With Class

After a win, it is a good idea to let the players enjoy the fruits of their labors and to go ahead and celebrate. But I believe it is equally important to keep a good perspective after a win. We tell our team that winning and losing are a part of life, not just of athletics, and that if they can handle both equally well, they will be successful in whatever they do.

Part of handling winning well is to win with class. I tell our team when we are victorious that we want to have the humility of a conquering hero. That includes not taunting an opponent. Instead, we want to remember how hard we worked and all of the things we did to be successful. And we want to remember that we are going to have to work even harder to stay successful. Mia Hamm once said, "It is more to stay on top than to get there." One way to stay successful is to win with class.

THOUGHT FOR THE DAY

A team of character will beat a team of characters every time.

Losing With Dignity

As coaches, one thing we should always be aware of is that we really have the attention of our team after a loss. In my experiences, the players are more receptive to what the coaches have to say after a defeat.

Athletes are competitors, and competitors will be disappointed in defeat. So when you go into the locker room after a loss, you know that the players will be a little down. But if the team has made a winning effort, let the players know that. Whenever your players give a winning effort, praise them for it, no matter what the outcome of the game. After a loss, help them keep their chins up and maintain a positive attitude that will carry over into the upcoming practices and games.

Lessons in Class

The first time we played Power Memorial High School and Lew Alcindor, we came up short by 3 points. Alcindor had had an unbelievable game, scoring 39 points and grabbing 22 rebounds, all in front of almost 13,000 people. In fact, during a time-out with about two minutes to go, the public address announcer said to the crowd, "Ladies and Gentlemen, no matter who wins this game, I think you will all agree that we are watching the two best high school teams in America." A standing ovation followed.

But despite Alcindor's incredible game, we had taken his team right down to the wire. I told the players I had never been prouder of them, and that I had never seen a more gallant effort than the one those guys had put forth. I told them I felt really good about the game because they had left their hearts and souls out there on the floor with their tremendous effort.

After the game, Lew Alcindor led his teammates into our locker room to shake the hands of all our players. They were a classy bunch of winners.

A year later, when we turned the tables and beat Power Memorial by 3 points, I told the players that we needed to get ready to go over to the opposition's locker room and congratulate them. But they beat us to the punch. Having just seen their 71-game winning streak come to an end, here was Lew Alcindor again leading his team into our locker room to congratulate us.

Lew Alcindor and Power Memorial demonstrated to us all what it is like to win with class and to lose with class. It heightened my respect for Alcindor and for his coach, Jack Donohue, who would become the coach of the Canadian national team. With such a combination of class and physical ability, it is no surprise that Lew Alcindor went on to become one of the greatest players our sport has ever known.

Setting the Tone

There are some teams that I love to play after they are coming off a loss. Why? Because in the locker room after the game their coach screamed and hollered at them so much that he all but guaranteed a couple more losses by destroying their confidence and their competitive spirit.

On the other hand, there are some teams that I hate to play if they lost their previous game. The coaches of these teams handle losses with dignity and can rally their team and fire their players up for the next game. And this is what I try to do with our teams.

After a loss, I tell the kids that I want to see them come back with the ferociousness of a wounded tiger. Telling players this helps set the tone for the next game and the practices leading up to that game. Here are some statements that I've found to be particularly effective after a loss:

- "Let's remember that basketball is not an undefeated sport."
- "We're going to learn from everything that didn't go well tonight so we can continue to improve."
- If you play each team in your league twice and lose the first game to a particular team, you can get your players looking forward to the rematch by saying something like, "Fellows, they won the wrong game."

Setting the tone for the team, after a win or a loss, is something that every coach should make an effort to do in the most positive way possible. In connection with that, I make it a point to shake the hand of every player after every game and thank the players for the effort they gave.

Even after a victory, a player may be a little discouraged because he didn't think he personally played particularly well. But you can always say, "Hey, Joe, the team did well, and that's what counts. Next game, you'll come back stronger than ever."

After a loss, most if not all of the players are going to be disappointed; you have to get them to lift their heads up. You have to set the tone by displaying the attitude, "We're coming back, and we're coming back strong."

Parting on a Positive Note

One of the biggest challenges that a coach faces is to pick up the spirit, enthusiasm, and confidence of a player who is very discouraged. Consequently, there is no greater reward than seeing a player whose chin was scraping the ground one day come back the next day with renewed vigor. How do you accomplish that? There's no magic answer. Just believe in the player, care about how he's feeling, and always be positive.

Taking the positive approach helped make my last season at DeMatha one of the most memorable. After losing a real heartbreaker to a league opponent on a long three-pointer (from NBA three-point range), our players were devastated. Some were even crying in the locker room after the game, and I knew that how they responded to the loss was going to be crucial to our success the rest of the season.

I stuck with the approach we've talked about and really tried to drive home positive messages to keep their spirits up and keep them focused on the next game. It worked. We went on an 18-game winning streak to end the season, finished with a 32-3 record, and won every championship we were eligible for. Had I taken a more negative approach and let my players have it when they were already down after a tough loss, I don't think I would have ended my coaching career at DeMatha in such memorable fashion.

Not a Time for Strategy

In my postgame comments, I never spend any time going over tactical problems or adjustments. I have found over the years that it is just a waste of time to do so, whether after a win or loss. The players are either so elated over a win or so dejected over a loss that they will not be able to fully absorb any tactical information at that point.

Tactical information should not be your first concern at that point anyway. The players' attitudes and mental well-being should occupy your time and efforts. You don't want them to be too high after a win or too low after a loss. Immediately after the game is the time when you can be most influential in helping them maintain an even keel. Save the tactical information for the next practice.

Besides keeping everything positive, the only other thing that needs to be mentioned after a game is the upcoming opponent. All you need to say is something like, "Fellows, our next game is against Central on Friday, and we're really going to have to be ready." Such a statement can help keep the players focused. After a loss, the upcoming game is an opportunity to redeem themselves. After a win, the mention of the next game serves as a reminder that there is still work to be done.

Summary

During game situations, keep the following points in mind:

- Try to keep some continuity in your starting five. Avoid making changes after a loss because it looks as if you are blaming the player who is no longer starting.

- Use your scouting reports to decide on matchups; the goal of any matchup should be to take away the other team's strengths. Make them beat you left-handed.

- Identify the critical matchups, including who will guard the other team's leading scorer and ball handler. When deciding on these matchups, consider other factors as well, such as potential foul trouble.

- Become involved with the game. Don't just be a spectator, and don't lose the feel of the game.

- As the coach and the leader of the team, make sure that you display exemplary conduct at all times. Coaches who lose their cool will have teams who do the same thing.

- Make minor adjustments in your game plan as dictated by game conditions. Never try to put in a new system during a game without having worked on it in practice.

- Have general guidelines in mind regarding how you want to handle personnel in all situations.
- Remember that sometimes you just have to trust your instincts.
- Try to use your time-outs as sparingly as possible so you will have enough for crucial points in the game.
- Organize your time-out procedures to maximize use of the limited time available to your team.

- Keep talks during time-outs, at halftime, and after the game as positive as possible.
- Try to keep your players' emotions as level as possible, not too high and not too low.
- Learn to handle winning and losing with equal class and dignity.
- Avoid discussing tactics with your team immediately after a game. Save it for the next practice.

PART VI

COACHING EVALUATION

CHAPTER 19

Evaluating Players

To become a successful basketball coach, you must have the resources and ability to evaluate your players, yourself, your assistants, and your overall program. You want these evaluations to be thorough and honest. Therefore, everyone involved must be open-minded enough to give and receive constructive criticism, assured that the evaluation process is for the good of the program. And one of the most difficult evaluations you'll make as a coach involves deciding which players will make the cut and what positions those players will play.

Summer Evaluations

We are fortunate to have an extensive summer league program that allows assistants to work with our players. The program also gives the head coach the opportunity to watch some of the players in action before practices begin. This gives us a big advantage in that we do not have to evaluate the players based on only a week or two of tryout performances.

The summer leagues in June, July, and early August provide tough competition at the varsity and junior varsity levels. Assistant coaches work with these teams, and whenever possible I attend these games and sit in the stands to observe and evaluate. Legally, I

am allowed to coach these teams if I choose to do so. But I think the players hear enough from me during the actual season; they're better off receiving instruction from staff members who will give them similar, but not the same, coaching. In addition, these games give my assistant coaches a chance to run the show, which is valuable experience for them and for me.

For high school basketball players to become the best they can be, they need to play basketball in the summer. Summer leagues and summer camps are available all over the country, and your players should be taking advantage of those opportunities to play more ball. In some cases, coaching staffs may not be allowed to coach the summer teams. When this is the case, you should at least try to observe your players. And if that is not possible, try to stay in touch with your players through frequent phone calls, e-mails, or postcards.

Our focus during the summer leagues is on observing the players and assisting them in their development. Before these leagues begin, I meet with my assistants and organize a detailed playing schedule for all of the players who will be competing. The varsity team is in two different leagues, and we start a different group of five in each of those leagues. This way, everybody learns how to start, everybody learns how to come off the bench, and many learn how to be finishers. This makes the kids better players, and it lets the coaching staff see how the players react in various situations.

During the course of the summer, I pull aside various players and chat with them, passing along some of the things I think they need to work on. I also go and speak to the team after each game that I attend. But I wait until after the head coach that day has made his comments. The postgame talks I give are very brief and are just pep talks to tell the guys they are doing a good job and should keep working hard.

After the final summer game, I make it a point to talk with the summer league participants and have them give the coaches a round of applause for working with them all summer. I tell the players to take a little bit of time off and maybe enjoy a family vacation.

But I remind the players that once school starts in September, it's time to get back to work for tryouts that begin in November. I stress to them that what they do between the beginning of school and the beginning of tryouts will probably determine whether they make the team. And if they do make the team, what they have done in that time will probably determine what kind of year they are going to have.

Summer Adjustments

When I first started at O'Connell, much like my father's teams, we participated in two varsity and one junior varsity summer leagues. Now, however, we not only participate in these summer leagues, but also participate in several team camps. Here are the reasons why:

1. Team camps increase players' opportunities to face great competition and to be seen by college coaches.

2. Team camps allow us to play as many as five games during a weekend. Thus, we can try to make corrections from one game to the next and see how players respond.

3. Team camps are set up in a format that is similar to a tournament, which puts our team in the kind of competitive situations that the players will encounter throughout the season as we take part in holiday, league, state, and national tournaments.

In addition to the team camps, we have our players participate in individual workouts and our shot board (see chapter 5 for more information). Therefore, while the players are improving their team play in the tournaments, they are also enhancing their individual skills.

Fall Evaluations

The school year begins in late August or early September. Around the middle of September, I suggest that you hold what I call a Fall Meeting. Perhaps you will want to have three different meetings, one each for the freshman, junior varsity (JV), and varsity teams. If your program is similar to ours, the varsity meeting room will be packed with young men who dream of making the team.

I open that meeting with motivational remarks, talk about how the summer league went, and go over our schedule for the upcoming season. Second, I introduce our academic advisor and remind the players that we will be checking on their academic progress every two weeks. I tell the candidates quite bluntly that if there is a tough choice regarding who will make the team, we will go with the better student. I also educate the players on college eligibility requirements and tell them of the importance of the SAT prep courses and exams.

I then have the players fill out pertinent information about themselves on index cards (see figure 19.1). This includes their class schedule so we will know where to find a player any time we need to get ahold of him.

Player Information Card

Name _____

Address _____

Phone _____

Year in school _____

Where you began the 9th grade _____

Height _____ Weight _____

Birth date (month-day-year) _____ Age as of today _____

Shoe size _____

Jacket size   XL   L   M   S

What team did you play on last year? _____

(Put class schedule on back of card.)

FIGURE 19.1 Player information card.

From M. Wootten and J. Wootten, 2013, *Coaching basketball successfully, third edition* (Champaign, IL: Human Kinetics).

Being a TEAM

At O'Connell, we take a similar approach to the fall period as my dad uses at DeMatha. We also work very hard to establish the right climate for the team to succeed the rest of the year. Early in my teaching career, a valued mentor and fellow faculty member, Richard Micheski, offered this pearl of wisdom: "Set the tone, and the content will follow." I believe this to be true, starting with the very first team meeting in the fall. You need to create the right culture within the program, because it will affect everything—the degree of respect with which everyone communicates, how the players perform academically, and so on.

In an effort to establish a winning culture, we stress the cornerstones of belief, trust, honesty, and collective responsibility at the fall meeting. We then introduce four themes based on these cornerstones that form the acronym *TEAM:*

Tough: Players must develop a mental and physical resilience to conquer challenges in all aspects of their lives. Our response to adversity will define us.

Eager: It's not sufficient for players to be willing to do what is asked and is needed; they must be enthusiastic and energized by those opportunities.

Attitude: Every player in our program must have his mind set on developing to his full potential as a person, athlete, student, and teammate.

Men: Maturity is a must. If each player is accountable and responsible for his actions and decisions, the group as a whole has a great chance to excel.

In fact, to remind players of our winning culture throughout the year, we give them wristbands with all four themes written on them.

We announce to the players that there will be open gym on Monday, Wednesday, and Friday for juniors and seniors; the gym will be available to freshmen and sophomores on Tuesday and Thursday. These open gyms are not organized practices, but merely an opportunity for the players to run and scrimmage in the gym as they work to get in shape. Legally, I am allowed to attend these gym sessions as long as I provide no instruction and do not organize anything.

I rarely attend open gym because I do not want the players to feel as if they are trying out. We are simply providing them with the facility where they can play. In addition to 5-on-5 scrimmages, we let our players play 2-on-2 and 3-on-3. We have found that this teaches them spacing, how to set screens, how to read screens, and so on. Open gym is also an opportunity for players to work on their individual skills—such as shooting and ballhandling—by focusing on repetition. One of the great benefits to an open gym is that the leaders of the team begin to emerge as they take charge of the time available.

Also at the Fall Meeting, I stress to the candidates the importance of being a member of the student body. I give the example (that I mentioned earlier) of James Brown, now a CBS sportscaster, who always had a friendly smile and hello for everyone at the school. He had plenty of ability as well, as evidenced by a great basketball career at Harvard and briefly in the NBA; but it was his pleasant and outgoing demeanor that made James one of the most popular players to ever go through DeMatha.

In addition, I hand out the Fall Evaluation sheets for the players to fill out (see figure 19.2). We encourage them to take their time and think about what they put on the form. One of the most important elements of the form is the section where we ask the player to write down his academic and athletic

---

Player's Fall Evaluation Form

Name _____

Address _____

Phone _____ Year in school _____ Height _____ Weight _____

Where do you see yourself on the team (role)?

1. What did you do this summer to make yourself a better student?

2. What did you do this summer to make yourself a better player?

3. What grade would you give yourself for your total effort to improve as a basketball player this summer? Circle one:

    Excellent   Very good   Good (average)   Below average   Poor

4. What do you plan on doing between now and November to make yourself a better player?

5. What weaknesses have become strengths since last May?

6. What do you think will be the strengths and weaknesses of this year's team?

7. List separately the following:
    a. Your academic goals for the year:
    b. Your athletic goals for the year:

FIGURE 19.2 Player's fall evaluation form.

goals for the year. These should be realistic, challenging targets to which the player is strongly committed—a promise to himself. I encourage the players to take their goal setting seriously.

Later on in the year, if a player is not doing as well academically as he should be, I might call him into the office, read back to him what his academic goals for the year were, and try to see what the problem might be. The same is true of athletic goals. If a certain player says that his goal is to become an outstanding defensive player but he's just not getting the job done, I will do the same thing: talk with him and remind him what his goals for the year were. Sometimes a little reminder is all it takes. In other instances, I may work with the player to revise his goals and aim for things that may be more attainable. Impossible goals will diminish, not increase, a player's efforts.

As we close the Fall Meeting, I remind the players that they are expected to report in shape and that all spots are open. I tell the candidates that there have been expected big contributors who became complacent and, unexpectedly, were beaten out by newcomers who had worked harder and improved more. I say this to encourage all candidates to come out and give it their best shot, because you never know what may happen when someone is given a chance. And I can promise them that they will get a fair chance.

A Chance Was All He Needed

I gave such a talk at the Fall Meeting in 1969. In the back of the room, a freshman named Adrian Dantley was listening. Little did I dream that he would make the varsity, much less become a starter, in his freshman year. Adrian is the only player in DeMatha history to be a four-year starter. He went on to become a high school and college All-American and an NBA all-star.

Dantley and other surprises serve as a reminder to me to avoid predetermining who will make the squad. We have to keep an open mind when evaluating our players for the upcoming season. When we say that all spots are open, we've got to really mean it. Almost every year, you'll find that someone you did not figure to start will end up cracking the first five.

Preseason Evaluations

Tryouts begin in early November. Typically, you'll use this time to see how players stack up against one another. Our first three days of tryouts are practically identical. First, we have players perform stretching exercises and warm-up drills. Then we hold scrimmages and simply watch the players play.

I have a rule that I will give every player at least three days of tryouts. I believe that these three days of scrimmaging are the best way to accurately evaluate a player. It gives the coaches a chance to watch the players under various conditions. We also have our managers keep statistics for all the scrimmages, which aid us in our evaluation of the players. We do not videotape these scrimmages and review the tapes to select the team. I think it's important to get a feel for the kind of players you have, and videotape does not capture all of the intensity and activity that occurs on the court.

We generally have about 40 students try out for the varsity team. I divide the candidates into five-player teams and have them scrimmage each other. I will move players from one team to another in an attempt to balance things as much as possible.

Balanced teams accomplish two things: (1) They afford the coaches a better opportunity to find that diamond in the rough, and (2) they are more fair to the players involved. When the teams are evenly balanced, it is easier to spot those players who rise above the other players' level of play. This allows you to make a better determination about a player's skills. It doesn't do anyone any good to have your five projected starters playing against five players who are likely to get cut.

THOUGHT FOR THE DAY

Be careful of the choices you make—they make you.

I do not necessarily have the team selected after the three days of scrimmaging. In fact, I may let only a few guys go at that point. But by that time, I do have a foundation on which to evaluate the remaining players. Generally, I try to have my 12- to 15-player team picked by the 10th day. I prefer to have it done sooner than that, but I want to allow myself enough time to get all the information I need to make the proper personnel decisions.

More Suggestions

At O'Connell, in addition to scrimmaging, we run drills that allow us to see how well players shoot the ball. Also, like many NBA teams that have players work out for them before the draft, we have the players play 2-on-2 or 3-on-3. In this way, we can really see if a player knows how to set and use a screen and if he has a good feel for the game.

Making the Cut

With DeMatha basketball, the kids usually start with the freshman team, work their way up to the junior varsity, and then try out for the varsity. Because of this system, it is unlikely that a very good player will slip through the cracks. Our largest turnout is always for the freshman team, which sometimes has 75 to 100 candidates try out. In this case, we run three separate tryouts for a few days, dividing the players alphabetically into teams for easier evaluation.

When you have a lot of candidates for your team, it can seem overwhelming to try to give each one a good look. But you will make the best decisions for your program and for the individuals trying out if you are willing to work hard and take the time to watch closely during the selection process.

Making cuts should not be an arbitrary decision. You can't just think someone looks like a player and decide on that basis. Sure, sometimes your instincts give you a feeling about a certain athlete. But you need more than that to go on.

When deciding whether or not to keep a player, consider these points:

- What kind of person the player is
- What kind of student the player is
- How quick the player is
- What kind of shooter the player is
- What kind of competitor the player is
- What kind of ball handler the player is
- What kind of passer the player is
- How the player gets along with teammates
- How coachable the player appears to be
- How high the player can jump
- How fast the player can run

One of the biggest mistakes that coaches make is to pick players by what I call the "eyeball test." Some coaches assume that if someone looks like a player, then he must be a player, and they keep him on the team.

I recommend staying away from the eyeball test. Instead, judge players by their performance. I've always said, "Don't play potential, play performance." And, similarly, "Don't keep potential, keep performance."

That does not mean you're mistaken if you keep some players who show potential but have failed to perform consistently. You can work with them to try to develop them. It is wise to keep such players as long as they have good attitudes, are coachable, and are willing to work hard to develop their potential. But, for the majority of your roster, keep players who perform and not those who may develop their potential.

Focus on Those Being Cut

When you are making decisions on whom you will cut, do not focus on the obvious players who will make the team. Focus on the players who are not likely to make it. For example, focus on thoughts such as, *I know that I am cutting Jim.* By focusing on whom you are cutting rather than whom you are keeping, you can help avoid having someone get lost in the shuffle.

The Most Difficult Part of Coaching

After the three days of scrimmaging and evaluating are completed, I then sit down with the rest of the staff to face what is the most difficult aspect of coaching. Together, we make the tough decisions about who we will keep and will not keep on the team. Cutting players is really the only part of my job that I have found to be disagreeable. When young men have dreams of playing varsity basketball and give their all during the tryouts, it is very difficult for me to tell them they are not going to make it.

For the players I am going to cut, I take the time to speak with each one individually in my office. I don't believe in posting lists that indicate who made the team or who got cut. I think that is a cruel, cold way of cutting players. When the player comes into my office, I start off by thanking him for coming out for the team and making such a great effort. I try my best to help the player keep things in perspective, tell him that life is a lot bigger than basketball, and generally just try to ease his disappointment as best I can.

If the players cut are not seniors, I invite them to come back out for the team next year. You might be surprised how much improved a player you cut one year can be the next season. One of the best examples of this for me was a young man named Perry Clark. When he was a junior, we were so loaded with talent that I didn't think he would play much. I encouraged him to take that year to play as much basketball as he could with the Boys' Club, Catholic Youth Organization (CYO), and so forth, and to work hard developing his game. When Perry returned the summer before his senior year, he was bigger, stronger, and much improved. He became one of the stars of our championship team and was an all-league selection. He received a full basketball scholarship to college, later joined my coaching staff, and then moved on to a successful college coaching career. Thank goodness I didn't make the mistake of cutting him as a junior and not encouraging him to continue playing and to come back the next year. You never know when a late bloomer will be ready to go.

After getting his start under Morgan at DeMatha, Perry Clark became a head coach himself, including a stint at Miami.

THOUGHT FOR THE DAY

Your talent is God's gift to you; what you do with it is your gift to God. –Leo Buscaglia

No matter what year they are in school, I encourage players I'm cutting to play in some of the local leagues, and I tell them that basketball is a great sport that can be played at a lot of different levels. I try to help the young men handle the fact that they are not going to make the school's team, and I emphasize that there are playing and coaching opportunities elsewhere.

Most players are able to take getting cut fairly well. Many of them are smart enough to see it coming. Understandably, all are disappointed, and some shed a few tears.

Maybe it is good that I was never a great player. Using myself as an example, I point out to the players I cut that there comes a time in everyone's life when the basketball will be taken out of their hands. And I try to get each young man to focus on the positives in his life.

I may say something like, "You are a great student. You get along well with people. And I know you are going to be a real success in life. But you're not going to win every game you play, and this is a great experience for you. My last year of organized basketball was after my first year of junior college. And I accepted that, just as you have to accept this. But what you have to do is go on and have the greatest year you can. You can continue to play basketball and have fun at it, and I hope you'll come out and support the team."

As hard as we may try not to make mistakes when cutting players, it inevitably happens. And that is the basis for another rule of mine. If, after a player has been cut, he truly thinks that he did not get a fair look, that he did not perform as well as he's capable of, or that the coaches just plain made a mistake, then he must wait one day and then come talk to me. I will give him another look. You might be surprised at how this can keep you from missing a potentially great player.

Putting Players in Positions

As mentioned in chapter 7, I prefer to assign players to only two positions: the perimeter and the post. Perimeter players, who face the basket, include guards, small forwards, and swing players (those who can play both the shooting guard and small forward positions). The post players, who play with their backs to the basket, include power forwards and centers. I am not sold on the designations of big guard, point guard, small forward, power forward, and center. As you have seen in previous chapters, I do assign numbers to players for alignment purposes. But in my way of thinking, there are two types of players on the floor rather than five.

I like to have as many complete basketball players as I can. These are players who possess, to some degree, all the necessary skills on the court. I am not satisfied with someone who can only rebound, or only dribble, or only

shoot from outside of 15 feet. To be a basketball player, you must possess all of the skills required of you while you are on the floor.

Every coach should at least once be blessed with a player who has all-around skills. I was when Danny Ferry attended DeMatha.

Courtesy of DeMatha Catholic High School

Morgan instructs Danny Ferry, who later went on to a great college and NBA career, at a DeMatha practice.

I remember one year when we played Archbishop Carroll High School for the league championship. Carroll featured Derrick Lewis, who went on to a successful career at Maryland and to pro ball in Europe. The inside matchup between Derrick and Danny was virtually dead even. But Danny was talented enough that he was able to pull away from the basket, and the odds shifted to his favor. Danny was just a little too quick for Derrick and had a good outside shot that very few post players were able to move out to the perimeter and defend.

Danny Ferry was one of the most complete players I ever coached. He was named the National Player of the Year at DeMatha and at Duke, and he went on to a great career in the NBA.

However, it is the coach's job to put players in positions that best utilize their strengths. If the best position for a player is playing facing the basket, make him a perimeter player. If he's stronger with his back to the basket, make him a post player. Of course, it's ideal when a player can play either position.

Putting Your Team in Position

Obviously, game situations often dictate certain coaching strategies. You can prepare by knowing in advance the combination of five players that you will put on the floor in all those various situations. You should identify your best starting team, your best ballhandling team (consisting of a combination of your five best ball handlers and foul shooters), your best rebounding team, your best pressing team, and so forth.

For example, if late in the game the other team is pressing, you will want the ball in the hands of your best ball handler. At that stage of the game, you will call for an offense that keeps the best dribbler and passer in control of the ball. Although I do not necessarily designate a point guard, I make sure that we are equipped to handle this and many other situations.

Watch Your Wallet Around This Team

We call one of our special situation teams, the all-out pressing team, the "Pickpockets." And over the years, they've earned their name.

In one game against Long Island Lutheran, we found ourselves down by 23 points going into the last quarter. I inserted the Pickpockets and told them that we couldn't let the other team get the ball over half-court. They did their job—in a hurry! Then, with a minute to go in the game, we put in our ball control team to protect our 4-point lead.

In a similar situation, we found ourselves down by 15 after the first quarter against Paint Branch High School. Once again we turned to the Pickpockets, and at the half we led by 13 points. That's a 28-point turnaround in one quarter!

I use these examples to illustrate that a coach has to know what five players will make up the best team to have on the floor in a particular situation. If you decide this ahead of time, you can get the most out of your team in each circumstance you face.

Practice Evaluations

As discussed in part II, I break our entire season down into a master season plan, monthly plan, weekly plan, and daily plan. When drawing up these long- and short-term practice plans, I always ask for the help of my staff. I have a practice plan for every practice that I have ever had at DeMatha High School.

Keeping records over the long term can be of particular help when evaluating the different squads from year to year. I can go back into the records if I'm interested in knowing where the team was at a certain point in the season the year before. Also, I can go back through the records and find teams that had similar talent as my present team. I use that information to help in deciding what to do in practice with my current team, knowing what has worked with past teams.

The more organized you are, the better coach you will be, and the better your team will be. As with everything in life, organization can be achieved through hard work. I suggest that you keep a written record of almost everything (practice plans, scouting reports, player files, and so forth) and a filing system that allows you to find what you are looking for without too much trouble.

Part of being organized is knowing what you want to accomplish for the season and for that particular month, week, and day. A high level of organization allows you to get the most out of every minute you spend out on the floor. As the old saying goes, "It's not the hours you put in your work that counts. It's the work you put in the hours" (Sam Ewing). And what you put into your hours with the team should be well planned in advance.

Practice Observations

The primary thing to look for during practice is how hard the players are working. I'm a believer in the coaching commandment, "As they practice, so shall they play." So I want my players out there giving it their all in practice as well as in games.

I pay particular attention to my best players to make sure they are out there working their hardest. Sometimes the very talented players can be so successful going at 90 percent speed that they fail to push themselves and do not improve.

It should be the ambition of every player to take himself to the next level. The way to get to that level is to practice as hard as you possibly can. So keep a sharp eye on all of your players to make sure they are not just going through the motions. I tell the players that every single day they are either going to get a little bit better or take a little step backward. There is no such thing as standing still. The only way to steadily improve is to give your best effort each day.

THOUGHT FOR THE DAY

Be not deceived; God is not mocked: for whatsoever a man soweth, so shall he also reap. –The Bible (King James Translation), Galatians 6:7

Assistant Input

I am fortunate to have two full-time assistants who help a great deal in observing and evaluating practices. We sit down and draw up that day's plan before we take the floor so we all know what we want to accomplish and look for. The assistant who works with the post players will concentrate on them, and the assistant who works with the perimeter players will be watching them. I keep an overall perspective on the practice.

After the practice is over and the team has been dismissed, I again meet with my assistants. We discuss the practice and look over the statistics that were kept by the team managers. The form on which we draw up our daily practice plan (see chapter 6) includes a section at the end for comments about that particular practice. This is our opportunity to record what we did well that day and what we need to work on. We then proceed to draw up the plan for the next day's practice.

The next day's practice plan should not necessarily depend on the success of the previous day's practice. Instead, pay more attention to your plan for that week. If you fluctuate daily, your players are likely to be

Courtesy of Bishop O'Connell High School/Tommy Orndorff

Assistant input is crucial to a successful ball club.

similarly inconsistent. When you're guided by your weekly plan, which was taken from the monthly plan, you'll be on course to meet the objectives outlined in your season plan.

Videotape

Videotapes are great tools with a variety of uses. They can be used for promotional reasons, such as making highlight films of your players to send to college coaches who want to see them in action. This is very popular among football coaches, but it can be equally effective in helping a basketball player win a college scholarship.

Videos can also be extremely effective teaching tools. Sometimes there is no better way to get a message across to a team or a player than being able to show them exactly what you are talking about. You can use tapes to illustrate both good and bad. For example, if you want to emphasize some of the good things your team is doing on offense, you can string together about eight high-quality possessions where they did just what you want them to do. Conversely, you can show your players six or eight bad series to help point out mistakes and what they need to do to correct them. I frequently have one of the managers videotape practices, but only when I have a specific purpose in mind.

On occasion, I sometimes make what I call a "lowlight" tape for individuals, say if a player is playing poorly or not hustling. Sometimes I'll videotape a drill to illustrate a point to one player. For example, I may tell a player that he's not running the lane as well as he thinks he is. If I can show him on film what I am talking about, he cannot disagree. As always, I don't do this to embarrass players, but to teach, and seeing themselves on tape really makes the point clear. If you do this, do not show the tape to the team. This should be done in private with just you and the player.

Sometimes when the team has played a disappointing game in which nothing seemed to go right from beginning to end, rather than dwell on those mistakes and rehash that entire game, I "burn the film." Not literally,

Candid Camera

Eddie Fogler, the former coach at South Carolina, played under Dean Smith at North Carolina University. He told me of a time when Coach Smith was really getting on him for not hustling. Eddie said he knew that he was going full speed and really working hard and that Coach Smith was wrong. But one film session convinced Eddie that Dean Smith was right. Pictures don't lie. Sometimes a player needs to see for himself what the coach is talking about for it to register.

of course, but I tell the team we're going to burn the film and move on. To continue to rehash a totally bad performance is often counterproductive. I'd rather move on and say, "We know we laid a real big egg out there the other night, and we know that's not going to happen again."

In sum, I cannot emphasize enough the importance of evaluating every single practice. How you practice is how you play. And through these daily evaluations you can determine if you are on course toward playing as you envisioned in your long-term plans. Of course, you need to evaluate games, too.

Game Evaluations

To ensure that you observe games as fully as you can, assign all of your coaches to watch specific things at certain times of the game. This should begin during the 20-minute warm-up; one of your assistants should monitor players' execution of the pregame routine just to make sure everything is going smoothly. At the same time, another coach should make sure the scorekeeper has the correct lineup with the correct numbers in the official book.

Game Duties

Once the game starts, every coach should perform an assigned role. As the head coach, my job is to observe the overall offensive and defensive picture of the game.

One of my assistants is assigned the role of sitting right next to me on the bench and taking notes on all the comments I make. He will jot down what I say as the game goes on, and I may want to refer to his notes for use during time-outs, halftime, or the next day in practice.

Generally, my comments are related to phases of the game that I think need improvement. I may say things like, "Joe just gave up the baseline" or "We're not changing ends of the floor" or "We're not looking up against their zone press." All of my verbal observations are written down by my assistant, and they provide us with a running account of significant concerns regarding individual and team performance during the game.

My other assistant is busy keeping track of the number of fouls on players from both teams, as well as the time-out situation. This assistant is responsible for letting me know immediately if one of our players picks up his second foul in the first half. He will also let me know if someone from the other team is getting into foul trouble. For example, if the other team's best rebounder picks up his third foul, my assistant should let me know. We then might try to work the ball inside, force that player to play defense, and possibly help him pick up his fourth foul. (But if he gives us the easy basket, we'll take that, too.)

The coach who keeps the fouls and time-outs is also responsible for watching the opposing team's huddle during those time-outs to see what substitutions the other team is making. He notifies me of any changes that are made during the time-out so that we have an opportunity to counteract their move with one of our own. Many teams have sneaked in a sub or two during time-outs and have gotten a cheap basket because the defending team didn't make the adjustment to the new personnel on the floor.

As part of his assignment in keeping an eye on the opposition, this assistant is also responsible for getting involved in any meetings during a time-out that the other coaches may be having with the officials. I want our team to be represented in all such meetings to make sure the opponent does not gain an unfair advantage. Although good officials go out of their way to make sure both teams are represented, I want an assistant coach to make sure we're a part of any discussions taking place.

As previously mentioned, during practices one of my assistants coaches perimeter players, and the other works with the post players. During games, in addition to the other duties I've described, the two assistants carefully observe the players they coach in practices.

I encourage my assistants' input at all times throughout the games and sometimes ask their opinion on trends in the game. But I make sure they tell me what they see and not the players. Meanwhile, I keep the bigger picture in mind and make any corrections I think are necessary. A rule we have is that there must be only one voice coming from the bench, and that voice is mine. Players on the floor can't benefit from three different coaches yelling three different things to them.

I strongly recommend that you really get into the game. Don't just be a spectator out there. As a coach, you've got to get a feel for games. Your assistants help you keep track of things, but you may not fully appreciate the meaning of what they tell you if you are removed from the nuances of the action. It's easy to become just a spectator, especially when things are going well. If your team hits three or four fast breaks in a row, you may have a tendency to jump up and down and cheer. But before you lead the cheering section, you should reflect on and understand why your team was able to get those easy scoring opportunities.

In addition to the coaches fulfilling their roles during games, we have one of our managers keeping stats, along with our faculty moderator. Another manager is our scorekeeper and keeps the book. A third manager videotapes the game. And the fourth manager, our student trainer, is on the bench to help with injuries and to provide water during time-outs.

Postgame Evaluation

With all the feedback I get, I have a pretty good record of what happened out on the floor once the game is completed. I have a list of my comments, the statistics, the time-out and foul charts, and a videotape of the game. In addition, as soon as possible after the game, my coaches and I meet and write down everything we can remember about the game.

From all of these information sources, we determine what we need to do as a result. We'll talk about what we need to work on the next day and whether there will be any change to our weekly or daily plan. As a coach, you should do these things right after the game when your memory of the game is still sharp.

At practice the next day, the first thing we do is go over a synopsis I've prepared from the preceding game. Win or lose, I have players walk through the trouble spots to try to help them understand my analysis. This helps players know why certain things worked or didn't work and how they can improve their performance.

Summary

Here are some tips to consider when evaluating your players throughout the season:

- If possible, get your players into summer leagues. This will make them better players and give you more information to evaluate.
- Tell candidates for your team that all spots are open during tryouts, and make it be the truth.
- Have your players write down their academic and athletic goals at the start of each year.

- Spend the first few days of tryouts just scrimmaging to get a good look at the candidates.
- Don't make arbitrary cuts based on casual observations. Arm yourself with specific information to make these decisions.
- Take time to speak individually with the players you are cutting.
- Consider having a procedure whereby any player who is cut can be given a second look.
- Encourage all players to be versatile on the court, but also make sure you put them in positions that best utilize their strengths.
- Identify your best five-player units for meeting various game conditions (that is, your best ballhandling team, your best rebounding team, and so forth).
- Draw up a practice plan daily and stick to it.
- Watch practices to make sure your players are working hard.
- Meet with your assistants to evaluate every practice.
- Videotape practices when you have a need to.
- Assign duties to your assistants and managers to ensure that careful observation and record keeping occur at all games.
- Meet with your assistants as soon as possible after games to evaluate and analyze.
- At the first practice after a game, take the time to walk through and demonstrate the points you want to cover from your analysis of the previous game.

CHAPTER 20

Evaluating Your Program

A coach's job is not over when the season ends; it just changes. Rather than working hands-on with players, you will be evaluating and planning for the future. In many ways, the work you do after the season determines whether your program improves the following year. It's not enough to just sit back at the end of the year and say, "Boy, we had a great year. Wasn't it wonderful?" Or, "We had a lousy year, and we'll have to do better next year."

Postseason Evaluation

No matter what kind of season you had, you need to sit down and thoroughly evaluate your program. What you want to find out is where you were, how you did with what you had, and where you are going. As I've mentioned, there is no progress without change. But all change is not necessarily progress. It is the evaluation process that will allow you to discover what needs to be changed and what needs to be left alone.

Program Assessment

The first step in analyzing your program is to have those involved write out their thoughts on the program. I learned a long time ago from

George Allen—the late, great coach of the NFL's Rams and Redskins—that if you really want someone's opinion, get it in writing.

Senior Feedback When seeking feedback from your graduating seniors, tell them that you are not looking for flowery accolades, but substantive ideas and criticisms that they believe will improve your program. It should be a private, personal evaluation by the seniors; for it to be helpful, they must be completely honest.

Through the years, I have received tremendous feedback from our graduating students. If I have a specific concern, I may ask them for their thoughts on that subject. Their responses may not always be what you want to hear, but realize that their insights can be for the good of the program. And responses are not always negative; what the seniors like about the program also comes through in these evaluations. But whether what's said is positive or negative, getting input from your graduating seniors is a great way to begin your program evaluation.

Assistant Coaches' Input I also ask all of my coaches for a written evaluation of the past season. If you call a meeting of all of the people associated with your program, there's a chance that only the outspoken among them will voice their thoughts, thus excluding some potentially valuable information from the quieter types. In writing, though, chances are better that what is on the paper will accurately represent that person's thoughts.

Performance Assessment

Performance evaluations should be completed for positive reasons, primarily so that all of the players and all of the coaches (including the head coach) can grow. From examining the strengths and weaknesses of the players, the coaches, and the overall program, I can get a pretty good picture of what I'm doing well or not doing well.

As the head coach, I view myself as the teacher. But, as the saying goes, sometimes the teacher learns more than the student. That may be particularly true in coaching. From these evaluations, we can learn quite a bit about ourselves as head coaches and about the kind of program we are running.

When conducting evaluations, we must be honest with ourselves and with others. We must be open-minded and flexible enough to incorporate changes that are for the good of the kids and the good of the program.

THOUGHT FOR THE DAY

Life is change; growth optional. Choose wisely. –Karen Kaiser Clark

Evaluation of Assistants' Performance After the season ends, you should evaluate your staff. Again, I suggest that you do this in writing. Then sit down with each member of the staff and go over that evaluation with him. Tell each staff member what you honestly see as his strengths and weaknesses, and what he can do to improve as a coach.

I have been blessed to have assistants who are interested in improving themselves and are receptive to constructive criticism, attitudes that help make these sessions valuable. Many former DeMatha assistants now coach at the collegiate and high school level.

I think each of them would say these yearly evaluations in some way contributed to his growth as a coach.

Player Evaluations My assistants and I evaluate our personnel the same way we evaluate ourselves and our program. We have each player submit a written evaluation of himself to the coaching staff. I will then meet individually with each player and discuss with him his own and the coaches' evaluations. At these meetings, I will share with each player the things that the coaching staff believes he needs to do to become a better basketball player. I remind each player that individual evaluations continue throughout the year, and that he will undergo the same process during summer league play.

I also give the players their off-season workout plans (see chapter 5) in writing. When they have a written copy of the complete program, this eliminates the possibility that something may be forgotten. And if they lose the written form, we have it on record and can give them another copy without having to sit down and go through the evaluation process all over again.

Personal Evaluation Since beginning my head coaching career at O'Connell, I also spend some time evaluating my own performance after each season. I go over the past season and examine things I did not get done, or things I did that I shouldn't have done. And I try to decide what I need to change.

A great evaluation tool for a coach is to watch one game film per week. As you watch that film, try to scout your team and pick apart your weaknesses and strengths. After you have watched at least 10 games, ask yourself these questions: Is my team exhibiting the style of play that I want? Are they taking care of the three or four most important points I emphasized throughout the season? This will allow you to evaluate what you are really getting across to your team and what areas you need to work on. After watching the games to scout your team, rewatch the same games to evaluate the strengths and weaknesses of your opponent.

30 Minutes Can Make a Difference

I can't emphasize enough how important these postseason evaluations can be to your players and your program. I talked earlier about Bill Langloh, who was a guard for DeMatha in the 1960s. In one of these meetings with Bill, I told him I thought he was a half step too slow to play big-time Division I basketball. He asked what he could do to correct that, and I prescribed a quickness program involving jumping rope, running hills and steps, and similar activities.

As a result of that meeting, for one entire summer Bill spent 30 minutes a day, 5 days a week, working on his quickness. Did it pay off? Bill Langloh went on to become a four-year starter at the University of Virginia and led the Cavaliers to their first ACC title. That might never have happened if we hadn't spent those 30 minutes talking during our evaluation meeting.

Adrian Dantley is another example. When we talked at the end of his first year, Adrian said he wanted to lose weight and gain strength. We went up the road to the University of Maryland, checked into its weight program, and Adrian got to work. Although Adrian was small at six-foot-five, the strength training habits he developed in high school helped him be a great inside force at both the collegiate and professional levels.

This will give you ideas on areas you can emphasize, help you understand why you hold the beliefs that you have, and also strengthen those beliefs.

Building the Future

It has often been said about the DeMatha program, "They never rebuild. They just reload." This can be true of any program if you have lower levels of the overall program, such as freshman and junior varsity teams, that contribute consistently to the varsity. If you have a basic structure to your program that allows players to develop as they work their way up to the varsity, you can continue to run your program without missing too much of a beat.

Evaluations are a big part of this. They can allow you to streamline and change the program, even as you adjust your style of play to the personnel in your system each year. Frequent evaluations can help the program to evolve and demonstrate a growth pattern, and they can help to eliminate overhauls of the system every couple of years.

THOUGHT FOR THE DAY

Don't knock success, analyze it.

This is not to say you won't have differences to deal with. Every player, team, and year will be different. But analyzing and evaluating each situation—how it was handled, what the result was, and how it could be improved—are the keys to building and maintaining a successful program.

One reminder: Conduct all of your evaluations and make any resulting adjustments within the framework of your own personality and philosophy. There are no magic coaching formulas that you can apply to a group of players for guaranteed success.

John Wooden's UCLA teams played one style of ball, game in and game out. Still, he admired North Carolina coach Dean Smith because he could teach so many different things and teach them all well. Smith, whose teams play multiple offenses and defenses, is one of the greatest coaches of all time. Yet so is John Wooden. Smith and Wooden are different people with different styles who are both among the best ever in our profession. As I said, the only way to succeed is by going about your work in a manner that is consistent with your personality and philosophy.

So be yourself at all times. Work hard at being a good coach. Listen to what people have to say and be open-minded enough to consider new ideas. Keep your program in perspective. Constantly reevaluate your program and incorporate positive changes. But most of all, have fun. If you do, you'll build a successful program that will win its share of games and, more important, produce young people who are well prepared for life—who will one day say they were proud to have you as a coach.

The Wootten Coaching Tree

Coaching has so many rewards that it is impossible for me to pick the greatest one or two. However, seeing my players go on to continue their education, lead successful lives, and become good citizens ranks right up there at the top. Some were fortunate enough to play in the NBA; others became teachers, lawyers, doctors, and successful professionals; a couple achieved fame in the media, such as James Brown of CBS Sports, and Adrian Branch, who works in the Washington, DC, area.

Certainly one of my greatest thrills as a coach and a father was to have the honor and privilege to coach both of my sons, Brendan and Joe Wootten. Both were starters and key members of championship teams: Brendan on the 1988 team, and Joe on the 1991 team, both of which won the league, city, and Alhambra tournament titles. It's still fun to hear them argue about which team was the best!

Brendan went on to play a year at the University of Pennsylvania, where he then got his degree. He is now a managing director with Goldman Sachs and is enjoying a very successful Wall Street career.

Joe played for a year under Gary Williams at the University of Maryland. After getting his degree, he became an assistant coach at Furman University, where he was the youngest assistant in the country. From there, he joined our staff at DeMatha, starting as the freshman coach before soon becoming my top assistant.

As you are aware from this book, Joe is now the head coach at Bishop O'Connell High School in Virginia, where he has built an extremely successful program. He took

Mark Goldman/Icon SMI

Mike Brey, once a player and assistant coach under Morgan, is now head coach at Notre Dame.

a team with only 6 victories the year before he arrived and transformed them into 16-, 17-, and 30-game winners in his first 3 seasons. Over the last 13 seasons, his teams have won 30 games three times (and 29 games once) and have averaged 23 wins a year. His teams have won five Virginia state titles and three Alhambra Catholic Invitational titles in those 13 seasons. He and I continue to run a summer basketball camp together at Frostburg State University that attracts players from all over the world.

Joe is one of many former players who have gone on to become teachers and coaches, which is a great thrill for me. It's both exciting and humbling to look at the list. Dozens of my former players and coaches have gone on to coach high school basketball. There are too many to mention individually, but they all take seriously their roles in touching the lives of young people.

Others have become college or pro coaches, such as Mike Brey (Notre Dame), Perry Clark (formerly Miami), Jack Bruen (formerly Colgate), Eddie Fogler (formerly South Carolina), Joe Mihalich (Niagra), Terry Truax (formerly Towson State), Murray Arnold (formerly Stetson University and Chicago Bulls assistant), Sidney Lowe (Utah Jazz assistant; formerly Minnesota Timberwolves and Vancouver Grizzlies), Dereck Whittenburg (formerly Fordham), Ron Everhart (formerly Northeastern), Rod Balanis (Notre Dame assistant), Darryl Bruce (Mount St. Mary's assistant), Marty Fletcher (formerly University of Colorado at Colorado Springs, men's and women's teams), Travis Lyons (formerly Fordham assistant), Heath Schroyer (UNLV assistant), Pete Strickland (George Washington assistant), Billy Hite (Virginia Tech assistant head football coach), Joe Cantafio (formerly Furman), Jeff Hathaway (Hofstra athletic director), Bill Mecca (Quinnipiac College associate athletic director), Derek Carter (Delaware State athletic director), Ken Blakeney (formerly Harvard and Delaware assistant), Kort Wickenheiser (formerly St. Bonaventure assistant), Scott McClary (Muhlenberg College), Ted Jeffries (formerly William and Mary assistant), Chris Parsons (Columbia assistant), and Kurtis Shultz (Cincinnati Bengals strength coach).

The list goes on. Coming from the DeMatha program, they all stress the fundamentals and pay attention to the details. Just as important, they all have their own styles that they bring to the art of coaching, and they have remained true to who they are. One of the things that I'm proudest of is that so many of our players saw teaching and coaching as a worthwhile vocation and avocation. It's a feeling I hope every head coach can experience.

O'Connell Assistants

If coaches know that you want to see them advance in their career, they will give you their best effort. I ask all of the coaches who come to work at O'Connell to help make the program better while they are with us. In turn, they have my word that I will do everything to help them advance. Assistant coaches also need to understand that, like a player, it is not where you begin, but where you finish.

Seth Goldberg is a great example of making the most out of a small opportunity. Seth came to me after working our summer camp and asked if he could join my staff. I did not have any spots open, but I liked his enthusiasm. I told him he could volunteer as my second assistant coach on the freshman team. He did a great job of showing his value by scouting, helping with the JV practices after completing the freshman practices, and always doing what needed to be done *before* he was asked. He showed so much growth in that first year that the next year I appointed him as the head JV coach. Seth eventually moved onto the varsity staff and currently is the head coach at St. Paul's in Baltimore, where he has led the program to incredible success.

My father said, "Surround yourself with good people," and I have always tried to follow that advice, not only with players but with coaches as well. I am very proud of the coaches I have worked with: Scott McClary (Muhlenberg College), Jason Donnelly (Villanova assistant), Ron Ginyard (St. Stephen's & St. Agnes), Mike Pegues (Xavier assistant), Duane Simpkins (UNC Greensboro assistant), Seth Goldberg (St. Paul's), Garrett O'Donnell (Maret School), Paul Easton (St. James), Stu Wilson (Montgomery College), and Hunter Taylor (Spring Hill High School, Texas).

Courtesy of DeMatha Catholic High School

Morgan, a legend, holds the most wins as a head coach in the history of basketball.

Summary

Here are some tips to consider when evaluating your program:

- At the end of the season, honestly evaluate all phases of your program.
- Have graduating seniors provide you with a written assessment of your program, describing the positives and negatives that they saw while they were a part of the program.
- Conduct all of your evaluations in two parts: a written assessment followed by a one-on-one talk.
- Have your assistant coaches submit a written evaluation.
- Be open-minded enough to evaluate yourself and honestly consider what new ideas may emerge during evaluations.
- For underclassmen, provide them with written workout programs structured to promote their development over the summer.
- Make all evaluations and adjustments within the framework of your personality and coaching philosophy.
- Have fun and be genuine in your efforts to promote the development of your program and the student-athletes who are in it.

APPENDIX A

AGENDA FOR FIRST BASKETBALL MEETING

Date: _____

1. Opening remarks–distribute the poem "Loyalty" (see chapter 2)
2. Philosophy and objectives
3. Personnel–collect all assistants' thoughts
4. Coaching and managing responsibilities*
5. Major tasks to be completed before the season starts–collect all assistants' thoughts*
6. Mass and dinner format*
7. Managers (home and away) and traveling squad*
8. Monitoring academics
9. Basketball clinic
10. Assign topics for second meeting
11. Thoughts for the season–collect all assistants' thoughts
12. Suggestions and additions

Date for next meeting: _____

* Topic assigned to an assistant coach for second meeting

AGENDA FOR SECOND BASKETBALL MEETING

Date: _____

1. Coaching and managing responsibilities–review and update on progress

2. Major tasks to be completed before the season starts–review and update on progress
   a. Man-to-man defense–name of coach responsible
   b. Pressure offense–name of coach responsible
   c. Fast break–name of coach responsible
   d. Jump balls–name of coach responsible
   e. Out-of-bounds plays–collect all assistants' thoughts
   f. Foul shots–name of coach responsible
   g. Time and score (offense and defense)–collect all assistants' thoughts

3. Mass and dinner format
4. Managers (home and away) and traveling squad
5. New business

Date for next meeting: _____

(continued)

AGENDA FOR THIRD BASKETBALL MEETING

Date: _____

1. Coaching and managing responsibilities—review and update on progress
2. Major tasks to be completed before the season starts—review and update on progress
   a. New drills—collect all assistants' thoughts
   b. Three-point plays—collect all assistants' thoughts
   c. Zone offense—name of coach responsible
   d. Zone defense—name of coach responsible
   e. Zone press—name of coach responsible
   f. Offense versus junk defense—collect all assistants' thoughts
3. Mass and dinner format—finalize
4. Managers (home and away) and traveling squad—finalize
5. New business

Date for next meeting: _____

AGENDA FOR FOURTH BASKETBALL MEETING

Date: _____

1. Major tasks to be completed before the season starts—review and update on progress
   a. Man-to-man offense—name of coach responsible
   b. Crazy situations (last-second shot, defense versus crazy offenses, and so on)—collect all assistants' thoughts
2. When team is selected
3. Teams for first practice
4. First day practice announcements
5. First week practice times
6. Film work
7. Travel procedure
8. Scouting for the year
   a. Available coaches
   b. Early-season opponents
   c. Films from last season
9. What is in place by first game
10. Season plans

APPENDIX B

Sample Monthly Practice Plan

Nov. 8	Nov. 9	Nov. 10	Nov. 11
Stretching	Stretching	Stretching	Stretching
Comments	Comments	Comments	Comments
Warm-up*	Warm-up*	Warm-up*	Warm-up*
Big 3 drills**	Big 3 drills**	Big 3 drills**	Big 3 drills**
Stance and steps	Stance and steps	Shooting stations	Shooting stations
Shooting stations	Screening	Free throws and sprints	Free throws and sprints
Free throws and sprints	Shooting stations	1-on-1 full court	1-on-1 full court
1-on-1 full court	Free throws and sprints	2-on-2 stations	2-on-2 full court
1-on-1 half court	1-on-1 full court	Scrimmage	2-on-2 stations
Scrimmage	2-on-2 stations	Box 1	3-on-3 full court
Forward and guard overplay	Scrimmage	Box 2	Man-to-man half court
Closing comments	Forward and guard overplay	Forward and guard overplay	Line
	Closing comments	Horseshoe drill	Fogler drill
		Closing comments	Explain number system
			22-Tough
			Closing comments

Nov. 12	Nov. 13	Nov. 14	Nov. 15
Stretching	Stretching	Off	Stretching
Comments	Comments		Comments
Warm-up*	Warm-up*		Warm-up*
Big 3 drills**	Big 3 drills**		Big 3 drills**
Shooting stations	Shooting stations		Free throws and sprints
Free throws and sprints	Free throws and sprints		1-on-1 full court
1-on-1 full court	1-on-1 full court		2-on-2 full court
2-on-2 full court	2-on-2 full court		3-on-3 full court
2-on-2 stations	2-on-2 stations		4-on-4 full court
3-on-3 full court	3-on-3 full court		5-on-5 full court
4-on-4 full court	Man-to-man half court		Four corners
5-on-5 full court	Box 3		Zone stations
Man-to-man half court	Box Out		Zone half court
Victory	Fogler drill		Half-court man-to-man
Fogler drill	2-2-1 zone press		25-Blitz Trap
25-Blitz Trap	Closing comments		26-Blitz Switch
Closing comments			2-2-1 zone press
			Closing comments

(continued)

Nov. 16	Nov. 17	Nov. 18	Nov. 19
Stretching	Stretching	Stretching	Stretching
Comments	Comments	Comments	Comments
Warm-up*	Warm-up*	Warm-up*	Warm-up*
Big 3 drills**	Big 3 drills**	Big 3 drills**	Big 3 drills**
Free throws and sprints	Free throws and sprints	Free throws and sprints	Shooting stations
1-on-1 full court	1-on-1 full court	1-on-1 full court	Post and perimeter stations
2-on-2 full court	Zone stations	Scrimmage	Free throws and sprints
Scrimmage	Zone half court	Man-to-man half court	1-on-1 full court
Zone stations	Forward and guard overplay	Zone stations	1-on-1 stations
Zone half court	Horseshoe drill	Stack options	2-on-2 full court
Drift	Fogler drill	Color	Release
Time and score	33 in the 2 area	Deep	Wide
Ladder	Closing comments	Half-court man-to-man	8 Play
Half-court man-to-man		Closing comments	Forward and guard overplay
25-Blitz Trap			Horseshoe drill
26-Blitz Switch			Fogler drill
2-2-1 zone press			Half-court man-to-man
44 zone to 43 trap			Zone sets
Closing comments			Closing comments

Nov. 20	Nov. 21	Nov. 22	Nov. 23
Stretching	Off	Scrimmage	Scrimmage
Warm-up*			
Scrimmage			

Nov. 24	Nov. 25	Nov. 26	Nov. 27
Stretching	Off	Stretching	Stretching
Comments		Warm-up*	Comments
Warm-up*		Scrimmage	Warm-up*
Big 3 drills**			Big 3 drills**
Shooting stations			Shooting stations
Post and perimeter stations			Rebounding drills
Free throws and sprints			Free throws and sprints
1-on-1 full court			1-on-1 full court
Man-to-man half court			2-on-2 full court
Zone half court			Stations
Out-of-bounds plays			Change
Line			Zone stations
Time and score			Zone half court
Forward and guard overplay			Time and score
Horseshoe drill			Vs. out-of-bounds plays
Fogler drill			Closing comments
Closing comments			

Nov. 28	Nov. 29	Nov. 30	Dec. 1
Off	Stretching	Stretching	Game
	Comments	Comments	
	Warm-up*	Warm-up*	
	Big 3 drills**	Big 3 drills**	
	Shooting stations	Shooting stations	
	Free throws and sprints	Free throws and sprints	
	1-on-1 full court	1-on-1 full court	
	2-on-2 full court	2-on-2 full court	
	3-on-3 full court	3-on-3 full court	
	Zone stations	4-on-4 full court	
	Zone half court	5-on-5 full court	
	Vs. 43	"21"	
	Forward and guard overplay	Dry run all (5-on-0)	
	Horseshoe drill	Man-to-man half court	
	Fogler drill	Zone stations	
	Recovery	33 in the 2 area	
	Intercept drill	Closing comments	
	33 in the 3 area		
	Closing comments		

Note: The skill listed indicates that this practice component is emphasized or first taught. A skill or strategy will be practiced in most practices subsequent to its introduction; therefore, the absence of a skill should not be interpreted as an omission.

* Warm-up includes single-exchange passing drill, full-court layup drill, and 10 free throws in a row.

** Big 3 includes 3-on-2, 2-on-1 drill; recognition drill; and 5 two-shot free-throw attempts.

INDEX

ABOUT THE AUTHORS

© Edward Potskowski

Morgan Wootten compiled a remarkable 1,274-192 (.869) record in his 46-year career at DeMatha High School in Hyattsville, Maryland. Under Wootten's helm, DeMatha won legendary national championships in 1962, 1965, 1968, and 1984. In 1984, *USA Today* named Wootten the National Coach of the Year. His teams recorded 44 consecutive seasons with at least 20 wins and won 33 Catholic League championships. Most impressive, DeMatha has finished the season ranked number 1 in the Washington, DC, area 20 times in the last 33 years.

Wootten first put DeMatha on the national map of high school basketball in 1965 when his team broke the 71-game winning streak of Lew Alcindor's club at Power Memorial Academy (New York). More than 160 of Wootten's former players have played college basketball, and a dozen have played in the NBA. Wootten was inducted into the Naismith National Basketball Hall of Fame in 2000. He retired in November 2002.

Wootten is regarded as one of the best teachers in the history of the game. Coaches throughout the world have read his books, watched his videos and DVDs, and sat rapt through his clinics for many years. He and his wife, Kathy, reside in Hyattsville, Maryland.

Courtesy of Bishop O'Connell High School/Tommy Orndorff

Joe Wootten played for and was an assistant coach for his dad and is now an accomplished high school coach in his own right. Upon his arrival at Bishop O'Connell High School (Arlington, Virginia) in 1999, he turned the program around from a 6-game winner the year before his arrival to an average of 23 wins per season as head coach. He also serves as athletic director of the school. Joe has led O'Connell to 5 Virginia State Independent titles, 3 Washington Catholic Athletic Conference (WCAC) regular season titles, 3 Alhambra Catholic Invitational titles, and 1 WCAC tournament title. He was selected as the Arlington County Coach of the Year three times, WCAC Coach of the Year once, and Virginia State Independent Coach of the Year four times. Well known for developing his assistant coaches, he has had one college head coach, four Division I assistant coaches, and 6 head high school coaches work with him before advancing in their careers. 32 of his O'Connell players have earned college basketball scholarships. Joe resides in Vienna, Virginia, with his wife, Terri Lynn, and their three children, Alexa, Reese, and Jackson.